ANCIENT EGYPT

Ancient Egypt

State and Society

ALAN B. LLOYD

OXFORD

UNIVERSITY PRESS

OXFORD

UNIVERSITY PRESS

Great Clarendon Street, Oxford, OX2 6DP,
United Kingdom

Oxford University Press is a department of the University of Oxford.
It furthers the University's objective of excellence in research, scholarship,
and education by publishing worldwide. Oxford is a registered trade mark of
Oxford University Press in the UK and in certain other countries

First Edition published in 2014

Impression: 1

Published in the United States of America by Oxford University Press
198 Madison Avenue, New York, NY 10016, United States of America

British Library Cataloguing in Publication Data

Data available

Library of Congress Control Number: 2013957451

ISBN 978-0-19-928618-8 (Hbk)
978-0-19-928619-5 (Pbk)

Printed and bound by
CPI Group (UK) Ltd, Croydon, CR0 4YY

In memoriam
Patricia Elizabeth Lloyd
1941–2012
uxoris amatissimae

ὥσπερ εἴ τις τὸ ἔαρ ἐκ τοῦ ἐνιαυτοῦ ἐξέλοι

Acknowledgements

I should like to express my deepest gratitude to the following colleagues who all read chapters of this book at various stages in their preparation: Professor Joseph Manning, Professor Anthony Spalinger, Professor David Wengrow, Dr Aidan Dodson, Dr Juan Carlos Moreno García, Dr Robert Morkot, Dr Joan Padgham, Dr Richard Parkinson, Dr Ian Shaw, and Dr Kasia Szpakowska. Their advice and guidance made significant improvements to my efforts, but any remaining deficiencies should be regarded as entirely my responsibility. I benefited from much assistance in assembling the images used in this book and am heavily indebted to Professor Béatrix Midant-Reynes, Dr Steve Vinson, Dr Renée Friedman, Mr W. V. Davies, Cambridge University Press, Oxford University Press, Oriental Institute Chicago, British Museum Images, Egypt Exploration Society, l'Institut français d'archéologie orientale, Taylor & Francis Books UK, Osprey Publishing, John Wiley & Sons, the Bodleian Library, and the National Trust. I should also like to thank The Picture Desk (Art Archive), Scala Archives, Erich Lessing Culture and Fine Arts Archives, Superstock, and Art Resource, New York, for supplying high-quality images for this publication, and Anna Ratcliffe of Swansea University for invaluable assistance in the production of maps. I should also like to thank the following for permission to use translations or other printed material from works published by them: Cambridge University Press; Dr Richard Parkinson, The Griffith Institute; Holt, Rinehart, & Winston; Oxford University Press; Pearson Education (for Heinemann); Professor John Baines; Professor Roger Bagnall; Routledge; Sheil Land Associates Ltd (extract from *Firing Line* by Richard Holmes, copyright 1985 by Richard Holmes, reproduced by permission); Stanford University Press; University of California Press; and University of Chicago Press. Every effort has been made to ensure that copyright has been safeguarded, but any deficiencies in this respect should be addressed to the publisher. Finally, it gives me particular pleasure to acknowledge the patience and expertise of Hilary O'Shea, Taryn Das Neves, Annie Rose, Kizzy Taylor-Richelieu, and Sylvie Jaffrey, my editors at Oxford University Press, who have done so much to make this long-drawn-out project a practical proposition. All translations of Egyptian and Classical texts are mine, except where explicitly stated to the contrary.

Contents

List of Colour Plates

List of Illustrations

List of Abbreviations

ÄF	Ägyptologische Forschungen
BAR	British Archaeological Reports
BAR	J. H. Breasted 1906–7. *Ancient Records of Egypt*. 6 vols. Chicago: University of Chicago Press
BdE	Bibliothèque d'étude
BIFAO	*Bulletin de l'Institut français d'archéologie orientale*
CdE	*Chronique d'Egypte*
EES	*Egypt Exploration Society*
GM	*Göttinger Miszellen. Beiträge zur ägyptologischen Diskussion*
IFAO	l'Institut français d'archéologie orientale
JARCE	*Journal of the American Research Center in Egypt*
JEA	*Journal of Egyptian Archaeology*
JEOL	*Jaarbericht van het Vooraziatisch-Genootschap (Gezelschap) 'Ex Oriente Lux'*
JESHO	*Journal of the Economic and Social History of the Orient*
JNES	*Journal of Near Eastern Studies*
KRI	K. A. Kitchen 1975–90. *Ramesside Inscriptions*. 8 vols. Oxford: Blackwell.
LÄ	*Lexikon der Ägyptologie*
MDAIK	*Mitteilungen des Deutschen Archäologischen Instituts. Abteilung Kairo*
OLA	Orientalia Lovaniensia Analecta
PdÄ	Probleme der Ägyptologie
RdE	*Revue d'Egyptologie*
Urk.	*Urkunden des aegyptischen Altertums*
Wb.	*Wörterbuch der aegyptischen Sprache*
ZÄS	*Zeitschrift für ägyptische Sprache und Altertumskunde*

Chronological Table[1]

THE PHARAONIC PERIOD

The Early Dynastic/Thinite/Archaic Period (c.3000–2686)

First Dynasty	c.3000–2890
Aha	
Djer	
Djet	
Den	
Merneith (Queen)	
Anedjib	
Qaa	
Second Dynasty	c.2890–2686
Hotepsekhemwy	
Raneb	
Nynetjer	
Weneg	
Senedj	
Peribsen	
Khasekhem/Khasekhemwy	

The Old Kingdom (c.2686–2125)

Third Dynasty	c.2686–2125
Nebka	c.2686–2667
Djoser	c.2667–2648
Sekhemkhet	c.2648–2640
Khaba	c.2640–2637
Neferkare?	?
Sanakht?	?
Huni	c.2637–2613
Fourth Dynasty	c.2613–2494
Snefru	c.2613–2589
Khufu (Cheops)	c.2589–2566

[1] Dates for the Pharaonic Period after Shaw (ed.) 2000; for the Ptolemaic Period after Hölbl 2001; for the Roman Period after Parsons 2007.

Djedefre/Redjedef	c.2566–2558
Khafre (Chephren)	c.2558–2532
Menkaure (Mycerinus)	c.2532–2503
Shepseskaf	c.2503–2498
Fifth Dynasty	c.2494–2345
Userkaf	c.2494–2487
Sahure	c.2487–2475
Neferirkare Kakai	c.2475–2455
Shepseskare	c.2455–2448
Neferefre (Reneferef)	c.2448–2445
Niuserre	c.2445–2421
Menkauhor	c.2421–2414
Djedkare Isesi	c.2414–2375
Unis	c.2375–2345
Sixth Dynasty	c.2345–2181
Teti	c.2345–2323
Userkare	?
Pepi I	c.2321–2287
Mernere I	c.2287–2278
Pepi II	c.2278–2184
	(traditional reign length but certainly too high)
Mernere II	c.2184

Queen Neithaqrit (Gk. Nitocris), inserted here in older literature but now regarded as the product of an ancient error.

THE FIRST INTERMEDIATE PERIOD (c.2160–2055)

The Middle Kingdom (c.2055–1650)

Eleventh Dynasty	c.2055–1985
Montuhotep II	c.2055–2004
Montuhotep III	c.2004–1992
Montuhotep IV	c.1992–1985
Twelfth Dynasty	c.1985–1773
Amenemhet I	c.1985–1956
Senwosret I	c.1956–1911
Amenemhet II	c.1911–1877
Senwosret II	c.1877–1870
Senwosret III	c.1870–1831
Amenemhet III	c.1831–1786
Amenemhet IV	c.1786–1777
Sobeknofru (Queen)	c.1777–1773
Thirteenth Dynasty	

THE SECOND INTERMEDIATE PERIOD (*c.*1650–1550)

The New Kingdom (*c.***1550–1069**)

Eighteenth Dynasty	*c.*1550–1295
	(reign overlaps indicate regencies)
Ahmose I	*c.*1550–1525
Amenhotep I	*c.*1525–1504
Tuthmose I	*c.*1504–1492
Tuthmose II	*c.*1492–1479
Tuthmose III	*c.*1479–1425
Hatshepsut (Queen)	*c.*1473–1458
Amenhotep II	*c.*1427–1400
Tuthmose IV	*c.*1400–1390
Amenhotep III	*c.*1390–1352
Akhenaten (Amenhotep IV)	*c.*1352–1336
Neferneferuaten (Nefertiti) (?)	Short reign of unknown duration
Smenkhkare (?)	Short reign of unknown duration
Tutankhaten/Tutankhamun	*c.*1336–1327
Ay	*c.*1327–1323
Horemheb (strictly Horonemheb)	*c.*1323–1295
Nineteenth Dynasty	*c.*1295–1186
Ramesses I	*c.*1295–1294
Sety I	*c.*1294–1279
Ramesses II	*c.*1279–1213
Merneptah	*c.*1213–1203
Amenmesse	*c.*1203–1200
Sety II	*c.*1200–1194
Siptah	*c.*1194–1188
Twosre (Queen)	*c.*1188–1186
Twentieth Dynasty	*c.*1186–1069
Sethnakht	*c.*1186–1184
Ramesses III	*c.*1184–1153
Ramesses IV	*c.*1153–1147
Ramesses V	*c.*1147–1143
Ramesses VI	*c.*1143–1136
Ramesses VII	*c.*1136–1129
Ramesses VIII	*c.*1129–1126
Ramesses IX	*c.*1126–1108
Ramesses X	*c.*1108–1099
Ramesses XI	*c.*1099–1069

THE THIRD INTERMEDIATE PERIOD (c. 1069–664)

Twenty-first Dynasty	c.1068–945
Smendes	c.1068–1043
Amenemnisu	c.1043–1039
Psusennes I	c.1039–993
Amenemope	c.993–984
Osorkon 'the Elder'	c.984–978
Psusennes II	c.959–945
Twenty-second Dynasty	c.945–739
Shoshenq I	c.945–924
Osorkon I	c.924–889
Shoshenq IIa	c.889–887 ? Ephemeral, very little
Shoshenq IIb	is known of these
Shoshenq IIc	kings.
Takelot I	c.887–874
Osorkon II	c.874–835
Shoshenq III	c.835–797
Shoshenq IIIa	c.797–783
Pimay	c.783–776
Shoshenq V	c.776–739

The Twenty-third and Twenty-fourth Dynasties consisted of petty kings with very limited power based in various parts of the country, the most famous of whom was Bakenrenef who achieved great fame in Classical tradition as Bocchoris.

Twenty-fifth Dynasty	?–664
Alara	?
Kashta	?–751
Piye	c.751–720
Shabaqa	c.720–706
Shebitqu	c.706–690
Taharqa	c.690–664
Tanutamun	664–656

THE LATE PERIOD (664–332; dates can now be accepted with confidence)

Twenty-sixth Dynasty	664–525
Psammetichus I	664–610
Necho II	610–595
Psammetichus II	595–589
Apries	589–570
Amasis	570–526
Psammetichus III	526–525
Twenty-seventh Dynasty (First Persian Period)	525–404
Cambyses	525–522
Darius I	522–486
Xerxes	486–465
Artaxerxes I	465–424
Darius II	424–405
Artaxerxes II	405–404
Twenty-eighth Dynasty	404–399
Amyrtaeus	404–399
Twenty-ninth Dynasty	399–380
Nepherites I	399–393
Psammuthis	393
Hakoris (Achoris)	393–380
Nepherites II	*c.*380
Thirtieth Dynasty	380–343
Nectanebo I	380–362
Teos (Tachos)	362–360
Nectanebo II	360–343
Thirty-first Dynasty (Second Persian Period)	
Artaxerxes III Ochus	343–338
Arses	338–336
Darius III Codomannus	336–332

THE GRAECO-ROMAN PERIOD (332 BC–AD 642)

The Macedonian Dynasty	332–305
Alexander the Great	332–323
Philip Arrhidaeus	323–317
Alexander II (IV of Macedon)	316–305

The Ptolemaic Period (323–30)

Ptolemy I Soter	305–282
Ptolemy II Philadelphus	282–246
Ptolemy III Euergetes I	246–221
Ptolemy IV Philopator	221–204
Ptolemy V Epiphanes	204–180
Ptolemy VI Philometor	180–145
Ptolemy VII Neos Philopator	(never reigned)
Ptolemy VIII Euergetes II (Physkon)	170–163, 145–116
Ptolemy IX Soter II (Lathyros)	116–107
Ptolemy X Alexander I	107–88
Ptolemy IX Soter II (restored)	88–81
Ptolemy XI Alexander II	80
Ptolemy XII Neos Dionysos (Auletes)	80–58
Cleopatra VI Tryphaina and Berenike IV Epiphaneia	58–55
Ptolemy XII Neos Dionysos (restored)	55–51
Cleopatra VII Philopator ruled jointly with	51–30
Ptolemy XIII and	51–47
Ptolemy XIV and	47–44
Ptolemy XV Caesarion	44–30

The Roman Period (30 BC–AD 323)
Roman Emperors (linked names indicate joint rulers)

Augustus/Octavian	30 BC–AD 14
Tiberius	14–37
Caligula	37–41
Claudius	41–54
Nero	54–68
Galba	68–9
Otho	69
Vitellius	69
Vespasian	69–79
Titus	79–81
Domitian	81–96
Nerva	96–8
Trajan	98–117
Hadrian	117–38
Antoninus Pius	138–61
Marcus Aurelius	} 161–180
Lucius Verus	} 161–169

Avidius Cassius (claimant recognized in Egypt)	*175*
Commodus	180–92
Pertinax	192–3
Didius Julianus	193
Septimius Severus	193–211
Pescennius Niger (claimant recognized in Egypt)	*193–4*
Caracalla	211–17
Geta	211
Macrinus	217–18
Elagabalus	218–22
Alexander Severus	222–35
Maximin	222–35
Gordian I and II	238
Pupienus	238
Balbinus	238
Gordian III	238–44
Philip	244–9
Decius	249–51
Gallus	251–3
Aemilian	253
Valerian	253–60
Gallienus	253–68
Macrianus	*260–1 (Claimants recognized in Egypt)*
Quietus	*260–1*
Claudius II	268–70
Palmyrene occupation of Egypt	*269–74*
Quintillus	270
Aurelian	270–5
Vaballathus	270–2
Tacitus	275–6
Florianus	276
Probus	276–82
Carus	282–3
Carinus	283–5
Numerian	283–4
Diocletian	284–305
Maximian	285–310
Constantius I	293–306
Galerius	293–311
L. Domitius Domitianus (claimant recognized in Egypt)	*?296–7*

Aurelius Achilleus (claimant recognized in Egypt)	*?297–8*
Maximin	305–13
Severus II	305–7
Maxentius	306–12
Licinius	308–24
Constantine I	306–37

The Byzantine Period (324–642)

This period is best begun in 324 when Constantine I became sole emperor. For our purposes three emperors are particularly important:

Constantine I	324–37
Theodosius	379–95
Justinian	527–65

Introduction

This book is not intended in any way to be yet another general study of Pharaonic Egypt. The market is already flooded with such offerings, and I see no need to swell it further. The focus of this study is an attempt to define, analyse, and evaluate the institutional and ideological systems that empowered and sustained one of the most successful civilizations of the ancient world for a period in excess of three and a half millennia. It begins in Chapter 1 with a conspectus of Egyptian prehistory and history down to the Roman Period which is designed to anchor the subsequent discussion firmly in its historical context, and there is no intention here to grapple with the many problems that bedevil the study of Egyptian history both because this is unnecessary for my purpose and because many of them are insoluble anyway, even though voluminous quantities of ink and effort have been, and will continue to be, expended upon them. The intention is rather to ensure that the student, the non-expert professional, and non-professional readers have a convenient point of reference within which they can locate the material in subsequent chapters and also to make clear, for better or worse, my view of what the key issues of Egyptian prehistory and history seem to be. No exposition of such matters, even at the level of description, is ever entirely objective, nor can it be, and it is as well for any writer engaged in the perilous enterprise on which I have embarked to make clear what he thinks the nature of the phenomenon to be.

With the historical context, or, at least, my concept of it, firmly established, the study proceeds to the discussion in a series of chapters of issues that have been the focus of much of my thought and research over many years. The fundamental premise here is that all societies are the product of a continuous dialogue between themselves and their physical context, understood in the broadest sense, and that in order to achieve a successful symbiosis with it they develop an interlocking set of systems, which historians, archaeologists, and anthropologists define as culture and which can be described as the sum total of the methods employed by a group of human beings to achieve some measure of control of their environment or, at least, to make that environment tractable. Understood in this way, culture has three main aspects, though separating out these aspects in specific cases can create difficulties since they not infrequently interrelate in complex ways. In the first place, and most obviously, the term embraces technology and the systems for applying technology, i.e. the corpus of tools, weapons, and engineering devices, and their modes of application by which a society attempts to extend the basic physical capacities of its members. In early societies these will amount to a very small and simple body of devices and systems of application, but in a modern technological society they will be extremely numerous and are frequently of high sophistication. The second ingredient of the cultural apparatus comprises social systems such as hunting-bands, tribes, and states, which presuppose, in varying degrees of complexity, a wide range of associated subsystems such as administrative organizations, economic structures, and systems for inculcating social norms. Finally, all cultures deploy systems that we may describe as intellectual or spiritual systems involving such phenomena as religions and ideologies whose essential function is to generate a mental picture of a society's world in the broadest sense and the position of that society within it. Social phenomena of this kind are essentially cosmicizing, i.e. they serve to impose a comprehensible order on the world inhabited by societies and thereby make it tractable—or at least make it possible to create an illusion of tractability. Without such processes it would be impossible for humans to locate themselves in a world with which they have to interact at a high level of self-consciousness, and they would quite simply not be able to negotiate terms with its many dimensions.

In accordance with these principles the main chapters of the book are concerned with the definition and analysis of what seem to me to be the main aspects of Egyptian culture that gave it its particular character and allowed the Egyptians to maintain that character for an extraordinary length of time and through cultural shocks of many different kinds. Chapter 2 addresses the prehistoric evolution of Egyptian society, inevitably with some degree of speculation since the absence of writing until the very end of the period frequently compels the social historian to employ comparative archaeological and anthropological data. The seeds of much that we associate with Pharaonic Egypt can be found at this stage, and Chapter 3 moves naturally to an analysis of the most significant institutional creation of Egypt's prehistoric cultures, i.e. kingship, the pivotal institution of Egyptian society and the embodiment of the Pharaonic state system throughout its history. This discussion involves the analysis of the concept of divine kingship which embraces both the concept of the divinity of the king in life and death and the distance between that conceptualization and the ways in which that divinity did or did not impact on those who came into contact with it. This analysis leads naturally in Chapter 4 to an examination of the role of violence in the state system since the Egyptian state was created through violence and maintained ultimately by the veiled threat or physical application of force. There is nothing unique in this. At the most basic level the power of all states is grounded in the capacity to mobilize force, however carefully that brutal truth is concealed, and it is necessary to consider what military and paramilitary means Egyptian rulers and administrators possessed to apply that force both to maintain order within Egypt and to guarantee the kingdom's capacity for self-defence and exploitation of resources in areas beyond its frontiers. Chapter 5 then describes the evolution of the administrative machinery through which the Egyptian state operated, once established, in an attempt to determine the ways in which the power of Pharaoh was articulated within the kingdom at large and, at some periods, beyond its frontiers. This topic links inevitably to the discussion in Chapter 6 of the all-important issue of dialogue with the physical environment since the physical context in which any culture is compelled to function must exercise a critical effect on what it can and cannot do. Most obviously it will require the development of technological and organizational systems which will make it possible for a culture to meet its physical needs, real and putative, and it is the opportunities, problems, and systems for dealing with them that form the focus of this chapter.

Societies do not simply live in a physical environment. At least as important, if not more so, is the way in which they conceptualize that environment to make it comprehensible and tractable, and this is the focus of Chapter 7. Such conceptualizations can, of course, differ enormously from one society to another, the criterion of validity being, in the final analysis, what makes sense to members of that society and what appears to work for them, but the process of developing their world pictures is crucial to their success. However, these are far from being static, once-and-for all creations. Circumstances, historical and otherwise, can change, and revision and adaptation are essential if the society's ethos is to be maintained. When that is no longer possible, societies collapse or transmute into something else, and Ancient Egypt is a classic example of the latter during the Graeco-Roman Period. The conceptualized environment, therefore, constitutes the theme of the seventh main chapter of the book.

States, cultures, and institutions do not survive untended. Their ideological underpinning and postulates need continuous restatement, reaffirmation, and reassessment, the latter process sometimes bringing with it considerable change. These processes can be carried through in many ways, but an important role is played by the arts, though this is often not explicit and frequently operates at a subliminal level on the part of the artists themselves. In the case of Ancient Egypt it is very easy to see the ways in which literature was used to restate, reaffirm, and even question ideological positions and social norms, and the role of the visual arts in such contexts is equally obvious. Chapter 8 is focused on trying to establish precisely how these processes operated. However, effective though these mechanisms were for millennia of Egyptian history, the conquest of Egypt by Alexander the Great in 332 BC marked the beginnings of an interaction between Egyptian and Graeco-Roman culture that led to the gradual and ultimately radical penetration of the culture of the Egyptian elite by that of the Greek and Roman world. This culminated during the Roman Period in the establishment throughout the country of the urban culture of the Roman world which achieved an ascendancy leading to the erosion of all aspects of traditional Egyptian civilization. The damage done by this process was completed by the introduction of Christianity which was enthusiastically welcomed and led swiftly to the replacement of the old conceptualized world and its manifestations by those of the Christian civilization of the Eastern Roman Empire. Chapter 9 attempts to unravel the main strands in this fascinating process of cultural transformation.

1

The Historical Context

PREHISTORY

The study of Egyptian prehistory is currently a major area of research which is yielding results of great importance, and will continue to do so (Midant-Reynes 2000; Hendrickx, Friedman, Ciałowicz, and Chłodnicki (eds) 2004; Connah 2005; Wengrow 2006; Koehler 2010; Friedman and Fiske (eds) 2011; Teeter (ed.) 2011). (See Fig. 1.1.) Its evolution is divided into the periods based on the materials used for making tools and weapons which are familiar to all prehistorians and prehistoric archaeologists, i.e. the Palaeolithic (Old Stone) Age, the Mesolithic (Middle Stone) Age, the Neolithic (New Stone) Age, and the Chalcolithic (Copper-stone) Age. These are all well represented in the Egyptian archaeological record, but, since prehistoric developments in the Nile Valley are discussed in detail in the next chapter, I shall confine myself at this stage simply to emphasizing that the evolution of proto-Egyptian society and civilization developed with increasing momentum during the Prehistoric Period until the latter half of the fourth millennium when it took a major leap forward under the influence of three major conurbations: first Naqada, whose culture swept all before it to dominate the entire country; then Hierakonpolis, which played a critical role in developing the ideology of Egyptian kingship; and finally Abydos which, in association with Hierakonpolis, laid the foundations for the Pharaonic Egyptian state.

THE HISTORIC PERIOD

It is a long-standing convention of Egyptology that Egyptian history is divided into dynasties, a system created by the Egyptian priest Manetho who wrote a history of Egypt in Greek during the third century BC at the behest of Ptolemy II (282–246 BC). He divided the narrative into thirty dynasties, or royal families, and this scheme was subsequently supplemented by another author who added a Thirty-first Dynasty to take account of the Persian kings who

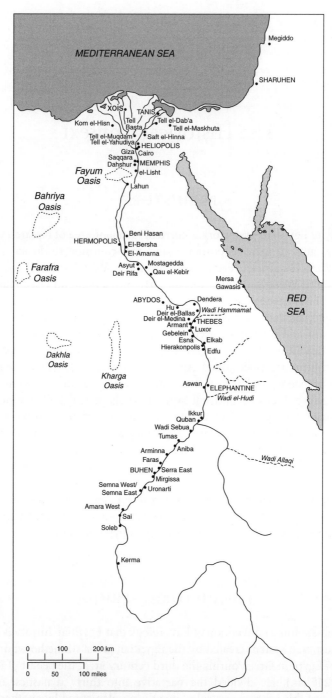

Fig. 1.1. Main sites of Pharaonic Egypt. After Lloyd (ed.) 2010*c*: map 1.

ruled the country from 342 until 332 BC. This system has many demonstrable deficiencies, but it is firmly established and universally accepted as a working framework. Since the nineteenth century this scheme has been divided up into larger units which are essentially based on the principle that some periods are characterized by firm centralized authority ('Kingdoms') whilst other periods see the country breaking up into smaller autonomous units with little, if any, centralized authority ('Intermediate Periods'). (For the details of this framework see above, p. xix.)

THE EARLY DYNASTIC PERIOD

This lengthy period begins with the unification of Egypt under a southern king and is of critical importance as the period that formed the bedrock of the Egyptian state and developments in Egyptian civilization that laid the foundations for its later greatness (Wilkinson 1999, 2003, 2010). According to tradition the figure responsible for the unification was Menes who is alleged to have established a capital at Memphis where he also constructed a fort and the first temple of Ptah. Which historical figure underlies this tradition has been a matter of much debate, the hot favourites being either the Horus Narmer or the Horus Aha of contemporary monuments, but a definitive decision is not possible on the basis of data currently available. Whilst historical information is not plentiful, there is enough to gain a picture of activity that both reflected current requirements and anticipated the later standard Pharaonic agenda. If Memphis was indeed founded at this period, it would not have stood on any of its later positions, but its *raison d'être* would have been the same, i.e. to provide a suitable administrative base from which to control the entire country, though the kings continued to be buried in the ancient royal necropolis at Abydos throughout the First Dynasty rather than in the readily available Saqqara necropolis. The presence of a fort at Memphis and the city's ancient name 'The White Wall' also point to a military role in overawing the recently acquired northern part of the country. The need to consolidate the unification is also illustrated by what looks like evidence of marriage with northern princesses, and we also find Aha founding a temple of Neith, a goddess closely associated with Lower Egyptian kingship. Care to show respect for northern gods is also illustrated by references to a festival of Sokaris, a northern deity, both in the First and Second Dynasties. The tightening of administrative control by the middle of the First Dynasty may well be illustrated by the appearance of the first attempt at year-dating and the census which becomes increasingly regular during the Second Dynasty. That the north was by no means reconciled to the conquest is suggested by the much later Saqqara King List which studiously omits all the kings of the First Dynasty before Adjib.

In line with this consolidation of royal control we find clear evidence of the evolution of royal ideology: the reign of Den, the fourth king of Dynasty I, provides us with the first example of the Double Crown that combined the crowns of Upper and Lower Egypt and symbolically asserted control of the entire country, and the title 'King of Upper and Lower Egypt' also appears for the first time. Dynasty I also yields the first evidence of the celebration of the *Heb-sed* Festival, a ritual of royal rejuvenation, and one ruler even contrived to perform two of them. None of this, however, prevented trouble at the top. There was clearly serious dynastic disruption at the end of the First Dynasty, and there was also turmoil in the royal house at the end of the Second Dynasty which seems to have been connected with religious differences arising from different views as to which god was incarnated in the person of the king.

External relations are very much in line with later practice: we hear of successful operations against the Libyans at the very beginning of the dynasty, and ivory fragments from the reign of Aha show them bringing tribute. Nubia was also on the receiving end of military activity, and aggressive operations to the east of Egypt are also in evidence, as well as expeditions into the Eastern Desert. The trade route to the western oases beyond Armant was being exploited too.

In the cultural area the Early Dynastic Period builds strongly on the fine traditions of the late Predynastic Period exemplified particularly by the finds at Hierakonpolis, and progress is considerable. Elaborate mortuary installations were constructed of mud-brick at Abydos, including the burial of wooden boats, and the tombs of officials at Saqqara are highly sophisticated structures. Sculpture is of high quality, both in the round and in relief, and the hiero-glyphic script developed quickly, though its earlier forms can often provide problems to the modern scholar.

THE OLD KINGDOM AND FIRST INTERMEDIATE PERIOD

The Old Kingdom was the consummation of all previous developments in organization, ideology, and culture and forms the first great age of Egyptian history (Baud 1999, 2010; Moreno Garcia 2004; Willems 2010). Internally the beginning of the period sees the rigorous application of the principle that the king is the incarnation of the god Horus, placing him at a level in the hierarchy of being which was never achieved previously or later. The most compelling illustration of this doctrine at this period is the pyramids of the Fourth Dynasty. The Great Pyramid at Giza, which, when complete, attained a height of 146.6 m and has a volume of *c*.2,500,000 cu, m, is alleged to have taken 20,000 men twenty years to build. This effort in itself indicates the capacity of the king to mobilize and direct huge bodies of labour and also demonstrates complete control of the manpower and material resources of the kingdom. The structure of the Giza pyramid field itself is an assertion of the pre-eminence of the king in that the pyramid is surrounded by orderly rows of much smaller tombs for members of the royal family and officials which, despite their high quality, are dwarfed into insignificance by the prodigious royal monument.

The high summer of the Fourth Dynasty did not last. The evolution of the pyramids of the later Old Kingdom illustrates the decline of de facto royal power in that they decrease significantly in size after the Fourth Dynasty, and the associated official cemeteries become smaller as provincial cemeteries are increasingly used by officialdom as their dependence on royal favour becomes, in practice, less crucial. Another factor in limiting royal power and prestige was the rise in the influence of the great solar temple at Heliopolis which led to a solarization of royal ideology in the Fifth Dynasty that effectively subordin-ated the king to the sun-god; it also led to a demand on royal resources for the construction of sun-temples which placed an additional burden on the royal exchequer. From the Fifth Dynasty onwards a further factor in the erosion of the king's pre-eminence was the rise of a provincial nobility (nomarchs), which was probably the most significant factor in the gradual fragmentation of political power within the kingdom. It may well be a result of this decline in royal prestige that the Sixth Dynasty, the last of the Old Kingdom, provides a number of examples of dynastic problems: Teti, the first king of the dynasty, is alleged by Manetho to have been assassinated by his bodyguard, and he is succeeded for a short time by an enigmatic ruler called Userkare who did not achieve universal recognition, and in the reign of Pepi I we hear of something that looks suspiciously like a harîm conspiracy. It would be wise to assume that such events were far from isolated phenomena.

Evidence of activity abroad is sporadic during the Old Kingdom, but, when we get it, it can be very full. Libya continued to attract military interventions that are clearly punitive in character but yielded rich economic returns in terms of booty, and Sinai is still a focus of interest for its copper and turquoise, though the constant threat posed by local Bedouin always required military protection. Commercial links with Asia were certainly maintained by sea and are strikingly illustrated by the presence of an Egyptian shrine at Byblos during the Fourth Dynasty; we are also informed of large-scale military operations into Palestine during the Fifth and Sixth Dynasties. In addition, we have evidence of maritime expeditions to the land of Punt (Eritrea–Somaliland–South Sudan), which was always a major source of incense, amongst other exotic commodities. It was, however, Nubia that loomed largest in Egyptian consciousness during this period and saw the major investment of effort. Here the motivation was pre-eminently its economic resources, but their exploit-ation required major expeditions which frequently had a marked military dimension as exemplified by the tomb inscriptions of Harkhuf, a governor of the administrative district at the First Cataract who describes large-scale operations to the south and west during the reign of Pepi II. This preoccupation also led to the establishment of a base at Buhen from which the rich local copper resources could be exploited, an initiative that had no parallel either in Libya or Asia and set a precedent for the colonizing activities of the Middle Kingdom.

The decline of the Old Kingdom at the end of the Sixth Dynasty and the transition to the First Intermediate Period was a complex phenomenon in which several factors played a part: for some time royal authority had been increasingly impaired by the growing autonomy of provincial governors who functioned more and more as kings in their own country, at best paying lip-service to the central government, and that process must have been aggravated by the unusually long reign of Pepi II, who in his later decades was not likely to have been in the best position to ensure the vigorous exercise of central government, but the critical factor was catastrophic environmental change which led to a major shift in the regime of the Nile's inundation, and that, in turn, brought with it disastrous economic consequences. In the north of the country the ensuing internal disruption was aggravated by infiltration of the Delta by Asiatics who established themselves as a major presence in that area, though this is best regarded not as a great novelty but as a significant and aggressive addition to a long-standing Asiatic element in the demographic mix of this area.

The first step in reversing the downturn of Egypt's fortunes was taken at Herakleopolis in Middle Egypt some time about 2160 BC with the rise of a dynasty of kings who are reflected, somewhat inaccurately, in the Manethonian Ninth and Tenth Dynasties. These rulers were successful not only in establishing their authority over Middle Egypt from the apex of the Delta to the Abydos area but also ultimately in gaining control of the Delta. Their expansion to the south was blocked by the rise of an energetic and able dynasty of rulers based at Thebes who achieved total control of southern Upper Egypt from the First Cataract to the southern limit of Herakleopolitan power at Abydos. Inevitably this line of demarcation became the context in which the struggle for domination of the whole of Egypt was fought out. This struggle led eventually to the victory of the south about 2040 BC under Nebhepetre Montuhotep II, one of the greatest of all Egyptian kings, who achieved the reunification of Egypt under one ruler.

THE MIDDLE KINGDOM AND SECOND INTERMEDIATE PERIOD

The Middle Kingdom was the second great flowering of Egyptian civilization (Grajetzki 2006; Willems 2010). Once in full military control of the kingdom its founder, Montuhotep II, had to guarantee its political control, and here the major obstacle was the power of the remaining provincial governors who had long since achieved the status of local barons. Ideally their positions would have been abolished, as had been done by the dynasty already through most of the southern part of the kingdom, and in the erstwhile domain of Herakleopolis this principle was certainly applied in dealing with the house of Asyut, which had been a strong supporter of the Herakleopolitan dynasty and may well have continued to be recalcitrant. However, this case seems to have been the exception since there is evidence of the continued presence of great baronial families elsewhere in Middle Egypt. The solution adopted to obviate the potential danger was to sideline the provincial nobility by replacing them for administrative purposes with a highly centralized bureaucracy run, as far as possible, by Thebans, i.e. officials from the place of origin of the royal house itself. Whilst this expedient went far to guarantee initially the peace of the kingdom, there is evidence that the latter part of the dynasty was afflicted by serious instability in the royal succession that led to its ultimate collapse and replacement by the Twelfth Dynasty inaugurated by Amenemhet I who had probably been the chief minister at the end of the Eleventh.

The upstart founder of the Twelfth Dynasty clearly felt a strong imperative to affirm and establish his legitimacy, and this was done in a number of ways: he used an epithet that amounted to claiming that his reign was inaugurating an Egyptian renaissance; links with the Eleventh Dynasty and with its base at Thebes were maintained; literary propaganda supporting the royal house was mobilized; and, in particular, the dynasty went to great lengths to present itself as restoring the glories of the Old Kingdom through a shift of the royal residence northwards to a site near Lisht which was named Itj-tawy ('Conqueror of the Two Lands') and the return to the use of pyramids for royal burials. It also appears that the provincial nobility benefited from this sense of insecurity; for the signs are that the survivors of this elite group experienced a resurgence of power in the early part of the Twelfth Dynasty, probably because Amenemhet needed its support. None of this, however, could preserve him from the daggers of assassins, and the nomarch policy was to prove a ticking time-bomb; predictably these potentates were gradually able to strengthen their position, particularly through intermarriage, to the point where they could once more pose a threat to the authority of the crown. The great conqueror Senwosret III grasped this nettle very firmly and solved the problem by converting the ambitious members of the local nobilities into civil servants whose position was entirely dependent upon the continued good will of the king, a situation vividly illustrated by the fact that their tombs were now built in proximity to that of the Pharaoh rather than in an ancient provincial family necropolis on such sites as Beni Hasan or el-Bersha. However, the internal policy of the dynasty was not confined to the problem of balancing royal authority against that of provincial barons, important though that issue was. There is also evidence of concern to strengthen the internal economy of the country by developing the agricultural potential of the Fayyum area, an enterprise particularly associated with Amenemhet III, the last major ruler of the dynasty with whom it reached the summit of its success. The presence of a pyramid of his at the entrance to the Fayyum at Hawara is, no doubt, an indication of this commitment.

Foreign involvements were a major feature of the Eleventh and Twelfth Dynasties. Initially the issue was the consolidation of Egypt's frontiers after the reunification, and this was vigorously addressed by Montuhotep II in successful campaigns against the Libyans and the neighbouring tribes of Sinai and Asia. Expeditions were also dispatched into Nubia both to guarantee Egypt's security to the south and also to ensure that Egypt had access to the valuable economic resources that existed in the area or passed through it en route from the south. The Eastern Desert was also a major focus of interest as a source of gold and stone as well as the favoured route to the land of Punt, which became once more a focus of Egyptian activity. The Twelfth Dynasty saw an intensification of foreign relations with all the old centres of interest: close contact with Byblos was maintained, but there is also evidence of major military activity in Asia which brought with it significant returns in booty of many different kinds with the penetration of an Egyptian army in the reign of Senwosret III as far as Shechem. Libya and the western oases also experienced Egyptian attention. However, it was in Nubia that the major effort was expended with the establishment of a permanent Egyptian presence between the First and Second Cataracts, its incorporation into the Egyptian state as an imperial province, and the consolidation of that control by the construction of a spectacular series of forts beginning at the Second Cataract and running northward to tie in with the southern defences of Egypt proper. Here a major inducement was to provide bases for economic exploitation, which was energetically pursued; moreover the forts also played a major defensive role in presenting a formidable obstacle to the young, vigorous, and enterprising Kerman kingdom to the south which posed an increasingly dangerous threat to Egypt.

The cultural achievements of the Middle Kingdom were very great, and the impression made on subsequent generations can hardly be overstated. The language of this period, known to modern Egyptology as Middle Egyptian, became the classic form of Egyptian and retained that status effectively until the demise of the hieroglyphic script in the Roman Period. Even the scribes of Cleopatra and the Roman emperors were trying to write this version of Egyptian, though they frequently fall victim to linguistic anachronisms and use spelling systems that are often quite at variance with Middle Kingdom practice. In line with this the literary texts of the period became the great classics used in education and read, quoted, and imitated for centuries by the small elite of literate Egyptians. The visual arts reached the highest standards, and sometimes moved in unexpected and even startling directions: sculpture frequently continued the traditions of the Old Kingdom, but some royal statuary displays a stark realism that is a long way from conveying the traditional calm and majestic image of divine kingship. We have only limited remains of royal temple building from the period, though some of this is of very high quality and some of it unique, such as the temple of Montuhotep III on Thoth Hill in Western Thebes, but mortuary architecture is much better served, and, though mortuary installations fall well short of Old Kingdom parallels in size, they show much innovation not only in the Eleventh Dynasty complex of Montuhotep II at Deir el-Bahri but also in the pyramid fields of the Twelfth Dynasty at Lisht, Dahshur, and Hawara. The pyramid complex of Amenemhet III at the latter site achieved enormous renown well beyond the frontiers of Egypt because of its spectacular associated cult temple which was known to the Greeks and Romans as the Labyrinth. This structure, now almost completely destroyed, was a combination of a mortuary temple to serve the king interred in the pyramid and also a composite shrine where the cults of the gods of the nearby Fayyum could be associated with that of the king.

The Thirteenth Dynasty is conventionally included in the Middle Kingdom because it carried on the cultural traditions of that great age of Egyptian civilization and evidently perceived itself in that light, but it was in all respects a pale shadow of its predecessor. Whilst it sometimes achieved at least a nominal control over the entire country, the reality was an increasing fragmentation of power that led ultimately to the Second Intermediate Period during which two of the major Egyptian nightmares became reality (Ryholt 1997; Bourriau 2000; Morenz and Popko 2010). Not only was Egypt subjected to a series of vicious raids by Nubians who ravaged Upper and Middle Egypt, including its major mortuary installations some of whose contents were transported bodily to their homeland, but a large part of the country was brought under the direct control of Asiatic rulers known to Manetho as the Hyksos. These able and ambitious conquerors had their origins in the Asiatic population which had settled peacefully in the Eastern Delta in some numbers during the latter part of the Twelfth Dynasty and the Thirteenth, encouraged to do so for military and commercial purposes by the Egyptians themselves, but during the Second Intermediate Period they established a state with a capital at Avaris (Tell Dab'a) in the eastern Delta and were supplemented by a large influx of Asiatics, an infiltration facilitated by the sheer impotence of the Egyptian state. From this springboard they were able to undertake the subjugation of most of the rest of Egypt, reaching Gebelein by about 1640, their success greatly promoted by a complete superiority in military technology and practice. At Gebelein direct Hyksos control stopped, and Theban dynasts effectively retained their hegemony over the southernmost nomes of the country.

The Hyksos were consistently given a bad press by the Ancient Egyptians, who present them as barbarians with no sympathy whatsoever for Egyptian culture. This image is demonstrably wide of the mark on both counts (Oren (ed.) 1997). Indeed, the Hyksos Period is probably one of the most influential in Egyptian history: in the first place, it seems to have badly shaken Egyptian feelings of self-sufficiency and security; secondly, Egypt acquired many cultural and technological benefits; and, thirdly the country was given the military capability and the motivation to create an Asiatic Empire, the most important new departure of the New Kingdom. Be that as it may, the Theban rulers associated with Manetho's Seventeenth Dynasty had no intention of tolerating a Hyksos presence in Egypt any longer than they had to and slowly built up sufficient strength to mount an increasingly successful struggle against the foreigners that eventually confined them to their old base in the Eastern Delta.

THE NEW KINGDOM: THE AGE OF EMPIRE

The expulsion of the Hyksos and the destruction of their last major base at Sharuhen in southern Palestine were both achievements of Ahmose, the first king of the Eighteenth Dynasty who came to the throne about 1550 BC. His reign marks the beginning of the New Kingdom, the most brilliant period in the history of Pharaonic civilization, which saw spectacular triumphs in all areas of activity (Bryan 2000; van Dijk 2000; Morenz and Popko 2010; Morris 2005, 2010). From its very beginning the dynasty expressed its energy and self-confidence in the vigorous exploitation of all available resources inside Egypt and beyond its frontiers with expeditions to such traditional areas of interest as Asia, the Eastern Desert, Punt, and the Sinai peninsula. These enterprises provided the material basis for artistic achievements of the highest order, particularly in architecture and sculpture, glorifying the rulers of the dynasty with such structures as the great tombs in the Valley of the Kings and the associated mortuary temples along the margins of the cultivation on the west bank of Thebes. Some of these buildings showed great originality in concept, the finest being the mortuary installation of Hatshepsut at Deir el-Bahri. The gods were also lavishly rewarded for their support with large-scale architectural works, above all in the major cult centre of the great god Amon-re at Thebes and the shrines of the two other major dynastic gods Ptah of Memphis and Re of Heliopolis. Amenhotep III was particularly active, developing a large-scale building programme which has left remains from the Delta to the Sudan, including a large and splendid palace at Malkata (Medinet Habu), which was the site of his first Heb-sed festival in RY30/1 and also those of RY 34 and 37, and a colossal funerary temple on the west bank now marked by the Colossi of Memnon that flanked the entrance, a great stele that stands at what was once the back of the shrine (O'Connor and Cline (eds) 2001), and a large number of spectacular recent finds unearthed on the site (Sourouzian 2011).

Egyptian activities abroad were a major success of the dynasty and yielded at their high point possession of territories stretching from the Euphrates in Asia to the lands beyond the Fourth Cataract in Nubia (Morris 2005; Cline and O'Connor (eds) 2006). Egyptian motivation for these military undertakings seems to have consisted of three elements: a strong sense of the need for self-defence, in which the determination to prevent a recurrence of the foreign occupations experienced during the Second Intermediate Period will have played a significant role; the ideology of kingship according to which the king was obliged to invade foreign territory for Egypt's benefit; and the very considerable economic returns that undoubtedly accrued in booty, tribute, and trading opportunities.

In Asia there were two main enemies during the Eighteenth Dynasty: the Mitannians, i.e. Hurrians with an Indo-European overlay, whose base lay in the great bend of the Euphrates in what is now largely Syria and northern Iraq, and the Hittites, though the latter only assume major importance at the end of the dynasty. There were five phases to Egyptian expansionism in Asia during the dynasty. The first ran from the reign of Ahmose to that of Tuthmose II and took the traditional form of military expeditions without any attempt at permanent occupation. The reign of Hatshepsut saw little action, but the third phase, covered by the reigns of Tuthmose III and Amenhotep II, presents us with a programme of full-blown imperialist expansion and occupation that continued into Phase 4 (Amenhotep II to Amenhotep III) in which the power of Mitanni was destroyed to be replaced by a much more serious enemy in the form of the Hittites. Phase 5 (Akhenaten–Horemheb) witnessed the serious erosion of Egypt's power and prestige in Asia, but not its total destruction. The organization of the territorial proceeds from these operations could hardly be said to have been particularly systematic and has sometimes given rise to the view that Egypt did not have an empire in Asia at all, but such negative judgements are ultimately a matter of definitions. Certainly the organization did not approach the tight control of a Roman imperial province, but Egyptian hegemony was formally structured and passed well beyond anything that could be described as a mere sphere of influence. The administrative basis was the local cities whose headmen were required to take an oath of allegiance to the Egyptian king, and they functioned very much like the governors or mayors of cities within Egypt itself. To help guarantee military control some of these cities became garrison towns, e.g. Gaza, with Kimudi being established as a headquarters city. Egyptian interests were also maintained by a large body of officials, many of whom were military officers, but some civilians are also encountered. Amongst this group we encounter Nubian police who had a bad reputation amongst the locals. Probably the most important function of all this infrastructure was to guarantee the system of taxation which was modelled on that which prevailed in Egypt itself and provided the major economic return on Egypt's investment in Syria-Palestine.

The recovery of Egyptian control in Nubia by the Eighteenth Dynasty was swift and effective, and in territorial terms went much further than the boundary of the Middle Kingdom, which had been set at the Second Cataract (W. Adams 1977: 217–45; Morkot 1991; S. Smith 1995, 2003). In the Eighteenth Dynasty direct control was extended as far as the Fourth Cataract with a further area of looser influence stretching as far south as Kurgus. The motivation was the same as that for Asia, though economic exploitation was even more important since Nubia and the lands further to the south had much to offer the exchequer. The administration was modelled on that of Egypt: structurally the Viceroy (called 'The King's Son and Overseer of Southern Countries') was the equivalent of the king, and second in importance to him was the army commander, who was known as the 'Battalion Commander of Kush'; just like Egypt, Nubia was divided into two main administrative districts, Wawat (Lower Nubia between the First and Second Cataracts) and Kush (Nubia as far as the Fourth Cataract); both districts were divided into townships like the *niut* (*niwt*), 'towns', of Egypt, each administered by a *haty-a* (*ḥȝty-ʿ*) or mayor; below him the administration was run by a large number of Egyptian officials and relied heavily on Egyptianized local princes. The wealth deriving from the exploitation of this area as well as Asia made a critical contribution to providing the resources needed to fund the large-scale building programmes, not only of the Eighteenth Dynasty but also of the New Kingdom in general.

The acquisition and maintenance of these imperial possessions required the development of a large, efficient, and, above all, permanently available military force and infrastructure, which gave the New Kingdom a pervasive military ethos (see Ch. 4), but the army was not the only novelty in the New Kingdom power structure. A particularly remarkable feature is the recurrent prominence of queens throughout the period, a trend already visible in the Seventeenth Dynasty. The most spectacular example was the case of Hatshepsut who set herself up in the middle of the dynasty as nothing short of a female Pharaoh (see Ch. 3). Yet another feature of the orchestration of power during the dynasty was the steady rise in the political influence of the priesthood of Amon-re at Thebes which made his high priest a major player in the high politics of the kingdom and a constant presence at the royal court. The explanation of this development is quite straightforward. Amon-re was the major dynastic god to whom the Egyptians ascribed the ultimate success of all royal enterprises at home or abroad. In recognition of this putative support, the god's cult centre at Thebes was showered with rich rewards in kind which were destined to make it by far the wealthiest ecclesiastical institution in the country. That, together with the intrinsic prestige brought by his office, gave the high priest a large degree of political power of which the royal house had to take account and that became ever stronger during the New Kingdom until the point was reached when the high priest could even mount a successful challenge to royal authority itself.

The Eighteenth Dynasty and, indeed, the New Kingdom itself reached their apogee in the reign of Amenhotep III who made such an impression on Egyptian historical consciousness that he even served as a model for no less a person than Ramesses II, but ideas were already abroad that were to lead to dire consequences in the following decades. The increasing solarization of Egyptian religion detectable in his reign was to be taken much further under his son Akhenaten whose obsessive concentration on his favoured sun-god Aten and the king's exclusive relationship with him had disastrous consequences for the kingdom both at home and abroad. These nefarious effects were only finally set to rights at the end of the dynasty with the accession of Horemheb, one of the great administrators of Egyptian history, to whom Egypt owed the full restoration of the old ways.

The work of recovery was ably continued by two great rulers of the Nineteenth Dynasty: Sety I and Ramesses II. Internally the reign of the first is characterized by large-scale architectural projects of extremely high quality for the gods, particularly at Abydos and Karnak, and also in his massive tomb in the Valley of the Kings. These projects were accompanied by expeditions to old sources of supply of valuable materials that helped to fund them. Sety also made significant progress in restoring the position that Egypt had lost in Asia as a result of the Amarna heresy. These policies were continued with great success by his son Ramesses II who came to the throne *c.*1279 and reigned for about sixty-seven years (Kitchen 1982). In foreign policy his major preoccupation was Asia where the aim was to push the Egyptian frontier as far north as possible against the firm opposition of the Hittites. Here success was certainly not as great as he would have wished, but the restoration of Egyptian control in southern Syria-Palestine was achieved before both the Egyptians and Hittites agreed that enough was enough, and a peace treaty was concluded *c.*1259 which was consolidated thirteen years later when the Hittite king Khattusilis III gave Ramesses his daughter in marriage. The long segment of Ramesses' reign that followed was devoted to peaceful development which included the establishment of a new Egyptian capital at Pi-Ramesse in the north-eastern Delta, marking a shift in the kingdom's centre of gravity to the north, and the execution of an enormous programme of building, e.g. at Karnak, Luxor, the Ramesseum, and Abu Simbel, that left virtually no site in Egypt untouched.

The period after the death of Ramesses II sees a downturn in Egypt's fortunes that gets steadily worse. Militarily the reign of his successor Merneptah was very active because the situation abroad had deteriorated considerably during the later years of Ramesses II. He had to deal with a major assault from the west by Libyans and the Sea Peoples, the latter being a loosely organized group of migratory peoples who may well have been displaced directly or indirectly by the gradual disintegration of the Hittite Empire from internal and external pressures. There was also trouble in Nubia, which was put down with great severity and may well have been connected with the attack from the west. The situation in Asia is far from clear, but it is likely that there was trouble early on in the reign in southern Palestine, but that this was swiftly brought to an end, and normal military, diplomatic, and trading relations were able to continue between Egypt and Syria/Palestine for the rest of the reign. Evidence for events after Merneptah is minuscule and often difficult to interpret (Dodson 2010a), but it should be noted that internally after his reign Egyptian history is marked by considerable dynastic instability, including, in the case of Twosre, yet another Egyptian queen who established herself as Pharaoh. For all that, continuity is certainly in evidence in some areas: Hori was vizier from the end of the reign of Sety II to the reign of Ramesses III in the Twentieth Dynasty, and the Egyptians do not seem to have had any difficulty in maintaining control of Nubia.

The early Twentieth Dynasty saw a brief resurgence of Egypt's fortunes. Its second ruler, Ramesses III, who modelled himself closely on Ramesses II, was the last great Pharaoh of the New Kingdom (Grandet 1993; Cline and O'Connor (eds) 2010). His reign is dominated by military activities arising from the collapse of the Hittite Empire that generated, directly or indirectly, further and much more serious attacks from the Libyans and Sea Peoples. Both were defeated, the Sea Peoples definitively, but the major reverses inflicted on the Libyans were simply a postponement of things to come. Beneath the umbrella of this great ruler's military prowess, Egypt was, in the main, rather prosperous, and his impressive mortuary temple at Medinet Habu is the last great monument of the New Kingdom. There are, however, signs of impending trouble, in particular serious economic and administrative problems, and after Ramesses' death Egypt quickly declined. There were several reasons for this: in the first place all rulers of the dynasty after Ramesses III were seriously deficient in the energy and drive needed to maintain a strong central government, and weakness and corruption became widespread features of government. In the second place, Pi-Ramesse, the royal residence located in the north-eastern Delta, was badly sited to serve as the administrative centre of the country. This factor, united with the mediocre quality of the rulers, encouraged a number of unfortunate developments that cast a long shadow: the establishment of an alternative centre of power in Upper Egypt by the priesthood of Amon-re which brought with it the development of the office of high priest into a quasi-hereditary position and an enormous enhancement of his political power. Indeed, at the end of the dynasty we find the High Priest Herihor taking the ultimate step, carrying out royal functions, sometimes wearing full royal regalia, and boasting full royal titles. The position of the crown in Upper Egypt was also weakened by the military intervention of the

Viceroy of Nubia in the reign of Ramesses XI and the establishment of his authority, albeit short-lived, in Upper and Middle Egypt. The depredations of Libyans were a further constant source of insecurity during the Twentieth Dynasty and will undoubtedly have led to further Libyan infiltration and settlement, increasing the already substantial Libyan permanent presence in Egypt. The end result of this miserable process of decline was that by the last years of the dynasty the country had dissolved into two power blocks: the north was ruled by Smendes, based at Tanis with a puppet Twentieth Dynasty Pharaoh resident in Pi-Ramesse, whilst the south was governed by the high priest of Amon-re who also had control of what remained of Egyptian Nubia.

THE LATE DYNASTIC PERIOD

Not surprisingly, when the Twenty-first Dynasty began *c.*1069 BC Egypt stood divided into two power blocks, the north under the direct control of the new Pharaoh Smendes, who had previously been governor of the northern province, and the south, for all practical purposes, under the authority of the high priest of Amon-re, though the royal status of Smendes was formally recognized in that area. This royal policy of 'live-and-let-live' in relation to the Theban theocracy was a major feature of first-millennium BC Egypt (Leahy 1985; Kitchen 1996*a*; Morkot 2000; Taylor 2000; Redford 2004; Bonnet and Valbelle 2005; Naunton 2010; Dodson 2012).

The succeeding dynasties (Manetho's Twenty-second–Twenty-fourth) were Libyan in origin and represent the end-result of major growth in the presence of Libyans in Egypt from the New Kingdom onwards, though there had always been a Libyan element in and along the western margins of the country since prehistoric times. The creators of the Libyan Period, however, were the product of two specific demographic phenomena: in the main they were probably Libyans who had been settled in Egypt from the Nineteenth Dynasty onwards, but these had been supplemented by Libyans who had been infiltrating the country during the Twentieth and Twenty-second Dynasties, availing themselves of the increasing inability of the Egyptians to prevent such movements.

The Libyan Period falls into two phases: initially Libyan kings succeeded in ruling a united country, bringing the priesthood of Amon-re under their control by judicious appointment of members of the royal family to key ecclesiastical offices, above all that of God's Wife of Amun, and also exploiting marriage alliances with powerful Theban families. However, this unity did not last. During the latter part of the period the country dissolved into a number of petty states ruled by kinglets who were to all intents and purposes autonomous. This political fragmentation was very much the situation encountered

by the great Nubian king Piy/Piankhi when he invaded Egypt from the south
*c.*730 BC and greatly facilitated his programme of conquest.

The Nubian Period (Manetho's Twenty-fifth Dynasty) was a time of mixed
fortunes for the ruling house. In cultural terms the Egyptians had little
difficulty in accommodating their southern conquerors since the Nubians
had by this stage become thoroughly Egyptianized with a particularly intense
devotion to the god Amun and his great shrine at Thebes. Indeed, in some
ways they were more Egyptian than the Egyptians themselves. However, their
fortunes in political and military terms were far from consistently favourable.
The first Nubian ruler to get control of the whole of Egypt was Shabaqa who
conquered the country *c.*715, but Nubian rule in Egypt was severely compromised by the military operations of the Assyrians whom the Nubian
dynasty was quite incapable of keeping at bay. This ferocious imperial
power from northern Iraq first invaded Egypt in 671, incensed by Egypt's
constant meddling in Syria-Palestine which the Assyrians regarded as part of
their empire. On this occasion they did not stay, but they returned in 667 and
conquered the entire country. However, as soon as the Assyrian king left, a
rebellion broke out that provoked a violent backlash, and a final defeat at the
hands of the Assyrians in 664 saw the end of the Nubian dynasty.

Conquest is one thing; maintaining control of conquered territory is quite
another, and Egypt was to prove quite simply too far from the heart of the
Assyrian Empire; the iron laws of strategic overextension dictated that the
Assyrian hold on this distant province was highly precarious. It was, therefore,
relatively easy for Psammetichus I of Sais, an erstwhile vassal of Assyria, to
mount a successful liberation campaign through a combination of judicious
support of rebellion in Asia and the military muscle provided mainly by Greek
and Carian mercenary troops. In 656 diplomacy gave him control of the
priesthood of Amon-re at Thebes and with it total control of the country,
inaugurating the Saite Period (Twenty-sixth Dynasty), one of the great ages of
Pharaonic history that not only saw Egypt once more playing a major role in
the political and military world of the Near East but also the resurgence of
high-quality artistic production on a national scale (Lloyd 2000*b*; Vittmann
2003; Perdu 2010).

A major feature of the Twenty-sixth Dynasty, which was to endure in some
form for well over a thousand years, was the great importance achieved by the
Greeks who had been coming to Egypt since the early seventh century in large
numbers and in a variety of capacities whether as mercenaries, merchants,
naval experts, allies, or students. Some were simply passing through with no
intention of a lengthy stay, but the active encouragement of the royal house,
which had a keen perception of the benefits to be gained, guaranteed that
permanent Greek settlements were established: the Greek trading base at
Naucratis in the western Delta was inaugurated sometime about the middle
of the seventh century as part of a network of bases intended to meet the

commercial requirements of Greeks and Egyptians alike, whilst military and naval bases in the north-eastern Delta ensured the continued presence of foreign mercenaries in the country as a major part of the military establishment and a significant support for the ruling house.

The Saite Period lasted until 525 when Egypt once again lost its independence as the country came under Persian control through the conquest by the Persian king Cambyses in 525, and for the next 120 years it formed part of the Persian Empire. To a considerable extent the Persians had the good sense to leave the old organization of the country in place, but the province was integrated into the Persian imperial system, being governed by a satrap and required to meet all imposts required of a province of the empire. These included not only taxes of a predictable kind but the requirement to supply ships and troops for Persian military adventures. It is, therefore, not surprising to find that Egypt naval resources were involved in Persian operations against Greek states in Asia Minor and on the mainland of Greece. The Egyptians did not prove easy to govern, and there was a series of revolts, the best known taking place about 460 and involving a heavy commitment and serious losses on the part of the Greek state of Athens and her allies. The Egyptians did achieve independence from 404 to 343 (Twenty-eighth–Thirtieth Dynasties), but a precarious and highly unpopular Persian authority was re-established in 343/2 that was brought to an end by the invasion of the country by Alexander the Great in 332.

ALEXANDER AND THE PTOLEMAIC PERIOD

The conquest of Egypt by Alexander the Great was one of the seminal events of Egyptian history, inaugurating a period of almost a millennium during which the country was governed by Greek-speaking rulers, and Greek culture became increasingly dominant, though the evolution of that domination was a slow process that did not reach its fulfilment until well into the Roman Period (Bowman 1990; Lloyd 2000c; Hölbl 2001; Bagnall and Rathbone (eds) 2004; Bingen 2007; Manning 2003, 2007a, 2007b, 2010; Vandorpe 2010). Initially all seemed well. Alexander, who had conquered the country as part of his larger agenda of subduing the Persian Empire, was widely accepted in Egypt as a liberator, and he did his utmost to win the population over, showing great respect for Egyptian religion and maintaining much of the old administrative structure. The Egyptians, in turn, recognized him as a new Pharaoh and accorded him all the traditional honours of that office. On the other hand, he ensured that military control lay firmly in the hands of Macedonian and Greek officers, and he founded a new city at Alexandria beyond the extreme north-west of the Delta, thereby serving notice of the intention to reorientate the focus of the kingdom, a focus destined to prevail for nearly a millennium: the Graeco-Macedonian rulers of Egypt had their gaze firmly fixed to the north and north-west, whilst for the Romans Egypt was a province, albeit a major one, of an empire whose epicentre was the Mediterranean Sea. Henceforth the Egyptians were to suffer history rather than make it.

Alexander did not live long enough to develop his perception of the potential of Egypt. That was left to one of his ablest generals, Ptolemy, son of Lagus, who had received Egypt, Libya, and part of Arabia as his portion of the empire after Alexander's death in 323, though initially under the overall authority of regents who tried to maintain the unity of the empire. Starting as satrap (governor) of Egypt, he eventually declared himself king in 305 in line with his major rivals elsewhere who had also received, or taken, sections of the erstwhile empire of Alexander. By this action he set the seal on the foundation of the Ptolemaic Dynasty which lasted until 30 BC.

The agenda of the Ptolemies emerged early and is easily defined. Some of their points of interest certainly replicate traditional preoccupations of native Egyptian Pharaohs, and it is indisputable that they felt an imperative to respond to the traditional external concerns of Egyptian kings not only for economic reasons but also to maintain their credibility as latter-day Pharaohs, but a lot of their activity passed well beyond what would have been expected of an Egyptian Pharaoh, even in the Late Period, and that is far from surprising since the main focus of these Ptolemaic rulers was not an Egyptian focus at all. The attentions of the Ptolemies, like those of Alexander, were directed overwhelmingly to the world to the north and north-west, and their overriding concern was to make their mark in the traditional areas of Greek and Macedonian political and military activity, i.e. the Aegean area and the Eastern Mediterranean, and these aspirations embraced not only military and political activities but cultural achievements as well. In a word, they were determined to make the Ptolemaic dynasty and the Ptolemaic kingdom the wonder of the age, but the wonder of the age in the eyes of the Graeco-Macedonian world to which they never ceased to owe their psychological allegiance.

Realizing these ambitions came at a price, and a very heavy one at that; for success required three things: an army, a fleet, and *lamprotēs* (splendour). The first two were needed in order to pursue with success the Ptolemies' campaigns against their rivals, above all the rival Hellenistic kingdoms of Macedon and Syria, and the third was required to raise the prestige of the kingdom to unparalleled heights by dazzling and bewitching the beholder through theatrical displays of royal pomp and the endless embellishment of Alexandria which soon had no equal anywhere in the Mediterranean world. All this required very substantial economic resources, and providing these resources was the most important function of their Egyptian subjects. Careful attention was devoted to economic exploitation on all fronts. Agriculture was managed, encouraged, and developed to achieve the maximum return either by ensuring that the old Pharaonic systems worked as well they could or by developing the potential of promising areas such as the Fayyum through the introduction of experts from the Greek world; trade was fostered both in the Mediterranean area and in the Red Sea and Indian Ocean for which the old Persian canal joining the Red Sea by way of the Bitter Lakes to Egypt was reopened; and the taxation system was run as tightly as possible to yield the maximum return. Throughout, the critical requirement was that the economy should generate the resources that the Ptolemies needed, and all options were on the table to achieve that aim. On their own, however, systems could not be enough. The acquiescence, ideally the enthusiasm, of the local population was essential if the maximum economic potential of the kingdom were to be realized, and that meant, above all, gaining the good will—or at least cooperation—of the Egyptian elites. The priests were key figures here, and their cooperation was carefully cultivated, particularly through a nationwide programme of temple building and reconstruction that has made Ptolemaic temples the largest surviving group of major religious buildings in the country. There is also evidence of great care to win over and soothe the susceptibilities of the great and ambitious indigenous elite families. There was, however, one group of the elite who did not enjoy great prominence in the early Ptolemaic Period, i.e. the military. They did not recover their old eminence until the reign of Ptolemy IV, and that only happened because this ruler was compelled by the inadequate availability of foreign troops to train Egyptians to operate as Macedonian heavy infantry which they did with conspicuous success at the Battle of Raphia in 217.

In cultural terms the Ptolemaic Period was an age of great achievement, very much continuing and building on developments of the Late Dynastic Period, and there can be no qualms in describing it as the last great age of Pharaonic civilization, but the wider world of grand politics was another matter, and here initial signal successes could not be maintained. Its longest and hardest struggles were fought out with the Seleucids, a rival Hellenistic kingdom, in six Syrian Wars beginning in 274, the first four of which were Ptolemaic successes, and the other two unmitigated disasters that the Ptolemies were able to survive only through the intervention of Rome, which regarded the continued existence of the Ptolemaic kingdom as very much in Rome's best interests. Indeed, it was only Roman support that enabled the dynasty to survive as long as it did. The reign of Ptolemy V sees the loss of nearly all Egypt's imperial possessions, but, to the very end, Ptolemaic political ambitions would not be gainsaid, and the brilliant Cleopatra VII made one last throw through the skilful manipulation of her putative Roman masters. Sadly for Egypt, her successes could be nothing but the briefest of triumphs in the face of inevitable and implacable Roman hostility to her machinations, and they were all abruptly wiped out by the Roman conquest under Octavian in 30 BC.

What went wrong? In the conflict with Macedon the Ptolemies, whatever other problems may have intervened, were bound to lose ultimately by the implacable laws of strategic overextension, but an analysis of the conflict with the Seleucids reveals some deep-rooted systemic problems that could hardly fail to lead to catastrophe. In the first place unrest in the kingdom impaired the resource base that was critical to successful military and naval operations: the first Egyptian revolt occurred in 245 during the reign of Ptolemy III and was followed by a long series of uprisings—in the north in 217; in 206 an independent kingdom was established in the Thebaid which lasted until 186; in 185 there was a rebellion in the Delta; about 165 there was widespread trouble including the revolt of Dionysius Petosarapis; and *c.*130 the revolt of Hariese occurred in Thebes. This, however, was only part of the problem. Dynastic instability was a recurrent malaise, frequently caused, or at least fomented by ambitious and powerful queens of whom Cleopatra VII is simply the most famous. This phenomenon fatally impaired the capacity of the Ptolemies to mount effective opposition to aggression abroad. In the end the dynasty crumbled, having long since lost an empire that at its height was the mightiest by far in the Eastern Mediterranean. At its peak the Ptolemaic kingdom projected an image compounded of a blend of the exotic, mysterious, dynamic, and powerful that no other contemporary could match, but, as with all imperial splendour and triumphs, none of this could last. Ultimately, the Empire of the Ptolemies succumbed, in some measure to forces that it was no longer able to control, but, in large part, it was institutional deficiencies within the kingdom itself that brought it low.

THE ROMAN PERIOD

The victory of Octavian (hereafter Augustus) led to the incorporation of Egypt into the Roman imperial system and, at the same time, initiated the last phase of Pharaonic civilization that was to see its decline and ultimate disappearance (Bagnall 1993, 2007; Peacock 2000; Jackson 2002; Bagnall and Rathbone (eds) 2004; Capponi 2010). Augustus and his successors were highly conscious of the economic strength and strategic importance of their prize and maintained a firm control over the province to ensure that these assets did not fall into the hands of potential rivals. During the first centuries of Roman rule the Egyptian elite continued the time-honoured practice whereby a foreign king of Egypt was conceptualized and depicted as Pharaoh, but, in practice, the head of the administration was an imperial prefect based in Alexandria who governed through an administrative structure that owed much to Ptolemaic practice but acquired an increasingly Roman stamp, particularly in legal and fiscal terms, so that by the middle of the third century the country presented the spectacle of a heavily Romanized province, particularly through the agency of the provincial capitals that acquired much the same ethos and appearance as cities elsewhere in the Roman world and played a major role in the attrition of Pharaonic culture.

Economic exploitation was very much part of the Roman agenda in Egypt. A carefully orchestrated fiscal regime was instituted whose major requirement was the annual delivery of a huge quantity of corn equivalent to one-third of the consumption of the city of Rome, but this formed only part of a raft of taxes that bore particularly heavily on the lower strata of Egyptian society. Other economic assets were also enthusiastically exploited: the extremely valuable trade in luxury goods with India through such Red Sea ports as Berenice brought rich returns, and the mines and quarries of the Eastern Desert were heavily worked. Control of the ancient trade routes running through the Western Desert also brought in rich rewards.

All these activities were ultimately dependent on the presence and effectiveness of the Roman army in the country. Support for the civilian authority formed a major part of its functions, and it had to deal with unrest and major disturbances caused by a number of factors. Resentment of the taxation system certainly featured, though to what extent and how often is open to debate, but there is no doubt that the hostility between Greeks and Jews was a significant source of unrest during the first two centuries: we hear of an attack against the Jews of Alexandria in 38 and a much more serious Jewish revolt in the years 115–17 which was put down with great bloodshed. The arrival of Christianity provided a further context for military intervention marked, in particular, by the persecution of Decius in 250 and the great persecution initiated under Diocletian that raged from 303 to 313. Policing of the Eastern and Western Deserts constituted a further internal role for the Roman forces in Egypt, a task that was organized through networks of military installations designed to guarantee security and, above all, efficient economic exploitation.

Intermittently, but very rarely, the army was required to deal with significant enemy penetrations of the frontiers of the province. In 22 BC the Nubians invaded southern Egypt, an attack that the Prefect Petronius successfully countered and repaid in kind by invading the Nubian kingdom and razing the city of Napata to the ground. The southern frontier again became a military problem in the mid third century when attacks by the nomadic Blemmyes began, and these remained a recurrent issue until the fifth century. For the first three centuries of Roman rule the eastern frontier was well insulated from attack by the presence of further Roman provinces to the east, but this situation changed spectacularly in the late third century with the invasion of the Palmyrenes who occupied the country between 269 and 274. Further invasions from this quarter were mounted later during the Byzantine Period by Sassanids (619–29) and Arabs (gaining complete control in 642), but these fall outside the chronological parameters of this book, which is concerned specifically with the institutional history of Pharaonic civilization that to all intents and purposes had disappeared when these events took place.

2

Genesis of a Society

The socio-political system of Pharaonic Egypt was the result of a long process of evolution that unfolded during millennia of prehistory, and therein lies our biggest problem in plotting the course of the process. Reconstructing the socio-political structure of any ancient prehistoric culture is fraught with peril because such cultures lack written documentation which is alone capable of providing the detailed information we require. Certainly it sometimes happens that information on the prehistoric past of a civilization is preserved and recorded at a later stage, and this is indeed the case for Ancient Egypt, but the Egyptian data are very few and, like all ancient historical tradition, are bedevilled by the consequences of the ancient attitude to historical recording, i.e. the past is there for the benefit of the present, and the past can, and should, be customized to fit what the present needs it to be with scant regard for what we should describe as historical truth. It follows that we simply cannot accept at the foot of the letter such records as the Ancient Egyptians chose to provide on what was happening before the First Dynasty. It is necessary, therefore, to fall back on other types of evidence. One approach is to focus on such archaeological remains as survive and try to flesh out this material using comparative data. We can plausibly argue that later societies at a similar level of material culture, which either survive in the anthropological record or still survive as living societies into the modern world, may well give us clues as to the social structure of their ancient material counterparts. As long as we recognize the intrinsic dangers of this process, we can certainly make some progress. In addition to extrapolating from material remains, we may be fortunate enough to have available material from contemporary, or near contemporary, societies that can also be used as part of a comparative methodology, and in the case of Ancient Egypt the evolution of society in the Near East, particularly Ancient Iraq, provides obvious possibilities.

I propose to begin by summarizing our current archaeological knowledge of Egyptian Prehistory and will then confront these data with a macrostructure model of the stages through which a prehistoric society could be expected to develop, provided that it had time and space to do so. This methodology should give us the basis for making an informed assessment of what the social evolution of the period is likely to have been.

THE ARCHAEOLOGY OF PREHISTORIC EGYPT

For the purposes of this chapter the term 'Egypt' covers both the valley of the Nile (including north Sudan), the Eastern Desert, and the Eastern Sahara. We should bear in mind that, despite a long tradition of research, it is still early days for Egyptian prehistory, particularly in its initial phases. Furthermore, like all archaeology, Egyptian prehistory has to work with what survives, and this surviving material may well yield a very partial picture of the phenomena that the archaeologist is trying to elucidate. For all that, great progress has been made, and further research is certain to bring a significant enhancement of our data.[1] (See Fig. 2.1.) Whatever the uncertainties, however, it is clear that Egypt and the surrounding deserts show the full range of prehistoric cultures expected in an Old World context: Palaeolithic (Pleistocene), Mesolithic (Early Holocene), Neolithic, and Chalcolithic. These phases will be examined in chronological order, in each case defining the main archaeological features that they present (See Fig. 2.2).

The Palaeolithic Period

Egyptian Palaeolithic cultures are identifiable from about 500,000 BC onwards. The evidence derives overwhelmingly from the desert areas surrounding Egypt to east and west, and they were all based on the exploitation of the numerous lacustrine or marshy environments created by seasonal or artesian water supplies, pre-eminently in the Western Desert, which, in turn, gave rise to savanna or steppe conditions and the food resources, both faunal and animal, that these conditions generated (cf. Midant-Reynes 2000: 40). The cultures themselves show the standard Palaeolithic diagnostic features: tool assemblages dominated by chipped-stone technology and an economy based on a largely nomadic hunting and gathering regime. Habitation remains have been identified: the site at Arqin 8 provided evidence of what appear to be tent rings to hold down temporary tent-like shelters (Hoffman 1991: 56); the plain of Kom Ombo has yielded hearths and kitchen middens; and the major site of

---

[1] In general see Hoffman 1991; Midant-Reynes 2000; Wengrow 2006; Wenke 2009; Koehler 2010.

Nile Valley + Deserts	Lower Egypt (Delta) + Deserts
Palaeolithic (Pleistocene)(earliest c.500, 000 BC)	*Palaeolithic*
Dungul Oasis, Bir Terfawi, Bir Sahara, Fayyum, Kom Ombo	Abbasiya (Cairo area)
Epipalaeolithic/Mesolithic (earliest probably c.8500 BC)	*Epipalaeolithic/Mesolithic*
Elkabian	Helwan, Lakeita Depression, Qarunian (old Fayum B)
Neolithic (begins early fifth millennium?)	*Neolithic*
Tasian, Nabta Playa, Badarian, pre-Kerma Khartoum Neolithic	Merimda Beni Salama, Fayumian (old Fayum A), el-Omari (*c.*3600–3200)
Chalcolithic	*Chalcolithic*
Amratian or Naqada I, and Early A-Group (*c.*4000–3500)	Minshat Abu Omar
Gerzean A or Naqada II, and Middle A-Group (*c.*3500–3100)	Maadi (gives its name to the Maadi culture widely exemplified in Delta)
Gerzean B or Naqada III (Semainian), and Terminal A Group (*c.*3100 into Thinite Period)	Buto

Fig. 2.1. Prehistoric cultures of the Nile Valley and deserts: major sites.

Bir Terfawi has provided what looks like a large butchery area where remains of many animal species were identified, including large bovids, gazelles, warthogs, ostriches, and turtles (Hoffman 1991: 68–9).

The Epipalaeolithic/Mesolithic Periods

The Epipalaeolithic/Mesolithic is a stage intermediate between the Palaeolithic and Neolithic phases of human history and is characterized by a technology heavily dependent on the use of microliths and a gradual shift from massive dependence on hunting and gathering to the beginnings of crop cultivation.

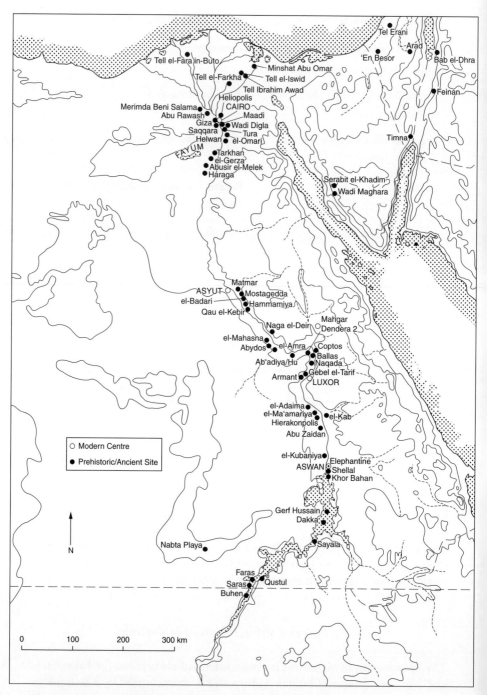

Fig. 2.2. Main sites of Prehistoric Egypt. After Wengrow 2006: p. xxi.

Currently it is not well represented in the archaeological record from Egypt, but that is certainly the result of the hazards of discovery rather than a genuine reflection of the evolution of Egyptian prehistoric culture. However, the Elkabian of Upper Egypt provides a conspicuous exception dating from *c.*6000 BC. Work at Elkab has revealed seasonal campsites that were used during the summer with plentiful evidence of a microlith tool assemblage. The inhabitants concentrated on fishing and animal resources that included aurochs, gazelles, hippopotami, and even porcupines, but no evidence came to light of the exploitation of plant foods (Hoffman 1991: 99–100, 102; Midant-Reynes 2000: 80–1, 87, 139), though it is most unlikely that this resource was excluded from the global diet. Lithic material from Helwan looks Mesolithic, though its precise chronological status has yet to be determined (Midant-Reynes 2000: 82–3, 124). The Qarunian sites of the Fayyum appear to show a variety of economic strategies, doubtless reflecting differences in local opportunities (Midant-Reynes 2000: 82, 87), but there is a Mesolithic look to them.

The Neolithic Period

The classic perception of a fully Neolithic culture runs as follows: tools and weapons continue to rely on lithic industries but are characterized pre-eminently by the use of polished stone, above all polished-stone axes. Despite the persistence of the use of stone this is the age that saw the most important development in human history, i.e. an economic revolution based on the cultivation of edible grasses, the exploitation of domesticated animals, textile manufacture, and the increased use of pottery. These developments brought with them ultimately a more sedentary mode of existence that created the possibility of evolving a more elaborate material culture than could ever have arisen in the largely nomadic lifestyle of Palaeolithic or Mesolithic cultures (e.g. Childe 1951, 1954: 48–51; Bender 1975: 9). There is no doubt that this model retains much of its validity, but it has long been recognized that cultures to which we should want to apply the Neolithic label do not present a homogeneous group and that there is considerable variability in the characteristics which they display.

In considering the Neolithic cultures of Egypt it is customary to make a distinction between Upper and Lower Egypt:

Lower Egypt and the Adjoining Deserts

Merimda beni Salama: Merimda is a permanent village site located on a terrace spur projecting into the valley *c.*60 km north-west of Cairo and well placed to exploit the possibilities of the valley as well as the semi-arid desert hinterland. It is very large, covering some 18 ha, and deposits reach a depth in parts of almost 3 m. Hoffman (1991: 169) suggested that it may have had as many as 5,000 inhabitants at its most populous, but in the current state of our knowledge of the site this figure should be treated with reserve. Excavation has been very partial, but five levels have been identified showing three cultural phases, all Neolithic, covering a time-span of over 400 years. The later phases seem to belong to the period *c.*4600–4100 BC (Wengrow 2006: 30), but the date of the foundation of the earliest settlement remains to be determined (Midant-Reynes 2000: 109). However, the signs at present are that it predates the Badarian of Upper Egypt (see p. 36).

In the village's fully developed form the houses were aligned in rows, a fact that indicates the operation of a considerable degree of organizational control. They were built of mud, wickerwork, and wooden posts, and were generally oval or horseshoe-shaped, about 1.6–3 m across, and partly sunk into the ground with one or two internal supports. Some examples show internal divisions, and occasionally the leg bones of hippopotami are inserted at entrances, apparently to act as doorsteps, though we should not exclude the possibility of a ritual, perhaps apotropaic function. Domestic equipment included hearths, grinding stones, baskets, mortars and pestles, and large quantities of pottery. Each household seems to have had its own granary (Midant-Reynes 2000: 116), and this, together with the size of the houses, may indicate that each house was the base of one nuclear family (Hoffman 1991: 176), but the presence of large threshing floors suggests that some aspects of grain processing had a more communal dimension. Burial practices are quite unlike those of the south: the dead were interred in a contracted position in oval pits with their heads orientated to the south and facing north north-east. Grave goods are very rare. The fact that the burials were located within the confines of the village has given rise to much discussion, but we should be cautious in our interpretation of this phenomenon since it is not certain that the relevant part of the village was being used for settlement at the time the burials were made (Kemp 1968). We should also not make too much of the fact that burials of adult males are rare amongst those known at present in view of the very partial excavation of the site. The low proportion of adult males certainly looks like evidence of differentiation in burial practice, but it could well be that they had a dedicated cemetery elsewhere.

The food economy was quintessentially Neolithic and lies firmly within Near Eastern tradition. Crop cultivation was practised, including emmer wheat, barley, and vetch. Pigs, sheep, cattle, and goats were raised, and dogs are also in evidence, and it may well be that the animal figurines occurring on the site had a ritual connection with these activities, though the precise species depicted are far from clear (for the problem of identification see Wengrow 2006: 55), but the shift to herding and crop cultivation did not mean that the inhabitants ignored other possibilities. The function of the human figurines discovered on the site may also have been ritual, but uncertainty on this score does not diminish their significance as very early examples of Egyptian three-dimensional representations of the human form (Midant-Reynes 2000: 115). There is ample evidence of hunting, and fishing was of particular importance. These activities were supported by a lithic technology of high quality, and it is of particular interest that the last phase of the site provides evidence of what may be a flint-knapping workshop, in which case we would have an early case of specialization of labour. Overall it is appears that, whilst the material culture of the earliest phase points to the Near East, that of later levels shows traces of African influence. However, whilst we must concede the possibility that Merimda drew on various cultural traditions, there is no doubt that the lifestyle of this site has a markedly oriental feel to it (Midant-Reynes 2000: 111–12, 118) and that the site has enormous importance as the first known example in Egypt of a settled village community.

The Fayyum: The earliest Neolithic culture in this area is the Fayumian (old Fayum A) which was made possible by the onset of a new humid phase at the beginning of the fifth millennium BC (Hoffman 1991: 185–90; Midant-Reynes 2000: 100–8; Wengrow 2006: 25, 29–30, 47).[2] Its remains are located in the Qasr el-Sagha area to the north of the present Birket Qarun, and its credentials as a classic Neolithic culture are impeccable. The tool-kit showed Near Eastern affinities and included polished or partially polished stone axes as well as tools of bone and sandstone mortars and pestles. Emmer wheat and barley were cultivated, and examples of wooden sickles with flint blades were uncovered. Flax was woven, and the full range of Near Eastern domesticated animals (sheep, goats, cattle, and pigs) was identified. It is clear that full use was made of all available alternative food resources and that fishing and hunting continued on some scale. Habitation sites have been identified, but, as yet, nothing that could be described as a village has come to light, and it would appear that we are not dealing with a community committed to a sedentary mode of life but rather with a population based on a mixed economy in which pastoralism, hunting, fishing, and the gathering of wild-plant resources all played their part. None of this excluded the exploitation of far-reaching trade connections and the use of prestige goods as items of conspicuous display (Wengrow 2006: 30–1, 47; Phillipps, Holdaway, Wendrich, and Cappers 2012).

El-Omari: El-Omari is a large Neolithic settlement consisting of three sites in elevated positions on the Eastern Desert margins adjacent to the modern town of Helwan. These sites are generally known as Omari A (at Wadi Hof), Omari B (at Gebel Tura), and Omari C, or simply Wadi Hof. Nine occupation phases have been postulated, and radio-carbon dates have yielded fixes *c.*4600–4400 BC (Midant-Reynes 2000: 124), but both Hoffman (1991: 194)

---

[2] There is a later Neolithic culture called Moerian that appeared about a century after the end of Fayumian and is also located at Qasr el-Sagha. Its origins have given rise to much debate (Midant-Reynes 2000: 106).

and Wengrow (2006: 84) incline to assign the settlement to the late fifth or
early fourth millennium, and Omari C may even be Early Dynastic. Omari
A contained over 100 circular or oval huts that were partly sunk below ground
level and had superstructures made of wattle and daub, sometimes supported by
wooden posts. As at Merimda, the houses looked like bases for nuclear families,
but Midant-Reynes (2000: 124) regarded the material as reflecting a less complex society than that at Merimda. Cemeteries yielded over forty graves with
bodies interred in a contracted position with faces to the west, and they show
distinctions in the location of burials of men, women, and children. They all take
the form of shallow oval pits, two of which may have had superstructures. If the
latter two were unique in this respect, they might well be evidence of social
differentiation, and such suspicions are further encouraged by the fact that one
grave contained the body of a man holding a stick, the latter attribute being a
feature that, in Pharaonic Egypt, indicated authority. Generally grave goods are
few, but the inclusion of pottery is common, and there is also some jewellery.
Most untypically the body of a child was buried with a set of ibex horns, which
may be the result of influence from the south (see p. 37).

The economy was based on agriculture (emmer, barley, rye, flax, and vetch)
and animal husbandry (pigs, cattle, sheep, and goats). There is possible
evidence of dogs, and the presence of donkey bones is certain, el-Omari
being the earliest Egyptian site to yield bones of this animal. This mixed
economy was greatly helped by the fact that the settlement enjoyed semi-
permanent water supplies that had not yet been wiped out by the gradual
process of desiccation afflicting the Eastern Desert. Hunting, for which dogs, if
they were available, would have been a major asset, and fishing were carried out
on some considerable scale. Trade relations were far-reaching, and this may
help to explain the presence of donkeys on the site. The lithic industry,
according to Hoffman (1991: 197), has Near Eastern affinities and uses a variety
of materials, some brought from outside Egypt. Stone was also exploited for
making vases, palettes, and mortars, but no copper artefacts are known. As for
pottery, this is not of the highest quality, but it should be borne in mind that
similarities to Palestinian types have been noted (Midant-Reynes 2000: 121–3).

Upper Egypt, Nubia, and Adjacent Deserts

The Western Desert: When considering the Neolithic of the Western Desert we
are inevitably drawn first to the much publicized finds of Nabta Playa and its
associated playa sites[3] that lie to the west of Abu Simbel (Hoffman 1991;

[3] Playas are basins in desert areas that receive periodic or seasonal supplies of water. Such
basins, created by wind erosion, were once a common feature of the Western Desert. Their fossil
descendants form a rich source of prehistoric archaeological data.

Davies and Friedman 1998; Wendorf and Schild 1998; Midant-Reynes 2000; Wendorf, Schild, and Associates 2001; Nelson and Associates 2002; Wengrow 2003, 2006; Connah 2005). Semi-arid conditions prevailing in this area from about 10,000 BC to *c.*3900 created an environment with numerous seasonal lakes and a water table accessible by deep wells able to support small mobile populations sufficiently flexible to adapt to its opportunities and rigours. Two Neolithic phases have been certainly identified at Nabta: Middle Neolithic (6300–5600 BC), and Late Neolithic (5500–4200 BC). At all periods the populations inhabiting the site were semi-nomadic, using the settlements there on a seasonal basis, probably during autumn. Hunting continued to play a crucial role in the economy, and bones of gazelle and hare are common. The introduction of sheep and goats from south-western Asia sometime in the sixth millennium made possible the addition of pastoral herding to the economic strategy and provided a major new element to the local diet. At that period we find tumuli containing cattle burials which may well reflect the presence of a cattle cult (Wendorf and Schild 1998: 108). Pottery showing Sudanese and Egyptian affinities occurs at all periods, though in variable quantities (Hoffman 1991: 218–21; Wendorf and Schild 1998: 100, 109), and remains of hearths and houses are plentiful. Differences in the size of houses may be evidence of increasing social differentiation, and Midant-Reynes is surely right when she comments in relation to site E75-6, 'The construction and spatial organization of the settlement . . . expresses a state of relatively sedentary organization, as well as undeniable signs of a social structure' (2000: 76). Of particular interest amongst Late Neolithic material is the presence of a small stone circle and groups of what are claimed to be megalithic structures (Wendorf and Schild 1998: 108). It has been argued that the circle had a calendrical function, but this remains no more than an interesting hypothesis, and the nature and date of the stone clusters described by the excavators as 'Megalithic' remain problematic (Wengrow 2006: 599). Nevertheless the evidence of the manipulation of large stone features is indisputable, and it is a sound working principle of archaeological exegesis that, if an ancient society goes to a great deal of trouble to construct or erect features that have no obvious material function and require significant labour and material resources, those features will have a ritual purpose. Therefore, Wendorf and Schild (1998: 106) may well be justified in suggesting that the adjacent Site E75-8 used both in the Middle and Late Neolithic had a cultic role. No cemetery site has yet been identified at Nabta, but 25 km to the north such a site has been discovered at Gebel Ramlah[4] which may give some insight into practice further south. This site, probably the base of 'a complex, prosperous community of . . . cattle-keepers' (Kobusiewicz et al. 2004: 577), dates to the

---

[4] The name was invented by the excavators (Kobusiewicz et al. 2004: 56).

early–mid fifth millennium BC and is, therefore, contemporaneous with the Late Neolithic at Nabta. Thirteen burials, richly supplied with grave goods, have been excavated, and the team came to the conclusion that 'The graveyard itself can probably be interpreted as a burial ground for an extended family', which would imply that the family was probably perceived as a corporation of the living and the dead.

The Badarian Culture: The Badarian Culture, named after the site of el-Badari in Middle Egypt, flourished in the second half of the fifth millennium BC. The bulk of the known sites occurs on desert spurs to the east of the Nile Valley stretching from Matmar in the north to Hemamia in the south, but one site, Mahgar Dendera 2, has recently been located on a desert ridge to the west of the Valley and offers a stern warning against making bold assumptions on the culture's spatial distribution.[5] There are also Badarian sites in the Eastern Desert in the Wadi Hammamat, the Wadi Atulla, and Ras Samadi (near the Red Sea coast), a distribution that should almost certainly be treated as an indication of a significant Badarian presence to the east whose archaeological remains have yet to be identified more fully. If the disposition of currently known sites in Egypt is a reliable indicator, we can assume that they form part of a much broader habitat embracing the east side of the Valley and areas of the Eastern Desert that still offered on a seasonal basis relatively benign climatic conditions. We can perhaps go still further. Since Badarian culture shows very close similarities to contemporaneous sites in the Sudan (Wengrow 2006: 50), we may reasonably postulate a broad cultural continuum during the second half of the fifth millennium running from Middle Egypt and the Eastern Desert well into the Upper Nile area (Wengrow 2003).

About forty Badarian habitation sites have been identified to date. Some scholars have been inclined to describe these as small villages (Midant-Reynes 2000: 158), but we must be very careful in our use of terminology in this context and should certainly avoid any suggestion of permanent settlement. Wengrow is clearly correct in insisting that the sites in question were inhabited only on a seasonal basis as part of a migratory pastoral economy (2006: 27–9), and we should think of them rather as campsites where shelter was provided essentially by easily portable tent-like structures. However, though numerous habitation sites are known. the major evidence for Badarian culture consists of cemeteries which usually contain 50–300 graves and may well reflect a social structure organized on the basis of 'numerous, relatively small social units' (Wengrow 2006: 50). Interments were made very carefully, placing the body on the left side with the head to the south and facing west, a practice that suggests that the Pharaonic conceptualization of the west as the land of the dead was already present, and that, in turn, might indicate that there was

---

[5] In general see Hoffman 1991: 136–44; Midant-Reynes 2000: 152–65; Wengrow 2006: 26–9, 46–7, 49–56, 75.

already a solar dimension to Badarian religion since the location of the land of the dead in the west almost certainly arises from the fact that this is where the sun sets. Grave goods are abundant and clearly reflect a belief in an afterlife where the requirements of the deceased mirrored those of the living, a further point of similarity with Pharaonic practice. Burials are often rich and show differences in wealth, i.e. they provide evidence of social differentiation, and they also demonstrate that bodily adornment by means of cosmetics and jewellery, some of it using material from Near Eastern sources, was of great importance and probably formed a major context for asserting social status. Figurines of humans and animals also occur as well as boat models. Four of the human figures are those of females in which the sexual dimensions are very marked, a fact that suggests either that sexual activity was expected in the afterlife, or that the point of emphasis lies rather in notions of fertility and rebirth which would be highly apposite in the mortuary contexts in which they occur. A combination of both ideas would also be possible.

A particularly intriguing feature of the cemeteries is the inclusion of animal burials and the common insertion of animal skulls in graves (Midant-Reynes 2000: 159–60; Wengrow 2006: 56–7). The interpretation of these practices is inevitably speculative since we are dealing with a culture dating well before the invention of writing and have no texts to provide explicit statements of belief. Nevertheless, there is no escaping the fact that the cemeteries and their contents closely reflect the world in which the Badarians lived and wished to continue to live beyond the grave, and in this world animals, both wild and domestic, were of critical importance not only in an economic sense but as a consistent element in the physical and conceptual world that the Badarians inhabited. It should also be remembered that in early societies the modern conception of the animal world as something inferior to that of humans did not exist. Animals were certainly different, but they were, nonetheless, regarded as cohabitors of the world which must be treated with respect and even deference and with which a close spiritual bond was assumed and maintained. Busia (1954: 194) comments on the Ashanti of the Gold Coast: 'Animals and trees are also believed to have souls, though not all are powerful enough to cause harm to men: but there are some plants and animals that have powerful souls, and these must be propitiated.' And (p. 205) 'Animals and inanimate objects too have spirits, and are to be propitiated according as their spirits are conceived to be strong and potentially harmful or not.' Fowler and Turner's (1999: 422) observations on the Paiute Indian concept of the interrelationship between plants, animals, and humans take us even further:

Southern Paiute people say that plants need to 'feel' a human presence, such as when people walk about on them, or prune, burn, or harvest them. Animals need this same interaction with humans: if they are not hunted, their numbers will dwindle; the animals will sense that people no longer depend upon, covet, and show concern for them. They must, of course, be hunted with respect; appropriate prayers must be offered to their spirits, if humans are to expect them to yield up their lives to the hunter. If humans cease their predatory interaction with the animals, the animal population will dwindle. Plants and animals also live together in associations . . . These associations are vital for the continuity and maintenance of a healthy world.

If, as is extremely probable, the Badarians conceptualized their relationship to the world of plants and animals in similar ways, the presence of animals and parts of animals in cemeteries and graves will have had a powerful spiritual dimension passing well beyond mere economic dependence. Overall, we are justified in concluding that, however the Badarians formulated their aims at a conscious level, the mortuary cult served not simply as a means of disposing of the dead and meeting their post-mortem requirements, but also functioned as one of their systems for recurrent restatement of fundamental cultural affinities as well as providing a means of asserting the essential permanence and unity of a society whose migratory *modus vivendi* could so easily have imperilled social cohesion (cf. the highly apposite comments of Frachetti 2008: 161).

When we turn to the more concrete aspects of this culture, we are confronted with some impressive achievements, and the range of artefacts is considerable. Excellent handmade pottery is a standard feature, and stone tools and weapons of very high quality are numerous, including slate palettes for grinding cosmetics that anticipate the superb examples typical of the Naqada and Early Dynastic Periods. Intriguingly, similarities have been noticed between Badarian lithics and industries in the eastern Sahara (Holmes 1989: 183) which may well constitute one of the varied influences contributing to the creation of Badarian culture. It is also worth noting that in the closely related culture of the Khartoum area polished stone maceheads make their appearance for the first time, pointing forward to their widespread use in the Naqada Period. Bone tools, some used in the production of clothing, are also frequent, and occasionally small and simple copper tools occur that may derive from copper imported from the Near East (Midant-Reynes 2000: 161). The economy was based on a mixture of agriculture, pastoralism, and hunting. Barley, emmer wheat, and flax, which all have their origins in the Near East, were grown, as well as the castor-oil plant, and features that might have been silos have been identified (Midant-Reynes 2000: 158; Wengrow 2006: 47). The pastoral side of the economy was based on cattle, goats, and sheep, which again have their origins in the Near East. Whether these elements passed into Egypt across the Isthmus of Suez or through the Eastern Desert with Sinai as one possible intermediary remains an open question, but a multiplicity of avenues of transmission must remain a distinct possibility. The one thing of which we can be certain is that Badarian culture is the product of numerous cultural influences of which the Near East is much the most important.

The Chalcolithic Period

Lower Egypt

Maadi and the Maadi–Buto Culture: Maadi lies on the east side of the Nile 10 km north of el-Omari on a ridge at the entrance to the Wadi el-Tih which placed it beyond the reach of the inundation. The site, which dates to the early–mid fourth millennium (contemporary with Naqada I-IIB), is large, covering an area of some 18 ha, but excavation has only been selective (Hartung 2004). The arrangement of the settlement shows little sign of systematic planning or of the dedication of parts of the site for specific activities, either economic, ritual, or social.

Houses are generally of typical Egyptian type, but four structures are either wholly or partly subterranean. Some mud-brick and stone blocks were used in their construction, and they appear to be living quarters. Their design falls well outside Egyptian norms, but they do have Near Eastern parallels and should be seen as one of the numerous Near Eastern influences on the site. Who inhabited these anomalous dwellings is an open question. They may have been migrants from Palestine or locals familiar with that area who decided to imitate this foreign style of housing. Whatever the truth of the matter, these houses can reasonably be regarded as evidence of social differentiation. Maadi was equipped with elaborate storage facilities which suggested to Hoffman (1991: 206) the operation of 'a rather well-organized, community-based system of storage' as distinct from storage facilities maintained by individual families as at Merimda. The dead were buried with few grave goods in shallow oval or circular pits in cemeteries set apart from the habitation area except for still-born babies who were interred within the settlement itself. Bodies in the final phase of the Wadi Digla cemetery show a facial orientation to the east, a practice at variance with contemporaneous southern practice as well as that of Pharaonic Egypt. In the earliest phase of the site there were some carefully buried dogs and ovicaprids the explanation for which may well be analogous to that suggested for Badarian sites (see p. 37).

Maadi operated a mixed economy that continues the Neolithic tradition. Agriculture was based on the cultivation of wheat, barley, and pulses, and cattle, sheep, goats, and pigs were also kept. Fishing also played a part in the food economy. Much play has been made of the fact that copper ingots and copper ore have been found on the site. This material appears to come from the Wadi Araba in Sinai (Midant-Reynes 2000: 213–14), but attempts to make Maadi into the base of a major metallurgical industry importing, processing, and disseminating copper and copper objects fall foul of the fact that there is no clear evidence of metallurgical activity on the site (Wengrow 2006: 84), and the material in question is best treated as one of the numerous trade items coming into the settlement down the Wadi el-Tih. Trade was certainly a major

activity at Maadi. The position of the site at the western exit of the Wadi el-Tih
made it ideally suited to benefit from trade connections to the east, and it is not
in the least surprising that some of the earliest remains of domesticated
donkeys occur there, a fact that squares neatly with contemporary evidence
from the Near East of donkeys being used for transporting pots (Wengrow
2006: 36; cf. Rossel et al. 2008). Apart from copper, imports from the south
and the Near East included carnelian, Palestinian pottery, slate palettes, stone
bowls, and resin; evidence on exports is not so plentiful but seems to have
included fishbone points made from the spines of the fins of catfish (Midant-
Reynes 2000: 213). The local pottery tradition is an amalgam of local features,
Palestinian elements, and Upper Egyptian practice, and the same holds true of
Maadi lithics.

As exploration of the Delta has proceeded it has become clear that Maadi is
far from being culturally unique. Buto and Heliopolis and numerous Lower
Egyptian *gezira* sites have so much in common with Maadi that it is now
customary to speak of a Maadi-Buto phase in the prehistoric archaeology of
this area, and it has become clear that an archaeological sequence running
right down to the Old Kingdom can be demonstrated in numerous cases
(Wengrow 2006: 87, 159). We can be confident that the discovery of further
sites is only a matter of time; Buto may even have been a site that was able to
draw on the Sumerian expansion towards the Mediterranean Sea during the
second half of the fourth millennium. As a port (at this period), it was well
placed to exploit the possibilities of maritime trade, and the presence of
pottery with features of the Amuq tradition of Syria (Midant-Reynes 2000:
219) suggests wide-ranging commercial enterprises, though the martial scenes
on the Gebel el-Araq knife handle (see Fig. 2.3) indicate that these contacts
were not always of the most peaceful.[6] The evolution of these cultures is
characterized by increased technological sophistication, enhanced efficiency
in food production, and the development of increasingly large settlements.
These trends reach their culmination in the late fourth millennium, showing
themselves first in villages/towns dating to the Naqada II/III divide that mark
a quantum leap forward, sometimes evolving on the locations of older Maadi-
Buto settlements, but sometimes establishing themselves in areas, as far as we
can tell, previously unexploited. There is good reason to believe that their
positioning was determined in some measure by trading opportunities, e.g.
Minshat Abu Omar in the far north-eastern Delta is ideally located to exploit
trade links with Syria-Palestine whilst the port of Buto was well placed to
benefit from commerce passing along the Delta littoral that may well have had
a Sumerian dimension. It is particularly important to note that settlements of

---

[6] It has been suggested that Sumerian-style architectural cones have been discovered at Buto
(e.g. Midant-Reynes 2000: 219), but it is now generally recognized that the relevant finds have
been misinterpreted. They are probably ceramic nails (R. F. Friedman 2000).

Fig. 2.3. The Gebel el-Araq knife handle, Musée du Louvre. After Adams and Ciało-wicz 1997: fig. 38.

this period such as the early levels at Tell el-Farkha (eastern Delta *c.*120 km north of Cairo) and Tell Ibrahim Awad (north-eastern Delta) show a marked increase in sophistication with mud-brick buildings of considerable size. Indeed, an ivory box from the cemetery at Minshat Abu Omar seems to depict an example of the palace-façade so typical of Late Predynastic and Early Dynastic monumental architecture (Midant-Reynes 2000: 236). There is also evidence of increased sophistication in agricultural production and output, and there are compelling indications of large-scale brewing, bread-making (cf. Hierakonpolis, discussed under 'Upper Egypt'), and ceramic production, which could only have taken place in communities with a high degree of centralized organization. Cemeteries also bear a Naqada stamp in that the simplicity and paucity of earlier Delta practice is now superseded by a taste for the splendour and conspicuous display so marked in contemporary burials in Upper Egypt (Wengrow 2006: 160–3). We are clearly getting very close to the world of Pharaonic Egypt, if we are not already there.

Upper Egypt

Naqada I (Amratian): The Naqada I or Amratian culture (*c.*4000–3500 BC) seems to grow organically out of Badarian from which it differs mainly in its ceramics. Indeed, it is likely that the two phases overlap in some areas. The type site is el-Amra near Abydos, and the culture's epicentre lies in the Naqada–Mahasna area from which Amratian spread north and south with sites eventually stretching from Matmar to beyond the First Cataract. There is even evidence of its presence in the Lakeita depression area in the Eastern Desert.[7]

Settlement patterns at this period are problematic. Naqada I habitation remains can sometimes cover a wide area, but their spatial extension cannot be taken as evidence of large permanent centres, not least because we need to take account of settlement drift over considerable periods of time. Site HK29 at Hierakonpolis suggests that the standard housing model was loosely linked hamlet-like communities consisting mainly of relatively flimsy structures supplemented by animal enclosures, and Amratian settlement remains at other sites such as Hemamia, Khattara, and el-Adaima point in the same direction (see Fig. 2.4). However, there is clear evidence of more substantial structures at this period: at Hierakonpolis site HK29 a rectangular house of Naqada I B–C date showed traces of mud-brick and formed a much more permanent structure (Davies and Friedman 1998: 25–6), though it was certainly associated with more ephemeral dwellings; Naqada provides us with what might be an Amratian town wall as well as rectangular houses made of mud-brick, and a late Amratian tomb at Abadiya yielded a model that depicts a crenellated wall behind which two human figures are shown staring outwards, though whether this is a town wall or part of some sort of fort is quite unclear. All this suggests that we are dealing with sites consisting mainly of clusters of settlements used by semi-mobile communities that are supplemented by more permanent structures dedicated to specific economic, social, military, or religious activities (Hoffman 1991: 147–8; Midant-Reynes 2000: 184; Wengrow 2006: 33–4, 77–9).

Naqada sites of all periods are characterized by extraordinarily large cemeteries that are increasingly dominated by the imperative towards conspicuous display. Amratian burials can range from small pits to large, rectangular structures equipped with rich grave goods, but, although social differentiation is clear, there does not appear to be any zoning by sex, wealth, or status. Interments are contracted with the head to the south and the face normally orientated to the west, and the physical type revealed by skeletal remains is dynastic (Hoffman 1991: 110). Coffins now appear for the first time, and grave goods continue to include figurines that emphasize sexual dimensions (see p. 37), though these are relatively rare. One large tomb contained a high-quality macehead, a clear indication of status and probably also of power, and a tomb at Naqada yielded a sherd bearing an image that looks like the

---

[7] In general see Hoffman 1991; Midant-Reynes 2000; Wengrow 2006.

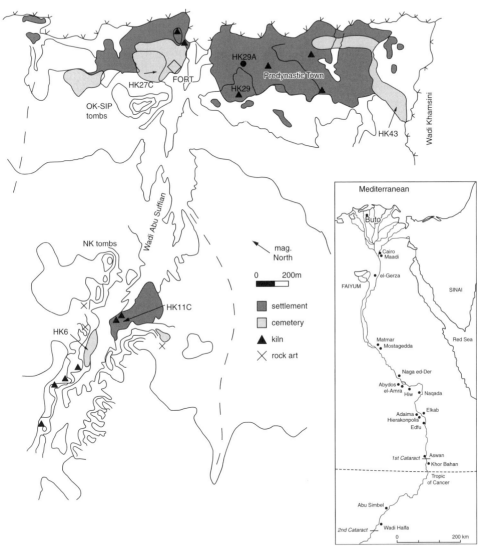

Fig. 2.4. The Prehistoric site at Hierakonpolis. Courtesy of the Hierakonpolis Expedition.

Pharaonic Red Crown of Lower Egypt (Midant-Reynes 2000: 170–1).[8] Whilst we should resist the temptation to over-interpret the latter find, the general picture emerging from Amratian cemeteries is of the slow but steady development of elites (cf. Castillos 2008).

The domestic economy continues the Badarian tradition with heavy reliance on emmer wheat, barley, and fish, and available evidence suggests that the diet of the majority was based mainly on plant sources. Cattle, goats, sheep, and pigs were all kept, and one site at Hierakonpolis (HK 11) seems to have been dedicated to the slaughtering of young animals, though the context in which this took place is quite unclear (Midant-Reynes 2000: 201–2). Gazelle remains indicate that hunting still played a part in the food economy, but such activities were evidently in decline. Pottery at Amratian sites can be of high quality (Hoffman 1991: 153), as are stone tools, though they do not feature in large quantities. Bone and ivory continue in use, but copper tools, although they increase in number, are relatively few. One notable development is the manufacture in stone of high-status items such as bowls and slate palettes for grinding pigments. Another innovation destined to a brilliant future is the first appearance of Egyptian faience. There is also evidence of wide-ranging trade activities, including in what was later to become Nubia, and Wengrow (2006: 33) rightly emphasizes the importance of the development of paddle boats in increasing the range of such contacts.

Naqada II (Gerzean A) (c.3500–3100 BC): The type-site of Naqada II lies at el-Gerza near the entrance to the Fayyum, but major sites in Upper Egypt, the Naqada II heartland, include Hemamia, Naqada, Abydos, Haraga, Abusir el-Melek, Mostagedda, el-Khattara, el-Adaima, and, above all, Hierakonpolis. Delta sites show gradual penetration of Naqada II culture, Minshat Abu Omar in the Eastern Delta being a particularly good example, and by the end of the period it had prevailed virtually everywhere in Egypt, either by immigration, imitation, or both (Wengrow 2006: 83–9). It also exercised a massive influence on the Nubian A-Group culture beyond the First Cataract. Whilst differing in many respects from Naqada I, there is no doubt that it was fundamentally a development of its predecessor (Midant-Reynes 2000: 189).

There are three major concentrations of settlement in Upper Egypt during Naqada II showing considerable progress in the evolution of urbanization, i.e. Naqada, Hierakonpolis, and Abydos all of which, in turn, dominated the area (cf. Wilkinson 1996: 89). The South Town at Naqada contained a large enclosure that might be a palace or temple, an enclosure wall, and the remains of rectangular houses. There was clear evidence of a gradual drift of the site away from the desert, and the same phenomenon was observable in the settlement area known as the North Town. There was a similar drift of the

---

[8] The two representations from the Wadi Gash discussed by Midant-Reynes (2000: 182–3) may well be of Naqada date, but there is no basis for allocating them to the Amratian Period.

inhabited area towards the river at Hierakonpolis where the currently access-ible remains of the Gerzean settlement consist of a 300 m-wide strip running along the outer margins of the cultivation and probably continuing under it. It is evident that this trend of movement towards the river was typical of the period (Midant-Reynes 2000: 198–207).

In general, settlement patterns still appear to be determined to a large extent by the mobile lifestyle of the majority of the population, but there is a clear tendency within settlements towards concentration into zones, even where these zones were used on a temporary basis. Sites can, therefore, present a picture of strings of village-like nuclei made up mainly of impermanent 'barnyard-style enclosures' where reed matting was the major building mater-ial (Wengrow 2006: 38, 78), but that is not the whole picture by any means. The remains of rectangular houses at Naqada have already been mentioned; we have a clay model house of Gerzean date from el-Amra that has a distinctly Pharaonic look to it; and there is clear increase in the use of mud-brick. Hierakonpolis is, as usual, particularly instructive: excavation at location HK29A has revealed the remains of an oval enclosure (Naqada IIb–IId with some reuse in Naqada III–early First Dynasty) which became more elaborate over time and possibly ended up looking rather like a later palace façade structure. This complex was indisputably a major ceremonial centre (R. F. Friedman 1996; Davies and Friedman 1998: 27–8; Jiménez Serrano 2002: 53–5; Hikade 2008; Friedman, van Neer, and Linseele 2011), but it also provided evidence of the quantity production of such trade goods as beadwork, very fine bifacial flint implements, and vessels made of a variety of hard stones, and exemplifies what must have been a growing tendency towards the development of specialized production areas within Naqada II settlements. The only contemporary evidence to offer some clue as to the deity in whose honour this complex was built consists of hawk figurines buried in the spectacular elite tombs at HK6 (Hendrickx and Förster 2010: 830–1; Hen-drickx, Friedman, and Eyckerman 2011). When the focus of settlement moved eastwards to Nekhen in Naqada III (Wilkinson 1996: 87; Hikade 2004: 183), it may well be that the major deity whose temple was built there was the same as that in HK29A. In later times that deity was Nekheny/Horus, the prototype of Egyptian kingship (see p. 65), and he may well have been the original tenant of the temple, but it has been suggested by McNamara (2008) that initially the focus of the earliest cultic activity on the site was not Horus but the king or kingship itself, though McNamara concedes that 'distinguish-ing between a temple to a king and one to the gods is a moot point' (p. 932). Either way it is reasonable to suspect that the ideological matrix underlying the ritual structure in HK29A is part of a trajectory taking the inhabitants firmly in the direction of the dynastic concept of kingship and that the complex was connected with the validation process applied to the prehistoric rulers of

Hierakonpolis.[9] If so, to this site goes the credit for generating a key element in the conceptual basis of Ancient Egyptian kingship.

Whilst the evidence for dwellings of the living is often meagre, the same is not true of cemeteries, which undergo significant expansion at this period and provide by far the richest source of information on its cultural evolution. They show the tentative beginnings of mummification, provide evidence of food offerings to the dead, and yield examples of animal burials alongside those of humans. Most intriguingly there is unequivocal evidence in some graves of the dismemberment of bodies before burial. The purpose of this practice is unclear, but Wengrow (2006: 121) points out that it did make possible the burial of parts of the body in different sites, and such a practice could have had obvious ritual and social value. Even a cursory survey reveals major differences in the size and equipment of graves that provide clear evidence of social stratification. Whilst some burials consist merely of pits containing a body and some grave goods, others anticipate the great tombs of the Pharaonic Period. Cemeteries B, G, and particularly T at Naqada are certainly the burial grounds of an elite class, and the best-known tomb of the period, Tomb 100 at Hierakonpolis, was almost certainly intended as the burial place of a local chief, and the large Naqada II tombs unearthed in HK6 very much point in the same direction (Wilkinson 1996: 86; Figueiredo 2004; Harrington 2004; van Neer, Linseele, and Friedman 2004; R. F. Friedman 2011). (See Fig. 2.5.) Of particular interest is the fact that Tomb 100 was decorated with scenes of warfare and hunting that show close affinities to the decoration of contemporary D-ware pottery and include the 'Lion-affronter' motif whose origins certainly lie in the Near East (see Fig. 2.6). Tombs of such splendour are patent examples of conspicuous display, asserting not only the status of the deceased but also of his lineage; for it is likely that family tombs of such worthies would be grouped together in the necropolis and *ipso facto* could constitute an ancestral claim to rights and power in the past and present as well as in the future. Intriguingly, craftsmen are also distinguished in burial practice (Midant-Reynes 2000: 188).

Economic activities are copiously documented (Hoffman 1991: 164, 207; Midant-Reynes 2000: 189–200, 204–7, 209, 223–4; Wengrow 2006: 33–6, 39–40, 76–7, 80–2). The food economy was based on agriculture, pastoral activities, fishing, and hunting, but it is clear that there was already a degree of specialization and standardization, e.g. site HK3 up the Great Wadi at

---

[9] Some of the late Prehistoric and Early Dynastic offerings discovered at Hierakonpolis in the Main Deposit and its environs are royal and bear witness to the continued importance of the shrine in the ideology of kingship even after the shift of political power to Abydos. It is also highly significant that as late as the end of the Second Dynasty Khasekhemwy constructed on the location of the prehistoric town a major ritual installation, now misleadingly known as the 'Fort' (Kemp 1963; Friedman and Raue 2007), and royal benefactions to the shrine continued well beyond that date (Hoffman 1991: 128).

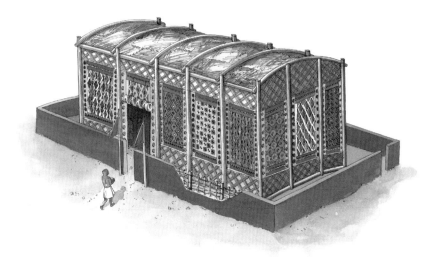

Fig. 2.5. Reconstruction of the Pillared Hall structure 07 in the elite cemetery at HK6, probably a funerary chapel.

Fig. 2.6. Tomb 100 at Hierakonpolis, drawing. From Kemp 2006.

Hierakonpolis to the west of the settlement has the appearance of a dedicated herding station whilst other parts of Gerzean Hierakonpolis were evidently concentrating on alternative economic activities, e.g. HK11C provides evidence of mass production of pottery (Baba 2011). A particularly striking example of this is the large-scale brewing installation discovered in the northern part of the site whose output passed well beyond the requirements of normal domestic consumption and only becomes explicable as part of a support system for highly organized elite activities (Davies and Friedman 1998: 270). Production of many different types of goods is exemplified in Gerzean contexts, and there is no doubt that numerous specialist workshops existed to meet demand: sites have yielded smelted and cast copper tools from the beginning of the period (Hoffman 1991: 207) and see a great expansion in such activities; there is a great variety in pottery types, D-ware being very distinctive. Some pottery types are Palestinian in origin but were adopted and adapted by local craftsmen, and there are major developments in stone-working that could have served only an elite market. Amongst other things the stone-workers were producing slate palettes and pear-shaped stone mace-heads that had probably already become symbols of power; Gerzean flintwork was of superb quality and reached its apogee in the production of ripple-chipped knives that have never been surpassed for technical brilliance. The major driver for all this production was undoubtedly trade, in which the exploitation of the Nile as an avenue of communication continues to play a major role. Manufactured goods are not, however, the whole story. Major population centres also had access to highly desirable raw materials: Naqada could tap the gold resources of the Eastern Desert through the wadis that reached the Nile on the east bank, and Hierakonpolis was well placed to exploit trade links with Nubia for such items as ebony. What we are dealing with in all this is patently an import–export trade in luxury items spanning not only Egypt but Lower Nubia and Asia, 'a prestige goods economy' (Wengrow 2006: 75) through which Egyptian products were exchanged for Near Eastern desiderata such as high-quality oils, resin, wine, and lapis lazuli via entrepôts such as Minshat Abu Omar and Maadi, and Nubia's riches in ivory and other raw materials were also tapped for home or external consumption.

Naqada III (Semainian) (3200–into the Old Kingdom): The Naqada III Period was one of the crucial stages in the evolution of Ancient Egyptian culture, bringing to fruition earlier trends in a spectacular burst of progress that propelled Egypt from its Prehistoric phase into the Dynastic Period. Large, well-organized settlements were a feature of the age, created, in part, by the decline of rainfall in the desert hinterland, which ultimately forced the pastoral element of the population into the valley on an essentially permanent basis (Midant-Reynes 2000: 232; Jeffreys 2004; Patch 2004; Campagno 2011), but demographic increase would also have been accelerated by more sophisticated economic systems such as emerge vividly in the Delta site of Tell Farkha (Wengrow 2006: 159–63; Koehler 2010: 36; Ciałowicz 2011), a process in which organized irrigation or, at least, some measure of water control seems to have played its part (Midant-Reynes 2000: 232). It is, therefore, no coincidence that walled settlements feature prominently on Late Predynastic slate palettes, though their appearance there must be regarded as only the latest phase in the development of a settlement pattern which was already of some antiquity. This increase in population may have been one of the factors behind the swift evolution of Naqada III (Hoffman 1991: 310), as well as creating contexts where rivalry and tension became endemic. As usual, the Hierakonpolis area provides the fullest picture, though interpretation of the evidence yielded by fieldwork is by no means straightforward. As we should expect, the settlement was not simply a habitation site but a centre of cult activity: evidence from the early levels of the Pharaonic town of Nekhen demonstrates the presence of temples at this time (Hoffman 1991: 131–2), and the large tombs excavated in the Great Wadi at HK6 provide clear proof of an elite stratum in the settlement's society in Naqada III, as, indeed, earlier (B. Adams 1996; van Neer, Linseele, and Friedman 2004). Evidence from Abydos, which achieved dominance in the late Predynastic Period, is more partial in that the town of This/Thinis that formed the settlement area has yet to be identified, but cemeteries are rich and very informative. The earliest, Cemetery U, began in Naqada I and continued in use into Naqada III when large, elite tombs set apart from lesser burials are encountered, in particular, tomb U-j (Naqada IIIa2) which was richly equipped with grave goods and may well have been a royal burial (Koehler 2010: 37–9).[10] Of particular importance is the fact that this tomb provides copious evidence of the use of an early form of the hieroglyphic script for record-keeping and also possibly for commemoration purposes (Kahl 2001; Hendrickx and Förster 2010: 848).[11] To the south lies Cemetery B containing tombs of rulers of Dynasty 0 and the Early Dynastic cemetery of Umm el-Qaʿab (O'Connor 2009: 137–57). Cemeteries also reveal that the process of social stratification applied at the other end of the scale, e.g. work at Elkab has identified the presence of a much less elevated stratum in Naqada III society at this period (Hendrickx 1994).

These urban conglomerations were major centres of manufacturing and commerce which led to a marked increase in wealth through the exploitation

---

[10] The excavator, Günter Dreyer, argued that it was the tomb of a King Scorpion because of the frequency of scorpion images on objects in the tomb (1998: 17, 86). The royal associations of the sign are indisputable, but there remains considerable doubt as to whether it represents a name or a title (cf. Midant-Reynes 2000: 249). The presence of the scorpion alongside other obvious symbols of kingship on the Cities Palette strongly supports the view that it is equivalent to the Horus hawk, i.e. it functioned as a title of a particular group of kings who would be regarded as The Scorpion *x*, The Scorpion *y*, etc. If this is correct, we do not have the name of a king on the famous Macehead of King Scorpion, only the animal symbolizing/embodying his status. It is intriguing that the earliest forms of the *serekh* do not contain any names, presumably because, at the relevant period, the important issue was to denote a royal connection of the objects on which they occur, the precise ruler involved being of quite secondary importance. The many cases of the scorpion sign on objects in tomb U-j are probably a mark of kingship and royal ownership or origins of the items in question, not the name of the ruler.

[11] Trigger (2003: 587–8) has argued that early writing systems served three functions: commemoration of the deeds of rulers, administrative record-keeping, and ritual. These earliest Egyptian examples would certainly be compatible with the first two functions.

of wide-ranging networks of trade embracing not only Egypt but Nubia, the surrounding deserts, and the Near East, though this wealth found its way mainly into the hands of the elite who were doubtless responsible for generating it in the first place. This trade was in prestige goods such as lapis lazuli, ivory, and timber, i.e. exotics that could be used to enhance the prestige of those privileged to enjoy them and could also be employed as gifts to those members of society whom a particular leading figure wished to tie to himself by bonds of obligation so that their possession could become a powerful instrument in building up political alliances and influence. A side-effect of the importation of the material from the Near East was that the Egyptians were exposed to artistic influences from Mesopotamia and Western Iran that enjoyed a short-term vogue during this period as objects of imitation, e.g. the Gebel el-Araq knife handle (see p. 40), but, as usual, the Egyptians took and customized what they needed and then went their own way. Although influence from the Near East is undeniable, it is evident that Naqada culture is, in essence, a native Egyptian product.[12] Indeed, by no means all high-status items were foreign imports, e.g. stone vases continue to show an increased presence, and these highly prized objects were certainly Egyptian.

Artistic production makes great strides in this period, particularly in the form of projections of elite power, as evidenced particularly by slate palettes of which the Narmer Palette is the prime example (see Fig. 2.7). One side of this monument, found in, or not far from, the Hierakonpolis cache,[13] shows three registers, the first of which depicts a horned goddess (Bat or Hathor) on either side flanking a *serekh* located in the centre bearing the name of Narmer. In the main register the king wears the white crown associated with Upper Egypt, a kilt with pendants adorned with bulls' heads, and a bull's tail. He is smiting an enemy who is designated as belonging to the Harpoon district which, in historic times, would denote an area in the Delta, perhaps the rough equivalent of the later Eastern Harpoon Nome, the Ninth of Lower Egypt. Above the enemy we find a hawk, symbolizing the king, taking prisoners in the Delta area, and, if we can treat each of the papyrus plants as denoting the numeral 1,000, as in the developed hieroglyphic script, the number amounted to 6,000. Behind the king stands an attendant carrying his sandals and also something that looks like a pot. In the third register we find two prostrate figures, obviously enemies, with what looks like glyphs denoting their places of origin. The other side of the monument contains four registers. The top is identical with the top register on the other side and is making the same statement.

---

[12] It has often been claimed that Near Eastern influence was considerably more pervasive, providing the Egyptians with the prototypes for palace-façade architecture, the hieroglyphic script, and subsidiary burials in association with royal tombs. It is now generally, and rightly, believed that it is more probable that we are dealing here with parallel developments, not imitations (Hendrickx and Förster 2010: 849–51).

[13] The exact location in which this find came to light is uncertain (Hoffman 1991: 129).

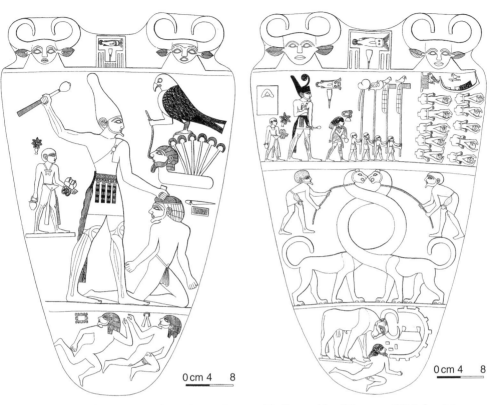

Fig. 2.7. The Narmer Palette, Cairo Museum. H. 63 cm. After Wengrow 2006: figs. 2.1 and 2.2.

In the second the king is wearing the Red Crown later associated with Lower Egypt, and he carries a flail, an attribute not connected with warfare, and a mace, which is not being used in any aggressive action. The king's name is placed over him, and his sandal-bearer again appears behind. The king is preceded by a figure who could well be the vizier, if we treat the hieroglyphs in front of him as an early writing of the word *tjaty* (*ṯꜣty*), the standard title of this official in later times. This individual, in turn, is preceded by four figures carrying standards which look like later nome standards and may indicate areas over which the king had control. They are all moving towards two rows of decapitated enemies over whom a group of signs is inscribed which can easily be read as *aa Hor* (*ꜥꜣ Ḥr*), 'The Gate of Horus', which could be a place-name on the north-east frontier, the exit route to the east that was known in later times as 'The Way of Horus'. This group is associated with the image of a ship and a hawk with a hoe, the two together probably referring to a military campaign in the north-east that involved naval activity. The third register consists of a scene depicting entwined long-necked leopard-like creatures which is inspired by Mesopotamian prototypes and can plausibly be decoded as a symbol of unification. The fourth register contains a scene of violent destruction of a city in which the agent is a bull, one of the classic symbols in later times of royal power. It is particularly important to note that both on the verso and the recto the king is represented as being much larger than anyone else, i.e. scale is being used to denote relative importance, a major element of Pharaonic artistic visual coding.[14]

THE EVOLUTION OF ANCIENT SOCIETIES: A MACROSTRUCTURE MODEL

Over fifty years ago Service (1962) argued that ancient social evolution passed through four phases: bands, tribes, chiefdoms, and states. Whilst there is much truth in this analysis, it is clear that the variabilities presented by historical and archaeological evidence make it impossible to use it as a rigid analytical template applicable to all societies, though I shall be using something like it in the following discussion. However, while we must avoid applying such models as rigidly predictive, imposing them mechanically on our very disparate and sparsely preserved data (cf. Yoffee 2005), it is permissible to construct a model of what the likely trends would have been in the evolution of prehistoric societies whilst accepting that the detail in individual cases will almost certainly lie beyond our grasp.

The Hunting Band

A survey of the evidence for the evolution of human societies reveals that there have been two principal ways in which societies have been organized, i.e. through kinship and the state. The state is very much a late arrival, and for most of human history it is kinship that has been used to create a cohesive community.[15] Whilst it is true that kinship can sometimes be fictitious, a convenient device for creating a working relationship that the societies in question need for their own purposes, it is generally based on a perception of genuine blood ties or on ties created by marriage. Its origins lie with the nuclear family, but, since the small size of the nuclear family imposes severe

---

[14] This feature is also present on the Scorpion King macehead.
[15] On kinship as an integrating social mechanism see, amongst many others, T. Parsons 1966: 35–47; Service 1966; Mair 1972: 69–108; Johnson and Earle 2000: 41–89; Panter-Brick, Layton, and Rowley-Conwy (eds) 2001; Barnard (ed.) 2004; Scarre (ed.) 2005.

limits on its survival value, the extended or composite family made up of several nuclear families linked by kinship relationships, real or fictitious, has often proved to be an operational necessity. The earliest form of human social grouping is the hunting band, which still persists as a going concern in some parts of the world, and other examples, now extinct, survived long enough to be the subject of ethnographic enquiry in relatively modern times (Lee and Daly 1999; Johnson and Earle 2000: 41–89). Therefore, our knowledge of these societies is very full, though it must be conceded that the possibilities for misunderstanding and for erroneous points of emphasis at various levels are legion. Their economies are based on hunting and gathering,[16] and, since their food supplies are usually transitory, their lifestyle is normally migratory and, therefore, relies on a very limited repertoire of equipment which provides what is needed for survival but little more. It follows that under normal circumstances such societies are small, though related groups may coalesce in certain circumstances for a short period of time to exploit seasonally available food supplies, to celebrate communal rituals, or to satisfy networking requirements of various kinds.[17]

Hunting bands invariably construct and maintain their groupings on a kinship basis though this can be orchestrated in a variety of different ways,[18] and the ramifications of kinship in such communities are pervasive. Not only is it the glue that binds the community together, but it determines nearly every aspect of life from the nature of leadership and the religious system to economic activity and the means by which the society deals with conflict and aberrant behaviour. There is a marked tendency to avoid institutionalized leaders. Since the band is made up of kinsmen, the prospect of one member becoming the permanent boss is deeply unpalatable. We find instead a situation where a temporary leader or 'Big Man' may come to the fore in particular activities, e.g. hunting or ritual, because he has a recognized expertise in those functions, but, once this role is discharged, he sinks back into the body of the society to assume the same status as everyone else. Since all societies develop the religious systems that reflect their social and economic needs, hunting-band systems reflect the specific social and economic imperatives of such societies and are, therefore, concerned with validating and maintaining their specific social order and guaranteeing their specific

---

[16] Once such societies came into contact with more advanced cultures, symbiotic economic relations involving mutually beneficial exchange strategies inevitably evolved, but this, in the long history of human development, was a relatively late phenomenon.

[17] The band is normally small, e.g. a camp of Aka pygmies may contain *c.*30 members (Bahuchet 1999: 192) and those of the Hadza of Tanzania an average of 18 adults (Kaare and Woodburn 1999: 202), but aggregation events that bring together a number of bands can be very large (e.g. Johnson and Earle 2000: 61–5).

[18] The pre-eminence of kinship does not exclude the operation of other integrating mechanisms such as the age-set found amongst the Okiek of Kenya (Kratz 1999: 222).

economic requirements. Resource acquisition is carried out on familistic principles, and exchange within the band is implemented on the basis of reciprocity between kinsmen which itself serves to enhance social cohesion. Sharing of resources of all kinds, particularly food, is, therefore, fundamental to the workings of the band. Since there is no institutionalized head and, therefore, no institutionalized control system, band members inevitably retain the right to exact retribution or vengeance for an injury on the basis of 'an eye for an eye and a tooth for a tooth', and such actions would bring honour, if carried through, and shame, if they were not. An injury perpetrated by the member of another band would be pursued on precisely that principle and with the support of the entire kin of the injured party, sometimes in the form of a long-term feud, but it is very rare for this policy to be implemented within the band itself since the social consequences of allowing such a system to prevail are so great that bands will go to extraordinary lengths to ensure that disputes are settled within the band itself to everyone's satisfaction (Service 1966: 54–7). The mechanisms employed generally reflect the familistic nature of the community, i.e. mechanisms are generated that enable the kin group to adjudicate on a matter of dispute: the offender can be 'sent to Coventry'; he can be expelled by common consent from the community; or, in extreme cases, he can be killed, though even that process will be conducted on a kinship basis. A particularly striking and instructive example of this phenomenon in an extreme case is provided by the !Kung of the Kalahari:

/Twi had killed three other people, when the community, in a rare move of unanimity, ambushed and fatally wounded him in full daylight. As he lay dying, all the men fired at him with poisoned arrows until, in the words of one informant, 'he looked like a porcupine.' Then, after he was dead, all the women as well as the men approached his body and stabbed him with spears, symbolically sharing the responsibility for his death.   (Lee 1984: 96)

The Local Group/Segmentary Tribe

Whilst some hunting and gathering communities have never abandoned their distinctive life-style, environmental conditions have made it possible in many contexts to move to a more sedentary mode of existence in hamlets or villages, initially through the exploitation of readily available natural resources but post-11,000 BC in the Old World through the cultivation of edible grasses and the domestication of animals.[19] The anthropological record suggests that such communities would have been based initially on an organizational system that

---

[19] The same evolutionary process is detectable in the New World but at a later date (Browman, Fritz, and Watson 2005).

Sahlins described as 'the Segmentary Tribe' (1968: 20–7) and Johnson and Earle as 'the Local Group' (2000: 123–241).[20] We may surmise that one of the starting points for such institutions would have been the development of some hunting-band communities into small autonomous settlements[21] still based on the same familistic principles of social interaction as the hunting band, though frequently displaying the beginnings of social differentiation. They follow a largely sedentary lifestyle usually based on cultivation supplemented by exploitation of any other food resources that might be available, though the migration of settlements to other sites is quite normal after periods of residence that might extend to several years. The domestication of animals such as cattle, sheep, and goats also introduced the possibility of herding and pastoralism which could assume various levels of importance in the subsistence strategy. Obviously it might simply be one item in a multifaceted economy, but the nomadic ethos of the hunting band would have made the transition of some bands to a pastoral-nomad mode of life a relatively easy process, and we must allow for that possibility, though there is a disinclination in current literature to accept such a shift.[22] However, whatever the mode of life, total autonomy for these communities is far from being a practical long-term option, and the establishment of links with similar settlements/communities within a viable radius of action swiftly follows to create the local group or segmentary tribe. These developments bring with them important consequences (Johnson and Earle 2000: 123–40): there is an enhanced need for leadership, but, whilst there are documented cases of something approaching a tribal chief, the model continues to be normally that of the 'Big Man', who maintains his somewhat precarious position through expertise in certain activities and, above all, through the judicious exploitation of patron/client networks of obligation cemented and maintained by lavish gift-giving; the need to maintain group solidarity leads to a heavy emphasis on group ceremonial activity that can only take place at group level and, therefore, acts as a powerful integrating mechanism; and the development of territoriality triggers a phenomenon that is extremely rare in hunting-band society, i.e. frequent and endemic warfare between groups. However, although these societies are more complex than band communities, institutional authority is still weak, and the prevailing familistic ethos ensures that the individual's right to self-

---

[20] The definition of the term 'tribe' has given rise to much debate. I prefer Crone's description of it as a 'descent group which constitutes a political community' (1986: 51). The Segmentary Tribe fits this definition only partially.

[21] 'The segmentary tribe is sharply divided into independent local communities ("primary political segments"). These communities are small. They rarely include more than a few hundred people, usually many less, and, except among hunters and pastoralists, rarely claim more than a few square miles as their own domain' (Sahlins 1968: 21).

[22] Theories of the origin of pastoral nomadism are discussed by Sadr 1991.

assertion and self-help within an honour/shame social framework will remain substantially unimpaired, and that will be particularly the case within pastoral communities (Mair 1972: 148–9; Ginat 1997).

The Chiefdom

Yoffee rightly insists (2005: 29) that the use of the term 'chiefdom' is bedevilled with ambiguities, but the classical view of chiefdoms, still widely current, provides a useful template for my purposes. According to this analysis chiefdoms are large consolidated communities that involved a quantum leap in size and, therefore, complexity as compared with segmentary institutions. The kinship nexus, with all its time-honoured ramifications, continues to play a role of fundamental importance but may work through a hierarchy of kinship units ranging from the family (nuclear and extended), through lineages, clans, and phratries to the tribe as the apex of society (Sahlins 1968). Inevitably, however, as groups became larger, the centripetal pull of kinship as an integrating mechanism would become less powerful than in a small group such as a hunting band, whilst, at the same time, the ad hoc systems for generating leaders both in bands and local groups would prove quite inadequate for meeting the leadership requirements of these large and complex communities. We find, therefore, that such societies generate the office of tribal chief as a permanent feature of their institutional structure, i.e. the leader's position is no longer a personal ascendancy that can be lost: 'Chiefs . . . "come to power" that is vested in an office—rather than building up power, as Big Men do, by amassing a personal following. Social status in chiefdoms is inherited, based upon an individual's genealogical position in a social hierarchy, and access to power through office is accordingly confined to specific elite personages' (Johnson and Earle 2000: 276). Amongst other things this development will gradually begin to impose limits on the individual's rights to unilateral self-help in matters of dispute, but it will not, and cannot, eradicate it completely.

Despite the enhanced status of the chief, he is still ultimately a kinsman, but he is a superior kinsman, and, as such, his extraordinary status requires a validation that lies beyond the kinship nexus. Johnson and Earle (p. 266) comment:

Within the chiefdom the regional organization is based on an elite class of chiefs, often considered descendants of the gods, who are socially separated and ritually marked. The organization is explicitly conceived as a kin-based, community like organization expanded into a regional governing body. The chiefs are related to each other through descent and marriage, and the idioms of kinship and personal bonds remain central in the political operation of the chiefdom. The tie between the developing economic system and developing social stratification is plain to all, and the chiefs come to dominate the economy as well as the social and political realm.

The State

The hunting band and the chiefdom are ultimately cemented into coherent communities by the integrating force of kinship ties. The state is different and altogether more complex. The distinctive integrating mechanism in all state systems, whatever their date, is an institutionalized power structure concentrated at the apex of the relevant society which imposes order from the top and which is not, in itself, a kinship mechanism, however it may work in practice. This does not mean that kinship is a dead letter—very far from it. It continues to function not only as the key mechanism determining self-perception, loyalties, and social cohesion but also as a structure through which political groupings are created and administrative functions organized. Whereas the chief is often regarded as a superior kinsman, the king is considered a superior being.

The City-State

The earliest type of state known is the city-state, which is exemplified in many parts of the ancient world. Such states consist of a city surrounded by the land that provides the economic basis for the community. That land could be very considerable in area and contain other urban communities that might, in some cases, be as large as towns or even cities. Particularly successful city-states may be able to impose their will on neighbouring city-states to create larger states or even empires, depending on resources and the ambitions and capacity of their rulers. Amongst the earliest known examples we are particularly well informed on the Sumerian city states of ancient Iraq, which evolved during the Late Uruk and Early Dynastic Periods (*c.*3500–2300 BC) and show very much the features we should expect: a ruler, whose apparatus of validation often, if not always, included a religious dimension; a society where kinship was still an important integrating mechanism beyond the boundaries of the family (Crawford 1991: 14, 20–5; Kuhrt 1995: 23–44; Yoffee 2005: 210–27); and endemic warfare between states living cheek by jowl with conflicting claims on available assets. All this raises a major question: why did the city-state arise at all? What led to the switch from chiefdom to kingship? There must have been some pressure that both necessitated the change and, at the same time, persuaded the members of the relevant societies that the change had to be accepted. In the case of Iraq there is not much difficulty in detecting the critical dynamic factor. Environmental and demographic influences forced

populations to move down from the north and east into the flood plain of
Mesopotamia where there was certainly huge agricultural potential—but
potential that could be realized only by the development of effective irrigation
systems, and such development could only take place if substantial bodies of
labour were mobilized to create it. Such mobilization might be achieved by
unalloyed persuasion, but this is an unsure and unpredictable solution to the
problem. By far the most effective and reliable mechanism would be concentrated authority at the top imposing its will on all below, i.e. kingship; or, at
least, an institutionalized ruler arose because it was essential to long-term
survival on the flood plain.

The Nation-State

The city-state by its very nature falls well short of embracing the entire ethnic
group to which its members belong. For long periods there were many
Sumerians living in many different independent Sumerian city-states. The
next stage in state evolution is the development of the nation-state, i.e. a state
that is essentially coextensive with the ethnic group, so that all Sumerians
could belong to one state. Two factors appear to determine whether this will
happen or not: military power and geographical circumstances. The latter
evidently played a major role in slowing down the process in Iraq where there
was a multiplicity of axes for expansion provided by the rivers Tigris, Euphrates, and Diyala as well as several smaller watercourses. The result was a deeply
rooted tendency to political fragmentation which was only intermittently
countered by the ambitions and military power of such figures as Eannatum
of Lagash (Kuhrt 1995: 42–3) and Sargon of Agade (Crawford 1991: 16–18).

THE MODEL AND PREHISTORIC EGYPT

The archaeological evidence, anthropological data, and historical parallels
previously described allow us with considerable confidence to generate the
following picture. I begin with socio-political structure. The remains of Egyptian Palaeolithic leave no doubt that we are dealing with hunting-band
societies that were, by definition, organized on a kinship basis, and the
presumption must be, in the absence of evidence to the contrary, that they
functioned broadly along the lines that we defined for such communities at
p. 52ff. Overall, the picture emerging from Epipalaeolithic/Mesolithic sites
is that of migratory hunting and gathering communities employing a microlith technology that significantly enhanced their capacities as compared with
their Upper Palaeolithic ancestors. However, the kinship-based social structure of the preceding phase will have remained essentially the same. When we

move to Neolithic cultures we must still be confronted with kinship structures, but they will be more sophisticated. Given Merimda's size and the clear evidence of substantial organizational control, it cannot be fitted into the segmentary tribe mould, and we must be dealing with a chiefdom-based tribal society with many, if not all, of the features described in our model for chiefdoms. Fayumian is another matter. In view of the apparent absence of a village settlement it is preferable to think of it as an example of an autonomous local group. On the basis of the archaeology there is no difficulty in locating el-Omari in the tribal range of societies, but its relatively small size and the presence of two contiguous settlement sites suggests that we may be confronted with a local group/segmentary tribe. The archaeology and the semi-nomadic mode of life at Nabta would suggest a local group/sedentary tribe system rather than a chiefdom, and a familistic ethos is certainly strongly suggested by the contemporaneous cemetery at the Gebel Ramlah. The evidence on Badarian settlement patterns is not compatible with a chiefdom social structure but would fit that of the local group/sedentary tribe very well, though it remains an open question whether we are dealing with numerous autonomous groups or local groups made up of linked segments in the form of loose federations.

The level of sophistication shown by Lower Egyptian Chalcolithic sites indicates that we are confronted with social structures that are initially at least at the chiefdom level but may well have evolved into city-state systems by the end of the period. Upper Egyptian evidence paints a complex picture. Naqada I looks transitional. Initially it probably exemplified Khazanov's type 3 form of pastoralism: 'Semi-sedentary pastoralism, where agriculture is the predominant economic activity' (Sadr 1991: 135), but the evolutionary trend probably involved a gradual shift away from the pastoral dimension. Settlement and cemetery remains strongly suggest a chiefdom organization, and Naqada II and III pursue that trend with increased momentum. We see concentrations of population such as Naqada, Hierakonpolis, and Abydos that would have created an imperative need for enhanced organization and leadership, and the presence of an elite ruling class is clearly evidenced by the large tombs excavated in the Hierakonpolis Great Wadi at HK6[23] and elite burials at Abydos. At what date we can begin to talk of kingship is a moot point. As tribal societies move through a city-state organization to a full-blown nation state, which Pharaonic Egypt became, the kinship ties binding the chief to his community would become increasingly attenuated and would eventually break, but the issue of validating the power of the ruler remains of paramount importance. Whenever we find this process of evolution it seems that the commonest way of justifying the ruler's position is to invoke religion

---

[23] It has been suggested that Tomb 1 is that of Scorpion, but see n. 10.

in some way. The chief then moves from being a superior kinsman to a divinely sanctioned king, a development made all the easier by the fact that the power of the tribal chief frequently benefits from a religious validation in addition to the kingship nexus. The development of the ideology to underpin this process seems to lie firmly to the credit of the major settlement of Hierakonpolis, which established the principle that the king was the incarnation of the god Horus of Hierakonpolis, thereby providing an acceptable validation for a degree of power that theoretically became all-embracing, though the existence of royal affinities to other animals in other communities is demonstrable.

It is in the highest degree likely that the elite cemetery in HK6 at Hierakonpolis contained the burials of kings, but there is no certainty on the matter. Tomb U-j at Abydos certainly looks like a royal tomb (Dreyer 1998), and Cemetery B at the same site is undoubtedly a royal cemetery, containing the burial places of the Pre-dynastic Dynasty 0 rulers Iry-hor and the Horus Ka, as well as those of the Horus Narmer and the Horus Aha (O'Connor 2009: 147, fig. 75). The latter is now normally allotted a position at, or near, the beginning of the First Dynasty, but the allocation of Narmer to the dynasty is more problematic. His name is widely distributed in contexts ranging not only through Upper and Lower Egypt but also in the Eastern Desert (a major avenue of trade) and the Near East, and a strong case can be made for identifying him as the prototype of the figure Menes who appears in Egyptian tradition as the founder of the First Dynasty and, *ipso facto*, the creator of a united Egypt (Lloyd 1988: 7).

The Narmer Palette bears eloquent visual testimony to this brave new world, though its interpretation has given rise to much debate (cf. Wengrow 2001; Jiménez Serrano 2002: 82–6; Wenke 2009: 181–8; Hendrickx and Förster 2010: 840–1; O'Connor 2011). It is indisputable from the association of the goddess and the royal register in the first register that the actions depicted are to be read as having divine sanction and that the king has a divine endorsement, and the identification of the king with Horus of Nekhen is equally clear. The large size of the king must surely indicate that any kinship nexus binding the ruler to his subjects is now at an end; he is no longer the *primus inter pares* but operates on a completely different and superior plane from common mortals. There has been much discussion as to whether the monument should be regarded as a statement about a specific historical event or as a symbolic assertion of royal power. It is both. If we accept that the hieroglyphic rubrics relating to geographical areas have been correctly interpreted, we must accept that there is a reference to successful military operations in the eastern Delta area. The narrative registers on the upper side of the monument are concerned exclusively with the military operations; those on the lower side, on the other hand, should be treated as depicting a triumphal procession celebrating success, the end of the operation being marked by the

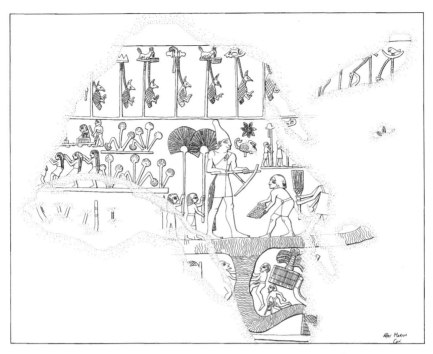

Fig. 2.8. The Scorpion Macehead, limestone, from Hierakonpolis. After Spencer 1993: 56 (36).

king's holding the flail, a symbol of rulership, and the macehead in a non-aggressive pose. The entwined animals can be treated as a symbol of the incorporation of the recently conquered area into Narmer's kingdom. At the same time these events are placed firmly into a context where royal action is located on the cosmic plane, and a cosmic plane where the ancient ritual and symbiotic association with cattle remains of cardinal importance.

Whatever view we take of the Narmer Palette's symbolic loading, there can be no doubt that it is associating the king with violence and the destruction of enemies and their cities (cf. Campagno 2004). This is a recurrent theme in monuments of the late Predynastic Period (cf. Wilkinson 1996: 95–6): the top register of the Scorpion Macehead shows a series of standards closely resembling later nome standards that all hold captive lapwings, symbols of defeated enemies (see Fig. 2.8); the Battlefield Palette depicts both captive enemies and a lion attacking or devouring prostrate foes, the lion doubtless functioning as a symbol of kingship; the fragmentary Cities Palette (see Fig. 2.9) shows seven cities (possibly Libyan or West Delta settlements), being destroyed by entities that look very much like embodiments of kingship and presumably represent

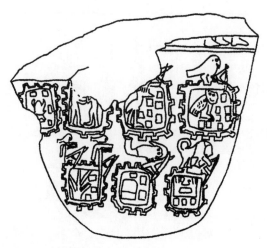

Fig. 2.9. The Cities Palette, Cairo Museum. H. 18.5 cm. After Midant-Reynes 2000: fig. 21.

an alliance of kings/kinglets;[24] and the Gebel el-Araq knife handle provides us with the earliest representation of a naval battle whose precise context is unclear but that may well involve conflict between Egyptian communities (Hoffman 1991: 340–2). These monuments add substance to hints in earlier Naqada material, particularly Tomb 100 at Hierakonpolis, of the increasing prevalence of an aggressive mindset, and it is also worth recording that the name 'Aha' borne by one of the earliest kings of the Pharaonic Period means 'The Fighter'. It may be that there were demographic or economic reasons behind this trait. The juxtaposition of city states would lead inevitably to conflicts, as it did in Sumer, but we cannot exclude the possibility that this martial dimension reflects the innate character of the late Predynastic rulers of Abydos/This and that the main driver behind the creation of the unified state was the ruthless determination of these warlords to bring the whole of Egypt under their control, by brute force if necessary. In this, as in other things, the Narmer Palette is iconic and expresses a perception of the king as an aggressive and successful warrior that was to remain a leitmotif of Egyptian royal iconography to the end of Pharaonic civilization.

If we try to construct a broad picture of the evolution of Egyptian urban polities in the Prehistoric Period, we are inevitably drawn in some measure into the sphere of speculation. However, both on the basis of evidence already presented and intrinsic probability we should expect something like the following: until the beginning of the Naqada Period villages/small towns of varying degrees of permanence, headed by chiefs, were the norm; from the

---

[24] Unless we adopt the hypothesis that the monument refers only to one king who had subsumed earlier dynasties into his own and, at the same time, acquired their sacred animals.

beginning of Naqada I concentrations of settlement developed of increasing density and permanence, which eventually consolidated into city-states dominated by elites headed by chiefs or kinglets; in due course contiguous city states were brought under the overall control of one of their number to form regional power blocks or confederations, without initially or necessarily being integrated into one homogeneous state, i.e. the subordinate cities could retain a considerable measure of independence. Such a confederation-structure is implied by the Cities Palette and was probably the basis for the hegemonies of Naqada, Hierakonpolis, and This/Abydos in Upper Egypt; in late Naqada III the hegemony of This/Abydos was extended to include the whole of the south; finally, once in control of the south, probably by a series of campaigns such as that depicted on the Narmer Palette, the hegemony of the south was extended to embrace the whole of the Delta, thereby creating the world's first nation-state (Wilkinson 1999: 28–59).

Socio-political structures, though crucial, are but part of the legacy of prehistory to the Pharaonic state. We also see a gradual move in economic structures from hunting and gathering strategies, through various combinations of pastoralism and agriculture, to an economy founded overwhelmingly on cultivation based on the exploitation of the waters of the Nile, though a strong herding dimension remained a constant feature of Egyptian farming activity throughout the Pharaonic Period. This process, which provided the economic base of Pharaonic society, was stimulated by influences from the Near East and owed nothing to the African context. We also see a long-drawn-out evolution of tools and weapons through millennia of lithic industries to the introduction and increased use of copper, though tools and weapons employing stone remained long in use in Pharaonic times. Here again, Near Eastern influences are of major importance, though there is also clear evidence of African stimuli. A similar picture holds true for ceramic production, but the use made of these contacts displays a consistent feature of Egyptian technological innovation, i.e. its ability to borrow, where required, and customize the borrowing to Egyptian needs and perceptions. Furthermore, we have identified the gradual increase in mud-brick architecture, and, above all, many features of later Egyptian religion, particularly in mortuary practice where the Pharaonic taste for using tombs as part of an apparatus of conspicuous display has obvious roots in prehistory, but we should also emphasize that the pastoral dimensions that we have so often identified cast a long shadow into the Historic Period where bull and cow deities are a frequent occurrence. Finally, important features of the visual arts in Egyptian prehistory carry over into the Pharaonic Period not only in terms of the visual code, which is in essence established by the beginning of the First Dynasty, but also in its role as a medium for making statements about political power and a device for the activation of various forms of ritual potency. In a word, we have *in toto* traced the evolution of the institutional core of Egyptian civilization.

3

Kingship

The formulation of the concept of kingship was the most important single institutional development of the late Prehistoric Period. It became the central feature of the structure of Ancient Egyptian society and formed the basis of state ideology throughout Pharaonic history (Frankfort 1948; O'Connor and Silverman (eds) 1995; Morris 2010). The Egyptians were incapable of conceiving of the mechanisms of government in any other terms; there are no words for 'politics' in Egyptian, but expressions referring to the monarch or kingship are many and various, encapsulating a wide range of nuances, political and religious. In theory all power lay with the Pharaoh and was exercised by others only as his representatives. However, as in all societies, the relationship between theory and practice was far from consistent, and the gulf could sometimes be surprisingly wide.

THEORY AND ITS RITUAL CONSEQUENCES

Every system of government must be grounded on a theoretical basis that makes it at least acceptable, if not entirely welcome, to the governed. Since all power was theoretically vested in the Pharaoh, it was essential that a theoretical formulation of his status should be generated that reflected and justified his unique position. From late prehistoric times onwards this conceptual basis took the form of the claim that the king was divine, the incarnation of the god Horus, the only exceptions occurring at the end of the Second Dynasty when the king Peribsen always and Khasekhem/Khasekhemwy sometimes claimed to be incarnations of Seth as well (T. Wilkinson 1999: 89–94; Dodson and Hilton 2004: 44; Kahl 2006: 105). This claim to divine status found formal expression in a number of ways. In the first place, from the Fifth Dynasty onwards all Egyptian kings, whatever their nationality, received a fivefold titulary whose thrust was overwhelmingly to insist on the divinity or divine associations of the ruler and whose format was standardized, though it was possible for anomalous examples to occur and for the order of titles to be modified to meet specific requirements (Müller 1938; Gardiner 1957: 71–6; von Beckerath 1999). The way in which the titulary normally worked may be illustrated by that of Senwosret III as it appears at the beginning of the Semna Stele of Regnal Year 16:

ʿnḫ Ḥr nṯr ḫprw nbty nṯr mswt nsw-bit(y) Ḫʿ-kȝw-rʿ di(w) ʿnḫ ʿnḫ Ḥr nbw Ḫpr(i) sȝ Rʿ n ḫt.f mr(y).f nb tȝwy S-n-wsrt di(w) ʿnḫ ḏd wȝs ḏt

Life to The Horus, *Divine of Manifestations*, the [Protected by the] Two Ladies, *Divine of Births*, King of Upper and Lower Egypt *Khakaure*, given life. Life to the Horus of Gold *Khopri*, the Son of Re, of his body, beloved of him, Lord of the Two Lands, *Senwosret*, given life, stability, and power eternally.

In this sequence the five generic titles are presented in Roman type, and the epithets, or names specific to the king, are indicated in italic. The first title insists on the status of the king as an incarnation of the god Horus, and the epithet that follows emphasizes the divine nature of his actions; the second title relates the king to the ancient royal protective goddesses of the kings of Upper Egypt (the vulture Nekhbet) and Lower Egypt (the cobra Wadjet), whilst the epithet insists on his divine birth; the third title is rendered here using the standard translation but means literally 'He of the Sedge Plant and He of the Bee', the first referring to the king's close affinity to the sacred heraldic plant of Upper Egypt and the second to his relationship to the sacred bee of the goddess Neith of Sais in the Delta; the fourth title again insists on the status of the king as an embodiment of Horus and reaffirms his divine status by associating Horus with gold, the colour and substance of the gods, and also by giving him the epithet 'Khopri' identifying the king with the sun-god as he appears over the eastern horizon in the morning. Finally, the king is stated to be the physical son of the sun-god Re and by that very token a divine being himself. Such titularies are frequently placed at the beginning of official documents, though they may take an abbreviated form, but they always serve in such contexts to insist on the basis of the king's power and on his legitimacy. It should be noted that, in addition to insisting on the king's divinity or divine affinities, the second and third titles in this list also empha-size the role of the king as the uniter of the two halves of the country. This is a recurrent theme in royal ideology and reflects the Egyptian conviction that there had been two parallel kingdoms in the north and south of the country before the Unification of Egypt, though this notion is now recognized to be a considerable oversimplification of the historical reality, and it is no longer generally held that there was a prehistoric kingdom of Lower Egypt compar-able to that known to have existed in Upper Egypt (cf. T. Wilkinson 1999: 50–2; Midant-Reynes 2000: 246–50).

Not surprisingly, the language used generally to refer to the king also emphasizes his divinity: the term *netjer* (*nṯr*), 'god', is frequently applied to him, either in isolation or in combination with other elements, one of which is the adjective *nefer* (*nfr*), which is often translated 'good' but whose connotations lie much deeper in that it evokes concepts of youth and pristine strength and power associated with the sun-god as he rises over the eastern horizon in the morning (cf. James 1953: 12). The king is also very frequently described as the son of gods or goddesses, as in the text quoted above, and his attributes are those of the great gods of the Egyptian pantheon: like them he enjoyed a superabundance of *hu* (*ḥw*), 'authoritative utterance', which is capable of bringing into being what the king commands by the very power of his word; he also claimed a superabundance of *sia* (*siʒ*) 'perception', which enabled him to define problems and their solutions more effectively than anyone else; he enjoyed *bau* (*bʒw*), 'power/s', i.e. a superhuman capacity to bring about change in the world about him; he also possessed a *ka* (*kʒ*), but a *ka* that was immeasurably more powerful than that of ordinary mortals, an idea strikingly expressed in the doctrine that the king has 14 *kas*, i.e. a superabundance of life force, and there is clear evidence of a cult of the royal *ka* from the New Kingdom onwards which was based on the concept that the royal *ka* was not specific to any king but a constant element of kingship that passed down from one legitimate king to another and was in need of constant cultic renewal (Bell 1985); the king was also endowed *ex officio* with *heka* (*ḥkʒ*), often translated 'magic', but it was quite devoid of the pejorative overtones of this English word and referred to a mastery of potent ritual words and actions that were capable of changing the physical world in which the Egyptians regarded themselves as living. The king also possessed the quality of *maat* (*mʒˁt*), a concept of wide-ranging application which, in his case, particularly related to the capacity to guarantee justice and order. Since the essence of the king was the essence of the gods, it is hardly surprising that the mode of representing the ruler is frequently indistinguishable from that of the gods of the pantheon.

Given the pre-eminent position of the king, the issue of the succession was of supreme importance, but the precise nature of the principles determining who was to become a Pharaoh has given rise to much discussion. For decades much play was made with the notion that, if anyone were to become king, he would have to marry the chief heiress, even if, as would often have been the case, that person was the king's full sister. This notion has now been thoroughly demolished, and it is now clear that choice by the living king played a critical role (Robins 1983). He would normally choose one of his sons, though, given the mortality rate in ancient Egypt, his first choice would not necessarily live to achieve this heady position, as is exemplified in the case of Ramesses II who lived at least into his ninetieth year and was succeeded by his thirteenth son Merneptah. However, it was by no means always the son who succeeded. Succession by a brother certainly took place, though the circumstances that gave rise to such a situation are never clear. Why Djedefre in the Fourth Dynasty was succeeded by his brother Khafre is unknown, though the event has given rise to much speculation (Dodson and Hilton 2004: 50–6), but in some cases it must simply have happened because the deceased king had no son to succeed. The example that appears quite explicitly at the end of the *Tale of Two Brothers* (Simpson (ed.) 2003: 90, 19.5), though fictional, must reflect Egyptian attitudes to such matters. The successor would then validate his position by carrying out the funeral of his predecessor, as exemplified in the case of Djedefre, who buried his father Khufu; Ay, who orchestrated the funeral of Tutankhamun (an event depicted in the latter's burial chamber); and Amasis, who interred his deposed predecessor in the royal necropolis at Sais.

Since the succession was determined de facto under normal circumstances by a decision of the living Pharaoh, incarnations of Horus were not incarnations at birth, though their potential for that role even before birth is often a matter of comment, and the question arises as to when this incarnation status was achieved. The answer is at the coronation, before which the putative ruler is only a potential incarnation and a potential king. No text or set of representations provides us with a full account of what took place at this event, and we should, in any case, make allowance for variations at different periods and also for different points of emphasis, but the general thrust of the ritual sequence is clear (H. Bonnet 1952: 395–400; Gardiner 1953: 24; Barta *LÄ* iii: 531–4). Where representations occur, the gods are shown playing a major part, and we can be confident that their role was enacted in practice by priests dressed to look like them and even wearing appropriate masks. As with all cultic acts, the starting point was a ritual of purification designed to raise the king to the highest level of cultic power. A crowning ritual then took place focusing on a kiosk containing two chapels in each of which the king sat in turn, first wearing the white crown of Upper Egypt and then the red crown of Lower Egypt. He also carried the crook and flail, the two classic symbols of royal power. These physical objects, as well as the thrones on which he sat, were suffused with divine power which flowed into the king during the ceremonies as part of the process of actualizing his divine status. There then followed the *sma tawy* (*smȝ tȝwy*) ('Unification of the Two Lands') ritual which was performed by two priests impersonating Horus and Seth (the latter sometimes replaced by Thoth) who wound around the *smȝ* sign (the hieroglyphic sign for unity) a lotus plant and a papyrus, respectively heraldic plants of Upper and Lower Egypt, a ritual that asserted that the new king fulfilled the key function of unifying the two lands but, at the same time, a ritual that actualized what it represented. Subsequently, there took place the *pekher ha inb* (*pḫr hȝ inb*) ('The Circling of the Wall') ritual involving visitations to shrines of all the gods supposed to be participating in the coronation events, an act that, amongst other things, affirmed the king's unique relationship with the divine order. At some stage a ritual was performed involving the formulation of the king's fivefold titulary, the king shot arrows to the four cardinal points to symbolize/actualize his mastery of the world, and four birds were released to the cardinal points to carry the news of the accession of the new Horus. It hardly needs saying that the accession was accompanied by nationwide festivities, and that these were greatly encouraged by the progress of the king throughout Egypt to present himself to his new subjects.

The coronation placed the king in the maximum state of divine potency to perform his functions, but this high level of capacity was not definitive. The notion was firmly established that the king might need recharging at some stage, and a ritual sequence was developed to achieve this purpose. This took the form of the *Heb-sed* Festival whose name was translated into Greek in the Ptolemaic Period as 'the Thirty Year Festival'. This fact has been taken to mean that it was celebrated in the Thirtieth Regnal Year, and this certainly holds true in some cases, e.g. Amenhotep III celebrated his first *Heb-sed* at that point, but once a ruler had performed the ritual it could be celebrated at much shorter intervals, e.g. three years, and as often as the ruler wished. However, the thirty-year rule did not apply throughout Egyptian history, e.g. Montuhotep IV celebrated it in Regnal Year 2 despite the fact that his reign lasted nowhere nearly the length of time later required, and it seems reasonable to assume that the date for celebration was a matter of personal choice at some periods. Be that as it may, despite the fact that again our evidence is very defective and scattered over a long period of time, we can see clearly that the ritual sequence followed by the festival bore many points of similarity to that of the coronation and that the conceptual thrust was very much to place the king back at the level of potency that he had enjoyed at his coronation (Gardiner 1953: 22; Murnane 1981; Hornung and Staehelin 2006).

The ideology of kingship gave the Pharaoh a clearly defined role not only in the working of the state but in the workings of the cosmos itself. Essentially his function was regarded as being the maintenance of *maat*, 'cosmic order (both material and moral)', which came into existence at the creation of the ordered universe and was the only possible order. This order was permanently under threat, and it was the duty of the king to ensure that the threats did not lead to the erosion and collapse of this order and the return of the universe to the orderless, undifferentiated matter from which the primordial god Atum had created it. In practical terms he fulfilled this function in three main contexts. In the first place, and most importantly as far as the Egyptians were concerned, he needed to maintain the gods themselves. As the human incarnation of a divine being, as man/god, he was ideally suited to function as the intermediary between the world of men and the world of the gods, though the Egyptians did not see the line of demarcation in anything like the rigid terms that modern man would deploy. As such, the king was technically the high priest of all the gods and goddesses of Egypt and was responsible for the performance of the daily rituals of maintenance which were conducted in temples the length and breadth of the country and without which the gods would weaken and die with catastrophic consequences for the entire cosmic order. If these rituals were performed, the gods would continue to flourish, and the king would receive from them the support the kingdom needed in order to survive, support that was conventionally represented in iconography by the conferment of the symbols ⸘, ꜥnḫ wꜣs ḏd (ankh was djed), 'life, power, eternity'. Of course this reciprocal relationship could not be actualized in practice every day in every part of the kingdom, and the function was normally delegated to the high priest of individual temples who was ritually converted into Pharaoh before the daily temple ritual began so that, in cult terms, the Pharaoh *was* carrying out the temple offices, and, in consequence, it is almost always the Pharaoh who is represented on temple walls as carrying out the rituals (A. Blackman 1919; Fairman 1954; Baines 1997; Wilson, 2010). If this task were properly performed by the Pharaoh, if only by proxy, he could be described as *menekh* (*mnḫ*), a word impossible to translate accurately into English, but which means basically 'efficient' in the very special sense that the Pharaoh is being described as carrying out to perfection his key role in the maintenance of order (Lloyd 1975: 57 n. 18). The gods could also, from to time to time, offer indications of their approval of a particular ruler by manufacturing *biayet* (*biꜣyt*), 'marvels', extraordinary events (see further at p. 238).

Whilst the priestly role of the Pharaoh was perceived to be his most important practical function, there were two other areas where his cosmicizing role was expected to manifest itself: he was responsible for the orderly running of the kingdom in all its aspects whether this involved administration, the operation of the law, or the maintenance of peace (see further Ch. 5). He was also expected to protect the kingdom against foreign attack, and, as such, he was commander-in-chief of the Egyptian armed forces and frequently led his troops in person on military operations, sometimes at the cost of his own life, though this is something that Egyptians were most disinclined to discuss (see further Ch. 4).

THE PROBLEM OF PHARAOH'S DEATH

The major obstacle to the maintenance of this canonical doctrine of the king's divine nature was obviously the king's physical humanity, above all, the fact that all kings sooner or later had to die. This the Egyptians dealt with very neatly by arguing that the death of the king was simply a transitional phase during which rituals of rejuvenation would take place that guaranteed his resurrection and survival beyond the grave on a new plane but without any loss of divine status or functions. The detailed conceptualization of this *post-mortem* existence could vary from period to period, but the overriding solar thrust of its thinking prevails to the very end of Egyptian civilization, despite recurrent references to the role of Osiris and the insistence that the resurrected king is 'an Osiris'. The earliest explicit statements appear in the *Pyramid Texts* which first become visible to us at the end of the Fifth Dynasty in the pyramid of Unis at Saqqara, though they are clearly considerably older and were probably in use as ritual texts as part of the royal funeral long before they were recorded in royal monuments. Spell 214 of this corpus describes the king's transition very clearly: 'Go in the wake of your Sun and become clean . . . that you may exist beside the god, and leave your house to your son of your begetting' (Allen 2005: 31, 147), i.e. the king's post-mortem existence is seen in the context of a close association with the sun-god himself. The process by which this goal was achieved had three main phases: first, the dead king must be reconstituted as a living entity as he had been on earth, i.e. like anyone else his body must be reintegrated with his *ka* and *ba* so that he can achieve the status of an *akh* (*ȝḫ*), 'a luminous one' (one of the resurrected dead, see p. 226), but, if he is to establish his pre-eminent position as ruler beyond the grave, he also needed to recover in full the royal attributes of *djed, sia, hu, heka*, and power (see p. 67), an outcome that is achieved at one level by assimilation to or even absorption of the gods themselves, the famous *Cannibal Hymn of Unis* being the most compelling statement of this concept (cf. Eyre 2002). Once through this phase he must be translated to the eastern horizon to join the sun-god, a process that is mediated in a variety of ways, e.g. elevation by the Circumpolar Stars or by means of a ladder. Finally, the resurrected ruler needs to be permanently associated with the sun in whose cyclical immortality he will share for eternity—or, at least, for as long as the cosmos survives. In the words of PT 210: 'Unis will circumnavigate the sky like the Sun' (Allen 2005: 30, 143).

The pre-eminence of the solar dimension is equally clear in the Middle Kingdom, though evidence from royal contexts is not as full for this period as for the Old Kingdom. A particularly explicit example is provided by the opening of the story of Sinuhe where the death and transfiguration of Ame-nemhet I are described in these terms: 'The god rose up to his horizon. The King of Upper and Lower Egypt Sehetepibre ascended to the sky, being united with the sun's disc, the god's limbs being united with him who made him' (R6). Here the unification of the resurrected king with the sun is made absolutely explicit, and this thinking continues into the New Kingdom in such texts as *The Litany of Re* where the issue of the assimilation of the king to the sun is heavily emphasized (Hornung 1999: 142–4). The solar dimension to the king's post-mortem existence is also evident in *The Myth of the Celestial Cow*, but the main thrust of this text lies in reaffirming and thereby reassuring the cosmic order of which the resurrection of kings is an integral part. This latter issue is central to other New Kingdom underworld books such as the *The Book of the Secret Chamber* (commonly called, incorrectly, *The Amduat*) and the *Books of the Sky*. The *Book of the Secret Chamber* is particularly interesting from this point of view since it expresses the concept that all deceased kings are to be found in the underworld in the section covered by the Sixth Hour of the text and that their immortality, along with that of the king in whose tomb the text appears, is dependent on the nightly resurrection of all the dead as Re/Amon-re brings life once more to the underworld in his nightly passage through its twelve sections from west to east (Hornung 1999: 34–8).

This body of concepts was backed up by an elaborate ritual system centred on royal mortuary installations which were essentially ritual devices designed to guarantee the resurrection and permanent survival of the king beyond the grave. Whilst such structures survive from the very beginnings of Egyptian history at Abydos, it is only in the Old Kingdom with the appearance of pyramid complexes that we are able to decode these buildings with some measure of confidence. The best starting point is the complex of Khafre for which the archaeological evidence is good and which sets the pattern for subsequent royal installations with clearly defined subdivisions consisting, from east to west, of a valley temple, a causeway, a mortuary temple, and a pyramid with associated subsidiary pyramids and boat graves. The most important element is the pyramid which is certainly a solar device, embodying the sacred *benben* stone, a pyramid-shaped stone fetish housed in the great solar temple at Heliopolis, which, in turn, embodied the primeval hill from which the creator god emerged at the genesis of the ordered universe. Just like the creator god at the birth of the cosmos, the deceased king was expected to rise from his own primeval hill to renewed life and power. The adjacent mortuary temple was pre-eminently the location for the rituals of maintenance that were crucial to the fulfilment of the function of the complex. The focus here was a false door at the back of the structure through which contact could be made between the deceased and the officiants providing the crucially important offerings and incantations. These ritual functions were also served by a group of five statues and storage chambers for ritual equipment, but with the passage of time the mortuary chapel also came to serve as a context where the king's successful reception by the gods could be asserted in representations that, simultaneously, were thought to bring about what they represented. The building also acquired a commemorative function, illustrating the achievements, real or alleged, of the royal owner, as illustrated by the superb reliefs from the mortuary installation of Sahure at Abusir. Ritual scenes might also appear as well as representations of triumph over animals, symbolizing the triumph of order over chaos. Of particular interest, in view of the decorative motifs found in later mortuary temples, are scenes relating to the *Heb-sed* festival, evidently asserting legitimacy, and the Min festival, presumably evoking rebirth. The causeway provided a link to the valley temple which some scholars have claimed was the context for the mummification and purification of the king's body before it was moved up into the pyramid, but, although this is by no means an implausible view, it awaits conclusive proof.

Royal mortuary installations of the New Kingdom from the Eighteenth to Twentieth Dynasties were located in Western Thebes along the margins of the cultivation. The tombs proper were excavated in the Valley of the Kings and the associated West Valley, all located beneath the pyramid-shaped hill now known as el-Qorn which probably served as the ritual equivalent of the man-made pyramids of earlier periods. These tombs were often of great size and, if completed, were copiously decorated with texts and representations designed to guarantee the ruler's survival and transfiguration as well as being richly equipped with grave goods to supply the deceased's post-mortem ritual and practical needs. Fundamentally, therefore, while detail may differ, there is no change in the tomb's ritual function (Reeves 1990*a*). However, there is a major innovation, undoubtedly motivated by security considerations, in the architectural orchestration of the mortuary complex as a whole in that the mortuary temples (called Mansions of Millions of Years), such as those at Deir el-Bahri, the Ramesseum, and Medinet Habu, were now completely separated from their associated tombs.

The Egyptian conceptualization of these temples has given rise to much perplexity and debate, some scholars describing them simply as mortuary temples, others as memorial temples (Haeny 1997: 86–126), and we must concede that their state of preservation is not entirely helpful in establishing function, but surely the difficulty is largely illusory. If we compare what we know of Old Kingdom mortuary temples with what we find in Mansions of Millions of Years, it will emerge that all the major points of emphasis of the latter—making offerings, association with the gods and ancestors, maintenance of the cosmic order, the concern with royal legitimacy, the emphasis on the *Heb-sed* and Min Festivals, the commemoration of royal achievements—are already there in the earlier period. There are certainly changes in the New Kingdom, both in concepts and cult practice: the shifting of at least some of the mortuary service to mortuary suites away from the central axis of the temple (B. Lesko 1969: 453–8) and the assimilation of the resurrected king to Amun as Amun-United-with-Eternity (Nelson 1942: 127–55; Morkot 1990: 326; Haeny 1997: 109) are certainly innovations, but they must both be seen as contexts within which offerings and other rituals of maintenance could be performed exactly as would have been the case in the Pyramid Age. Essentially what seems to have happened is that the old focus of cult with its false door adjacent to the pyramid has been shifted to the south of the main axis in the form of a mortuary suite to be superseded by a cult place for the heavily Amonized ruler in the form of Amun-United-with-Eternity. Another distinctive New Kingdom feature is the pre-eminent position given to the Theban triad headed by Amon-re who is often described as the deity in whose honour a temple was built, i.e. on the face of it, he subordinates the king, but since the king, as we have already seen, is identified as a version or hypostasis of Amun, the departure from earlier practice is not as great as it appears. At the same time the cult practice in honour of these and all other deities in the temple serves to maintain the cosmic order and, by the same token, guarantees the resurrection of all deceased rulers. We may also have another novelty in the practice whereby in some cases, if not all, these Mansions of Millions of Years were activated as soon as they were completed while the king was still living, but we are not in a position to say whether this has antecedents in the Old or Middle Kingdoms. If all this is correct, the Mansions are neither simply mortuary nor memorial temples. Like pyramid mortuary temples before them they are both—as well as serving the living king as a cult temple for such events as the *Heb-sed*, as and when required, hence the palaces still detectable in some extant examples.

THE PRACTICE

The concepts described in the previous section dominate overwhelmingly the large corpus of surviving iconographic evidence as well as the texts, inscriptional and otherwise, that have survived into modern times, forming part of the Pharaonic media image of kingship that has often been described, not without reason, as the 'propaganda of kingship'. This material might well create the impression that the king lived a life of hieratic splendour that kept him far removed from the world of ordinary men. Indeed, if we were to invoke the style of Chinese or Japanese emperors, we might even begin to think of him as being far from easy to access and generally closeted in the palace in a state of splendid isolation, only emerging to fulfil the religious and military duties that feature so prominently on temple walls. However, this was far from being the case. In Ancient Egypt, as elsewhere, theory and practice functioned in a complex dialectic in which the main emphasis could swing markedly from one pole to the other, depending on a variety of factors. This shows itself in numerous contexts:

Humanity v. Divinity

In the previous discussion we have described the ideology underpinning Pharaonic kingship as the insistence that the king was the living incarnation of a god and that the most problematic aspect of this doctrine was the king's evident humanity, as demonstrated most obviously by the fact that, like ordinary mortals, he was subject to death. However, this was not the only context where the problem arose, and the tension between the alleged divinity of the king and his obvious humanity can show itself in other ways. Indeed, the point of emphasis can come down at many points on the divine–human spectrum. Sometimes the divine aspect will predominate; at other times the king's humanity prevails.

A particularly vivid illustration of these trends is presented by royal iconography. If we consider the well-known statue of Khafre from his Valley Temple at Giza (Fig. 3.1), it would be difficult to imagine a more compelling image of the divinity of kingship; the serene figure looks into the far distance well above and beyond common humanity, and the hawk at his shoulders leaves us in no doubt that we are confronted with an incarnation of Horus. It can hardly be denied that here an all-powerful king of the Fourth Dynasty with its highly centralized governmental system is at issue, and the same point

Fig. 3.1. Seated diorite statue of Khafre from his pyramid complex at Giza, Cairo Museum. H. 160 cm.

could be made about the Menkaure triads, though this image of kingship is by no means universal in the Old Kingdom, as the Sixth Dynasty copper royal statues from Hierakonpolis demonstrate clearly (Robins 2008: 65 no. 59). The Middle Kingdom can persist in projecting the divine dimension of kingship, but the Twelfth Dynasty shows a remarkable willingness to concede the humanity of the ruler in the facial rendering of statues of Senwosret III and Amenemhet III (Fig. 3.2) of which Stevenson Smith (1981: 185–6) aptly commented:

Fig. 3.2. Black granite statue of Amenemhet III. Luxor Museum.

The dominating quality of such heads is that of an intelligent consciousness of a ruler's responsibilities and an awareness of the bitterness this can bring... A brooding seriousness appears even in the face of the young Amenemhat III in a seated limestone statue from his Hawara pyramid temple which has more of the idealized character of the earlier seated figures of Sesostris I. Although there is here none of the hardness or the signs of weary age to be found in other heads of Amenemhat III, it is immediately apparent that this man lived in a different time from that which produced the serene confidence of the people of the Old Kingdom.

The humanity of the ruler is very much in evidence here, and this closing of the gap is also reflected in movement at the human end of the social order with Pharaoh's subjects sometimes abrogating attributes that are more often associated with kingship, as is startlingly illustrated in the tomb of Djehutyhotep II at el-Bersha where the nomarch set up a colossal statue in his tomb garden that might well be compared with the colossi later located at Biahmu by Amenemhet III.

The image projected by this humanizing royal iconographic material is strongly supported by *The Instruction of Amenemhet*, one of only two surviving examples of a royal instruction text, both, intriguingly enough, belonging to the late First Intermediate Period–Early Middle Kingdom period. It is a carefully wrought literary text that takes the form of the king advising his son and successor Senwosret I on how to rule the kingdom, another intriguing phenomenon since this function involves an admission that the king might not know how to do his job, a concession diametrically opposed to the standard image of the Pharaoh as omnipotent and omniscient. It is evident from several passages that it is the ghost of Amenemhet which is speaking from beyond the grave and that the king, in fact, had no part in the preparation of the text (Simpson (ed.) 2003: 166–71).

The king's advice is full of pessimism, painting the bleakest view of the position in which a ruler finds himself, prey, as he is, to treachery and ingratitude:

> Be wary towards your [?] subordinates
> Who are not really such,
> In whose respect no trust can be placed;
> Do not approach them when you are alone.
> When you rest at night, let your own heart keep watch over you,
> For no man has any supporters on the day of trouble.
> I gave to the poor, I raised the orphan,
> I caused him who had nothing to approach [me] like a man of means.
> Yet it was one who ate my bread who raised complaint,
> Someone to whom I had given my support devised dread deeds therefrom.
> Those clothed in my fine linen looked upon me as though I were nothing,
> And those anointed with [my] myrrh poured water in return.   (M.1, 3–9)

And this was his reward, despite the fact that he has fulfilled the agenda of the Pharaonic office in an exemplary manner, but none of this could guarantee his safety; for the text then proceeds in an astonishing passage to describe an assassination attempt that was clearly successful (see p. 81). For our purposes the important issue is that in his account of this episode the king speaks without inhibition of having to resist his assailants alone and not being in a fit state to defend himself, presenting a picture of royal and all too human vulnerability that is spectacularly at variance with the masterly and omnipresent control attributed to the Pharaoh in so many other contexts.

The Middle Kingdom perspective did not last. The latter part of the Eighteenth Dynasty shows royal ideology swinging to the other end of the spectrum with the functional divinity of the king being elevated to a particularly high level. We find Amenhotep III describing himself as 'The Dazzling Aten' and developing a cult of himself, while still living, at Soleb and Sesebi (O'Connor and Cline (eds) 2001: 80, 89–90, 142, 179, 294–5). This practice was followed by Tutankhamun at Kawa and Faras (Darnell and Manassa, 2007: 112) and in the Nineteenth Dynasty by Ramesses II at Aksha (R. Wilkinson 2000: 229), Gerf Hussein (p. 219), Wadi es-Sebua (p. 220), ed-Derr (pp. 221–2), and Abu Simbel (pp. 223–7). Amenhotep III's son Akhenaten took the divinity of the ruler to even greater heights:

Not only did Akhenaten elevate the Aten to the position of chief deity, but he actively suppressed the worship of all other gods (except Re and Atum, whom he saw as manifestations of the Aten). At the same time, he elevated the role of the living king to that of sole intermediary with the god. He insisted on exclusivity not only for the god but also for himself as the god's representative on earth. In his iconoclasm, he restricted the avenues of access to the god practically to his own person. The god has no Prophet (hm-ntr) except the king, whereas the living king now has his own Prophet. It is difficult to tell when the Aten is acting and when the king is acting; the two merge into one another to an astonishing degree.

(Bell 1985: 291–2)

A factor that might be expected to lead to modifications of the standard ideology is foreign invasion and the establishment of non-Egyptians on the throne, but this was by no means always the case. All the signs are that the Asiatic Hyksos who gained control of most of the country during the Second Intermediate Period quickly adopted Pharaonic imagery and practice. On the other hand, the Libyan dynasts who ruled Egypt during the first millennium seem to have taken a much more eclectic stance, either because the finer points of Egyptian ideology were lost on them or—and perhaps more likely—were of no interest. The eighth-century Victory Stela of Piye (Piankhi) provides an excellent illustration of the way in which the vocabulary, iconography, and, *ipso facto*, the conceptualization of kingship were adjusted to the circumstances of the Libyan Period (Simpson (ed.) 2003: 367–85). Whilst Piye, the victorious Nubian invader from the south bent on reasserting Nubian domination of Egypt, presents himself in all respects in the guise of a traditional Egyptian Pharaoh, above all as a divinely sanctioned 'King of Upper and Lower Egypt', the stela presents, at the same time, a vivid picture of the extent to which the tribal fragmentation characteristic of Libyan society had led to the dissolution of Egypt into a large number of essentially independent fiefdoms, though there is mention of four kings, two based in Upper Egypt, two in Lower, who presumably exercised some sort of suzerainty over contiguous grandees who boasted less elevated titles. However, from our point of view, the most interesting aspect of the situation is that these four rulers are given the old title *nsw,* 'king', have their names written in a cartouche, and are said to be 'wearers of the uraeus'. Indeed, they are all four represented wearing this attribute in the lunette at the top of the stela (Fig. 3.3). These features are as far as the text is willing to go in treating them as Egyptian kings, and that may well indicate the limits of what Piye was willing to concede to these recalcitrant vassals. However, it could equally, and perhaps more plausibly, be argued that the Libyan dynasts themselves wanted to go this far and no further, i.e. it was a matter of prestige to present themselves to some degree with some of the trappings, linguistic and otherwise, of Egyptian kingship, but they still felt themselves to be, at heart, heirs of the Libyan tradition of tribal chiefs, and the persistence of such Libyan features as the feather head adornment and such Libyan titles as 'Great Chief of the Ma' (*wr ꜥꜣ n M*) lend support to this view. In general, however, foreign rule did not lead to significant modifications of royal ideology. The Egyptian priesthood had no other means of validating supreme power within an Egyptian conceptual framework, and, irrespective of whether their rulers were Persian Great Kings, Macedonian Ptolemies, or Roman Emperors, they converted them into Egyptian Pharaohs with a self-interested enthusiasm visibly attested in many surviving late temples and decrees (e.g. Austin 2006: texts 271, 276, 283).

Fig. 3.3. The lunette at the top of the Piye (Piankhi) stele. After Grimal 1981: pl. v.

Conspiracies against Pharaoh

The ideology of kingship did nothing to preserve the Pharaoh from conspiracies and assassination plots, some of which were undoubtedly successful—and there must have been considerably more such events than our severely biased evidence reveals. The earliest extant case of the assassination of a king appears in Manetho's account of the reign of Teti, which reads: 'Othoes 30 years, who was killed by his bodyguard' (*FgrH* III C: 26, F.2). Whilst the wildly incorrect reign-length does not initially inspire confidence, the subsequent notice is compatible with other evidence: not only was Teti the first king of the dynasty, and thereby probably subject to risk from rivals, but three of the epithets in his titulary may indicate an unstable situation (Horus Name: Seheteptawy ('He who pacifies the Two Lands'); Golden Horus: Zema ('He who unites'); Praenomen: Sehetepnebty (The one who pacifies the Two Ladies')); most telling of all is the enigmatic presence of the short-lived Userkare between Teti and Pepi I whose status has never been established, but a role as a successful opponent of his predecessor must be a possibility (cf. Strudwick 2005: 75).

Evidence from the Middle Kingdom is altogether fuller, consisting of documentary material, inscriptions, and a major literary text. We begin with the case of Montuhotep IV. This ruler, generally regarded as the last king of the Eleventh Dynasty, is a somewhat mysterious figure on whom the documentation casts an intriguing light (Grajetzki 2006: 25–9, 169, 172). It strongly suggests that his reign was a precarious one and prompts the question whether he died of natural causes. Nowhere among the Karnak, Abydos, Saqqara, or Turin kings do we find the name of Montuhotep IV. This means that, as far as all the authors of these texts were concerned, he was not a legitimate king. Furthermore, a partial king-list discovered at Karnak shows two Eleventh Dynasty kings, Nebhepetre (Montuhotep II) and Sankhkare (Montuhotep III), with their names written in cartouches followed by someone called 'The God's Father Senwosret' without a cartouche (Winlock 1941: 117–18). It is intriguing that Senwosret is the name of several kings of the Twelfth Dynasty, and, since it was common practice in Egypt to name grandsons after their grandfathers, it may be that this Senwosret was the father of the Amenemhet who founded that dynasty. The well-known texts of Montuhotep IV in the Wadi Hammamat dealing with an expedition to the area to obtain greywacke for his sarcophagus and also to mine for gold gives further grounds for suspecting that his position was somewhat precarious: in the first place, the mention of his mother called Imi is startling; for I know of no other case where a royal mother appears in such a context. Why does it happen here? Surely it is because Montuhotep's claim to the throne was suspect: presumably it was seen to come from Imi, and a need was felt to insist on that point. Secondly we need to grasp the significance of the term *biayet* (*bi3yt*) used to refer to two extraordinary events that occurred during the expedition. It means 'marvel' and denotes something that the gods use to indicate to a ruler, or anyone else for that matter, that what is taking place has their approval. Again, therefore, the legitimacy agenda is being met in a particularly acute case. A further point to emphasize is that the Pharaoh is here associated with the acquisition of water, and that is one of the classic functions of an Egyptian king. Finally, there is a particular insistence in the text on Min's approval of what Montuhotep is doing, i.e. his holding of the royal office has divine approval (Lloyd 2013). Whatever the truth of the matter, this document justifies the strong suspicion that the Eleventh Dynasty ended in dynastic turbulence in which probably more than a measure of dynastic murder played its baleful part.

The case of Amenemhet I is much less obscure. He was the first king of the Twelfth Dynasty and is generally regarded, though absolute proof is not available, as being identical with the Vizier Amenemhet whom we encounter in one of the Montuhotep IV inscriptions from the Wadi Hammamat. That his position was felt to be insecure is indicated by *The Prophecy of Neferti* which is a *post-eventum* messianic prophecy allegedly delivered in the reign of the great Old Kingdom Pharaoh Snofru and foretelling the accession of Amenemhet from a non-royal family as a ruler who would re-establish order after chaos, i.e. he would be fulfilling the cosmicizing role that was fundamental to Egyptian royal ideology (Simpson (ed.) 2003: 214–20). Other factors that may spring from the same perception of insecurity can also be suggested: he took as his Horus name the epithet *wehem mesut* (*whm mswt*), 'Repeater of Births', an epithet that always seems to imply that the holder is to be regarded as inaugurating a renaissance; he initiated the practice of establishing his successor as co-regent before he died; furthermore, instead of basing himself in the Theban area, the power-base of the Eleventh Dynasty, he moved northwards to establish a new capital at Itjtawy at, or near, Lisht, thus placing himself firmly in the context of the Old Kingdom rulers. His choice of a pyramid as a burial place may also be seen in the same context (in general, see Grajetzki 2006: 28–35). Overall it would seem that we can build a plausible, if slightly speculative, case that an important part of Amenemhet's agenda to strengthen his weak position was to present himself as inaugurating a new great age by returning Egypt to the glories of the Old Kingdom. For all that, his reign provides us with one of the few absolutely clear cases of an assassination attempt against a Pharaoh, which is graphically described in *The Instruction of Amenemhet*:

> It was after supper, when darkness had fallen,
> When I had taken an hour of relaxation,
> lying on my bed, for I was tired,
> And my heart had begun to drift into sleep.
> Lo, weapons for my protection were raised against me,
> While I became like a worm of the necropolis.
> When I woke up to the fighting, I pulled myself together,
> Finding that it was an attack of the guard.
> If I had quickly taken weapons in my hand,
> I would have made the punks turn tail in confusion (?).
> But no one is valiant at night, and no one can fight alone;
> No success can arise without a protector.   (M. 1. 11–2. 4)
> . . . .
> Had women [of the harîm] organized troops?
> Were rebels nurtured within the palace [itself]?   (M. 2. 7–8)

It will be noted that there is a suggestion that the harîm may have been involved and that the conspiracy had its origins within the palace; indeed, it appears that he was attacked by at least some members of his own guard who had presumably been suborned (cf. the case of Teti above). Though the text is far from being as explicit as we should like, we seem to be confronted with an event suspiciously similar to the harîm conspiracy in the reign of Ramesses III (to be discussed), and nothing could be less surprising. We may well have a similar issue in biography of the Sixth Dynasty magnate Weni in which he claims:

Proceedings were initiated in the royal harîm against the King's Wife, 'Great of Affection', in private, and His Majesty caused me to proceed to judge [the matter], I being alone. There was no chief justice and vizier nor any official there save for me alone because I was excellent, because I was firmly planted in the heart of His Majesty, and because His Majesty had confidence in me. I was the one who set it down in writing, I being alone, together with one other judge-and-warden of Nekhen, while my office was a [mere] overseer of *khentyw-she* of the palace.[1] Never had any of my peers heard a secret of the harîm before, but His Majesty caused me to act as judge.   (*Urk.* i. 100–2)

The text is remarkably discreet, but treasonous activities directed against the Pharaoh himself would be a highly plausible explanation for these secretive proceedings, and we should not forget that the polygamous practices of Ancient Egyptian kings created a major source of danger for the succession. Whatever the position of the children of the Chief Wife, there was always the possibility that other royal women would aspire to set their own sons on the throne, as a host of later parallels from the Orient amply demonstrate. This situation emerges clearly in the harîm conspiracy which occurred at the reign of Ramesses III in the early Twentieth Dynasty (De Buck 1937: 152–64; Goedicke 1963: 71–92; S. Redford 2001; Vernus 2003: 108–20). While the detail is not entirely clear from the extant documentation, the Turin Juridical

---

[1] For this title see p. 189.

Papyrus, which provides an account of the proceedings, leaves us in no doubt that we are confronted with an attempt emanating from the harîm to place the son of one of Ramesses III's queens on the throne by assassination:

The great criminal, Paibekkamen, who was [then] chief of the chamber. He was brought in because he had been in collusion with Teye [i.e. the queen] and the women of the harem; he had made common cause with them; he had begun to bring out their words to their mothers and their brothers who were there, saying: 'Stir up the people! Incite enmity in order to make rebellion against their lord!' He was placed before the great officials of the Court of Examination; they examined his crimes; they found that he had committed them; his crimes seized him; the officials who examined him caused his punishment to overtake him.   (trans. De Buck 1937: 154)

Whilst, however, the majority of those involved were connected with the harîm, they were by no means unique, and the textual evidence also lists court officials and military officers all of whom, no doubt, expected to benefit greatly from the success of the conspiracy. It would appear that Ramesses did not die immediately as the result of the plot, though he did not long outlive it, but the fate of most of the conspirators was death, either by some unspecified method covered by the last line of the quotation printed above or by an encouragement to suicide that could not be refused, though we do hear also that some relatively minor participants were deprived of their noses and ears whilst one other escaped with no more than a brisk telling-off!

When we move to the Late Period, we are fortunate enough to possess non-Egyptian, above all Greek, sources which are free from the distorting influences that bedevil the interpretation of Pharaonic textual material, though they are by no means free of error. Herodotus (2. 161–3, 169) describes in some detail the deposition of the Twenty-sixth Dynasty Pharaoh Apries in 570. This episode was quite unlike anything described to date in that it started as a revolt by native Egyptian troops who had been sent on an unsuccessful expedition to Cyrene. Apries then sent Amasis to bring them to heel, but the rebels elected him king, and he then led his forces against Apries who mobilized his foreign mercenaries to meet them. Apries was defeated and forced to flee the country. He attempted a return by military means in 568 with the assistance of the forces of the Chaldaean king Nebuchadrezzar II, but this effort failed disastrously and led to Apries' death by drowning in the Nile after which he was duly buried in the royal necropolis at Sais (Lloyd 1988: 176–202). Our Greek accounts of the Thirtieth Dynasty present an equally unsavoury picture, this time in the form of the jockeying for power by major elite families in the Delta. Plutarch, for example, describes the dynastic gyrations leading to the deposition of Teos (Tachos) in these terms, illustrating the major role played by the Spartan king Agesilaus:

For Nectanabis, who was Tachos' cousin and had part of the forces under his command, revolted, and, having been proclaimed king by the Egyptians, sent to Agesilaus asking for his assistance. He made the same request to Chabrias also, promising large gifts to both. When Tachos heard of this and resorted to entreaties to them, Chabrias tried through persuasion and entreaties to hold Agesilaus also to his friendship with Tachos.   (*Agesilaus* 37. 3–4)

There then took place a series of diplomatic exchanges in Sparta as a result of which Agesilaus changed sides, taking his mercenaries over to Nectanabis. This grizzly tale then continues:

Tachos, therefore, having been abandoned by his mercenaries, took flight, but from Mendes another rival rose up against Nectanabis, having been proclaimed king, and having collected a hundred thousand men, marched against him . . . the Mendesian also sent and tried to win over Agesilaus. Nectanabis was, therefore, alarmed, and, when Agesilaus commanded him to fight it out as speedily as possible, and not to procrastinate in making war against men who were inexperienced in fighting but had the numbers to surround him and hedge him in and anticipate him in many ways and gain the initiative over him, he became even more suspicious and fearful toward him and withdrew into a well-fortified city which had a large enclosed area. Agesilaus was incensed at such a lack of confidence, and full of indignation, but, being ashamed yet again to go over to the rival ruler and to return home without achieving anything, he followed him and entered the walled city.   (38. 1–4)

Nectanabis (Nectanebo II) eventually emerged the victor, but nothing can conceal the ease with which hard-nosed opportunism, self-interest, and ambition could erode any inhibitions in attacking an incarnation of Horus. These examples are, of course, late, but the imperatives that they reveal are as old as the Pharaonic office itself. We should not be far wrong if we worked on the basis that Egyptian royal courts were just as familiar with conspiracy, subterfuge, ruthlessness, and murder as the courts of the sultans of Ottoman Turkey.

The Man in the God: Some Literary Portrayals of Pharaoh

Egyptian literary texts can be surprisingly frank in lifting the veil on the humanity of the Pharaoh in ways that yield a very different picture from that on temple walls. We have already discussed the portrayal of Amenemhet I in his *Instruction* in another context (see p. 81), but this is by no means an isolated case. We turn first to the *Westcar Papyrus* which has much to offer in this respect. The text in its surviving form dates from the Thirteenth Dynasty and presents us with a sequence of carefully linked tales dealing with feats performed by a series of magicians, concluding with an account of the divine birth of the first three kings of the Fifth Dynasty (Simpson (ed.) 2003: 13–24). A passage in the second of the fully preserved tales runs thus:

<One day King Snofru wandered through all the rooms> of the palace (life, prosperity, health) to seek for himself <recreation, but he found none. Then he said>, 'Go, bring me <the chief lector-priest, the scribe of books, Djadjaemankh. Then was he brought to

him straightaway. Then did His Majesty say to him, 'I have traversed all the rooms> of the palace (life, prosperity, health) in search of recreation, but I have found none.' Then did Djadjaemankh say to him, 'May Your Majesty proceed to the lake of the palace (life, prosperity, health). Equip a boat with all the beautiful girls of your palace. Your Majesty's heart will be refreshed at seeing them rowing up and down.' . . . <Then did His Majesty say> 'Indeed, I shall go boating! Let there be brought to me twenty oars of ebony plated with gold, their handles of *sekheb*-wood plated with electrum. Let there be brought to me twenty women with the most beautiful bodies, well-formed breasts, and braided tresses, who have not yet given birth. Also, let there be brought to me twenty nets, and let these nets be given to these women when their clothes have been set aside.' Then was everything done as His Majesty commanded. (4. 22–5. 13)

The women then set about their rowing to the extreme delight of the king, but then disaster struck in that the fish-shaped pendant in the hair of one of the oarswomen got tangled in the loom of her oar and fell into the water. She stopped rowing and thereby brought the entire operation to a standstill. The text then continues:

Then did His Majesty say, 'Do you not row?' Then did they say, 'Our leader has stopped rowing.' Then did His Majesty say to her, 'Why have you stopped rowing?' Then she replied, 'It is because a pendant of new turquoise has fallen into the water.' <Then His Majesty said to her, 'Row! It is I who shall replace it for you.'> Then she replied, 'I prefer my own thing to one like it.' His Majesty replied, 'Go, bring me the chief lector-priest <Djadjaemankh . . .' (5. 18–24)

Another passage of the story is equally revealing. At this point in the narrative another famous magician called Djedi has been brought to the palace of Khufu by the king's son Hardedef:

After he had reached the residence, Prince Hardedef entered in to report to the Majesty of King Khufu, justified. Then did Prince Hardedef say, 'O Sovereign, my lord, I have brought Djedi.' Then did His Majesty say, 'Go, bring him to me.' Then His Majesty proceeded to the columned hall of the palace (life, prosperity, health). Then Djedi was ushered in to him, and His Majesty said, 'How is it Djedi, that I was not allowed to see you?' Then Djedi said, 'It is the one who is summoned who comes, O Sovereign (life, prosperity, health). Summon. Behold, I am here.' Then did His Majesty say, 'Is it true, what they say, that you can rejoin a severed head?' Then Djedi replied, 'Yes, I can, O Sovereign, my lord.' Then His Majesty said, 'Let there be brought to me the prisoner who is in the prison, that his sentence may be executed.' Then did Djedi say, 'But not to a human being, O Sovereign, my lord! Surely, it is not permitted to do the like thereof to the noble cattle'. (8. 5–17)

In all three of these passages we are a long way from the official, religiously orientated image of kingship. In the first the king, far from being totally in control of the situation, is represented as being thoroughly bored and also as being dependent on the lector priest Djadjaemankh for a solution to his problem. In addition he shows an enthusiastic interest in setting up some highly sexually charged entertainment. The second passage, if anything, is even more surprising: the king is presented as a model of politeness in the exchange with the oarswoman and at no point takes refuge in an imperious command, as might be expected. Indeed, the oarswoman's response that she wants her own pendant back rather than a replacement could even be described as impertinent, though it is not received as such by the king. In the third quotation Djedi's response to the king is, to say the least, pert, if not impertinent, but there are no dire consequences, and at the end he not only puts the king firmly in his place but goes so far as to indicate that the king's request is morally reprehensible.

Even more intriguing are the activities described in a story of the New Kingdom (P.Chassinat 1) involving the relationship between the Pharaoh Neferkare (Pepi II) and the general Sisene (Posener 1957: 119–37; van Dijk 1994: 387–93):

Then did he [i.e. Tjeti, son of Henet] see the Majesty of the King of Upper and Lower Egypt Neferkare going off in the night for a solitary walk, with no-one with him. Then he distanced himself from him to prevent the king seeing him. Tjeti, son of Henet, remained motionless, thinking and saying to himself, 'Since this is what he is at, it is then true what people say, "... he goes out at night".' Tjeti, son of Henet, followed this god without his heart making any reproach to him to see everything which he was going to do. He [the king] reached the house of the general Sisene. He threw a brick ... at which a ladder was caused to go down for him. He climbed up, while Tjeti, son of Henet, stayed there, waiting until His Majesty came out. After His Majesty had done that which he had desired with him, he went to his palace ... He had spent four ... hours in the house of the general Sisene. And he had returned to the Great House where he remained four hours until dawn.　　(trans. Lloyd after Posener 1957)

This passage begins by depicting the king taking himself off for a solitary walk at night, like any ordinary mortal. Admittedly, the king is subsequently described as 'this god', but this is clearly very much a matter of form, a recognition of the king's technical status that simply shows respect without any significant implication beyond that. It is the phrase 'After His Majesty had done that which he had desired with him ...' which is truly startling because this language is a coded reference to sexual congress, i.e. the king is engaging in a homosexual liaison with his general, a form of activity of which the Egyptians would have deeply disapproved.

Yet another text that presents the king in a distinctly undivine light is a tale preserved in a papyrus of the early Ptolemaic Period now in the Bibliothèque Nationale in Paris. It is known to modern Egytologists as the *Tale of Amasis and the Sailor* or simply as *The Tale of a Sailor*. It is largely destroyed, but for our purposes it is the beginning which matters:

Once in the time of Pharaoh Amasis Pharaoh said to his great ones, 'I want to drink a vat [approximately 12 litres!] of Egyptian wine.' Then did they say, 'Our great lord, it is difficult to drink a vat of Egyptian wine.' Then he said to them, 'Do not gainsay what I say.' Then they said, 'Our great Lord, may Pharaoh do his will'. Then Pharaoh said, 'Let us hasten to the seashore.' Then it was done as Pharaoh commanded. Then Pharaoh washed himself and ate with his women, no wine in the world standing before them but a vat of Egyptian wine. Then Pharaoh was merry with his women and drank a very large amount of wine because of the desire which Pharaoh had for a vat of Egyptian wine. Then Pharaoh gave himself up to sleep on the sea shore that same night. He slept under a vine on the north side. When it was morning, Pharaoh could not get up because of the size of his hangover. When the time approached, he could not get up. Then the courtiers lamented, saying, 'Is such a thing possible? It has come to pass that Pharaoh has a big hangover. No-one in the world can speak with Pharaoh . . .' (trans. after Spiegelberg 1914: 27, with some modifications)

Here we find courtiers expostulating with the king very much in the manner of Djedi in the *Westcar Papyrus*. Again Pharaoh is partying with the harîm, but on this occasion he devotes himself to drinking wine in such quantity that he is incapable of functioning the following day. Indeed, he could not even stand up, and anyone who spoke to him did so at their peril! Other Demotic texts such as P. Rylands IX and *Setne I* also display the king operating in human mode, if with rather more dignity, and give no indication that his technically divine status was at issue in the practical business of running the country.

What are we to make of all this? One reaction might be to argue that these are all fictional contexts, and that the Egyptians are simply taking a holiday from their respect and awe of kingship in much the same way that comedy traditions operate in all cultures: the most important institution in Egyptian culture is held up to ridicule or subversion within the confines of the stories, but this involves reversal of what would normally happen, not a reflection of it in any way; under normal circumstances a much more formal relationship would have existed. There is certainly something to be said for this reaction, but the argument should not be pushed too far. It is of the essence of comedy that it must have a firm purchase on reality. The heightening or distortion of reality does not mean the negation of reality. If contact on a human-to-human basis had not been conceivable, stories of this kind would not have been written in the first place. Indeed, the Neferkare tale shows clearly the ease with which the king's functional divinity could be recognized without its impeding the acknowledgement of some very human activity. Our confidence in accepting the basic trend of these stories is greatly strengthened by consideration of a passage in the Middle Kingdom *Story of Sinuhe*. Here, of course, we are again confronted with a fictional context, but this is a text that is firmly rooted in the historical here-and-now, and no one could claim that it was intended to be subversive of royalty in any way. On the contrary, the main thrust of the tale is that the Pharaoh is crucial if an Egyptian is to live a full life and achieve a good hereafter (cf. Baines 1982: 31–44). The relevant passage occurs towards the end of the narrative when Sinuhe returns home at the invitation of the king after a long exile in Asia and is ushered in to an audience in the royal presence:

On the great throne in a kiosk of electrum did I find His Majesty. I was stretched out on my belly, not knowing myself before him, while this god greeted me cheerful-ly... Then did His Majesty say to one of the Companions, 'Lift him up, let him speak to me.' Then did His Majesty say, 'Behold, you have come, after having roamed foreign lands, after flight has ravaged you. The years have prevailed over you, and you have reached old age. It is no small matter that your body will be buried without being escorted by foreigners...' Then the royal daughters were brought in, and His Majesty said to the queen, 'Here is Sinuhe...' She let out a very great cry, and the royal daughters shrieked all together... Then did His Majesty say, 'He shall not fear, he shall not dread. He shall be a Companion amongst the officials. He shall be placed among the courtiers. Proceed to the robing chamber to wait on him.'   (253–83)

As in the preceding texts, we find the king described as 'this god', and his elevated status is reflected in Sinuhe's prostration before him; we are also left in no doubt that the court environment in which all this takes place is one of great splendour. However, once the court preliminaries are over, the situation becomes much less formal, the king showing consideration, kindliness, and generosity towards his wayward subject, and the episode even acquires a family dimension when the royal daughters are invited in to enjoy the occasion. Both they and the queen are suitably, and rather comically, horrified at the spectacle of Sinuhe's Asiatic appearance.

   The conviction that the king's theoretic divinity was largely context-specific is strongly encouraged by classical texts. Greeks were going to Egypt during the first millennium BC from at least the seventh century, and Greek writers have left detailed records of the Greek experience of the country from the fifth century BC onwards at a time when Pharaonic civilization was still a going concern, and the Pharaonic office was still the basis of Egyptian ideology. It is most remarkable that none of these writers shows any awareness of the alleged divinity of the Egyptian kings. Herodotus, who visited Egypt some time about 450 BC, has much to say about Pharaohs of all periods, but his account of those who ruled from the time Greeks began to appear is particularly apposite because it must reflect Greek perceptions of these kings. They are presented as doing all the classic things expected of rulers in ancient society: they make war, they rebel, they intermarry, they engage in building and engineering projects, and, rather less plausibly, they can even engage in scientific enquiry and African exploration. Greek writers clearly believed that access to the king for business purposes was perfectly possible, even for them, and that some kings could behave in a distinctly unregal manner. They will, of course, have been aware that there were special modes of address and courtly behaviour that had to be observed, but these must have been regarded as part of the apparatus of kingship comparable to such phenomena in any other monarchical system. However, nowhere is there any indication that Herodotus was aware of any divine pretensions on their part. That can only mean that in their dealings with Greeks—and there were plenty of them—this was not something that impinged to any significant degree. If we turn to the evidence for the Thirtieth Dynasty, which is particularly illuminating, these suspicions are amply confirmed. Plutarch in his *Life of Agesilaus* presents a most vivid picture of the foreign relations that characterized the dynasty, and that picture presupposes close accessibility for Greeks to the rulers in question. He speaks of King Teos (Tachos) as being arrogant and full of empty pretensions and vividly describes the deficiencies of Nectanebo II who shows, in turn, considerable inexperience, vacillation, and failure of nerve. The wording of some of the speech placed in the mouth of the Spartan general at one point and addressed to Nectanebo is particularly revealing: 'This is the moment of deliverance, young man . . . Come, now, be eager to show yourself a man of courage. Follow us in the attack, and save both yourself and your army' (39. 2–3). In Diodorus Siculus' account of the reconquest of Egypt by Artaxerxes III in 343/2, inexperience and failure of nerve are equally in evidence, and this heady brew, laced with a big dose of overconfidence, led to the end of the dynasty and the flight of Nectanebo to Nubia. At no point in any of our classical sources on this issue does the theoretical divinity of the king make any impact in any shape or form.

THE QUEEN

Any discussion of the status and role of the Egyptian king brings with it the question of the status and role of the queen, i.e. the chief royal wife. If the king is a god incarnate, what then is the queen? We might expect that her close proximity to the king would ensure that some of his divinity would percolate down to her, but the degree to which this happened, when it happened, differed from one period to another. Two sequences of queenly titles from an architrave in the tomb of Khamerernebty I, the mother of Khafre, are most instructive on the perception of the queen's status in the Old Kingdom:

1. Mother of the King of Upper and Lower Egypt, Daughter of the God, She who sees Horus and Seth, the Great One of the *Iamet*-Sceptre (?),[2] the Great of Praise, the God's Servant of Thoth, the God's Servant of Tjasep, the King's Wife, beloved of him, the King's Daughter of his Body, the Possessor of Reverence[3] with the Great God, Khamerernebty.

---

[2] For this problematic title see Jones 2000: 401.
[3] For this title see Strudwick 2005: 30.

2. The Eldest Daughter, She who sees Horus and Seth, the Great One of the *Iamet*-Sceptre [?], the Great of Praise, the God's Servant of Thoth, the God's Servant of Tjasep the Partner of Horus, She who joins the One Beloved of the Two Ladies.

The King's Wife, beloved of him, the King's Daughter of his Body, the Possessor of Reverence with her father, Khamerernebty.   (*Urk.* i. 5(96))

In these texts the queen is not described at any point as a goddess; she is stated to be the daughter of a god, i.e. in this case, the king, but the potential for divinization in this situation is not pursued. The queen is also given priestly titles that may or may not have brought with them priestly functions, but that falls well short of attributing divinity. An affinity with a sceptre is stated, if the translation is correct, and it should be noted that sceptres, like other royal regalia, were believed to be endowed with divine potency, but, if there was any practical significance to this affinity, it would probably not have passed beyond a ritual function. The main emphasis is on the queen's role as consort of the king, in which affection and personal favour play a part, and it is evident that her position is ultimately dependent on her relationship with the king; it is of cardinal importance that we grasp the point that there is no Egyptian word for 'queen'; the standard term is *hemet nesu* (*ḥmt nsw*), 'King's Wife', which defines her role, quite explicitly, as emanating from her relationship with Pharaoh. At no point do we get anything approaching the assertion of divinity which we find in the titulary of the king. At the same time we cannot ignore the fact that the vulture headdress, originally an attribute of the goddess Nekhbet, already appears as an attribute of the queen during the Old Kingdom, and that must indicate an association with the goddess, though the precise ontological significance is open to debate.

If we look elsewhere in the Old Kingdom, it emerges that it was possible for factors other than royal birth to lead to queenly status. In an inscription from the latter part of the Sixth Dynasty referring to a vizier named Djau, who was a member of a powerful family, probably provincial governors, of the Abydos nome (Strudwick 2005: 257), we find the following text over the heads of two queens:

1. The Royal Wife of Mennefermeryre, the Great One of the *Iamet*-sceptre, the Great of Favour, the Great of Possessions, the Companion of Horus, the Partner of Horus, the Mother of the King of Upper and Lower Egypt Khanefermerenre, Ankhenesmeryre.

2. The Royal Wife of Mennefermeryre, the Great One of the *Iamet*-sceptre, the Great of Favour, the Great of Possessions, the Companion of Horus, the Partner of Horus, The Mother of the King of Upper and Lower Egypt Menankhneferkare, Ankhenesmeryre (*Urk.* i. 24).

In this instance the issue of personal relationship to the king is as prominent as in the previous text, as well as the role of the queen as the royal consort, but the queens in question are not of royal ancestry. This is an instance of marriage being used as a political stratagem whereby the king strengthened his position in the southern part of the country by marrying women of a great provincial family. Nonetheless, it should be noted that two of the titles refer to the king as Horus, and the relationship that they affirm must have led to some seepage of the royal divinity in the queen's direction.

It is evident from the well-known inscription of Weni from the Sixth Dynasty that things did not always go well with these Old Kingdom queens (see p. 82), but this basic pattern, once established, remained the norm for most of Egyptian history, though the details of titles do change from one period to another, sometimes significantly (Troy 1986: Registers A and B). The best example of this is the establishment of the title *hemet nesu weret* (*ḥmt nsw wrt*), 'Great King's Wife', as a standard part of the title sequence of the New Kingdom Chief Wife, though it does occasionally occur earlier. However, there were two factors that were likely to yield, in favourable circumstances, to a radical advancement of the queen's position. In the first place, queens were physically very close to the source of power in the Egyptian kingdom, and that greatly facilitated the acquisition of real power on their part; secondly, far more often than not, queens could claim to have the blood of a god, i.e. their royal father, in their veins. It is, therefore, not in the least surprising that from time to time we find queens running the country and sometimes assuming the attributes and forms of the Pharaonic office. The earliest case occurs in the latter part of the First Dynasty with Mer(t)neith, whose name appears on an Early Dynastic seal impression on the same terms as those of the kings who precede her, though she is described here as 'royal mother', not as a king (Fig. 3.4); her name also occurs on one occasion in a *serekh*, i.e. in a context normally reserved for a king; she has a standard royal tomb at Abydos equipped with two stelae of the type used for kings' tombs, though they do not show the *serekh*; and there is a good chance that her name appeared on the Palermo Stone (recto, second divider right) on the same terms as those of kings. We are clearly confronted with a woman who achieved an extraordinary position of power and influence which made it possible for her to be treated in a number of respects on the same terms as a Pharaoh. The standard, and perfectly reasonable, guess is that she was a queen regent who ran the country while her son was in his minority, but this situation, as we can see from later Egyptian history, would not be an entirely adequate explanation since it was perfectly possible for eminent courtiers and administrators to work through a Pharaoh who was a minor, the case of Tutankhamun being a very obvious example. Where such a situation arose, we must assume that the queen involved was an unusually potent personality who insisted on assuming the reins of power against whatever opposition confronted her.

Another figure who has featured prominently in discussions of early queens who assumed royal power is a Nitocris at the end of the Sixth Dynasty. Sadly, it

Kingship

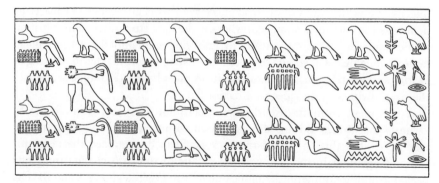

Fig. 3.4. First Dynasty jar sealing containing a king list of rulers of the dynasty. After Spencer 1993: 63 (43).

has now been demonstrated that she is the product of an ancient error in the reading of a king list (Ryholt 2000: 87–100), but it is significant that Manetho and Herodotus record the presence of a queen called Nitocris on the throne, and that must mean that the Egyptian tradition to which they had access found no difficulty in accepting the possibility of such an historical event. Indeed, the Herodotean account claims that the queen exploited dynastic instability to enhance her position, and that fact, at the very least, indicates the kind of situation that Late Period Egyptians regarded as likely to give rise to such an unusual event.

With Sobeknofru at the end of the Twelfth Dynasty we are on much firmer ground. She appears in the Turin Canon immediately after Amenemhet IV with her name supplemented by that of the sun-god and is allocated a reign of 3 years, 10 months, 27 days. Manetho also knows of her as the ruler who succeeded Amenemhet IV, giving her a reign of 4 years, obviously by rounding up the true figure, and he adds the interesting information that she was the sister of her predecessor. If we accept Manetho's claim of affinity, we might well argue that she succeeded to the throne because there was no available male heir. Alternatively we could invoke the parallel of Hatshepsut (see further) and guess that the male heir was too young to rule, Sobeknofru did the job for him, and subsequently promoted herself or was promoted to the Pharaonic office. We shall probably never know the truth of the matter, but contemporary monuments have no compunction about giving her a full royal titulary, though her iconography shows that her gender was something of an embarrassment; for her statuary shows an awkward mixture of male and female characteristics.

The Eighteenth and Nineteenth Dynasties show a remarkable enhancement of the power of the chief queen who is frequently described as the *ḥmt nsw wrt*, 'the Great King's Wife', a title that explicitly marks out the person in question as the queen par excellence. The question immediately presents itself as to why this development should have taken place. Given the clear evidence that the Eighteenth Dynasty had more than its fair share of strong characters in the queenly office, we may plausibly guess that it arose through the insistence of such individuals as Ahhotep, chief wife of Seqenenre Tao II, and Ahmose Nefertari, chief wife of Amenhotep I (Troy 1986: 140–3). Another novelty is the introduction of the title 'God's Wife of Amun' (*ḥmt nṯr n imn*) or more briefly *ḥmt nṯr*, which was formally established as a queen's title for the benefit of Ahhotep (Robins 1993: 149–56) and down to the reign of Ramesses VI was normally held by the chief royal wife (otherwise by a princess of the royal house). At one level it may have referred to the doctrine of the royal theogamy, insisting on the queen's role as the mother of the next king, but it brought with it also ritual functions in the temple of Amon-re at Karnak as well as substantial economic benefits and the political influence that high-ranking and prestigious office in this powerful temple inevitably conferred. The office also had the advantage of giving the king a firm foothold in the richest and most powerful temple in the country, and the political benefits of that position should not be underestimated. Certainly, the political dimension was predominant from the time of Ramesses VI down to the end of the Twenty-sixth Dynasty in 525 when the office seems normally to have been restricted to a royal daughter (see further, p. 150ff.).

Titles, however, are one thing, real power is quite another. There is no reason to suspect that the two queens just mentioned fell short in this respect, but the Eighteenth Dynasty presents a number of examples of queens obtaining an extraordinary degree of prominence. The best-known case is Hatshepsut, the daughter of Tuthmose I, who began her rise to prominence as regent because Tuthmose III came to the throne as a minor. For this reason Hatshepsut's regnal years and those of Tuthmose are identical. This position she was prepared to accept until regnal year 7, but from that point she claimed royal honours and maintained that status until her death in regnal year 22. Whilst there is no good evidence of hostility on the part of Tuthmose III during her lifetime, her extraordinary position needed consolidating, and this she did, in practical terms, by building up a powerful coterie of high-ranking officials, such as Senenmut ('Chief Steward', amongst many other functions) (Dorman 1988, 1991) and Hapuseneb ('High Priest of Amon-re' and holder of many other offices, ecclesiastical and secular) (O'Connor and Cline (eds) 2001: 107, 110), but she went far beyond this and developed a carefully orchestrated propaganda campaign to justify her position: she represented herself unequivocally as a king in sculpture and painting; she used masculine grammatical elements in her titulary, though the practice here is not consistent; she abandoned her original tomb in the Wadi Sikkat Taqa el-Zeide (WA D) (Carter 1917: 114–18) and used a tomb in the Valley of the Kings that might have been started by her father (KV20; Reeves 1990*a*: 13–17); this tomb was served by the construction of one of the finest mortuary temples in

Western Thebes at Deir el-Bahri, located, significantly, next to that of Montuhotep II and on the site of the mortuary complex of Amenhotep I, two of the
greatest rulers of Egyptian history in whose reflected glory and, above all,
legitimacy, she doubtless expected to share; her temple-building projects and
the great expedition to Punt formed part of the classic corpus of activities
expected of an Egyptian king; and in her mortuary temple she caused to be
carved the best surviving representation of a royal theogamy, insisting that,
like any male Pharaoh, she was the product of a union between the god Amon-
re and the queen (Desroches Noblecourt 2002; Cline and O'Connor (eds)
2006: 39–68).

The case of Tiyi, Chief Wife of Amenhotep III, is more nuanced, but
nonetheless provides another example of the enhanced status and influence
that an Eighteenth Dynasty queen might achieve: in iconography and texts she
occupies a position of prominence that has no earlier parallel for someone of
queenly status; on one occasion she is represented as a sphinx, normally a
prerogative of the king, and the sphinx is depicted in a Pharaonic role as
trampling the enemies of Egypt; and Tiyi is closely aligned, if not fully
identified with, a string of goddesses including Hathor, Isis, Maat, Nekhbet,
Wadjet, Maat, Mut, Tefnut, and Taweret, a process signalled iconographically
by the attribution to the queen of a number of divine characteristics. One
motive for assimilation is that all these goddesses can serve as the solar eye, i.e.
as protectors of the king, and thereby form part of the intense solarization of
kingship that characterizes the reign of Amenhotep III and continues with
disastrous results into the reign of Akhenaten, but this list of divine prototypes
also encodes the concepts of joy and sexuality, concepts that are far from
inappropriate to an Egyptian queen (Kozloff and Bryan 1992). Finally, like
Amenhotep III at Soleb, Tiyi is divinized in her temple at Sedeinga as Hathor,
possibly the local version of the goddess Hathor of Ibshek. (Ramesses II's wife
Nefertari occupies a parallel position at Abu Simbel, one of numerous points
of convergence between the reign of Ramesses II and Amenhotep III.) All
these features are reflections of an eminent and powerful role in royal activity
that can be described at the very least as that of a semi-divine consort to a ruler
who saw himself to a much greater degree than any previous Pharaoh as a
living god on earth (Robins 1993: 52; Dorothea Arnold 1996).

The precedent set by Tiyi was continued by her daughter-in-law Nefertiti
without hesitation. From the very beginning of the reign of her husband
Amenhotep IV/Akhenaten she is depicted in a similarly prominent position
and features in the divinizing Atenist triad consisting of Atum = Aten, Shu =
Akhenaten, and Tefnut = Nefertiti. She also features as the dominant figure in
one of the temples built at Karnak during the early years of Akhenaten's reign
as a smiter of Egypt's enemies quite independently of Akhenaten himself. Her
status after Regnal Year 12 has been the subject of much discussion and
disagreement, but the most plausible interpretation of the evidence would be

that her position was further enhanced from that point by her establishment as co-regent with Akhenaten, endowed with royal attributes, and that after Akhenaten's death she exercised independent authority as Pharaoh for a short time, with or without the enigmatic Smenkhkare as titular consort (for the issues see Murnane 1995: 205–11; Reeves 2001: 163–73).

The Nineteenth Dynasty presents us with the only other known case of a female Pharaoh in the form of Twosre, the last ruler of the dynasty. We can be sure that her elevation to Pharaonic status was greatly assisted by the dynastic turbulence at the end of the dynasty created by the rivalry of Sety II and Amenmesse, and the problematic legitimacy of Siptah, her immediate predecessor, who came to the throne as a minor. She began her career as the wife of the short-lived Sety II (*c.*1201–1196) and probably acted as regent, at least, in the latter years of Siptah's six-year reign before emerging as a full-blown Pharaoh *c.*1188 (Dodson and Hilton 2004: 176–7; R. Wilkinson 2012). As befitted a Pharaoh, she was buried in the Valley of the Kings in KV14 in the same tomb as her husband Sety II, but they were both removed from this site at the beginning of the Twentieth Dynasty, though whether this act reflected hostility to the female Pharaoh cannot be determined. The tomb was certainly intended for reuse at this point, possibly by Sethnakht, and the previous owners may simply have fallen victim to an urgent need for a tomb by a later ruler (Reeves 1990*a*: 109–11). Intriguingly, Twosre's memory survived long after her death to be included in Manetho's *Aigyptiaka* where she features as Thuoris, though she is converted to a king in the surviving tradition on the Manethonian text at this point.

CONCLUSIONS

Any system of government must have a theoretical validation that will make it acceptable to the governed if that system of government is to survive. In the Egyptian case that validation took the form of claiming not simply that the king, the embodiment of the state, was of divine birth but that he was indeed a god himself. This provided the perfect justification for the all-pervasive power that the Egyptians vested in the king, and it remained the theory of the state in Egypt until the end of Pharaonic civilization in the late Roman Period. Such a theory threw up the practical problem of how the Egyptians were to reconcile the obvious humanity of the king's bodily person with his alleged divinity. This tension between divinity and humanity recurs throughout Egyptian history, and in literature and the visual arts sometimes the divinity is emphasized at the expense of the humanity, and sometimes the opposite takes place. It is, however, evident that, whilst an Egyptian's perception of the Pharaoh's office, his modes of address, and, to some degree, his modes of behaviour were determined by the concept of divine kingship, this did not inhibit close contact, formal and informal, with the king and that in practical terms, behind the formulaic behaviour and modes of address, relationships were determined in large measure on the basis of one human being interacting with another on human terms. The queen's role was subservient to the needs of her divine consort as chief wife, king's mother, or ritual assistant. No doubt she often exercised considerable de facto power in the land, but that would very much depend on circumstances and personalities at the time, and only occasionally did she break the mould to establish herself as a full-blown Pharaoh. The extent to which the queen was regarded as divine is a fluid matter. Her bodily proximity to the king and her fictional role as the consort of Amun could not fail to raise her ontological status above that of common mortals, but, although full divinity came the way of living queens in the Eighteenth and Nineteenth Dynasty, this was never written into royal ideology in a manner comparable to the divine status of the king until we reach the Ptolemaic Period when ruthless and powerful women in the mould of Macedonian queens could lay claim to full royal titles and the status of rulers of the land.

4

Violence and the State

In an important study published over forty years ago the distinguished American social anthropologist Lawrence Krader (1968: 21) wrote: 'The concentration of all physical force in the hands of the central authority is the primary function of the state and is its decisive characteristic.' Ancient Egypt was no exception. Certainly, within the Nile Valley and, to a lesser extent, within Egypt's imperial possessions there was an extremely effective, highly visible, and ubiquitous ideological support structure for the state system, but none of this conceals the fact that the Pharaonic state was ultimately created, maintained, and extended by the threat and frequent application of institutionalized violence. Within Egypt, as in most states, the mailed fist was normally concealed within the proverbial velvet glove, but it is highly significant that the most pervasive and strident theme of royal iconography throughout Egyptian history—and even before—is the king as victorious warrior. Naturally, the right to have recourse to violence was a right that percolated down from Pharaoh to all state officials who proved anything but reluctant to avail themselves of it.

Institutionalized force was conceptualized and activated within the Egyptian state essentially in two ways, i.e. policing and the theory and practice of war. The discussion of the former is reserved for Ch. 5, and the current chapter will concentrate on the latter.

THE THEORY AND PRACTICE OF WAR

War is the organized pursuit of the aims of a society, or, at least, the dominant group in a society, by means of force. Such aims can be of many different kinds. They may be ideological (including religious), involving a clash of ideologies or, more narrowly, an ideological motivation to conflict on the part of one or other of the combatants. Self-defence is a recurrent explicit factor throughout recorded history, but the aim may also be economic. The latter can operate in a number of ways, e.g. a simple desire to acquire the wealth of other communities, deficiencies in a state's resources that need to be made up, or severe economic pressures at home. Social ethos can also be a factor if making war becomes an essential part of the behavioural and aspirational structure of certain offices or groups within a society. Organization is an intrinsic ingredient of war. A disorganized and uncoordinated series of raids or even an individual attack would not normally be described as a war. War is a discrete human event involving violent confrontation of some duration which is intended to achieve an agreed purpose and has a clearly defined beginning, often characterized by a formal declaration of war, and a clearly definable end, frequently characterized by formal treaty arrangements. It will often have a ritualized dimension to the extent that it will be conducted according to agreed rules of war, of which the best-known example in recent years has been the Geneva Convention, which is simply one of a long line of agreed bodies of principles for the conduct of conflicts. Such rules can, of course, break down completely when severe cross-cultural differences arise as, for example, in warfare between Europeans and Asians. Finally, military success will often be concluded with a triumphal celebration of victory.

Egyptian sources reveal evidence of all the standard motives for military operations:

Ideology

The Sphinx Stele of Amenhotep II describes the king's military role beyond the Egyptian frontiers thus:

He trampled the barbarians under his feet. The northerners bow down to his power. All foreign lands are filled with fear of him . . . His borders reach the circuit of heaven, The low lands are in his hand in a single knot . . . He [sc. Amon-re] commanded him to conquer all lands without exception . . . His portion is that which Re illuminates, to him belongs what Ocean encircles; . . . To the pillars of Horus he has no equal . . . As <Amon>-re-atum, Lord of the Gods, has decreed, he seized the lands in triumph, and none will [need to] repeat it.   (*Urk.* iv. 1276–83)

This text is giving expression to the classic theory of Egyptian kingship. At the most basic level Pharaoh's role was the maintenance of the cosmic order (*maat*) in all its aspects (see p. 65ff.), and his duty in this respect extended to the ends of the earth. Pharaoh was king of everyone and of all lands because only in that capacity could he fulfil his cosmic mission. Whilst this view features in many ancient texts, it appears with particular frequency in visual form in contexts where the king is represented treading on or subduing 'The Nine Bows' who symbolically represent the totality of his enemies, i.e. all the inhabitants of the lands beyond Egypt and sometimes even within it. Since it was the king's duty to rule the world, it is hardly surprising that the Sphinx

Stele presents his imperial mission as something that has been decreed by Amon-re, the king of the gods himself. Exactly the same concept emerges in the *Annals* of Tuthmose III where his assault on Asia is stated to be commanded by Amun, and victory is claimed to have been given by him and vouchsafed by Re (Lichtheim 2006: 30) (Fig. 4.1). The activities of the Asiatics are also treated as an act of rebellion against what is obviously supposed to be their rightful lord, and there is no doubt whatsoever in this text that the gods were considered to be on the side of Tuthmose. In the late eighth century Piye, although a Nubian, presents himself in his Victory Stele as a classic embodiment of an Egyptian Pharaoh (Grimal 1981) and, as such, he too insists on the centrality of the support of Amun when he issues the command to his troops:

Boast not as [though you are] a possessor of might. No man has might in ignorance of him [i.e. Amon-re]. He makes the weak-armed strong-armed, and the many flee before the few, and a single one defeats a thousand men! Sprinkle yourselves with water of his altars; kiss the earth before him. Say to him, 'Give us the way, that we may fight in the shade of your strong arm! As for the troop which you sent, when it charges, may the many tremble before it!'   (*Urk.* iii. 13–14)

It is within this context where conquest is part of Pharaoh's divine mission that we must also interpret the frequent references to the king's intention to extend the frontiers of Egypt. In the Boundary Stele of Regnal Year 16 of Senwosret III the king insists: 'I have made my boundary further south than my fathers. I have added to what was bequeathed me' (Sethe 1928: 83), and the *Annals* of Tuthmose III also insist on this aspect of the king's role. There might be a temptation to regard these statements as raw imperialism, but that would be a mistake. The subtext in all such cases is that the king's divinely appointed cosmicizing mission is being fulfilled. It is within this complex of ideas that we must also interpret the frequent claims made in Egyptian texts that the king is dealing with foreign rebels against his authority. Sometimes there is a historical justification for such assertions, but it would be possible for the Egyptians to conceptualize as rebels any foreign foe who took up arms against them since theoretically they were all subjects of Pharaoh, whatever they themselves might think of the matter. These attitudes to foreigners and their relationship to Egypt were greatly facilitated by the Egyptian conviction that only Egyptians were, in the fullest sense, 'human beings' (*remetj, rmṯ*). Foreigners could certainly cross the divide by adopting Egyptian culture, but, if they failed to do so, they were consigned to a lower level in the hierarchy of being. Inevitably, therefore, contempt for, and loathing of, foreigners came easily: the adjective 'vile' (*hesi, ḫsi*) was routinely applied to Nubia and Asia as well as to their rulers, and the ethnic 'Asiatics' (*Setetiu, sttyw*) is used as a term of abuse in the stele of Piye to refer to *Egyptian* enemies. This ideological mindset, *in toto*, helped greatly in providing the Egyptians with what they considered to be the

Fig. 4.1. The Near East during the New Kingdom. After Shaw (ed.) 2000: 233.

moral basis for war, one of the earliest forms of the concept of *Bellum Iustum* ('the just war').

Self-defence

However exalted the role of the king might be in ideological terms, harsh realities inevitably impinged on a regular basis, and the Egyptians were far from ignoring this brutal fact. Amongst these realities the recurrent need to defend the borders of Egypt against foreign enemies is frequently expressed in textual sources, and here again the Egyptians were able to claim that they were waging a *Bellum Iustum*. To take some paradigmatic examples of attacks on northern enemies first: in the Sixth Dynasty Weni insists in his account of a military expedition into Asia that the king is not simply an aggressor but is responding to a threat: '. . . His Majesty took [preventive] action (*ḥsf ḥt*) against the Asiatic Sand-dwellers' (*Urk.* i: 101). The significance of the phrase *ḥsf ḥt n* has not always been fully grasped, but the word *ḥsf* always seems to convey the notion of 'repelling' and suggests a reaction to a threat, an interpretation that fits beautifully with the comment later in the text: 'His Majesty sent me to lead these armies five times to destroy the land of the Sand-dwellers, as often as they rebelled, with these troops' (*Urk.* i. 104). This text implies that the war is defensive, and the message being pumped out is that Pharaoh was justified in his actions. In the Middle Kingdom the need to defend the Asian frontier is strongly emphasized by the fictitious royal author of the *Instruction for Merikare*, and the *Prophecy of Neferti* informs us that the fortification known as 'The Walls of the Ruler' in the Wadi Tumilat area was designed specifically to keep Asiatics out of Egypt. The motive for subsequent Twelfth Dynasty operations in Asia is not explicitly stated, but the fragmentary annalistic text of Amenemhet II from Memphis, although it speaks of economic benefits, makes it clear that aggressive action was taken against some Asiatic states and peoples (Marcus 2007), and the Stele of Sobekkhu[1] composed later in the dynasty describes a hard-fought campaign in Syria-Palestine that was intended 'to cast down' (*sḥrt*) the Asiatic Beduin and had exclusively military dimensions. The early Twelfth Dynasty Nesumontju Stele points in the same direction (Obsomer 1995: 546–52), and it is impossible not to suspect that we are dealing in all these cases with strikes, pre-emptive or otherwise, against perceived threats. Defence of Egypt is also mentioned as a motive for Tuthmose III's campaign into Asia in Regnal Year 23. In Merneptah's Regnal Year 5 a mass invasion of Egypt by Libyans and their allies was defeated by the Egyptians in a campaign that the king's Karnak Stele explicitly

---

[1] The name is also read Khusobek.

describes as defensive, and the inscriptional record of the Libyan campaign of Regnal Year 5 of Ramesses III describes Egyptian operations in the same light, as do inscriptions relating the actions against the Sea Peoples in Regnal Year 8 and the Libyans in Regnal Year 11. Somewhat later the great Karnak inscription of Shoshenq I also insists on self-defence as a motive.

Self-defence also features in accounts of military operations to the south of Egypt. The Senwosret III boundary stele of Regnal Year 16 previously mentioned, apart from making the interesting point that a military response should be calibrated to fit the particular circumstances, indicates that the king's Nubian campaign was motivated by self-defence when he describes himself as:

One who takes thought for inferiors, one who stands up for mercy, but who shows no mercy to the enemy who attacks him,

One who attacks when he is attacked, but who ceases when the enemy ceases,

Who responds to a matter in accordance with that which comes forth from it;

for, as for ceasing after an attack, it is a strengthening of the heart of the enemy.

Aggression is valour; to retreat is a vile thing.

He who is driven from his frontier is a true punk.   (Sethe 1928: 83–4)

In the case of the Nubians his bellicose stance was entirely justified; for there was a very real threat to Egyptian security from the Kerma peoples to the south of the Second Cataract, a threat that became a disastrous reality during the Second Intermediate Period when a wide-ranging alliance of invaders from the south ravaged Egypt at least as far as Asyut (W. V. Davies 2003: 5–6), and that threat also emerges quite explicitly in the first Kamose Stele (Redford 1997). Given this situation, it is hardly surprising that the Egyptians constructed a series of massive fortresses in Lower Nubia during the Middle Kingdom and extended their grip on the area to well beyond the Fourth Cataract during the New Kingdom. The biography of Ahmose, son of Abana, reveals that there was unrest in Nubia in the time of Ahmose and Tuthmose I, and that the king also had to deal with intruders from the desert, a consistent problem throughout Egyptian history (Lichtheim 2006: 13–14).[2] The danger was further illustrated in the eighth century when the Nubian king Piye invaded Egypt and established the Twenty-fifth Dynasty which exercised a rather intermittent and often partial control of the country until the mid seventh century. The Tanis Stele of Regnal Year 3 (593–2) of Psammetichus II speaks of the Nubians 'planning to fight' with him and describes a pre-emptive strike put in by the Egyptians to forestall this endeavour (Der Manuelian 1994: 367).

---

[2] The Nubian campaign of Amenhotep I is presented in this text as aggressive rather than a response to a threat.

Whilst we have been able to identify several first-millennium texts that provide explicit statements on the motivation for Egyptian military operations, such statements are rare for that period. Consequently, although we have information on numerous military operations, we do not have the texts to indicate what the Egyptians thought they were doing. Nevertheless, the information available can leave little doubt that the primary motive was defensive. This must hold true of the operations of Psammetichus I against the Assyrians between 655 and 630 and his confrontation of the Chaldaeans from 616 onwards, a policy followed by his son Necho II, his great grandson Apries, and the usurper Amasis from 570 onwards. Psammetichus III's operations against the Persians and those of the Thirtieth Dynasty against the same enemy must also fall into the same category (Perdu 2010: 149–57).

The wars of reunification, which occur at several points in Egyptian history, can also be seen as examples of protection of borders in so far as they are concerned with re-establishing frontiers that had been lost to enemy action, sometimes to rival Egyptian dynasts and sometimes to foreign invasion. An example of the first is the reunification of Egypt by Montuhotep II through the defeat of the Herakleopolitan Dynasty. The second is exemplified by the Kamose Stelae which present us with a king determined to deliver northern Egypt from Asiatic domination, at the same time exacting vengeance on the Asiatics for alleged injuries perpetrated against Egypt. The reunification of Egypt under Psammetichus I which was achieved in 656 BC belongs in the same order of things.

Economic Motivation

There is no doubt whatsoever that Egyptian military operations both in Egypt and beyond could generate considerable economic benefits for the crown as well as the individual soldier (cf. Na'aman 1981), but it is not so clear that economic factors were a primary motive for these operations. The Palermo Stone lists a successful campaign in Nubia that allegedly brought in 7,000 captives and 200,000 small and large cattle, and also a campaign in Libya that yielded 1,100 captives and 13,100 (or 23,100) small cattle (Strudwick 2005: 66–7), though we should be cautious in accepting the startlingly high figures for animals. The Second Kamose Stele speaks fulsomely of the booty acquired by the troops engaged in the war of liberation against the Hyksos, and the Piye Stele describes the economic benefits accruing from the king's successful invasion of Egypt, including 'silver, gold, copper, and clothing; everything of Lower Egypt, every product of Syria, and all plants of God's Land' (*Urk.* iii. 55), but in both latter cases the primary motivation was the determination to gain, or regain, complete control of Egypt. The textual evidence for Asia already discussed strongly suggests that the pre-eminent issue in that area was self-defence, and the same will have held true for Libya, but we should beware of accepting such texts entirely at face value. Most of this material consists of official royal documents that are designed to present the king's motives in an impeccable ideological framework where mundane economic factors would have no place. Even if, in some cases, the economic motive had been pre-eminent, the texts would not be likely to admit that fact. Nevertheless, the booty acquired by Tuthmose III in the Megiddo campaign of Regnal Year 23 and listed in his Annals makes most impressive reading:

<List of the booty which His Majesty's army brought from the town of> Megiddo: prisoners 340; hands 83; horses 2,041; foals 191; stallions 6; colts ...; 1 chariot decorated with gold, with a pole [?] of gold, belonging to that enemy; <1> fine chariot decorated with gold belonging to the Prince of <*Megiddo*> ...; chariots of his vile army 892. Total: 924. 1 fine bronze coat of mail belonging to that enemy, <1> fine bronze coat of mail belonging to the Prince of Meg<iddo; ... coats of mail belonging to his vile army 200; bows 502; tent-poles of *meru*-wood, inlaid with silver, of the tent of that enemy 7.

Now the army <of His Majesty> took away <cattle> ...: 387 ...; cows 1,929; goats 2,000; sheep 20,500. List of what was carried off subsequently by the king from the household effects of that enemy, who was <in> Yenoam, in Nuges, and in Herenkeru, together with the property of those towns which had allied themselves with him ...; <*maryannu*> belonging to them 38; children of that enemy and of the princes who were with him 84; *maryannu* belonging to them 5; male and female slaves, as well as their children, 1,796; non-combatants who had come out from that enemy because of hunger. Total: 2,503. In addition bowls of costly stones and gold, sundry vessels ..., a large *akunu-jar* of Syrian workmanship, jars, bowls, dishes, various drinking vessels, large kettles, knives <x + 17>, amounting to 1,784 *deben*; gold in discs, found in the hands of craftsmen, as well as large quantities of silver in disc form, [amounting to] 966 *deben* and 1 *kite*; a silver statue in the form of ... <a statue> ..., with a gold head; staves with human heads 3; carrying-chairs of that enemy, of ivory, ebony, and carob-wood, inlaid with gold 6; the footstools belonging to them 6; large tables of ivory and carob-wood 6; 1 bed belonging to that enemy, of carob-wood, inlaid with gold and with all manner of precious stones, in the manner of a *kerker*, 5 completely worked in gold; a statue of that enemy which was there, of ebony worked with gold, its head of lapis <lazuli> ...; bronze vessels, and large quantities of clothing of that enemy.

Now the fields were made into arable plots, allocated to inspectors of the palace (life, prosperity, health) in order to reap their harvest. List of the harvest which His Majesty carried off from the Megiddo land plots: wheat 207,300 <+ x> sacks of, apart from what was cut as forage by the army of His Majesty ...   (*Urk.* iv. 663–7)

This and comparable New Kingdom texts reveal that booty and the foreign donations generated by military operations in Asia yielded a copious econom-ic return not only from Palestine and Syria but also from states as far afield as

Assyria, Babylonia, Khatti, and Cyprus.[3] This income consisted of luxury items of many different kinds—oil, cosmetics, incense, wine, animal skins, ivory, cattle, goats, sheep, considerable quantities of agricultural produce, prisoners of war (including the elite charioteers called *maryannu*), slaves, military equipment, including horses and chariots that were of immense value to the elite chariot corps of the Egyptian army, metals (both precious and industrial), a great deal of timber of various kinds, and even the occasional Asiatic princess. As in all ages, some of this ended up in the hands of individual soldiers as one of the standard rewards of the military life, but the major beneficiaries were the royal exchequer and, by association, the Egyptian temples, above all, the great shrine of Amon-re at Thebes. Sadly, the blessings of Empire were not enjoyed to anything like the same extent by the large towns and population of Palestine which seem to have suffered a severe economic decline during the period of Egyptian occupation (Weinstein 2001: 223–4), though to what extent this was a direct result of Egyptian hegemony remains an open question.

The data for Nubia are altogether more equivocal and indicate that the primary motive changed over time. Archaeological evidence demonstrates that the relationship between Egypt and the A-Group peoples of Lower Nubia underwent a radical transformation at the beginning of the First Dynasty (Wengrow 2006: 146–7). From an association of equal partners in the late Predynastic Period it became a relationship where the recently unified northern power assumed a dominant role that placed the A-Group in an emphatically subordinate position where the Egyptians basically did what they liked in Lower Nubia, and even beyond, simply because they had the military muscle to impose their will. The establishment of the Old Kingdom settlement of Buhen for the exploitation of local copper resources exemplifies this imperious mindset, and the great biographical inscription of Harkhuf illustrates it perfectly in its description of an expedition into the far south:

I found the ruler of Irtjet, Setju, and Wawat . . . With three hundred donkeys did I go down, laden with frankincense, ebony, *hekenu*-oil, *sat*-oil, panther skins, elephant tusks, throw sticks, and every goodly product. *When the ruler of Irtjet, Setju, and Wawat saw the strength and numbers of the force of Yam which went down with me to the residence together with the expeditionary force which had been sent with me*, then did this ruler escort me, giving me cattle and goats, and acting as a guide for me on the mountain roads of Irtjet. (*Urk.* i. 126–7)

Here Pharaoh had sent a heavily escorted expedition southwards to acquire the goods which the Nubians had available, and in the face of Egyptian

---

[3] Not all the resources described as *inw*, lit. 'things brought', were the product of direct military action. Some took the form of presents from independent states on the basis that it was a good idea to maintain good relations with the top power in Western Asia.

military force the Nubians recognized that they had no alternative but to cooperate. There is no suggestion here of trade relations; the Egyptians demanded with menaces, and the Nubians provided. It is, of course, significant that this is a non-royal inscription whose author/s could afford to be a little more frank about motivation than those responsible for the formulation of royal texts. The Egyptians renewed their aggressive activities in Nubia during the Eleventh Dynasty (Darnell 2003, 2004). These may have been motivated by self-defence, if we accept that there was an independent kingdom in Lower Nubia at this period (cf. Grajetzki 2006: 27–8), but we have already seen that the Semna Stele of Regnal Year 16 of Senwosret III insists that self-defence was an issue during the Twelfth Dynasty, and his canal inscription of Regnal Year 8 at Sehel is quite explicit that the expedition preceding the construction of the canal was intended to 'overthrow vile Kush'. The spectacular series of forts of this period constructed in Lower Nubia bearing bellicose names such as 'Warding off the Bows' (Semna East/Kumma) and 'Repelling the Nomads' (Uronarti) point in the same direction (see p. 121), and the rigid control on movement northwards described in the Semna Stele of Regnal Year 8 of the same monarch (see below) betrays a clear nervousness about the permeability of the southern frontier as well as the possibility of diplomatic contacts with the Kerma peoples to the south (see next paragraph). The invasion and ravaging of southern Egypt by Nubians during the Second Intermediate Period and the hostile machinations of the Nubian ruler mentioned in the Kamose Stelae demonstrate that Egyptian anxiety in relation to the southerners was entirely justified and explain the determination of the Eighteenth Dynasty to initiate a programme of conquest that led eventually to the destruction of the Classic Kerma kingdom and the establishment of Egyptian influence beyond the Fourth Cataract.

Having said all this, we must concede that economic exploitation was also a major inducement in Nubia, if not the primary motive. Gold and copper were available in abundance, and it is significant that some of the Middle Kingdom forts, following the Old Kingdom precedent at Buhen, were constructed near mining areas, e.g. Kuban and Askut, and quarries yielding high-quality stone and gemstones were also exploited at this period. The Semna Stele of Regnal Year 8 of Senwosret III reveals the currency of trade between Egyptian Nubia and the Kerma people to the south:

The southern frontier made in Regnal Year 8 under the Majesty of the King of Upper and Lower Egypt Khakaure (may he live for ever and ever) in order to prevent it being passed by any Nubian journeying north by land or in a *kai*-boat as well as any livestock belonging to Nubians, with the exception of a Nubian who shall come to traffic at Iken [i.e. Mirgissa] or on an embassy, or on any matter that may lawfully be done with them; but it is forbidden for any *kai*-boat of the Nubians to pass northwards beyond Heh [i.e. Semneh] for ever.   (Sethe 1928: 84–5)

During the New Kingdom the expansion south which extended the Egyptian sphere of influence at least as far as Kurgus between the Fourth and Fifth Cataracts yielded substantial trade benefits, and large quantities of taxes (*bakut, b3kwt*) and 'gifts' (*inu, inw*) were paid both into temple coffers and those of the king (see p. 184).

THE METHODOLOGY OF WAR

Wars are won in one of two ways: either the enemy's will to continue is eroded or the enemy is deprived of the means to continue. The first phenomenon is much the commoner. In pursuit of these aims wars are fought at three interlocking levels: strategy, operational planning, and tactics. 'Strategy' embraces the aim or aims formulated as the means of bringing a war to a successful conclusion; 'tactics' covers the methods by which a *battle* is fought; and the much less familiar operational level embraces the way in which military action is orchestrated within a theatre of operations to achieve strategic aims (on 'the operational art' see Glantz and Orenstein 1995). Excellence in one area does not necessarily mean excellence in others, e.g. the British in the American Revolutionary War suffered very few tactical reverses but fought a poor war at the operational and strategic levels, and a similar situation held true of the Germans in the Second World War; their tactical expertise was incomparable whereas operational and strategic grip was often precarious, if not worse. In the formulation of strategy and operational planning there are many factors that must be taken into consideration: geography, terrain (particularly lines of communication), supply, the nature and positioning of enemy forces, and the political and economic organization of the enemy. At the tactical level critical issues are terrain, the relative numbers of opposing forces, levels of training and morale of troops involved, the way in which a general disposes his forces to meet his enemy, the ways in which he controls those forces in battle; the tactical formations used by the enemy; and the offensive and defensive equipment available to both sides.

Unlike Imperial China (Sawyer 1993) the Ancient Egyptians do not seem to have produced military manuals, and we are, therefore, usually thrown back on deduction in trying to establish their thinking on the conduct of campaigns or lesser military enterprises. Our discussion of motives for war has already covered the broad strategic aims of Egyptian warfare, though specific enemies changed over time, e.g. Mitanni was the main opponent in Asia during much of the Eighteenth Dynasty, and the Hittites in the latter part of that dynasty and the early part of the Nineteenth, whilst the Sea Peoples were a growing menace from the Nineteenth Dynasty into the Twentieth. When we turn to operational planning, it is evident that the Egyptians had a very firm grip on the principles that might govern this aspect of war, and the literary record of Ramesses II's Battle of Kadesh reveals that, when the army set out, an operational plan had already been formulated and, very surprisingly, disseminated to the whole army (Gardiner 1960: 7).

As early as the late Sixth Dynasty we find Weni describing a variety of operational techniques in his assaults on Egypt's Asiatic neighbours:

1. It was said that there were rebels amongst these foreigners in Gazelle's-Nose Land. I crossed in ships together with these contingents [i.e. those given by the king]. Behind the heights of the mountain range did I land, to the north of the land of the Sand-dwellers, while [the other] half of this army came by road (*Urk.* i. 104–5).

2. In safety has this army returned, having hacked up the land of the Sand-dwellers . . . flattened the land of the Sand-dwellers . . . having cut down its fig trees and its vines . . . having cast flames in all its <houses> (103–4),

3. having cast down its strongholds . . . having slain its troops by many tens of thousands . . . <having carried off> from it many <troops> as captives (103–4).

4. I returned home only after I had seized them all, slaying every rebel amongst them (105).

The first passage displays a grasp of the value of combined operations, a technique that came very naturally to the Ancient Egyptians since the Nile and its associated waterways were by far the easiest way to move troops within their own country (Spalinger 2005: ch. 1; 2010). Water transport formed a major part of operations in Nubia at all periods, and the Kamose Stelae leave us in no doubt of the crucial role of the fleet in the king's successful operations against the Hyksos. A comparable picture emerges in the not dissimilar circumstances of Piye's conquest of Egypt. The New Kingdom offers some spectacular developments of the techniques learned on the Nile as applied to operations beyond the frontier. From at least the time of Tuthmose III the Lebanese ports became standard operational bases for supply and reinforcement of military contingents campaigning inland (Säve-Söderbergh 1946: 31–70), and that policy was continued well into the Nineteenth Dynasty. Tuthmose III's Eighth Campaign into Asia in Regnal Year 33 is a particularly impressive example of this system in that the movement of his land forces to the Euphrates was complemented by the construction of prefabricated boats near Byblos which were then transported in sections on carts a distance in excess of 250 miles to the Euphrates where they facilitated the forcing of a crossing at Carchemish and also the pursuit of the defeated enemy on the river (Faulkner 1946: 39–42; Redford 2003: 220–8). A recurrent type of combined operation is Egyptian reactive responses to the threat or actuality of coordinated land and sea attacks on Egypt proper. Here the operational posture was mainly defensive and determined by the actions of the enemy to which the Egyptians responded in kind. Ramesses III exemplifies this operational response in the First Libyan War of Regnal Year 5, and in his Great Inscription dated to that year he also speaks of a two-pronged attack mounted by the Peleset and Tjeker by land and sea in Regnal Year 8 which he succeeded in defeating (KRI v. 20–7). The king describes his countermeasures to this later assault in these terms:

I fixed my frontier in Djahi, prepared before them, the princes, troop-commanders, and *maryannu*. I caused the waters to be equipped like a mighty wall with ships of war, galleys, and freighters < . . . >.[4] They were furnished completely from stem to stern with valiant fighting men carrying their weapons and infantry from all the best of Egypt . . . the chariotry consisting of skilful fighters, men of rank [?], and every good and efficient officer whose hands were competent, their horses quivering in all their limbs ready to trample the foreign lands under their hoofs . . . Those who came forward united on the sea, the full flame was in front of them at the river mouths, and a barricade of spears enclosed them on the shore, they being dragged in, hurled down, prostrated on the beach, slain, and made into piles from head to toe,[5] their ships and their possessions being like what has fallen into water.   (KRI v. 40–1)

During the first millennium the problem of dealing with a two-pronged attack became a recurrent issue when the Egyptians were faced with meeting assaults by the Assyrians, Babylonians, and Persians, and the solution inevitably remained largely the same (Lloyd 2000*a*, 2000*b*).

To return to Weni: our first passage (see p. 108) also demonstrates the employment of another operational technique that has been widely used since, i.e. the pincer movement, the *Kesselschlacht* so successfully employed by the German army during the Second World War. In this beautifully simple and highly effective procedure one arm of Weni's pincer is provided by a naval manoeuvre to the north of the enemy's position and the other by a dedicated land force coming up from the south. The use of the verb *nedjer* (*nḏr*), translated 'seized' in the passage (4), is particularly apt to describe its results since it powerfully evokes the concept of grasping or holding something fast in the hand. A later Egyptian parallel to this action is not easy to find, but it may well be that the Battle of Kadesh provides something similar in the arrival from Amor of the Na'arn force at the city of Kadesh whilst the outcome is still very much in the balance. It is perfectly possible that the appearance of this contingent was not accidental but part of a wider operational plan to attack the city from the west whilst the main force came up from the south (Fig. 4.2).

---

[4] At the end of this list of ships the text has the unique word *nsk* whose meaning has never been established. It is determined by two signs that suggest that it may denote violent and destructive action. This and the talk of the ships forming a wall may mean that the mix of ships in question was deliberately sunk as block ships at the mouths of the Nile.

[5] Literally 'from tail to head'. My translation assumes that this is an idiomatic expression that was not confined to animals and could be generally applied.

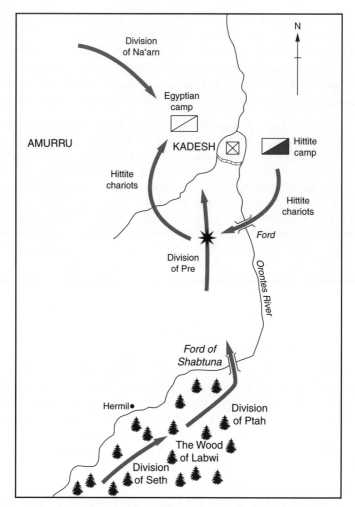

Fig. 4.2. The Battle of Kadesh. After Spalinger 2005: map 5.

The second of our Weni passages reveals another dimension to his campaigning, i.e. the application of economic warfare in an attempt to impair the military capacity of the enemy by destroying his economic infrastructure, a technique destined to a brilliant future in the history of war, the most grizzly instance probably being the massacre by the United States Army under General Philip Sheridan of the bison on which the economy of the Plains Indians depended and whose loss brought inevitable disaster on its unfortunate victims. Such assaults on the enemy's economy were a standard Egyptian operational procedure of which the great Semna Stele of Senwosret III provides an excellent example, in this case used against Nubians:

I captured their women.
I carried off their dependants,
Proceeding against their wells, killing their cattle,
Cutting down their grain and setting fire to it.   (Sethe 1928: 84)

Here the methods governing the assault on the economic basis of Nubian societies are self-evident, but the passage also gives an insight into another closely related operational technique, i.e. the disruption of the very social fabric of the enemy. There is no mention of males in this catalogue of malevolence, and presumably most of these were killed, but the removal of surviving members of the defeated Nubian communities would have meant, in effect, their annihilation, and the massacre of the cattle, certainly a major, if not *the* major, criterion of wealth and social status as well as being an economic asset, would have been equally disastrous.

The third and fourth Weni passages reveal yet another operational procedure that was again part of the standard repertoire of Egyptian warfare, i.e. the policy of degrading the enemies' military assets to forestall immediate retaliation. Killing off the enemy in large numbers gets very close to the 'strategy of annihilation' as well as exemplifying yet again that the victor can acquire valuable manpower resources through successful military operations. Symbolic depictions of this process begin in the late Predynastic Period with such images as those on the Narmer Palette (see p. 51) and subsequently occur on monuments throughout Egyptian history with unrelenting enthusiasm in the form of Pharaoh smiting enemies or assaulting them in various poses from a war chariot, but, as in the case of Weni, these blood-thirsty predilections did not blind the Egyptians to the economic and military benefits of taking prisoners which might be used for economic production in Egypt or, like the Sherden and *maryannu* so prominent in the New Kingdom, enrolled in the Egyptian army.

Another operational procedure exemplified in Egyptian texts is operations on interior lines, i.e. a commander faced with more than one enemy will place himself between them and try to defeat them separately as Napoleon tried to do, unsuccessfully, during the Waterloo campaign in 1815. In the situation described in the Kamose Stelae (see p. 102) the king found himself occupying Middle and Upper Egypt but confronted with an enemy to the north in the form of the Hyksos, who controlled the country as far south as Cusae, and a Nubian kingdom beyond the First Cataract. It was critically important to ensure that they could not join forces to present a united front so that he could deal with his two enemies separately. The solution to the problem was to exploit his position between them to keep them apart. His enemies could only join up, or produce a coordinated assault from the north and the south, if they could communicate, and the only practical way for them to do that was by means of the western desert road since Kamose had control of the Nile route.

This Kamose clearly realized and had a watch kept on the desert road that eventually led to the capture of a Hyksos messenger travelling south to mobilize assistance for the Hyksos ruler. This made it possible for Kamose to defeat the Hyksos first and then turn his attention to his enemy to the south.

Egyptian texts are not fulsome on tactics. Evidence from the Late Predynastic and Thinite Periods provides snapshots of action, but no coordinated sequence emerges. It is more than likely that confrontations, at the most, would have involved two groups of warriors coming face-to-face, discharging several rounds of missiles at each other, and then closing in to fight it out hand-to-hand in the close-range butchery characteristic of all warfare until relatively recently. The Old Kingdom material is equally unhelpful. The inscription of Weni, for all its value, says nothing about what happened tactically when Egyptian forces confronted those of the enemy, and it is likely that battles unfolded in much the same way as we have surmised for the earlier period. The Middle Kingdom is rather more explicit. Nesumontju in the early Twelfth Dynasty speaks of training his soldiers in ambush tactics and makes the following interesting claims: 'I cast down the Montju nomads . . . and the sand-dwellers, having overthrown their fastnesses, creeping like a desert-fox along the desert margins. Along their (own) highways did I go out and return' (Sethe 1928: 82 ll. 13–15; cf. Obsomer 1995: 549). These attacks look very much like classic light-infantry commando tactics designed to hit a totally unsuspecting enemy. The mind-numbing effects of surprise and its value as a force-multiplier were certainly something that Egyptians understood well, the Battle of Megiddo fought by Tuthmose III in the campaign of Regnal Year 23 being an excellent example (Fig. 4.3). He had marched north towards the city of Megiddo where the enemy had concentrated his forces. There were three possible roads to the city through the Carmel Ridge that Tuthmose might have taken, and the enemy clearly expected him to follow either the northern route via the Djefti road or the southern route, which would have brought him to Megiddo via Taanach, and they drew up the southern wing of their forces at Taanach and the northern in the Valley of Kina[6] clearly in the expectation that they would have time to combine these two wings once Egyptian intentions had become clear. However, Tuthmose decided to use the least likely route along a narrow pass running between Aruna and Megiddo. If successful, this dangerous manoeuvre would threaten the right flank of the enemy force at Taanach and also offer the possibility of severing links with the northern force in the Kina Valley, thus throwing the enemy completely off balance and forcing him into a hasty redeployment in order to bring his full force to bear effectively on the Egyptian army. This course of events is precisely what ensued, a situation that will have done nothing to improve the morale of

---

[6] Here I follow the reconstruction of the damaged text offered by Lichtheim 2006: 31.

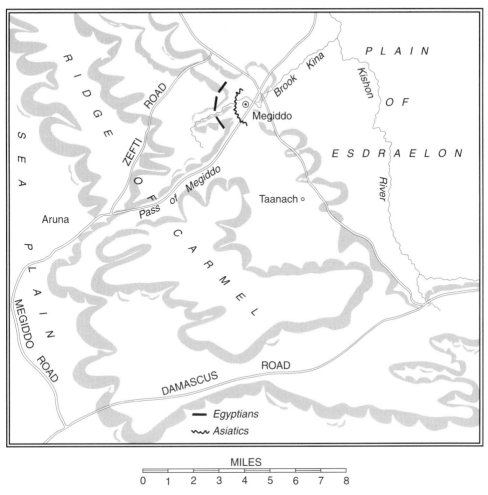

Fig. 4.3. The Battle of Megiddo. After Breasted 1909: map 4.

Megiddo's army, but the detailed tactics employed, once the armies confronted each other, are not described. We are informed that the Egyptian army was drawn up in a line consisting of three divisions (north, centre, south), an arrangement that would have facilitated control and tactical flexibility, but how exactly the Egyptian army defeated the opposition we are not told. It may well be that Tuthmose exploited the sheer fighting power of his well-trained and largely homogeneous army in a vigorous frontal assault against the heterogeneous allied force before him which led to its swift collapse, and he certainly succeeded in completely routing the enemy and driving them pell-mell into the city of Megiddo itself (cf. Redford 2003: 18–43, 206–9). Whilst, however, the standard Late Bronze Age tactic in pitched battles may well have been the all-out frontal attack, it is evident that more sophisticated tactics could be employed. In the case of the Battle of Kadesh the Hittites mounted a large-scale ambush against the right flank of the advancing Egyptian army with devastating consequences from which the Egyptians only extricated themselves through a combination of the undoubted courage of Ramesses II himself and the timely arrival of reinforcements from the west (see Fig. 4.2). Training in ambush tactics is also mentioned on the Stele of Nesumontju.

Given the ideological rationale of Egyptian inscriptions it is inevitable that the emphasis in military narratives is firmly placed on Pharaoh as victorious aggressor, but it is evident, if rarely mentioned, that the tactics of defence were well understood. The inscription of Sobekkhu describes a campaign of Senwosret III against the Beduin of Asia which extended as far as the site of Shechem. After an allegedly successful campaign[7] the army turned for home, but nothing was left to chance in this intrinsically dangerous manoeuvre. As in any similar modern operation, the retreat was carefully screened by a rearguard (*peh(wy)*, *ph̭(wy)*), a force described as being under the command of Sobekkhu himself, and this fought vigorously and successfully to cover the withdrawal of the main force.

We cannot conclude this discussion of the Egyptian methodology of war without some discussion of diplomacy as an adjunct to military operations. Of the fighting power of the Egyptian army during the New Kingdom there can be no doubt, but its success at its apogee in the Eighteenth Dynasty was in some measure due to its being confronted by enemies of inferior military capacity such as Palestinian and Syrian city states and the kingdom of Mitanni. However, from the end of the Eighteenth Dynasty the military balance of power in Asia was slowly changing, and the rise of the mighty Hittite Empire which was able to mobilize first-rate military assets on a large scale placed a strict limit on the capacity of the Egyptians to establish and maintain direct control of Syria-Palestine. This was ultimately recognized by the great treaty concluded between Ramesses II and Hattusilis III in Ramesses' Regnal Year 21 which provides the most spectacular piece of documentary evidence of the growth of diplomacy and formal treaty obligations as a means beyond force of guaranteeing Egypt's military position (Kitchen *c.*1982: 75–81). To what extent this event had precedents before the New Kingdom we cannot say, but it is quite clear that the diplomacy option was increasingly forced on the Egyptians from the late New Kingdom onwards by the rise in Asia of a series of great powers—Hittites, Assyrians, Babylonians, and Persians—which were at least their equal in military might and usually their superiors. Egypt, singlehanded, was no longer capable of mobilizing sufficient fighting power to defeat the most potent of its Asiatic enemies and was increasingly compelled to have

---

[7] The vigour with which the enemy attacked the Egyptian force on its journey home suggests that the Egyptians were not as successful as the text claims.

recourse to the defensive alliance with states threatened by the same enemies in the hope that a combination of fighting power would prevail. An excellent example of this methodology is the international mutual defence pact concluded by Twenty-sixth Dynasty Pharaoh Amasis (570–26) to meet the growing threat of a Persian attack. This involved the creation of a wide-ranging alliance with Sparta, Lydia, Babylonia, and, initially, Samos. Not very surprisingly the inherent geographic difficulties presented by this scheme guaranteed its failure with the last surviving partner, Egypt, being utterly defeated in 525 to initiate more than a century of Persian domination.[8]

THE INSTRUMENTS OF WAR

Hegemony and Empire are things states do to people when they can get away with it, and that requires either superior military institutions, superior technology, or both. Until the end of the New Kingdom Egypt was generally well served in this respect.

The Army

We have little information on the organization of armies during the Prehistoric and Thinite Periods. The evidence that does survive (e.g. slate palettes and the Scorpion Macehead) strongly suggests that royal armies were made up of local contingents, each distinguished by its own standard, called up by the crown and serving under local grandees. The data improve greatly during the Old Kingdom when, above all, the autobiography of Weni throws a flood of light on the way that a large force designed for major operations beyond the Egyptian frontier was organized. In the first place, it reveals that we are not dealing with a full-time professional force. The army was under the command of Weni, who was himself a civilian royal official, and the subordinate commanders were also amateurs, consisting of:

counts, chancellors of the king of Lower Egypt, sole companions of the palace, governors, and estate-controllers of Upper and Lower Egypt, companions, chiefs of dragomans, overseers of priests of Upper and Lower Egypt, and overseers of the work centres being at the head of the contingents of Upper and Lower Egypt, from the estates and towns that they governed and from the Nubians of those foreign lands.

(*Urk.* i. 102)

---

[8] On the fascinating question of Late Bronze Age diplomatic relations see Beckman 1999; Cohen and Westbrook 2000; Lloyd 2007.

His force was a large one, though it was certainly nowhere remotely near the tens of thousands that he claims, and it was drawn from the whole of Egypt as well as containing contingents from various parts of Nubia and also from Libya. Whether these non-Egyptian troops should be treated as mercenaries or troops from areas over which the Egyptians had some sort of control cannot be determined. At all events it is self-evident that the Egyptians, not very surprisingly, regarded large numbers as a critical element in enhancing the fighting-power of their military forces.

The local basis of much of the manpower used in military operations emerges very clearly from Middle Kingdom inscriptions. At the beginning of the Twelfth Dynasty the nomarch Amenemhet describes himself as the commander of the troops of the Oryx Nome and speaks of contributing 400 men of the nome for one Nubian expedition and 600 for another enterprise (Simpson (ed.) 2003: 419–20). Sobekkhu, who bore the title 'Commander-in-Chief of a Town (Regiment)' (*ḥtw ʿꜣ n niwt*), also speaks of his nome regiment in an expedition of Senwosret III to Nubia. The efficiency of these contingents was dependent on their physical fitness and training at local level, and that commitment is probably illustrated in representations of vigorous physical exercise in the tombs at Beni Hasan. Whilst, however, such militia contingents formed the basis of the army at this period, texts reveal that there was another level to the military organization which was linked to the palace and was essentially a professional military force. There was certainly a royal bodyguard for the close protection of the king which is denoted by a number of different terms: Sobekkhu speaks of serving with 'seven men of the Residence' (*s(w) 7 n ḫnw*), who must have belonged to this force, and it seems probable that the high-ranking figures bearing the title 'Follower' or 'Follower of the Ruler' (*šmsw/šmsw n ḥḳꜣ*) should be seen as an elite group within the royal bodyguard, though the term is not exclusively military in its implications. The guard is also mentioned in the *Instruction of Amenemhet* where it is designated by the term 'soldiers of my body' (*ʿḥꜣw n ḥʿw.i*). These troops presumably formed part of the 'Ruler's Forces' (*ṯt ḥḳꜣ*) who were probably all professionals and the elite of the Egyptian military establishment (Quirke 1990: 81–4, 118, 191–3).

The heavy military commitments created by the development of the New Kingdom Empire in Asia and Nubia as well as technological changes in equipment necessitated a radical reorganization of the military system. This led to the creation of a body of 30,000–40,000 effectives consisting of two major components, chariotry (the elite) and infantry. However, very few of these troops were full-time soldiers. The vast majority were settled on agricultural allotments and were called out, as required, for periods of service of three or four months a year, an arrangement highly reminiscent of the Territorial Army in the British military establishment. This system is graphically described by Ramesses II in an address to his troops after Kadesh:

'I caused you to dwell in your towns without doing soldier's service. My chariotry likewise, I dismissed them to their villages saying: "I shall find them like today in the hour of joining battle"' (Gardiner 1960: 11). When called up for military service, they were supplied with equipment from royal arsenals by the state, with the exception that chariot troops were required to pay for their own chariots, though horses, which were infinitely more valuable, were provided by the central government (Caminos 1954: 95–6). Evidently these troops were required to maintain a high level of physical fitness, when not serving with the colours, but that would not have been difficult since many of them would have been engaged in agricultural activities for most of the year. This force was divided into divisions which increased in number over time; there appear to have been two during the Eighteenth Dynasty, one each for Upper and Lower Egypt; we know of three under Sety I named after the three dynastic gods Amun, Pre, and Sutekh and at least four under Ramesses II, the earlier list being supplemented by a division named after the god Ptah. It is believed, but undemonstrable, that each division contained 5,000 men (Faulkner 1953: 41–7; Spalinger 2005: 150, 155–6, 203–4, 260). This much more professional military establishment provided a new career path for many Egyptians, and high-ranking soldiers frequently acquired very elevated status in society and government, even, on occasion, gaining the Pharaonic office, though it should always be borne in mind that such officers were still firmly embedded in the ruling civilian elite and frequently held and exercised non-military offices. Inevitably, however, the importance of military action during the New Kingdom led to a progressive increase in the power and importance of military officers both in society and administration. In addition to Egyptian troops New Kingdom Pharaohs also had available substantial bodies of excellent foreign soldiers such as the elite Asiatic *maryannu* chariotry, Sherden, and Libyans, who had frequently been captured in battle and then incorporated into the Egyptian army. Indeed, we are informed in the Great Harris Papyrus that such troops were located in 'strongholds' (*nḫtw*) within Egypt itself where they constituted a significant increment to the defences of the country as well as a useful addition to the forces that the Pharaoh himself could call on as required (cf. Morris 2005: 820–1). These contingents are often described as 'mercenaries', but Spalinger is correct in insisting that this is a misnomer since they were clearly permanently settled in the country as part of the Egyptian army, which was in sore need of an increment in high-quality military personnel. This is not to say that the Egyptians did not, at some periods, use mercenary troops, i.e. troops employed and paid for a specific period and then released. During the Late Period there is ample evidence of Carian and Greek mercenaries functioning as part of the military establishment, and troops of other ethnic origins, such as Jews and Phoenicians, are also detectable (Lloyd 1988: 55, 133–9, 180).

It is probable that the *Machimoi* ('Warriors') frequently mentioned in classical sources were, at least in part, the descendants of foreign troops, mainly Libyans, permanently settled in the country from the New Kingdom onwards. They are described in the Late Period as a military class in Egyptian society and survived into the Ptolemaic Period. Herodotus, our earliest source, informs us that they were based in settlements mainly located in the Delta and that, at their maximum, they numbered 410,000 men, a figure that could not possibly reflect the number of military effectives and would only become even remotely plausible if it included family, dependants, and descendants. Herodotus states that their position was hereditary, and that every year 2,000 of them served in rotation as a royal bodyguard. He also claims that they were all allotted 12 *arourai* of land (3.2 ha), but this rule could hardly have been universally applied since the size of allotments must have taken account of differences of rank. He also claims that they were required to devote themselves entirely to military concerns, but there is good reason to doubt this claim (Lloyd 1988: 189–91). The *Machimoi* had to maintain themselves fit and capable of military operations, but they would have been able to engage in other activities as and when they chose. This probably explains the description, no doubt seriously exaggerated, of the force raised by an unnamed Mendesian claimant to the throne in the Thirtieth Dynasty as consisting of 'newly raised men, who, though many in number, were of no skill in war being most of them mechanics and tradesmen, never bred to war' (Plutarch, *Agesilaus*: 38). The *Machimoi* could certainly be effective kingmakers, when they chose, and were responsible for the deposition of the Pharaoh Apries in 570 and the enthronement of Amasis, one of the greatest of Late Period Pharaohs. They could also be highly effective in battle and greatly distinguished themselves fighting as marines as part of the Persian fleet at the Battle of Artemisium in 480 BC (Herodotus 8. 17).

Equipment

Until the New Kingdom the equipment of Egyptian soldiers lagged behind that of their counterparts in the Near East and achieved parity only in the mid second millennium. Close-quarter weaponry took a variety of forms. Maces appear at an early period, those typical of the Naqada I Period being tipped with disc-shaped heads whilst those of Naqada II date show the pear-shaped head that became the classic form throughout later Egyptian history. The Egyptians also used maces with pointed heads that were wielded essentially like picks. Axes were very common, initially of stone but subsequently of metal, and in the New Kingdom the pole-axe appears. Spears form a standard element in military equipment from prehistoric times. The shafts were about 1.5+ m long, and initially they were stone-tipped, but later spears had metal blades, the leaf-shaped form being common. In military contexts such spears were used as pikes rather than as missiles, but there is good evidence of the use of javelins. Knives and daggers, originally of stone, later of metal, were widely used as stabbing weapons, but from the New Kingdom the much more effective scimitar or sickle sword came into use, usually in the simple form, but weapons that combined the scimitar and mace are also exemplified. *Machimoi* troops in the fifth century were equipped as heavy infantry with spears, battle-axes, and large knives (Herodotus 7. 89, 3).

Missile weaponry was a consistent feature of Egyptian military equipment from prehistoric times. Slings, which could have a range of 200 m, were certainly employed for military purposes, but the dominant missile weapon was the bow of which there were three types: the most basic was the simple or self bow which was a maximum of about 2 m long, made of acacia, and furnished with strings made of animal gut or linen. It had a maximum range of about 200 m, which was useful for volley fire, but the range for accurate aimed shooting was much less. The double-convex bow, which gave a greater range, was also used, but the quantum leap in archery came with the introduction of the composite bow in the mid second millennium. These bows were constructed of a laminate of layers of wood, horn, and sinew, and, when strung, they assumed a triangular shape. The maximum range was in the region of 300 m, but they were not good for aimed fire beyond 120 m. Though they were extremely effective and greatly superior to the other two types of bow, they were expensive and very temperamental so that they were normally kept in bow cases and functioned as elite weapons used particularly by chariotry. Arrows for all types were normally of reed, though wood was sometimes used; tips were made of a variety of materials; and feathers to stablilize the arrows in flight were employed. There is also evidence of wrist guards.

Defensive equipment was initially simple and for much of earlier Egyptian history consisted of nothing more than shields, sometimes very large and commonly made of wood and cowhide. Given their size, their defensive value extended well beyond that of protecting the body of the owner, and at least as early as the New Kingdom they could be set up around a marching camp to shield it from enemy attack or the attentions of enterprising Bedouin thieves. Known royal shields are much more elaborate and very ornate, but in many cases such equipment would have been intended for use as parade or cere-monial items only. During the New Kingdom metal scale armour appears in Egyptian contexts, but it was probably rarely used, and here again royal examples could be very elaborate and richly embellished with precious metals. Leather armour, sometimes in scale form, is also exemplified. For many soldiers, however, such elaborate defensive armour was out of the question, and the furthest they would have gone was to bind the body with bands of linen. Before the New Kingdom head protection would not have extended beyond a mop of greased hair, but, even when metal helmets became available, they were not in general use and formed an item of equipment solely for the elite. The Late Period *Machimoi* seem to have been much better protected than their predecessors; for Herodotus (l.c.) informs us that they were equipped with helmets of mesh work, saucer-shaped shields with large rims, and, in most cases, breastplates.

Mobility in warfare was greatly enhanced by the introduction of the horse to Egypt during the Second Intermediate Period. By modern standards the animals were small with an average height of about 1.35 m. They were certainly ridden in military contexts, but they do not seem to have formed the basis for significant cavalry contingents in the Egyptian army until the Late Period. Their most important role by far was to provide the motive force for the chariot which enjoyed a great vogue in the warfare of the Eastern Mediterranean and the Near East until the late fourth century, though it remained current in the Far East considerably longer. Egyptian war chariots were lightly constructed of wood and leather, and the lightness of their build meant that they could easily be taken apart and carried in pieces in territory that was unsuitable for their deployment. They ran on wheels whose spokes could vary in number, but six eventually became standard. The wheels were attached to a very long axle that greatly enhanced stability, and the axle was fixed to the body of the chariot much closer to the rear than was the case with Hittite chariots so that the vehicle could be turned with the greatest possible speed. Power was provided by two horses, and there were two crew, one to drive the chariot and the other to fight, whereas Hittite chariots supported three crew, offering a significant enhancement in fighting power at the expense of greater overall weight.

Though they were spectacular military assets, the value of chariots in combat was limited by their dependence on suitable terrain. To be used to full advantage they needed a considerable expanse of flat ground where they could be drawn up in serried ranks and could exploit their mobility, though they would retain some value as transport vehicles for the elite of the army in less favourable conditions. Most of Egypt proper, criss-crossed by canals, would have been a charioteer's nightmare, but Asia offered more favourable conditions where chariots could be spectacularly successful, as the surprise Hittite attack at the Battle of Kadesh vividly demonstrates. How exactly they would have been used in a formal battle such as Megiddo is a matter of speculation. In all probability they would have advanced on the enemy as quickly as conditions allowed and loosed off several volleys of arrows from composite bows before closing the range to engage the enemy at close quarters. If the enemy broke, they could then pursue, inflicting further loss, followed by the infantry (for further detail on weaponry see Partridge 2002; McDermott 2004; Spalinger 2005, 2010).

Military Engineering

Military engineering is indisputably one of the most impressive aspects of Ancient Egyptian military practice. It is evident that urban settlements were surrounded by mud-brick fortified walls even in prehistoric times (see p. 61ff.), and that forts and fortified installations were a standard feature of the Egyptian landscape, no doubt forming a significant element in the apparatus of state control as well as protecting Egypt from foreign assaults (Gardiner 1916: 192; Faulkner 1953: 36; Moreno Garcia 1999: 28–9, 180–2, 185, 279–80; and see here p. 160), but the most spectacular and instructive examples of Egyptian prowess in this aspect of warfare consist of the fort system running from the First to the Second Cataract area which reached its apogee in the reign of Senwosret III (Emery 1965: 141–65; W. Adams 1997: 175–92; Williams 1999; Kemp 2006: 231–41). Documentary evidence provides us with the names of fourteen of these forts (Gardiner 1916)[9] which were disposed in three zones: the First Cataract Group, the Plains Group, and the Second Cataract Group (Fig. 4.4). As demonstrated by many of their names, they were designed pre-eminently as protection from attack by the Kerma peoples to the south and, to a lesser extent, to overawe the C-Group inhabitants of Lower Nubia, though some forts also served as bases for the exploitation of local gold and copper resources and also as trading posts. Their siting shows a keen eye for terrain, and available topography is well exploited, as illustrated by the forts of Semna and Kumma (Fig. 4.5). Their design displays a mastery of military engineering never surpassed and rarely equalled in the ancient world, the Second Cataract Group running from Buhen to Semna South being particularly impressive. The headquarters for this entire southern complex lay at Buhen, the structure of which shows a remarkable grasp of the principles of fortification (Fig. 4.6). It covered an area 172 m×160 m and presented a fearsome obstacle to any assailant. An enemy mounting an attack would first have to negotiate a glacis surmounted by a wall and would then have to cross a ditch 9 m wide and 7 m deep which was protected by a rampart pierced with loopholes for archers and punctuated by semicircular bastions that helped to create three-sided killing zones into which an attacking force would be channelled. Behind that stood the main defensive wall, a massive mud-brick structure 11 m high and 4.8 m thick strengthened with beams of wood and mats of halfa grass and topped with battlements equipped with firing steps and arrow ports of an ingenious design which gave maximum protection to the defenders whilst allowing them three different arrow ports pointing in different directions to bring down fire on the enemy. This wall also was equipped with bastions, this time rectangular in shape, and these also would have created killing zones in the same way as

---

[9] Three forts within Egypt proper are also listed, the northernmost at Silsila.

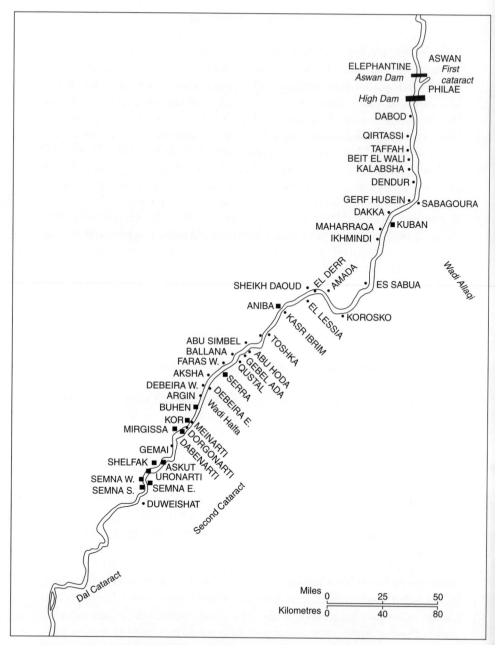

Fig. 4.4. The fortress sites of Lower Nubia. Drawing by Anna Ratcliffe.

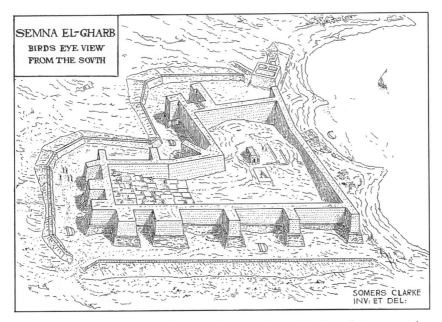

Fig. 4.5. The Middle Kingdom fortress of Semna West at the Second Cataract. After Clarke 1916: pl. xxxi.

the bastions in the rampart. Small gates gave access to the river, but the main gate in the middle of the west wall was a massive structure fitted with a drawbridge that could be pulled back on rollers in an emergency. This feature could only have been stormed, if at all, at very heavy and probably prohibitive cost to the enemy. This sequence of fortifications was linked to Egypt by the Nile whose role in this respect was greatly facilitated by engineering works such as the canal at the First Cataract first excavated by Senwosret III (see p. 106) and the slipway circumventing the dangerous cataracts at Mirgissa (Vercoutter 1970: 13), though both of these structures would also have had economic value.

It has often been said, with good reason, that these forts were far larger than was necessary to achieve their military purpose. This judgement was, to some extent, influenced by a low estimation of the threat posed by the C-Group inhabitants of Lower Nubia but has lost a great deal of its force with the realization that the Kerma peoples to the south of the Second Cataract were much more formidable and advanced than was once thought. However, practical matters are only part of the equation. Gigantism is a standard ingredient in the architectural vocabulary of Pharaonic Egypt and is used frequently to emphasize the power of the Egyptian state. The size of these forts is much more than a matter of military or economic function. It is propaganda

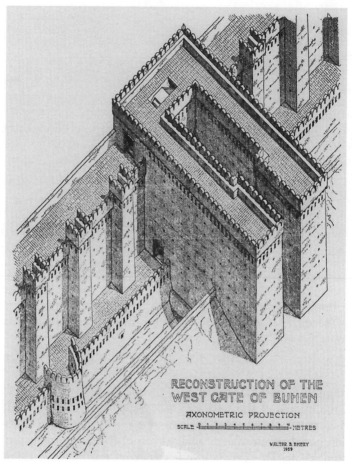

Fig. 4.6. The west gate area of the Middle Kingdom fortress of Buhen. After Emery 1979: pl. XI.

in mud-brick, projecting the invincible power and majesty of the Pharaonic kingdom and leaving no one in any doubt who was in control of the Nile Valley below the Second Cataract.

The Nubian forts are by far the most impressive examples of Egyptian military architecture to survive into modern times, but they should be seen as examples of an expertise in military engineering that remained a constant feature of Egyptian warfare until the end of the Dynastic Period, and there is substantial evidence from the New Kingdom of a range of fortifications in Egypt itself as well as in Libya, Asia, and Nubia to protect Egyptian interests abroad (Morris 2005). In the Persian invasion of 374 this expertise played a major part in the successful defensive measures taken by Nectanebo I to meet the Persian attack: all entrance-points along the north coast of Egypt were blocked and defended with fortified settlements;[10] large towers were erected on each bank joined by a wooden bridge; and the Pelusiac, i.e. easternmost, branch, was particularly heavily fortified (Diodorus Siculus 15: 42). Water channels were also dug; points where ships might enter were carefully fortified; defensive embankments were constructed; and points of access by land were flooded.

Egyptian military engineering was not, however, confined to defence and shows to good advantage in siege warfare. The taking of fortified positions appears very early in Egyptian history (see p. 61), but in its simplest form consisted of either storming the enemy's walls using ladders and protective coverings like the Roman *testudo*, or a set-piece siege to starve the enemy into submission, or a combination of both. The description of the siege of Megiddo in the *Annals* of Tuthmose III reveals that techniques had become considerably more elaborate by the mid Eighteenth Dynasty. In this case local timber was used to construct a wall of circumvallation around the city backed up by a ditch that effectively insulated Megiddo from its hinterland and forced its surrender (Lichtheim 2006: 33). The Piye Stele provides much information on the state of military engineering in the eighth century BC, informing us that siege towers were employed to bring down fire from archers and slingers on defending troops at Hermopolis, and a wall of circumvallation was also constructed to invest the city; the use of an assault ramp to take Piye's forces up to the ramparts of Memphis was also considered, though never implemented.

The Navy

As already indicated, the topography of Egypt ensured that military operations, far more often than not, had to be combined operations in which ships played an indispensable role. The existence of a Royal Navy alongside the army is firmly established, and there is a close similarity in the terminology used of naval personnel and that employed in the army. The commanders of these naval resources are frequently mentioned under such titles as 'Great Commander in Chief of ꜥḥꜥw-ships in the Palace' (*imy-r ꜥḥꜥw wr m pr-nsw*) or 'Commander of all the ꜥḥꜥw-ships of the King' (*imy-r ꜥḥꜥ(w) nbw n nsw*), though these vessels were more often used for peaceful purposes such as trade and the transport of tribute than for strictly military functions. Indeed, until the New Kingdom, there is no evidence of vessels designed specifically for

---

[10] Diodorus Siculus uses the Greek word *polis*, 'town', to describe these installations. This would be entirely compatible with established Egyptian practice. Some New Kingdom fortresses are known to have exceeded 66.000 m² in extent (Morris 2005: 807).

military purposes (Säve-Söderbergh 1946; Landström 1970: 108–115; Fabre 2004: 91–101).

There are only two ways to fight a naval battle: it can be fought as a land battle at sea where the military function of ships is to act as troop-carriers and as decks from which a land battle can be conducted on water. Alternatively, the ship can be used as a ship-destroyer—basically, there is no functional difference between a ramming war-galley and an aircraft-carrier or a nuclear submarine. Through much of Egyptian history it was the former method that prevailed so that the navy functioned essentially as a fighting platform for soldiers or as a transport arm for troops and supplies. This situation still obtained in the Twentieth Dynasty battle against the Sea Peoples depicted at Medinet Habu (see p. 262ff.). The hulls of the Egyptian ships in this engagement follow the traditional Egyptian spoon shape, and they show cross thwarts of the standard type. The deck houses forward and aft also have many earlier parallels, and the pavisade protecting the oarsmen may be compared to traditional screens, though the gap between them and the gunwale does not seem to be exemplified elsewhere. The crow's nest is a novelty and functions here as a fighting top, but it may well have been employed as an observation post on non-military vessels. The figurehead has sometimes been described as a ram, but this is most improbable: its position is too high, and the hull is of the traditional Egyptian type and would, therefore, not have been strong enough to withstand the impact of ramming. Clearly these vessels have been customized for naval warfare, but, despite the modifications, they should be seen essentially as vessels of traditional Egyptian design intended for fighting land battles at sea.

The great divide appears when the ram became firmly established as the major instrument of naval warfare; for a vessel whose hull was constructed according to traditional Egyptian principles was incapable of absorbing the shock of ramming and was, therefore, incompatible with the new style of warfare. Foreign techniques had to be adopted, either from Greeks, or Phoenicians, or both, and the importation of large quantities of high-quality timber capable of yielding long planks was essential, the Lebanon and Cyprus being obvious sources of supply. It is probable that ramming war-galleys were already in service during the eighth century in Egypt, but we have to wait until the seventh century for clear evidence of such vessels which first appear in the reign of the Saite Pharaoh Necho II (610–595 BC) (Lloyd 2000a). The earliest extant representation of such a vessel occurs on a Carian stele from Egypt now in the Musée Historique at Lausanne (Fig. 4.7). It is almost certainly from Saqqara, and there is good reason to believe that its context was Saite. The case for this date is considerably strengthened by the fact that the stele presents us with warships in association with Carians; for Carians are not known to have formed part of the Egyptian military establishment after

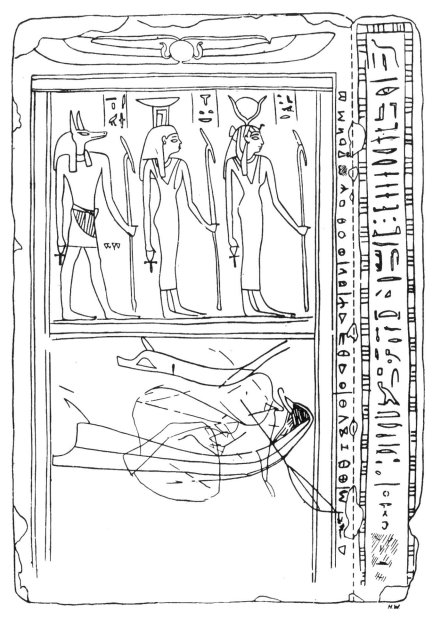

Fig. 4.7. The Lausanne stele. After Masson and Yoyotte 1956: 21 (13).

the Saite Period. It should, however, be emphasized that for normal purposes traditional designs continued to be employed.

Once established, fleets of ramming war-galleys became a standard feature of Egyptian naval activities, but the military performance of these fleets was distinctly uneven. There is no sign of their activity in meeting the invasion by the Persian emperor Cambyses in 525, and there is no indication of a fleet action in meeting Persian attacks during the Thirtieth Dynasty. It is always possible that this was the result of treachery, but it may well be that, given the large size of Persian fleets, Egyptian commanders preferred the Persians to come to them so that Egypt could benefit from the significant natural defensive advantages that the Delta had to offer (Lloyd 2000*a*: 89; and see here, p. 124). On the other hand, we hear of successful Egyptian naval operations in the Eastern Mediterranean against the Phoenicians and Cypriots in the reign of Apries (589–70), which must have used ramming war-galleys, and the Egyptians distinguished themselves greatly as an element in the Persian fleet in the attacks on Greek cities by Darius I and Xerxes during the early fifth century, particularly at the Battle of Artemisium in 480 (see p. 118).

The Attunement of Troops to Battle

We have spoken much of organization and hardware, but an effective military machine needs more than that. Soldiers are created not born, and soldiers and civilians are very different beings since the ethos under which they have to operate is, and must be, very different (Lloyd 1995). The soldier must be able to kill without too much compunction whereas the civilian functions under a deeply ingrained taboo against such actions. Militarization is, therefore, a key procedure in the creation of an army. The training process is critical here, and frequently in military traditions the world over this involves the brutalization or dehumanization of recruits. They are quite simply taken apart and remade in the requisite mould.

When we consider Egyptian evidence from this point of view, it emerges, not very surprisingly, that the fate of the Ancient Egyptian soldier was very much like that of his modern counterpart. A grim picture of the militarization process in New Kingdom Egypt is provided by P. Anastasi III:

Come, let me describe to you the condition of the soldier, that much tormented one. He is taken as a child of two cubits and imprisoned in a barrack. A searing [?] blow is dealt his body, a knock-down blow to his eye, a splitting blow his eyebrows. His head is split open with a wound. He is laid down and beaten like papyrus and battered with castigations.   (trans. Caminos 1954: 91–5)

Egyptian drill sergeants clearly had no compunction in applying the most vicious regime and quite literally knocked the tyro into shape. This demonstrable lack of finesse at the initial stage of training would also suggest that there were some equally vicious initiation rituals every bit as unpleasant as those that the most sadistic of modern military installations can boast, but there does not seem to be any evidence of that as yet. Whether there was an oath of allegiance we do not know for certain, but, Egypt being Egypt, it is extremely improbable that there was not something of the sort, and the comments of Ramesses II after Kadesh (see p. 117) suggest that there was, at the very least, a tacit contract between the king and his troops. All this, however, would only have been the beginning. When not being beaten up and drilled in the basics of the profession of arms, the young Egyptian recruit would also have been toughened up by physically challenging games such as wrestling, boxing, stick-fights, and archery contests like those graphically represented in Middle Kingdom tombs (e.g. at Beni Hasan) and our accounts of the martial prowess of Amenhotep II (Decker 1992: 208).

The absorption of the individual into his unit was carefully fostered by the development of group loyalty. We hear in the *Annals* of Tuthmose III of units with troop commanders, and in New Kingdom texts we are informed that the army was divided into a number of divisions (see p. 117). A sense of unit individuality was consolidated by giving units standards that could act as an embodiment of the identity of the group, probably functioning rather like the regimental colours in the British army or the eagles of Roman legions, though we should be wary of pushing the comparison too far. Nevertheless, Faulkner (1941: 18) rightly comments:

that some attachment was felt for them is suggested by the fact that the bearer of the standard was an officer of some rank, about whom it doubtless shed an aura of additional authority. Whether it was considered a disgrace to lose your standard in battle we do not know, but it is safe to assume that the sight of his standard swaying over the press on occasion inspired the Egyptian soldier to feats of valour of which he would otherwise have been incapable.

In this context it is particularly important to emphasize the role of small-group solidarity whose part in maintaining fighting capacity cannot be overrated. Soldiers do not like to let their comrades down and will go to very great lengths to ensure that this does not happen. We can be confident that the Ancient Egyptian squaddy (wᶜ, wa, or ᶜnḥw, ankhu) was no exception. The process of group-integration would have been promoted by the use of uniform dress of which there is ample representational evidence in the form of Middle Kingdom models and in tomb scenes at el-Amarna and the copious reliefs in New Kingdom temples such as the Ramesseum and Medinet Habu.

These processes might conceivably be enough in themselves to make a man into a killer on command, but, if they were not, there were other techniques available that can easily be paralleled in much more modem contexts. In the first place the soldier can justify what he is doing by claiming that it is right to do it, and we have already discussed the concept of 'the Just War' or *Bellum Iustum* in Ancient Egypt (see p. 101). Denigration of the enemy is another method of stiffening the resolve of the fighting man and is frequently in evidence in Egyptian texts. The Semna Stele of Regnal Year 16 of Senwosret III provides an excellent example of this point:

the Nubian hearkens to the mere sound of the voice; it is answering him which causes him to turn tail; if you are aggressive against him, he bolts; turn tail, and he presumes to be aggressive. They are not people worthy of respect, they are despicable people, craven-hearted. My Majesty has seen it; there is no untruth [in this].   (Sethe 1928: 83)

The *Annals* of Tuthmose III describe opponents as 'the wretched enemy', 'the wretched enemy of Kadesh', and 'the enemies whom Re abominates'; the Kadesh inscriptions of Ramesses II refer with equally eloquent disgust to 'the Wretched Fallen One of Kadesh'; and the Piye Stele speaks particularly intriguingly of his enemies at Hermopolis, of all places, as 'the Asiatics' (see p. 99)!

A further factor, which operates in all armies to attenuate distaste for killing, is simply long exposure to the experience of war. Put crudely, the more one kills, the easier it gets. The lack of moral finesse of the battle-hardened veteran is easily deprecated, but it is the indispensable adjunct to the successful soldier in the military world of 'close-range butchery' that characterized ancient warfare. We can hardly expect that point to be consciously stated in our texts, but this must have been one of the great strengths of battle-hardened foreign troops such as the Medjay and Sherden and was surely one of the main reasons for their prominence in Egyptian warfare.

Once an army has been created by such dubious but essential methods, it must be prevailed upon to fight. Here all commentators would emphasize the critical role of leadership in motivating troops to confront the trauma of battle, and this is a topic on which the Egyptians have much to say, either by depicting the commander as a model and inspiration or, and less obviously, by reflecting the personal relationship or bonding with his subordinates both at officer level and lower down the military hierarchy. At Kadesh Ramesses II's vigorous counter-attacks led to the recovery of his shattered forces and made it possible for the army to attack the Hittites the following day. At a more basic level he and Tuthmose III show the solicitude for their troops that leads to effective bonding between commander and army: Tuthmose III at Megiddo listens to the officers who advise him to be cautious when the vanguard emerges. They urge him to wait until the force is concentrated, and this good advice is accepted; he also displays an awareness of the need to keep his troops in good physical shape; Ramesses II shows concern for the equipment of his troops and also nurtures the morale of his soldiers in ensuring that they should know the plan; and Piye displays a willingness to consult which would have had the same effect.

The pre-battle pep-talk is a conspicuous feature of Egyptian texts: Tuthmose III provided one before going onto the Aruna road and after emerging from it, and also offers a rousing exhortation the night before the battle. In the Piye Stele Tefnakht insists on the capacity of Memphis to resist the Nubian assault whilst Piye delivers a stirring speech before his attack on the same city. Of course, the vast majority of the troops would not have been able to hear a word of what was said, but the troops at the front of the army would have acted as 'cheer leaders' injecting into the force as a whole a rousing response to the words of encouragement. Another motive for engaging in battle is the urge to glory, a point well brought out in the fictitious exhortation to the soldier in P. Lansing: 'The enemy is come and surrounds him with arrows, and life is far from him. They say: "Hurry up, forward, o valiant soldier, win for yourself a good name!"' (trans. Caminos 1954: 401). Martial music has also often been used in military contexts to cheer the troops on, and there is certainly evidence that, even if the Egyptians did not march into battle with their equivalent of fifes and drums, musical instruments in the form of trumpets and drums were employed in Egyptian armies. The use of such instruments for signalling can be accepted, but there can be little doubt that the shrill note of the Egyptian trumpet rising over the din of battle had something of the morale-stirring effect that the beat of the drum had in moving on the columns of Napoleon's shock troops.

The use or threat of force to keep troops from bolting in the face of the enemy is a well-known device in later armies, but coercion of the crudest type is not easily found in Egyptian sources, and we should not expect it to be mentioned explicitly, even if it were employed. However, we *can* identify Egyptian commanders shaming their troops into action. Ramesses II has recourse to this device at Kadesh, and Piye deploys the same technique. The delights of promotion are another inducement, and these are described with relish by a text in Anastasi V:

I have received the letter which you wrote to say: 'Pharaoh (life, prosperity, health), my good lord (l.p.h.), has carried out for me his good designs. Pharaoh (l.p.h.) has put me to be captain of troops of the well'—thus you wrote to me. It is a benefit of Pre your being [now] in the post of your father. (trans. Caminos 1954: 239)

The Stele of Sobekkhu speaks with similar enthusiasm of his promotion for conspicuous service in Nubia under Senwosret III. Decorations for valour were also available, and here again we think of Sobekkhu who received field decorations consisting of a *metpenet*-dagger, a *bagsu*-dagger, and a handful of arrows, and there are numerous New Kingdom references to the 'gold of valour' (*nbw n ḵnt*), the Egyptian equivalent of the DSO. Trophies of valour acquired from defeated enemies are also described in Sobekkhu as they are in *Sinuhe*, these, of course, hovering between the status of trophies to demonstrate the bravery of the victorious warrior and economically valuable rewards of military activity. Raw economic benefits certainly feature prominently in our sources: the Semna Stele speaks of carrying off people as slaves, as does P. Lansing. The *Annals* of Tuthmose III describe the collapse of the attack of the victorious Egyptian army as the troops gave themselves up to plundering the enemy camp, and they also describe at some length the booty derived from victory. Piye is equally unreticent about the economic rewards of successful military action (see p. 134).

On the point of engaging the enemy a number of psychological tricks could be employed to stiffen the resolve of an army. The war cry can be a particularly effective way of expressing and generating a corporate commitment to action, but there is rather more to it than that:

War cries are a time-honoured means of boosting one's own fighting spirit and attempting to diminish the enemy's . . . Grunts and growls have both psychological and physiological motives, as professional tennis-players know. Not only do they help to unsettle an opponent, but they also accompany the expulsion of air by the diaphragm at a moment of intense muscular effort, thus fixing the chest wall and coordinating the movement.   (R. Holmes 1985: 164–5)

The power of Pharaoh's war cry of (*hemhemet, hmhmt*) is mentioned in a number of texts (e.g. *Urk.* iv. 18, 6; 612, 11), and we can be confident that it was accompanied by hundreds of others on the field of battle.

Another time-honoured method of coping with battlefield stress is flight. This remedy is not conspicuous by its absence in our texts: the enemy takes to spectacular flight at Megiddo; the division of Pre does likewise at Kadesh; and the Piye Stele speaks of it on several occasions. There is, however, such a thing as flight to the front, i.e. a frantic assault on the enemy either through desperation or on the principle of 'let's get this over with as soon as possible'. It is not unreasonable to regard the actions of Ramesses II at Kadesh as an example of this phenomenon.

Other factors well known as palliatives for battlefield stress are humour, narcosis through strong drink or drugs, or fantasy. The first is unlikely to reveal itself in our Egyptian sources, though Egyptian humour being what it was, e.g. the cartoon of the battle between cats and mice, we can be confident that the alleviation of panic by military jokesmiths was far from unheard of in Ancient Egypt. Over-indulgence in alcohol before battle we can accept without demur even if we cannot find a text to prove it, since meals before battle would inevitably have involved alcoholic drink. Fantasy could be subsumed in an equally potent instrument, i.e. religion. In the account of the Megiddo campaign we are told that a statue of Amon-re was carried before the army; the king is brought into relation with several deities before the battle; there is talk of the serpent diadem overpowering the enemy in battle; victory is ascribed to Amun; and Re is said to have brought about the confinement of the enemy in Megiddo. In the *Poem* version of the Battle of Kadesh Ramesses II is compared to the gods, and in his appeal to Amun at the height of the crisis he pleads that he has a moral claim on divine support. It is evident that, when he gets it, it is considered to be the source of his victory. In the Piye Stele the king is claimed to be making war on behalf of Amun whose agent he is. This firm conviction that the gods are working through Egyptian rulers (the *Gott-mit-uns* syndrome) presumably percolated some way down in the army and will certainly have done a great deal to bolster the morale of troops at all levels confronting the challenge of battle.

Triumphs and Triumphalism

Wars are traumatic experiences in the history of societies raising issues of many different kinds, religious, political, and psychological. They are normally begun in a formal way and concluded with elaborate ceremonies such as the Roman triumph and modern victory parades. Ancient Egypt was no exception. Pharaoh's wars were brought to an end by formal triumphs which can be detected as early as the time of Narmer (see p. 60). On the right-hand side of the verso of his slate palette two neat rows of decapitated enemies are shown, evidently the result of a successful campaign in the north-east Delta area. The king, dressed in the Red Crown and adorned with the bull's tail, strides towards these unfortunates accompanied by a sandal-bearer and someone who is probably the vizier. They all march behind four figures carrying standards and representing military contingents. This scene has a very formalized look to it and can hardly refer to anything other than a ritualized celebration of victory. It may well be that the scene on the recto in which Narmer is slaying an enemy anticipates New Kingdom representations of the execution of defeated enemies in the temple of Amon-re.

The biography of Weni takes us further in the same direction. As usual with biographical texts of any length, the inscription is a very carefully composed document with painstaking attention to literary effect, and the military section is no exception. The second part of this passage is clearly in verse and takes the form of a triumph song. It may have been composed specifically for inclusion in this biography, but it reads rather oddly in the context and certainly has the feel of an insertion from some other source. It seems at the least possible that it was composed for the triumphal return home of the victorious army and was sung by the troops in some sort of ritual context. It must surely have been the case that the return of the victorious army was greeted by unofficial expressions of joy comparable to those described in the local reactions to the transport of the colossus of Djehutyhotep II at el-Bersha in the Twelfth Dynasty (*BAR* i. §§697–704), but there must have been a ceremonial event on its return to base or the capital of the type with which we seem to be confronted on the Narmer Palette.

The New Kingdom provides a number of examples of ritualized triumphal conclusions to military campaigns. Tuthmose III established at least three festivals of victory of five days' duration and with copious offerings at Thebes. The Karnak Stele of Amenhotep II states that the booty obtained from his early Asiatic campaign was seen by everyone and strongly suggests a triumphal voyage through the country with the proceeds of victory very much on display to the acclamation of all who could line the banks. The Karnak reliefs of Sety I relating to his Asiatic victories describe wild rejoicing on the king's return as well as the ceremonial presentation of booty to Amun, including the execution before the god of chiefs who were his prisoners. After his Kadesh campaign Ramesses II also presented captives to Amun, though it would appear in this case that they were not slain but added to the god's workforce. In all these instances a beautifully symmetrical scheme is evidently being applied: Pharaohs go forth to do the will of Amun, and, when Pharaoh returns in victory, this is recognized by victory celebrations that include presentations of booty and prisoners to Amun who demanded the campaign in the first place and gave the king his victory.

The Piye Stele provides the clearest evidence in any extant text of a triumphal progress celebrating victory. The relevant part of the text runs as follows:

Then the ships were loaded with silver, gold, copper, and clothing; everything of Lower Egypt, every product of Syria, and all plants of God's Land. His Majesty sailed south, his heart joyful, and all those near him shouting. West and East took up the announcement, shouting around his majesty. This was their song of jubilation:

> O mighty ruler, O mighty ruler,
> Piye, mighty ruler!
> You have returned, having established rule over Lower Egypt,
> Making bulls into women!
> Joyful is the mother who bore you,
> And the man who engendered you!
> The valley dwellers praise her,
> The cow that bore the bull!
> You are eternal,
> Your might abiding,
> O ruler beloved of Thebes!   (*Urk*. iii. 55–6)

The victory song here is functionally comparable to that in the inscription of Weni, but how was it generated? The singing seems to have taken place in two stages, first on the part of those contiguous to the king, and it was then taken up by others who were clearly on the banks of the river. It may have been basically a traditional and widely known song, the singers changing the royal name and other details according to circumstances, and that would explain neatly how the celebrants on the banks knew it. Alternatively, it may have been composed for the occasion and sung by men on the ships, being picked up, at least in part, by others who heard it. However, perhaps the best explanation would be that various traditional songs of triumph were sung throughout the journey, and this example was included in the victory stele to represent the genre as a whole, either as a song actually sung or as something composed specifically for this text.

5

Government of the Kingdom

Theoretically the Pharaoh was the ultimate source of all power in Ancient Egypt and the driving motor of the entire administrative system, but the extent to which he could exercise that power was dependent not only on his own personality and abilities but also on the political environment in which he found himself. It is also important to resist the temptation to exaggerate the extent to which it was ever possible to operate a truly centralized governmental structure. Throughout Egyptian history, however powerful the ruler might be, royal authority became progressively less real the further a district lay from the royal residence, not least because of difficulties in communication, and we should never forget that for long periods there was no ruler whose writ ran the length and breadth of the country as the unitary Pharaonic system disintegrated to create smaller independent kingdoms that were sometimes, as in the Libyan Period, startlingly numerous. Nevertheless, even in these lesser realms, the classic model of Egyptian kingship continued to exercise a profound influence, above all in providing basic administrative structures and the theoretical validation for royal authority. Fragmentation, however, was exceptional. In the great days of Egyptian civilization, such as the Old, Middle, and New Kingdoms, royal authority prevailed throughout the country, either directly or by proxy, and that authority was exercised through two main mechanisms: a central administration based on a palace located in the capital city and a provincial system integrated with it that could be organized in a variety of ways, depending on the period in question. In the following discussion I do not propose to map the detailed chronological evolution of this governmental system from the beginning of Egyptian history to its demise but rather to identify and discuss its major features as a system of state control.

THE PALACE

Whilst the king at all periods had the use of numerous temporary residences throughout the country, e.g. temple- and harîm-palaces, his principal base was the residential palace located in the capital, usually Memphis, which functioned as the central node of the entire governmental system. This building, or rather complex of buildings, could be denoted by a variety of terms, depending on the point of emphasis the Egyptians wished to highlight in a given text. Some words simply emphasize its role as a dwelling (*pr*, 'house', *pr-nsw*, 'king's house', *pr ꜥꜣ*, 'the Great House', or *ḥwt-ꜥꜣt*, 'the Great Mansion'). Others have a religious colouring (*ꜥḥ*, and *ist*, which both mean 'dwelling (of king or of a divine being)'), and, to some degree, the odour of divinity even hangs over the phrase *ḥwt-ꜥꜣt* (cf. van den Boorn 1988: 99), whilst the term *ḥnw*, 'Residence' (lit. 'the Innermost Part'), insists on the centrality of the palace within the kingdom (see p. 206). The residential palace functioned in a number of ways.

The Palace as Propaganda

As in all state systems, the ethos of the Egyptian state required continual reaffirmation. The palace had a major role to play in this process in that it served as a context where the king could be accessed by lesser beings, and, as such, it could be employed as a major device for constant image projection. Indeed, literary texts and archaeological evidence leave us in no doubt of the role of the palace as an instrument for generating a potent image of the majesty, wealth, power, splendour, and divinity of the Egyptian king targeted not only at Egyptian consumers but also at any foreign dignitaries who might have cause to visit the ruler (Spence 2007: 288–9, 320).[1] Typically it would be surrounded by a great mud-brick wall of the type depicted in the *serekh* element in the Horus title (see Fig. 2.7 top) and represented in stone by the temenos wall of the Step Pyramid at Saqqara, creating a complex that could sometimes be extremely large, e.g. the late Eighteenth Dynasty palace complex of Malkata on the western margins of the cultivation at Thebes occupied about 33 ha.[2] How impressive these walls could be in practice may be seen from the great wall surrounding the Tuthmosid palace complex at Tell Daba (Bietak 2005), the double wall of mud-brick surrounding the North Riverside Palace at el-Amarna (Lacovara 1997*a*: 31), and the massive palace complex of Apries at Memphis whose impact was further enhanced by placing the main palace

---

[1] This function of the palace had its parallels in other ancient Oriental kingdoms, e.g. Han China (van Ess 2007: 238) and Achaemenid Persia (Brosius 2007: 46–9). The advice given to the Han emperor Liu Pang in 200 BC encapsulates the issue perfectly: 'Without great and elegant <buildings> you will not <be able to display> your authority and majesty. We should not moreover let it be that later generations should find anything to be despised.'

[2] For the palace of Malkata, the best known of all Egyptian palaces, see W. Johnson 2001: 75–7; O'Connor 2001: 160–2; Kemp 2006: 277–9. This impressive complex served both as a *Heb-sed* palace (see p. 142) and as a residential palace during the last decade of the life of Amenhotep III.

building on a colossal mud-brick platform so that it towered over the surrounding landscape (Petrie 1909; Kaiser 1987), a device also exploited in the Eighteenth Dynasty palaces at Deir el-Ballas (Lacovara 1990, 2006). In addition to their role in image-projection, these walls and their monumental gateways also served another major function, i.e. to ensure that access to the king was carefully and rigorously controlled.

The *Westcar Papyrus* provides vivid literary evidence that the palace complex might contain a substantial lake that could be used for royal entertainments, though an accessory ritual function is likely enough, and archaeological evidence of this feature has survived in the Tuthmosid palace complex at Tell Daba and the great lake at Malkata which covered an area of about 103 ha in its latest form. Lakes were, of course, a common element of houses of the elite and were, in themselves, a mark of elite status, but the size of these royal examples far exceeded anything available even to the highest officials and constituted another element emphasizing the unique nature of the palace and its occupant. We should also bear in mind that artificial lakes were a common ingredient of temple complexes and that their presence in palaces serves as one of several devices establishing a conceptual link between temples and palaces; the House of the King and the House of the God are using the same architectural vocabulary not only because they were both regarded as houses but because the king himself was considered to be divine. At a more mundane level, in addition to the royal dwelling or dwellings,[3] the palace complex contained a large number of ancillary structures ranging from storehouses and workshops to houses and offices for workmen and officials, and this hive of activity also could not have failed to send out a powerful message to anyone entering the complex that the palace was the working power-house of the kingdom. We should not, however, forget that all administrative buildings need not have been constructed within the palace complex itself, and that some would have been located elsewhere in the residence city, e.g. state granaries and other storage facilities which were an essential part of the redistribution network of the state economy.

An important element in the image-projection repertoire of the palace proper was the Window of Appearance (*seshed n kha(u)*, *sšd n ḥꜥ(w)*). 'In temple palaces, the Window is generally the central feature in the façade, whereas in the residential palace it seems to have been placed in a side wall at the opposite end of the central hall across from the throne room and overlooking an outer court' (Lacovara 1997*a*: 36). The Window served the eminently practical purpose of providing a context, again carefully controlled, where the king could display himself to his adoring subjects and even shower them with gifts, a practice well illustrated by representations in tombs at

---

[3] There were at least three palaces at Malkata (W. Smith 1981: 282).

Fig. 5.1. Akhenaten and Nefertiti at a Window of Appearance in el-Amarna. After Davies 1903–8 ii. pl. 10.

el-Amarna (Kemp 2006: 275–6; Spence 2007: 313–18; see Fig. 5.1). Another feature which set the palace apart from all other dwellings and further asserted the unique status of the king amongst the inhabitants of the earth was the harîm (*ipt, ḥnrt*), and it is certainly no coincidence that the only other entity within the Egyptian world to possess a harîm was the god Amun, one of whose epithets was 'Lord of his Harîm' (*ḫnty ipt.f Wb.* i. 68 l. 4). This institution was a self-contained element within the palace complex consisting of royal women and their offspring, which boasted its own administrative staff and its own very considerable income as well as functioning as a centre of economic production in its own right (Reiser 1972). It even contained an inner group that served as a travelling corps, distinguished by the epithet 'in the Suite, in attendance' (*ḥr šmsw*), to accompany the king on his peregrinations, guaranteeing that no one lost sight of this highly distinctive feature of the king's status. At Malkata part of the harîm was located in two suites of rooms running along both sides of the main columned hall in the King's Palace (W. Smith 1981: 285), but other members of the harîm will have been housed elsewhere in the complex, and the existence of harîm palaces outside the residence city is well established (cf. Shaw 2007, 2008, 2009). It should, however, be noted that, wherever the members of the harîm were located, there does not seem to have been a strict policy of seclusion comparable to that prevailing in the palaces of the Ottoman sultan, and we can be quite confident that the ladies of the harîm often exercised considerable de facto influence on events, whatever the *de iure* situation may have been. Closely connected with the harîm and probably physically part of it was the *kap* (*kꜣp*), which served as a royal school not only for princes but also for the sons of favoured members of the elite so that we frequently encounter officials who proudly boast that they held the status of 'Child of the *Kap*' (*ḥrd n kꜣp*) (Quirke 1990: 246; al-Ayedi 2006: 466–7). This title points to the same practice as that indicated, amongst other texts, in the Twelfth Dynasty stele of Ikhernofret where the king reminds him: ' it is indeed the case that you were brought up as the pupil of My Majesty. Indeed, you were a foster-child of My Majesty, the unique pupil of my palace' (Sethe 1928: 70 ll. 21–2). In all such cases the object of the exercise was to tie the individuals in question to the palace and its agenda as closely as possible from the earliest possible age and thereby strengthen the ties binding the crown to key members of the elite.

The physical impact of the palace proper was also carefully calculated to impress. Excavations at Malkata and el-Amarna have provided a wealth of evidence of the brilliance of its decoration during the Eighteenth Dynasty, every surface, horizontal or vertical, apparently being embellished with brightly painted scenes, sometimes showing a marked affinity to the artistic traditions of the Aegean area, and palace furnishings would certainly have been equally splendid (Kozloff 2001: 95; Weatherhead 2007). The palace ambience is filled out particularly well in the *Story of Sinuhe* at the point where Sinuhe is described as being brought to the Twelfth Dynasty palace at Itj-tawy to be interviewed by the king: 'I bowed my head to the ground between the sphinxes, the royal children standing in the gateway to meet me. The Companions who showed me into the columned hall (*wꜣḥ*) set me on the route to the audience chamber (*ꜥ-ḫnwty*, a-khenuty). Upon a throne in a recess of electrum did I find His Majesty' (B249–52). The presence of the sphinxes (as guardians of the entrance) is significant since this feature is shared with temples and yet again reflects the divine nature of the royal tenant of the palace. The gateway is as impressive as we should expect since it is later described as 'a great double gate' (*rwty wrty*), and we are also confronted with a columned hall which also appears in the *Westcar Papyrus* and was evidently regarded as a major feature of the palace. This architectural element, which has obvious counterparts in the hypostyle halls of temples, is well represented in the palaces at Deir el-Ballas and at Malkata, where there are at least four, all provided with a throne dais. They would, amongst other things, have served as royal audience chambers and probably marked the limit of access in the palace for the vast majority of those allowed to enter the building. Beyond that point lay the private suite of the king to which access was severely restricted, and Lacovara (1997a: 36) rightly comments: 'It may well be the case with royal palaces as it was with temples, that entry became more selective as one went deeper into the palace building, with the private apartments being the equivalent of the holy of holies at the rear of the temple'. It is, therefore hardly surprising that the palace complex at Malkata contained a temple in honour of the god Amun, though in this case there is an added inducement to construct ritual buildings since the initial rationale for the complex was to serve as a context for Amenhotep III's *Heb-sed* Festivals.

The Royal Family

The second major function of the palace was to act as a base for the royal family.[4] An image of close-knit solidarity is a constant feature of the image of the royal family in our surviving evidence and emerges with utmost clarity in burial practices that show a marked tendency for members of the royal family to be buried alongside each other and in close proximity to the king. Pyramid cemeteries consistently illustrate this practice, and the massive tomb for the sons of Ramesses II in the Valley of the Kings a short distance from that of their father, is a potent, though unique, statement of the same principle (Weeks 1998, 2006). This familistic dimension also appears in texts such as the *Story of Sinuhe* (see previous section) and with increasing frequency in representations of royal activity. The examples from the reign of Akhenaten are, of course, an extreme case in the degree of informality which they display, but they do reflect a recurrent perception of kingship as something function- ing within a family context which is far from confined to the Amarna Period. This becomes increasingly evident from the Nineteenth Dynasty onwards as long lines of princes and princesses become a common feature of royal monumental decoration. However, despite these images of solidarity, the visible formal employment of members of the royal family in high-status administrative functions is nowhere nearly as prevalent as we should expect, though we must always bear in mind that in any given reign or any given period there can be a wide gulf between practical realities and what is visible in our evidence.

We have already discussed the role of the queen in a previous chapter and have established the point that she rarely had an explicit active involvement in governmental matters. The same does not, however, hold true for the 'Royal

---

[4] Since the Royal Family does not seem to have formed part of the *shenyt*-court (see next section), I am discussing them separately. However, princes presumably often mingled with courtiers both in formal and informal contexts.

Children' (*msw nsw*), though it could hardly be claimed that their full potential was ever exploited. In the passage from *Sinuhe* quoted above the 'Royal Children' play an active role in greeting Sinuhe at the palace gate, and later in the tale they are instructed by the king to take him to a house within the palace complex. In the course of their interaction with the king they deliver a lengthy and highly flattering passage of theologically orientated court rhetoric, a practice that must have been common in public contexts and that illustrates the ritualistic character of much of the interaction between the king and lesser beings. However, whilst the children are throughout this passage functioning as the Pharaoh's agents, there is no indication that they have formal administrative roles in the workings of the palace or the kingdom, though the inner logic of the narrative does not require anything more of them at this point than to execute the royal will. Nevertheless, though our evidence is very uneven in its coverage from one period to the next, it is possible to establish that kings did avail themselves of the talents of some of their children and also of other blood relatives, conferring upon them some of the major offices and titles that the state had to offer.

Princes

The study of the role of princes in the Old Kingdom reveals a process of evolution. Establishing a completely accurate genealogical table for Fourth Dynasty kings and their families is impossible since it is not always feasible to establish what the genealogical links were, and the titles 'King's Son (of His Body)' and 'Eldest King's Son (of His Body)' can be misleading in that they may be honorific and do not always refer to sons in our sense but may denote grandsons or descent from an even more remote royal ancestor (Dodson and Hilton 2004: 32–4). Nevertheless it is absolutely clear that the rulers of the dynasty made copious use of members of the royal family for high-level administrative purposes, e.g. Ankhhaf, a son of Snofru, was the vizier of his nephew Khafre; Ankhmare, a son of Khafre, was the vizier of his half-brother Menkaure; Babaef, a grandson of Khafre, was vizier under Shepseskaf; and Sekhemkare, a son of Khafre, managed to maintain himself as a major figure not only in the reign of Khafre but also under Menkaure, Shepseskaf, Userkaf, and Sahure. However, whilst there is a clear policy of keeping the office of vizier within the family, there was a marked disinclination on the part of kings of the Fourth Dynasty to appoint their *sons* to that position, though Khufukhaf may be an exception since he was possibly a son of Khufu and probably vizier under that king. At a slightly lower level we find Rahotep, probably a son of Snofru, holding the office of 'High Priest of Heliopolis', at this period the most important priestly office in the kingdom, and also functioning as an 'Overseer of an Expeditionary Force' and 'Controller of Archers'. On the other hand, we encounter certain or probable 'King's Sons', such as Ranefer, a possible son of

Snofru, and Snofrukhaf, a great grandson of Snofru, who are not known from surviving monuments to have exercised any administrative functions, though this does not exclude the possibility that they were used to discharge specific royal commissions (*wp(w) nsw*) as and when required.

The evidence for the Fifth and Sixth Dynasties is much less full, but what there is paints a very different picture. In the Fifth Dynasty only Isesiankhu, a son of Djedkare Isesi, is given administrative titles ('Overseer of Works' and 'Overseer of an Expeditionary Force/General').[5] We do hear of sons of Sahure, Menkauhor (probably), Djedkare Isesi, Neferirkare, and Unis, but none of them are known to have held government office. In the Sixth Dynasty certain or possible sons or grandsons of Teti, Pepi I, and Pepi II are identifiable, but only Meryteti, a grandson of Teti, is known to have held an administrative post, in his case the office of vizier.

Overall, the pattern that emerges in the Old Kingdom in the administrative use of members of the royal family is that, whilst the Fourth Dynasty preferred to keep the highest offices in the hands of close blood relatives of the king, the Fifth and Sixth made much less use of this practice, preferring to bind the holders of functions to the royal house by careful use of royal daughters to cement marriage alliances (see p. 149). This change, in all probability, was designed to forestall attempts by ambitious sons to usurp the throne, a phenomenon that had probably already occurred in cases now lost to us through the discreet Egyptian policy of ignoring unpalatable historical events.[6]

Evidence for the Middle Kingdom is much less revealing. We know of very few cases from the Twelfth Dynasty of the title 'King's Son' or of individuals discharging duties in that capacity (Dodson and Hilton 2004: 82–113). Apart from Senwosret, the son of Amenemhet I, who features as the leader of a successful military expedition into Libya at the end of his father's reign,[7] only the 'King's Son' Ameny, the later Amenemhet II, operates as a significant agent in that he was involved, as a prince, in the military expedition to Nubia mentioned in the biography of the nomarch Amenemhet at Beni Hasan (Simpson (ed.) 2003: 419). Apart from that we hear of the 'King's Son' Amenemhetankhu, probably a son of Amenemhet II, who was an 'Acquaintance of the King' and held a number of priestly offices, but he shows no sign of high-level administrative activity. We also encounter a Senwosretsonbu, son of Senwosret II, who is not known to have borne any administrative titles, though

---

[5] Here and subsequently, except where the Egyptian prototypes are obvious, I have reserved the transliterations of titles for an Appendix to avoid burdening the text with a mass of linguistic material that is only of value to the philologically trained.

[6] For details of the figures discussed in the Old Kingdom section see Baud 1999, 2010; Dodson and Hilton 2004: 50–61. On conspiracies in the Old Kingdom, real or alleged, see Kanawati 2003.

[7] Admittedly *Sinuhe* is a work of fiction, but, since it is firmly based in an historical context and would greatly gain in impact by the insertion of genuine historical events, I have no qualms in regarding this event as historical.

we must concede that the one source in which he appears would not be likely to provide much information on that score. This very sparse range of evidence may be the result of the chances of discovery, but it certainly looks, at present, as though the Pharaohs of the Twelfth Dynasty went to some lengths to ensure that major sources of power were kept at arm's length from princes of the royal house with the exception of Crown Princes whose succession during the dynasty was assured in a number of cases by establishing them as co-regents alongside their fathers in the latter part of the reign (Murnane 1977: 1–29; Grajetzki 2006: 33–4). As for the Thirteenth Dynasty, about eighteen princes are known, but we have no information on careers with the exception of Sobekhotep, brother of Neferhotep I, who served as a co-regent and subsequently became king as Sobekhotep IV, and Sankhptahi who seems also eventually to have become king.

We should expect the Second Intermediate Period to offer little, and we are not disappointed. Evidence for the Fourteenth to the Seventeenth Dynasties is sparse and amounts largely to names. However, some use was made of princes, two of whom held military office during this period: Khonsuemwaset, possibly a son of Dedumose I, was a general, and Nakht, possibly a son of Inyotef VI, bears the title 'Troop Commander'. Qinen, a possible son of Inyotef VI, was Commander of Coptos, which may have been an administrative office but would certainly have had military dimensions at this period.

Evidence for the New Kingdom is much fuller, and princes of the Eighteenth Dynasty are relatively well attested (Robins 1987: 15–17). Six of the 'King's Sons' recorded have titles beyond the statement of filiation. These are sometimes administrative: Amenemhet, 'Eldest King's Son' of Tuthmose III, was 'Overseer of Cattle (of Amun)', as was Khaemwese, probably 'King's Son' of Amenhotep II; and Amenhotep, a son of Amenhotep II, featured as 'Executive at the Head of the Two Lands'. Other titles are priestly: Ahmose, probably a son of Amenhotep II, was 'High Priest of Heliopolis'; Amenhotep, son of Amenhotep II, was '*Sem*-priest of Ptah' (at Memphis); and Tuthmose, son of Amenhotep III, was 'High Priest of Ptah', '*Sem*-priest of Ptah', and 'Overseer of the God's Servants of Upper and Lower Egypt'. Three are military: Amenmose, 'Eldest King's Son' of Tuthmose I, held the rank of 'Commander-in-Chief of the Army'; Tuthmose, 'King's Son' of an unknown ruler, was 'Captain of the Troops'; and Nakhtmin, probably a son of Ay, was 'Commander-in-Chief of the Army'. Numerous other 'King's Sons' have been identified in the dynasty, but they bear no titles beyond 'King's Son' in extant documentation.

The reign of Sety I provides little information on family relations, but he did make use of his son Ramesses who held the title 'Executive at the Head of the Two Lands' before ascending the throne as Ramesses II, and the prince was certainly active in administrative and military affairs before his accession (Kitchen 1982: 27–41). We can be confident that Sety's policy of bringing his son early into the governmental arena was strongly motivated by his desire to guarantee the succession in the light of the instability of the late Eighteenth Dynasty and the non-royal antecedents of his father Ramesses I. The related issue of legitimization of the dynasty was also a major concern to Sety, as emerges from his construction of a large and splendid temple at Abydos, a site whose connection to Egyptian kingship went back well beyond the Dynastic Period, i.e. he was asserting a right to rule on the same basis as all the earlier Egyptians kings buried in, or associated with, the site, and the same point is also being made by the insertion of a king-list in this temple depicting Sety making offerings to a long sequence of rulers perceived to be legitimate going back to the beginning of the First Dynasty. All these precedents were followed by Ramesses II who constructed a similar Abydos temple containing a similar king list just to the north of that of his father, but in his dynastic strategy for the use of sons he went much further in that he not only guaranteed the succession by begetting an extraordinarily large number of sons (approximately fifty), but ensured that the eldest fourteen, at least, were given high-profile roles in all aspects of royal action (Kitchen 1996*b*: 559–97, 1999: 571–619; Fisher 2001). Their status as a 'Son of the King' is frequently asserted, and the enhanced title of 'Eldest/First King's Son' was held by Amenherkhopeshef,[8] Ramesses, Khaemwese, and Meryatum, a status that might simply have indicated a position of particular importance and prestige but more probably reflected the status of the eldest as crown-prince which inevitably passed down the line with the death of older tenants of the position. Prince Ramesses also bore the rare title 'Son of the God (i.e. the King)'. High status is also conveyed by the title 'Fanbearer' borne by Amenherkhopeshef, Ramesses, Preherwenemef, and Ramesses Merysutekh, marking a position that brought the holder into close physical proximity to the king, and representational evidence proves that this could be a real function. Other high-status ranking titles borne by princes include 'Hereditary Lord', 'Count', and 'Hereditary Lord and Count' but do not imply administrative functions. Titles with clear administrative dimensions are held by few of the sons, but Amenherkhopeshef featured prominently in this area, bearing the titles 'Delegate', 'Chief of Secrets of the King's House', and 'Lord in Charge of the Entire Land'. His title 'Controller of the Hau-nebu' is particularly intriguing in that it fits in perfectly with his known involvement in foreign relations, and Meryatum bears the title 'Eyes of the King at the Head of his Two Lands' which suggests a wide supervisory role. Amenherkhopeshef, Ramesses, Preherwenemef, and Merneptah are all described as a 'Royal Scribe' which probably should not be taken too literally, but, since Amenherkhopeshef and Ramesses are known to have

---

[8] It is now generally held that Amenherkhopeshef was also called Amenherwenemef and Sethherkhopeshef (Kitchen 1999: 577; Fisher 2001: 57–62), and I have proceeded on that basis in the following discussion.

exercised civil authority and engaged in diplomatic activity on behalf of the king, the title may well have some substance—a British 'Foreign Secretary' does very little secretarial work! Not surprisingly, given the warlike character of the early part of the reign of Ramesses II, military titles are common. The office of '(First) Commander-in-Chief of the Army' was held by the princes Amenherkhopeshef, Ramesses, and Merneptah whilst titles held by Preherwenemef, Montuherkhopeshef, and Meryatum connect them with elite forces: 'Overseer of Horse (of the Lord of the Two Lands)', 'First Charioteer of His Majesty (Father)'. Other military titles that feature are 'First Lieutenant of the Army', 'Marshaller of Troops', and 'Troop Commander'. If we can trust the inscriptional evidence, these titles were not empty labels but often, if not always, reflected some measure of direct involvement in military activities, and we have reason to believe that a number of princes saw active service or were, at least, present during campaigns.[9]

Some of the sons were allocated religious functions, partly as a means of controlling major priesthoods but also as initiation into the Pharaoh's priestly role which they would have had to assume if they ever ascended the throne. Two sons held high-level priestly titles: 'High Priest of Ptah' (Khaemwese) and 'High Priest of Re (at Heliopolis)' (Meryatum). These titles meant that these sons were in control of two of the three most important temples in the kingdom and held considerable economic and, therefore, political power. It is, however, striking that *no* son was placed in charge of Karnak, the richest and most powerful ecclesiastical centre in the kingdom—too much power in the hands of a prince was potentially a threat and carefully avoided! Sons also commonly bore high-ranking priestly titles: Amenherkhopeshef, Khaemwese, and Meryatum were all '*Sem*-priests'; Khaemwese and Sety were both '*iunmutef* priests';[10] Khaemwese was 'Chief of Secrets in Ro-setau'; and Meryatum was 'Chief of Secrets in the Mansion of the Phoenix', a title that he presumably held in his capacity as 'High Priest of Re (Heliopolis)'.

Khaemwese was the son who made, in the long term, the deepest impression on Egyptian historical consciousness, an impression, indeed, that survived into the last days of Pharaonic civilization. In his lifetime his influence spread far and wide. Apart from being 'High Priest of Ptah', which brought considerable economic and political power, he is also described as 'Controller of All (Memphite) Temples' and 'Controller of All "Priestly" (?) Offices', both of which suggest wide administrative functions conferring considerable powers of patronage and opportunities for building up a formidable power base. His title sequences frequently refer to ritual functions that he would

---

[9] Amenherkhopeshef, Preherwenemef, Khaemwese, Montuherkhopeshef, Meryamun, Amenemwia/Sethemwia, Nebenkharu, Sety, Setepenre, Merire I, Horherwenemef, Merneptah, and Amenhotep.

[10] Both of these titles are confined to the inner elite circle (Fisher 2001: 47–9).

certainly have discharged in person, but the heaviest emphasis in our sources is on his activities as a restorer of ancient monuments. On the Old Kingdom statue of Kawab Khaemwese described his motivation for such work as a love of 'antiquity and the noble folk who were before time, along with the excellence [of] all that they had made'. Whilst we need not deny a personal commitment of this kind, we can hardly be wrong in suspecting that Khaemwese was also acting to a large extent as his father's agent, as he certainly was in his work on the pyramid of Unis and the tomb of Shepseskaf at Saqqara (Kitchen 1999: 584). Surely, this programme of restoration should be seen as pre-eminently part of the dynastic aim of linking the dynasty firmly with the great achievements of the past and, therefore, as part of the legitimization agenda.

We are nowhere nearly as well informed on the rest of the New Kingdom, but the pattern already described for the early Nineteenth Dynasty seems to have been followed closely. Princes with high-ranking military functions are common, and they continue to hold important priestly offices such as 'Sem-priest of Ptah' at Memphis and 'High Priest of Heliopolis'. However, this period provides the most vivid extant object lesson on the potential danger posed to the crown by royal princes in the abortive and well-documented palace conspiracy at the end of the reign of Ramesses III (see p. 82).

Many 'King's Sons' are known from the Third Intermediate Period, but all too often they are names only. Nevertheless, the evidence available amply demonstrates their use to establish and maintain royal authority in important parts of the kingdom, particularly since political instability was endemic for long periods. Military titles such as 'Generalissimo', 'General', and 'Army Leader' appear frequently, and Bakenptah, a son of Takelot I, also held, amongst other standard military distinctions, the rank of 'General of Herakleopolis', a city of major strategic importance in Middle Egypt. In several cases during the Twenty-second Dynasty high-ranking military titles were held by 'King's Sons' who were also 'High Priests of Amun', a practice reflecting the use of princes of the royal house to control the powerful priesthood of Amun at Thebes which held, in effect, an independent sacerdotal fiefdom in Upper Egypt. Nothing illustrates this better than the case of Nimlot, a son of Osorkon II, who was 'Governor of Upper Egypt', 'High Priest of Amun', 'High Priest of Arsaphes' (at Herakleopolis), 'General', and 'Army Leader'. The appointment of 'King's Sons' to the office of 'High Priest of Amun' is also exemplified in the Twenty-fifth Dynasty when we find Haremakhet, a son of Shabaqa, occupying that position. Other priestly titles came the way of several princes: Harnakhte, a son of Osorkon II, was 'High Priest of Amun' at Tanis, a considerable office, but, since he seems to have died while still a young boy, this appointment looks like a particularly blatant attempt at royal control of an important shrine. Control was probably also at issue in the appointment of Osorkon, a 'King's Son' of the Twenty-third Dynasty, as a 'God's Servant' of Amun and

Nesishutefnut, a son of Taharqa, to the major office of 'Second God's Servant of Amun' in the Twenty-fifth Dynasty. After that date down to the end of native Egyptian rule references to 'King's Sons' are rare and usually unenlightening, but we do find Ahmose, 'King's Son' of Amasis, holding the office of 'General' in the later Twenty-sixth Dynasty, and at the end of the Thirtieth Dynasty–Early Ptolemaic Period we find the eldest son of Nectanebo II holding the office of 'Commander-in-Chief of the Army of His Majesty' (Lloyd 2002: 119).

Princesses

Princesses are mentioned very frequently in our sources but did not normally function in any formal sense in government, though they could play an important role in the orchestration of the power structure at the highest level. In the Fourth Dynasty we know of numerous royal wives and daughters, but there is no evidence of any role in administration. Even so, we can be quite confident that informal influence was not infrequently exercised. In the cult sphere we do find Bunefer, a King's Wife (*ḥmt nsw, hemet nesu*) and King's Daughter (*sȝt nsw, sat nesu*), functioning as a (Female) 'God's Servant' of Shepseskaf, though whether this was simply a title that brought with it an income or a title involving genuine participation in ritual we cannot tell. Similarly, in the Fifth Dynasty Hemetre Hemi, daughter of Unis, held a cult position in a temple of Teti. Khentaues I was an altogether different matter and seems to have functioned as regent, probably during the minority of a son. Of particular interest is the case of the daughter of Unis who appears to have been married to Mehu who held the office of vizier. This looks very much like an instance of the royal house using a daughter to bind a high official firmly to the king, and the Sixth Dynasty provides a number of examples of this: Teti gave three daughters in marriage to eminent officials, two of whom either were or became viziers (Kagemni and Mereruka) and the third, Neferseshemptah, eventually achieved a rank not far below that. Rather later we find Nebet, a daughter of Neferkauhor, appearing as the wife of Shemay, nomarch of Coptos, Governor of Upper Egypt, and vizier.

The catalogue of 'King's Daughters' of the Middle Kingdom offers a positive embarrassment of riches; for the sources provide the names of a large number of bearers of this title in the Twelfth Dynasty. Since many of them were buried in close proximity to their royal fathers, occasionally in their father's pyramid but more often in pyramids of their own, they were clearly regarded as significant adjuncts to the royal person, but very few of them appear to have been involved explicitly in notable governmental activity. Their formal contribution, as far as we can tell, was generally restricted to two areas. In the first place several of them were certainly or probably married to Pharaohs who were presumably all half-brothers at least, e.g. Nofret, a 'King's Daughter of his

Body' of Amenemhet II, was the wife of Senwosret II, and Nofru, 'King's Daughter' of Amenemhet I, was the wife of Senwosret I. Of considerably greater significance is the fact that the dynasty provides one certain case of a 'King's Daughter' becoming Pharaoh (Sobeknofru, 'King's Daughter' of Amenemhet III) (see p. 92) and another case where it looks as though a similar intention existed, though it was never fulfilled; for Nofruptah, 'King's Daughter of his Body' of Amenemhet III acquired a cartouche at the end of her life, an honour presumably bestowed in anticipation of her becoming ruler at some stage. Both cases belong to the same reign, but they nevertheless go some way towards confirming the high regard in which 'King's Daughters' were held during the dynasty, and it is impossible to repress the strong suspicion that they must have exercised considerable informal influence in the decision-making process. Not the least interesting feature of princesses of the Twelfth Dynasty is the fact that there does not seem to be any evidence of their marrying powerful officials to tie them in to the royal family. The majority must surely have been married to someone, and it seems probable that they were used as pawns in dynastic politics, but we cannot identify who benefited from such largesse. The names of numerous 'King's Daughters' of the Thirteenth Dynasty have survived, but there is little evidence of their role beyond the title. However, a 'King's Daughter' named Dedetamun was married to a 'Chancellor (Seal-bearer) of the God' (*ḥtmty nṯr*) named Nebsenet whose father's name Bembu has a distinctly unregal sound to it, and Hatshepsut, wife of Nedjesankh-Iu, and Nofru, wife of a Chief of Police at a temple of Anubis, may be similar cases. There may well have been political dimensions to these marriages, but paucity of evidence makes it impossible to establish any detail.

There is a long list of 'King's Daughters' for the Eighteenth Dynasty, many of them with no additional titles (Robins 1987: 15–17). However, a number certainly or probably became queens: Hatshepsut, daughter of Tuthmose I (also 'God's Wife'), Iaret, daughter of Amenhotep II and wife of Tuthmose IV, Iset, daughter and wife of Amenhotep III, Ankhesenpaaten, daughter of Akhenaten and wife of Tutankhamun, and Meritaten, daughter of Akhenaten and wife of Smenkhkare. Others (Sitkamose, probably a daughter of Kamose, Sitamun, a daughter of Ahmose, and Merytamun, a daughter of Tuthmose III) did not achieve such eminence but were appointed as 'God's Wife' (*ḥmt nṯr*) (see p. 93), though in the first case the title may have been granted posthumously.

In contrast to sons, the Nineteenth Dynasty has little to offer on princesses. Henutmire, wife of Ramesses II, was probably a daughter of Sety I, in which case she would have been at least a half-sister of Ramesses. Over fifty daughters of Ramesses II are known, but there is little detail on their lives (Kitchen 1996*b*: 597–606; 1999: 619–31). At least three (Bintanath, Meritamun, and

Nebettawy) functioned in some sense as his wife (*ḥmt-nsw* or *ḥmt-nsw wrt*).[11] Bintanath also bears the titles 'Hereditary Princess' and 'Chief of the Harîm'. Meritamun is also 'Hereditary Princess', 'Lady of the Rattle and Mistress of the Sistrum', 'God's Servant of Hathor', and 'Princess Child of Horus'. Later known princesses of the Nineteenth and Twentieth Dynasties usually end up as royal wives: Takhat, 'King's Daughter of his Body' probably of Ramesses II, was probably a wife of Sety II, Tyti became the wife of Ramesses III, (Dua)tentopet became the wife of Ramesses IV, Henttawy, perhaps 'King's Daughter' of Ramesses XI, also became a Royal Wife, and Tyti was possibly the wife of Ramesses X. (Dua)tentopet was also 'Divine Adoratrix', as was Iset, 'King's Daughter' of Ramesses VI. The latter also held the title of 'God's Wife of Amun', an office that had developed into an independent female counterpart of the High Priest of Amun.

Many daughters are known by name from later dynasties, but usually we have little detail (Dodson and Hilton 2004: 196–257). A number feature predictably as wives of kings, but they are particularly prominent in ecclesiastical contexts, e.g. Henttawy, 'King's Daughter' of Pinudjem I, was appointed 'Chantress of Amun', and 'Flautist of the House of Mut'; Mutnodjmet, 'King's Daughter of his Body', probably of Pinudjem I, was 'Second God's Servant of Amun' at Tanis; and Maatkare, 'King's Daughter' of Psusennes II, held the office of 'God's Servant of Hathor'. Above all, however, they occupy positions of the highest rank in the cult of Amon-re at Thebes as 'God's Wife', 'Adoratrix', and 'God's Hand'; Ankhenesneferibre, 'King's Daughter of his Body' of Psammetichus II, and Nitocris II, daughter of Amasis, even held the office of High Priest of Amun. The practice of allocating women of the royal house to these posts probably always had a political dimension, but in the Twenty-fifth and Twenty-sixth Dynasties it functioned transparently as a device for maintaining royal control over the powerful and wealthy priesthood of Thebes. In the Third Intermediate Period it is possible to find not infrequent examples of royal princesses marrying commoners of middling status: Ankhenesshoshenq, 'King's Daughter' of Shoshenq III, was married to a Iufa who bears the title 'God's Father', but the precise implication of that title is unclear. Marriages within the royal family were probably common (e.g. Tjesbastperu, 'King's Daughter' of Osorkon II, married her nephew Takelot, grandson of the same king), as were marriages with high officials, e.g. Irbastwedjanefu, 'King's Daughter' of Takelot III, was the wife of the vizier Pakhuru; Shepensopdet, 'King's Daughter' of Takelot I was the wife of Djedkhonsiufankh, 'Fourth God's Servant of Amun' and a descendant of the Pharaoh Harsiese; and Tentsai, 'King's Daughter' of Takelot III, was married to Nakhtefmut, *'lesonis* of Khonsu'.

---

[11] Kitchen (1999: 624) has no doubt that these princesses were wives of the king in the fullest sense.

THE *SHENYT*-COURT (*ŠNYT/ŠNWT*)

A crucially important element within the palace was the court. The standard word for this institution was *šnyt* which derived from the verb *šni*, 'to surround, encircle', and means literally 'that which surrounds (the king), the entourage'. It functioned in a number of ways. In the first place, very much like the court of Louis XIV, it served as a theatre for displays of royal splendour and majesty and, therefore, a context for repeated reaffirmation both of royal status and of the loyalty to the crown of key members of the elite; secondly, it provided a pool of administrators to carry out the business of central government; and, thirdly, it supplied the personnel who tended the royal person and ran the royal household.[12] The word that would cover most members of the court was *srw*, sometimes translated 'nobleman' or 'magistrate', but best rendered by the more neutral term 'officials'. In modern terminology the executive functions of government lay with them whilst the legislative functions lay with the king. Within this group officials holding the title 'Companion' or 'Sole Companion' occupied a highly privileged position as particularly close associates of the ruler with immediate access to his person and, therefore, immediate access to his favour and power, a position that could not fail to confer very considerable de facto authority on the officials themselves. We can be quite confident that the *shenyt* was as riddled with faction and self-serving ambition as courtiers in any other society, ancient or modern, and the *Instruction of Amenemhet* paints a grizzly picture of the reliability of royal subordinates in the early Twelfth Dynasty which probably held true for the whole of Egyptian history (see p. 82).

One of the ways in which the king might interact with his *srw* to arrive at decisions is suggested by such texts as the Kuban Stele of Ramesses II where the king is presented as sitting on a throne of electrum at Memphis wearing a diadem embellished with the double-feathers and considering the problem of supplying water for gold-mining expeditions into the Eastern Desert (Kitchen 1996*b*: 190–3). He then instructs the 'Chancellor (Seal-bearer) of the God' to summon the court officials (*srw imyw bꜣḥ*, literally 'the officials in the presence') to discuss the matter. Once introduced, the officials embark on a long programme of typical ritualistic adulation of the king which ends with the king making a decision and the officials prostrating themselves with their heads touching the ground in the customary 'kissing-the-earth' (*sn-tꜣ*) act of obeisance. The king then instructs the 'Overseer of Royal Scribes' to write to the Viceroy of Nubia to dig the necessary wells. It must be conceded that the text is

---

[12] Modern studies devoted to royal courts often make a distinction between the 'inner' and the 'outer' court (Spawforth (ed.) 2007). This is a useful division. In our case the king's personal attendants and staff would constitute the 'inner' court and all others the 'outer' court.

using the traditional motif of the *Königsnovelle*,[13] and that this motif always presents an intrinsically distorted and one-sided picture whose basic purpose is to convey the message that kings decide and officials execute, but we should not dismiss the value of the text out of hand. The narrative certainly presents an exaggerated picture, but it must have some basis in the procedure frequently followed in the decision-making process at the palace; otherwise the narrative would lose any claim to plausibility. Kings of the calibre of Ramesses II or Tuthmose III may well have functioned in this omniscient mode from time to time, but other sources suggest that genuine consultation and discussion with officials were perfectly possible: at the beginning of the mythical *Destruction of Mankind* we encounter a narrative based on the *Königsnovelle* motif that unfolds rather differently in that advisers are summoned by Re, their opinion requested, a proposal offered by the advisers, and their proposal actioned; in the *Westcar Papyrus* King Snofru is presented as asking advice from the lector priest Djadjaemankh which he accepts; and in the council-of-war preceding the Battle of Megiddo described in the *Annals* of Tuthmose III we find a description of an exchange of ideas taking place between the relevant officers and the king that the king certainly wins but that, nevertheless, demonstrates that discussion with the king on possible courses of action was conceivable. All this can leave us in no doubt that royal decisions were often the result of debates and proposals, both formal and informal, public and private, even though they were presented as royal decisions. In other words, policy and decision-making in ancient Egypt was determined exactly as intrinsic probability would lead us to expect.

The most important of the 'officials' by far was the vizier whose classic title *t3yty s3b t3ty*, conventionally usually rendered in English as 'Chief Justice and Vizier', first appears for certain during the Second Dynasty (Grajetski 2009: 15), though it may already have existed at the very beginning of Egyptian history (see p. 51). During the Sixth Dynasty, in a unique divergence from the norm, the title was held by Nebet, the mother-in-law of Pepi I, but it is probable that the title in her case was honorific only. It is likely that the office was held by more than one person simultaneously during the Old Kingdom (Strudwick 1985: 323–8), and it is certain that there could be two during the New Kingdom when separate, contemporaneous viziers for Upper and Lower Egypt are well attested (van den Boorn 1988: 18–22). Viziers specifically of Upper Egypt are also exemplified in the Third Intermediate Period (Kitchen 1996a: 483–4). Throughout Egyptian history the vizier acted as the king's deputy, though the relationship between the two functions could vary considerably from one period to another, e.g. it may well be that the Ankhu family of

---

[13] The motif is designed to emphasize the king's omniscience and has standard elements: there is a problem that the king is considering; the courtiers or troops are nonplussed; they refer the matter back to the king, and he provides the solution.

viziers responsible for running the country during the Thirteenth Dynasty were the de facto rulers of the country as Pharaohs came and went with awesome regularity, but evidence is too sparse to determine more than the family's rare capacity for survival in an ever changing world (Quirke 1990: 214–16). Nothing better describes the vizier's position as supreme executive authority than a passage in the tomb biography of the Eighteenth Dynasty vizier Rekhmire:

Now I was the heart of my lord (life, prosperity, health), the ears and eyes of the sovereign. Behold, I was his ship's captain, who knew no sleep by night or day. Whether I was standing or sitting, my heart held the bow rope and the stern rope. The sounding pole was not idle in my hands, and I was watchful for a case of grounding.   (*Urk.* iv. 1077 l. 3)

As the king's deputy the vizier lived and had his office (*ḥȝ*) either in the palace complex or in its immediate vicinity since he was required to open business daily at the palace, a process vividly described in the text now known as *The Duties of the Vizier*:

Now he [i.e. the vizier] shall enter to greet the Lord (life, prosperity, health), when the affairs of the Two Lands have been reported to him in his residence each day. He shall enter the Great House [i.e. Palace] before the Overseer of the Treasury when he stands at the northern flagstaff. Then the vizier shall move from the east from the doorway of the great double gate. Then the Overseer of the Treasury shall come, meeting him and reporting to him saying: 'All your affairs are sound and prosperous. Every functionary has reported to me saying: "All your affairs are sound and prosperous; the palace is sound and prosperous"'.   (R5–6)

This document,[14] together with a substantial body of inscriptions, provides a wealth of information on the vizier's activities, and from this material it is clear that viziers were answerable only to the king and were ultimately responsible for ensuring the orderly functioning of the entire Egyptian state machinery (Helck 1958: 17–64; Grajetski 2009: 16–19; Murnane 2001: 200–6). Theoretically, therefore, they exercised an all-embracing supervisory authority which was powerfully expressed through the enormous list of titles to which they frequently lay claim, though these titles need not, in reality, reflect functions actually discharged. In practice, however, the vizier features most prominently in the supervision of civil administration, running the royal secretariat, supervising major building operations, guaranteeing the efficient operation of the economic system, and dealing with a host of judicial matters. Given his enormous work-load, he inevitably relied a great deal on delegation, and the

---

[14] This document survives in several New Kingdom tombs, most completely in that of Rekhmire, vizier of Upper Egypt in the reign of Tuthmose III. It is usually dated to the late Middle Kingdom (Quirke 2004: 18), and I share that view, but van den Boorn assigns it to the early Eighteenth Dynasty (1988).

need for an army of scribes to deal with the huge volume of paperwork involved is self-evident. It is hardly surprising, therefore, that we frequently encounter during the Middle and New Kingdoms the title 'Scribe of the Vizier' (van den Boorn 1988: 36, 327; J. A. Taylor 2001: 218 (2136)). Communication was also a major issue, and to guarantee that this worked effectively the viziers employed a corps of 'Messengers of the Vizier' who commanded great respect and authority. Mistreatment of these emissaries brought with it dire penalties!

Below the vizier the nexus of administrators in the palace complex consisted of numerous high-ranking officials of whom the most important were those who controlled the treasury and its departments such as the 'Overseer of the Treasury' (Grajetski 2009: 43–66; J. A. Taylor 2001: 42 (387)), the 'Overseers of the (Double) Granary', who administered the state granary, and the closely linked 'Overseers of the (Double) Treasury' of which there could be several at any one time. Also associated with the state economy were 'Seal-bearers (Chancellors) of the God' (Jones 2000: 767; Quirke 2004: 78) who occur commonly as expedition leaders despatched by the Crown to acquire raw or precious materials which would be stored in or near the palace complex until needed (see p. 194). All these officials were of critical importance to the royal power structure since they ultimately guaranteed the economic well-being of the state and, thereby, of the king himself. Other important palace functions included the 'Royal Heralds', responsible for communicating the royal will, 'Overseers of the King's Documents' and 'Overseers of Royal Scribes', who were responsible for running the royal secretariat, and the 'Overseers of Works' who were essentially ministers of public works. Other important officials were the 'butlers' (*wdpw*) who acquired great importance during the New Kingdom, doubtless through their daily close proximity to the king, the 'King's Adjutant', the 'Chief of the Chamber', and, particularly, the 'Royal Stewards' (J. A. Taylor 2001: 19–28; Murnane 2001: 212–14) in charge of the royal household whose immediate association with the ruler inevitably conferred great and potentially dangerous power.[15] Others form part of the large secretarial staff of the palace, such as the 'Scribes of the Archives', the 'Scribe of the Treasury', and the 'Scribes of the House of Life'. We hear also of numerous harîm officials: 'Overseer of the Royal Harîm', the 'Deputy of the Harîm in the Suite', 'Administrators of the Harîm in the Suite', the 'Scribe of the Royal Harîm in the Suite', and 'Men of the Gate of the Harîm'. Military and police officers were also to be found there; the *Turin Juridical Papyrus* mentions a 'Commander of the Army', a 'Captain of Archers of Nubia' and 'a Standard-bearer of the Garrison', and a 'Captain of Police', though there will have been many more than that. Palace guards were also a standard element in the staff. We also hear in Middle Kingdom documents of the presence of a 'Magician'

---

[15] The Achaemenid court provides another example of precisely this phenomenon (Brosius 2007: 26).

(*ḥkȝy*) who would have guaranteed that the palace had ready access to expertise in the manipulation of *heka* (see p. 232), and that duty was probably also discharged by the conspirator Prekhamenef listed in the *Turin Juridical Papyrus* as a 'Chief (Lector Priest)'; in the same order of things both categories of source speak in the palace context of priests of Sekhmet who probably functioned as part of the palace's medical services (De Buck 1937: 163; Quirke 2004: 28, 37–8).

Tomb inscriptions of all periods demonstrate that plurality of function was common amongst senior members of the court, and they can move from one activity to something totally different with astonishing facility, i.e. professionalism was conspicuous by its absence. If we consider the case of Neferseshemptah, son-in-law of Teti, first king of the Sixth Dynasty, one of many who might be cited, we find that, although a number of his titles are ranking titles, such as 'Hereditary Lord', 'Count', 'Keeper of Nekhen', 'Overlord of Nekheb', 'Keeper of Pe', and 'Sole Companion',[16] the majority point to three areas of activity, though it is sometimes difficult to establish what, exactly, those activities were, and there is also some overlap in function. Many refer to responsibilities in tending the king's person and running the royal household, i.e. to his status as a member of the 'inner' court. Other titles relate to priestly functions or, at least, to functions in the administration of priesthoods or temples. Yet others relate to administration, particularly to legal duties. Less specific but, nevertheless, wide-ranging administrative functions are indicated by offices such as 'Secretary of all Commands'; 'Overseer of Attendants';[17] 'Head of His Two Banks'; 'Secretary of the King in all his Places'; 'Overseer of Everything which Heaven produces and Earth creates'; 'Overseer of the God's Palace of Upper Egypt'; 'Overseer of the Two Workshops';[18] and 'Overseer of the Two Houses of Gold'.[19]

Texts of all periods insist on the point that the position of officials was entirely dependent on the favour of the king, expressions such as 'Favourite of the King' being extremely common. There was doubtless a strong element of truth in these claims, though it is certain that family connections also played an important part in promoting the career of many individuals: in his biography the Sixth Dynasty official Weni repeatedly asserts his favoured status with the king and claims that his promotions were dependent on his own

---

[16] Titles fall into two broad categories, i.e. ranking or honorific titles, which indicate status, and administrative titles, which relate to offices held and, to a greater or lesser degree, exercised (Strudwick 2005: 26–30). For indexes of titles see Jones 2000 (Old Kingdom), Ward 1982 and Fischer 1997 (Middle Kingdom), and J. A. Taylor 2001 and al-Ayedi 2006 (New Kingdom).

[17] See n. 12.

[18] The *wabt* workshops seem to have had mortuary functions involving the preparation of tombs and the bodies of members of the elite (cf. Jones 2000: i. 87–8). The use of the dual presumably reflects their royal status.

[19] A treasury title (Strudwick 1985: 284–6).

merits, but in this text he completely conceals the fact that his father Iuu had been a vizier before him (Richards 2000, 2002; Simpson (ed.) 2003: 401–7; Strudwick 2005: 352–7), despite the fact that this can hardly have been irrelevant to his success. Similarly, the Eighteenth Dynasty vizier Ramose was a member of a large extended family cemented by blood and carefully calculated marriages whose corporate success in attaining high office can be plotted over several generations. The Crown, for its part, cemented these relationships by a wide-ranging programme of calculated generosity. During the Old Kingdom Weni, Neferseshemptah, and countless others received a tomb or, at least, elements for their tombs. The Fifth Dynasty inscription of Nyankhsekhmet is a particularly striking case of this form of emolument, informing us that, when Nyankhsekhmet asked the king to give him a false door for his tomb, the king provided not one but two made of the finest material and had them manufactured under the king's personal supervision in the royal audience chamber (Strudwick 2005: 303). In the same way we can assume that the large land-holdings, with their concomitant staffs, mentioned frequently in Old Kingdom tombs were not only payments for services rendered but also, and more importantly, tokens of royal esteem. The *Story of Sinuhe* is particularly fulsome in its description of what might accrue to a 'top Companion' (*smr tpy*, *smer tepy*) in the Middle Kingdom. Until his own house had been constructed, he was given the use of a prince's house, which contained:

precious things, a bathroom being in it and divine images of the horizon.[20] Valuables of the treasury were in it, and clothing of royal linen was in every apartment, and myrrh of the highest quality, officials of the king whom he loved being in every chamber, and every servant being about his duty. (B286–90).

A high-quality house was then built for him, and he was regularly supplied with food from the palace, a service that implies that the house was either in the palace compound or very close to it. He also received a superb mortuary installation built and equipped to the very highest standards. Similarly, royal favour determined the allocation of tombs at el-Amarna (Murnane 2001: 214), and Paser, a vizier of Ramesses II, also speaks of receiving a tomb from the king (Kitchen 2000: 8), but New Kingdom inscriptions are much more reticent about the origins of tombs than those of earlier periods and sometimes go so far as to insist that the owner built the tomb himself (e.g. Ahmose, son of Abana, Lichtheim 2006: 14). However, they can be most emphatic about other forms of royal approval. In the Eighteenth Dynasty Ineni, amongst other

---

[20] The reference to 'divine images of the horizon' (ꜥẖmw nw ꜣẖt) is intriguing. It would most naturally relate to statues, but the phrase might refer to wall paintings (Parkinson 1998: 52 n. 80) or relief sculptures, both of which are copiously represented in surviving palace remains, particularly at el-Amarna and Malkata.

things, 'Superintendent of Granaries', speaks on several occasions of the rewards of office accruing to a king's favourite:

My praise endured in the palace, love of me being with the court. His Majesty endowed me with serfs, and my provisions came from the granary of the palace each day.

(Sethe 1928: 58 ll. 7–10)

I was supplied from the table of the king with offering bread [intended] for the king, beer likewise, fatty meat, vegetables, various fruits, honey, cakes, and jars of wine. I was greeted with 'health and life', as His Majesty himself said, for love of me.   (59 ll. 6–12)

By the same token the claim that officials had been singled out for special attention by the king is commonly made in tomb biographies, and there are numerous examples in Old Kingdom tombs of the inscriptional recording of letters from the king to tomb owners in which the latter are presented as unparalleled recipients of royal favour. The withdrawal of such favour would be catastrophic for the individual, and a disaster to be avoided at all costs. A recent description of the workings of the Achaemenid court fits Egyptian practice perfectly:

The key to the successful workings of the . . . court was personal recognition by the king and his bestowal of gifts to reward service . . . this 'service aristocracy' was based not only on personal ambition, but also on fear of loss of status. Accordingly, it fostered loyalty on the one hand, but also intrigue and rivalry on the other, with ambitious nobles and royal scions becoming allies in the plotting of potential palace coups.   (Brosius 2007: 55)

THE PROVINCES

The phrase 'Upper and Lower Egypt' runs like a mantra through Ancient Egyptian studies, and it is indisputably correct to regard the underlying concept of Pharaonic governance as the principle of unity-in-duality. Nevertheless, Upper and Lower Egypt very rarely figure as discrete administrative entities in their own right. That position is held, for many periods of Egyptian history, by institutions called in English 'nomes' (Egyptian *sepat (spȝt)*; Greek *nomos*) which were much smaller subdivisions of the country comparable to English counties or modern Egyptian governorates. However, whether the units were nomes or something smaller two principles consistently dominate the workings of provincial administration: the need to ensure the effective exploitation by the Crown of the economic resources of the provinces and the need to ensure that the power placed in the hands of provincial administrators did not rise to a level where it threatened the pre-eminence of the king.

There is a temptation to argue that the nome system had its origins in local units already evident in the Predynastic Period which are probably reflected by the standards carried on the Narmer Palette and those that feature in representations of ships displayed on Naqada II D-ware pots, but Martin-Pardey (1976: 14–16) has rightly observed that few of the standards in question reappear as nome-standards at a later period, and that there does not seem to be any lineal connection with later administrative units. Given the lack of concrete evidence, the most reasonable assumption would be that the early standards reflect previously independent, or largely independent, polities that were brought together in stages by Upper Egyptian warlords and whose identity was subsequently eroded as they were replaced by new administrative units, i.e. nomes, over which the king could exercise direct control. Nevertheless, Moreno García (1999: 252–3) may well be correct in suggesting that some of the old elite families might have retained their pre-eminence well into the Old Kingdom in ancient centres of power such as the Third and Fifth Nomes of Upper Egypt.

The precise date at which the nomes were introduced cannot be established, but they certainly existed by the reign of Djoser at the beginning of the Third Dynasty and may go back well beyond that point. The canonical nome lists inscribed in temples from the New Kingdom onwards enumerate forty-two nomes, twenty-two in Upper and twenty in Lower Egypt, but the total of twenty for the Delta was achieved only gradually as the economic exploitation and political organization of the area progressed; the nome list on the kiosk of Senwosret I at Karnak (the White Chapel) gives only fourteen for Lower Egypt, though the number twenty-two for Upper Egypt is already present (Helck 1974).

Whilst the nomes are a recurrent feature of the physical and conceptual landscape for most of Egyptian history, their use as the major units in provincial administration is not consistent, and our conception of how precisely they functioned during the Old Kingdom has undergone a radical revision in recent years as a result of the rigorous and sensitive re-evaluation of the written data conducted, in particular, by Moreno-García (1999, 2007). It has long been recognized that their organization evolved considerably from the Fourth to Sixth Dynasties, and it is now evident that they were anything but the monolithic administrative units ruled by provincial governors resident in the province beloved of some older literature. Some were certainly administered by governors designated by titles that vary according to period and include *sšm-tꜣ*, 'District-leader', *ḥry-tp ꜥꜣ*, 'Great Chief', *ḥꜣty-ꜥ*, 'Count, Governor',[21] and *ḥqꜣ*, 'Ruler'; in Greek the terms used were *nomarchos*, 'nomarch, nome-governor', or *strategos* ('general'). During the Fourth and Fifth Dynasties they were royal officials some of whom governed their nomes from the

---

[21] As pointed out previously this title is frequently used as an honorific, but there are numerous examples during this period where it is employed as an administrative title with the meaning 'governor'.

Residence itself, and that seems to have been typically the case for the Delta nomes and those in the northern part of Upper Egypt. Others were sent out from the Residence and moved on as and when the king saw fit, but the Sixth Dynasty saw a marked tendency for nomarchs to become more nome-based and for the hereditary principle to establish itself with the inevitable result that they gradually evolved from royal officials into local barons with a strong sense of their own worth and power, a process that inevitably led to a de facto weakening of royal authority (Martin-Pardey 1976: 41–170; Moreno García 1999: 242–8, 2007: 323; Baud 2010: 76–80; Martinet 2011). However, hereditary lords or not, they were always locked into the Residence by the overarching pre-eminence of the king, which they frequently acknowledge in inscriptions, and, in particular, by the state's taxation and requisition system which it was their major function to operate within the boundaries of their provinces.[22] The nomarch's responsibility for delivering taxes and workforce personnel was, of course, based on his overriding responsibility for guaranteeing the economic well-being of his province in all its aspects, which is again evident from inscriptional sources. Beyond that he carried out judicial duties, supervised the execution of public works within his province, held responsibility for the delivery and command of militia contingents for military service or corvée duty, as required by central government, had oversight of some of the *mnw*-forts, if any, within his nome, and, in general, could be called on to discharge such other commissions as the Residence might require from time to time.

The nomarch, however, was only part of the picture. His province might contain a veritable mosaic of institutions some of which were under the control of local elites and others part of the royal administrative system into which they were closely integrated, and in both cases the nomarch exercised little, if any, authority over them. Elite families controlled the nome's major temples which functioned as units independent of the nomarch, as did the *ka*-chapels established in some nomes as part of the royal mortuary service (Seidlmayer 1996: 117, 125–6). Apart from the prestige-value accruing to local elites from their control of these important institutions, such worthies also benefited from the fact that the temples were significant economic powerhouses in their own right, though their special status did not exclude them from the orbit of the royal taxation and requisition system. We also hear frequently in early Old Kingdom texts of 'foundations' (*grg(w)t*) which look very much like royal establishments designed to open up underdeveloped territories in such areas as the Delta, and from the end of the Fifth Dynasty

---

[22] At the end of the Third Dynasty and the beginning of the Fourth we encounter a particularly intriguing device for asserting royal authority: distinctively royal monuments in the form of small, solid step pyramids were constructed at various points in the kingdom, including Elephantine on the southern frontier (Seidlmayer 1996: 119–20, 122).

we encounter the 'New Towns' (Jones 2000: 150) established in the nomes as instruments for the extension of the royal economy which were sometimes under the supervisory authority of nomarchs but were very much part of the king's demesne, as demonstrated by a passage at the end of the letter of Pepi II to Harkhuf which mentions that instructions had been sent to the 'Governor(s) of the New Towns, Companion(s), and Overseer(s) of God's Servants' (*ḥḳꜣ(w) niwt mꜣ(w)t smr(w) (i)m(iw)-r ḥm(w) nṯr*, *Urk.* i. 131: 4–7) to provide supplies for Harkhuf's expeditionary force 'from every estate of the storehouse [i.e. the royal magazines] and from every temple without exception', i.e. the 'Rulers of the New Towns', like the chief executives of temples, were subject to an overriding royal right of requisition whenever the king chose to exercise it. The 'Estates' (*ḥwt*) mentioned here are a common feature of Old Kingdom documentation, and 'Governors of Estates' (*ḥḳꜣ(w) ḥwt*) are mentioned alongside, though after, nomarchs in the list of officials providing troops for Weni's Asiatic expedition and are stated to occur, like them, in Upper and Lower Egypt (*Urk.* i. 102, 3–8). These institutions formed yet another element in the administrative apparatus of central government and yet another means by which the crown could develop and exploit the economic resources of the provinces, a function that led to the installation of large-scale commissariat arrangements of the type exemplified from the Third–Fourth Dynasties on the western side of Elephantine. These activities could lead to the 'estates' acquiring a military dimension possibly inherited from the '*swnw*-forts/towers' that disappear from the record in the Fifth Dynasty (Moreno-García 1999: 28–9), and it is in this context that we must locate the fort at Elephantine which had its beginnings in the First Dynasty (Seidlmayer 1996: 112). In all this it is impossible to mistake the state's intense concern with fiscal and requisition issues, a fact perfectly illustrated by the introduction of the office of 'Overseer of Upper Egypt' in the middle of the Fifth Dynasty (Martin-Pardey 1976: 152–70) whose fiscal dimensions emerge unequivocally in the biography of Weni who was appointed to this office by Mernere. He boasts, amongst his other achievements in post, that: 'I assessed everything which was assessable to the Residence in this Upper Egypt on two occasions and every compulsory service assessable to the Residence in this Upper Egypt on two occasions' (*Urk.* i. 106, 7–8). However, whilst the fiscal dimension was certainly pre-eminent, this office also provided a mechanism through which a general supervisory control could be exercised in Upper Egypt and the royal *Diktat* mobilized whenever and wherever required. A similar situation is probably indicated in the tomb of Nyankhpepi at Zawiyet el-Maietin who is described as 'Overseer of Commissions in Nine Nomes', and by the title 'Overseer of Upper Egypt in the Middle Nomes' held, amongst others, by Pepiankh the Middle of Meir. The only evidence of a comparable situation in the Delta is provided by the title 'Overseer of the Nomes of Lower Egypt' borne by Ishti-Tjeti in the reign of Pepi II. Whilst, however, state authority in the provinces is pervasive during the Old Kingdom, there was one innovation that showed the beginnings of private property, i.e. the 'per djet' (pr-ḏt), 'private estate', a phenomenon whose character is in some measure revealed by the Gebelein archive. These were private estates conferred by the crown on an official as remuneration for services rendered and transferable, at least in certain circumstances, to other members of their family (Moreno García 1999: 210–29).

Whether the officials in the nomes were royal agents or local elites, they wielded very considerable power that could easily be abused, and we can be quite confident that this was frequently the case. The Egyptians were not unaware of this, and it is very much to their credit that they put in place systems that at least attempted to address this problem. The most surprising Old Kingdom example of this occurs in the tomb of Pepiankh the Middle at Meir:

> I spent all that part of my life which I spent on a board of officials in a seal office to the very end. Never did I sleep with the seal far from me since I was appointed an official. Never was I placed under guard; never was I imprisoned. As for everything which was said in the presence of the officials, I emerged successfully on that score while it rebounded upon those who said it, since I was innocent of it in the presence of the officials, and, to be sure, they spoke concerning me in slander.   (*Urk.* i. 223)

Pepiankh reached the highest level in Egyptian administration, at some stage becoming vizier. We do not know to what stage, or stages, of his career this text refers, but it vividly expresses the perils of official life where jealousy and intrigue must have been common. However, the most important point about these claims is that they demonstrate that even someone of the Pepiankh's status could be called before a board of officials to answer charges. He claims that he got off scot free, but evidently this was by no means a foregone conclusion.

The re-establishment by Montuhotep II of a unified kingdom after the First Intermediate Period saw significant changes in provincial administration. The Theban dynasts of the Eleventh Dynasty who created the new state had rid themselves of nomarchs in their southern kingdom, preferring to govern through an elite corps of officials concentrated at Thebes, though nomarchs survived in the territory previously controlled by their Herakleopolitan rivals (Willems 2007, 2010: 84–5). However, the Twelfth Dynasty saw, to some degree, a retreat from this position and marks the high summer of the nomarch system, though, as with the Old Kingdom, evidence of resident nomarchs is restricted to relatively few areas, and we must still avoid the assumption that the existence of a nome implies the existence of a nomarch. In Upper and Middle Egypt they are known at present only from Nomes 1, 3, 4, 9, and 13–17 (Gestermann 1987: 172–90; Lloyd 1992), but the Delta yields very little information; governors or mayors are known from a number of sites, including Heliopolis, Bubastis, Avaris, and the Third Nome of Lower

Egypt, but we have nothing from the area comparable to the wealth of inscriptional evidence from Upper Egypt where tombs of Twelfth Dynasty nomarchs in Middle Egypt provide the fullest picture from any period of the way in which these officials worked and demonstrate that their powers and authority surpassed by some way those of their Old Kingdom predecessors. One of the earliest of these tombs (No. 2 at Beni Hasan) is that of Amenemhet, nomarch of the Oryx Nome (Sixteenth of Upper Egypt), whose long biographical inscription contains a wealth of information on his activities and self-perception. Unusually, it is dated not only by Regnal Year 43 of Senwosret I but also by Year 25 of Amenemhet himself, a striking indication of his sense of self-importance, despite his fulsome and recurrent claims of dependence on royal favour and his impressive list of court ranking-titles. Indeed, we are informed by his nephew Khnumhotep II that the family owed its essentially hereditary position in the Sixteenth Nome to Khnumhotep I who had been appointed there by the founder of the Twelfth Dynasty. Amenemhet also held high rank in the military establishment as 'Commander-in-Chief of the Expeditionary Force of the Oryx Nome' ((*i*)*m*(*y*)-*r mšꜥ wr n Mḥt*), and he himself was a participant in several royal expeditions into Nubia as leader of a military contingent from the nome. He particularly emphasized his responsibility for meeting the fiscal liabilities of the nome, in which an important role was played by an official called 'The Overseer of the Gangs of the Administrative Districts of the Guardians of the Oryx Nome', and he also insists on his success in meeting a famine crisis there. We should, of course, be a little cautious in accepting the literal truth of this latter claim, but it does, at the very least, indicate that such general concern for the well-being of the nome's population was a virtue expected of a nomarch. Another impressive feature was Amenemhet's pervasive grip on the religious life of the nome, with all that implies in terms of prestige and economic power: he held the office of 'Overseer of God's Servants' of Khnum, 'God's Servant' of Shu, Tefnut, and Anubis, '*Sem*-priest', and 'lector priest'.

A similar picture of wide-ranging power and immense self-satisfaction is presented at Asyut by the contemporaneous tomb of Hapydjefa, nomarch of the Thirteenth (Lycopolitan) Nome, the largest private tomb of the Middle Kingdom. Whilst, at one level, he behaves in quasi-royal mode, even using material in his tomb from the royal textual and architectural repertoire (Kahl 2007: 130–2), he can still boast such titles as 'Sole Companion', 'Acquaintance of the King', 'Controller of the Two Thrones in the Two Houses', 'Beloved Sole Companion', and 'Noble of the King, beloved of him'. Like Amenemhet he also held priestly titles, both cultic and administrative, and he makes particular play of his role in the cults of Wepwawet and Anubis, the major nome deities. He also describes himself as 'Chief Lector Priest' and lays claim to a knowledge of hieroglyphs. Of particular interest is the fact that he reveals explicitly that the nomarch had an estate that went with the office and was quite separate from his personal estate, i.e. the nomarch's estate functioned as his salary (see p. 190). This situation is paralleled in the Old Kingdom (see p. 162) and was probably standard practice, but the evidence is not forthcoming to prove the point. It is equally uncertain how the nomarch's personal estate came into existence, but it clearly functioned as his private property.

Djehutyhotep II, nomarch of the Fifteenth Nome provides further details of nomarch activities in texts preserved—or once preserved—in his badly damaged tomb at el-Bersha. He and his family had a hereditary claim to office (Willems 1983–4), but, like other nomarchs of the period, he strongly emphasizes his favour with the king, laying claim to a string of high-status ranking-titles and also asserting that he was a 'foster-child of the king' (*sḏty nsw*). He exercised both administrative and priestly functions, including the office of 'High Priest of Hermopolis' (*wr diw*, lit. 'Chief of the Five') and states that nomarchs in his province were responsible for making legal judgments in their capacity as 'judge and boundary official' (*sꜣb ꜥḏ mr*) and also for levying taxes on the river. He leaves us in no doubt that he had authority throughout the nome and informs us that he was able to summon the manpower resources of the entire nome on corvée duty to drag a colossal statue of himself from the Hatnub quarry to his tomb complex and also to provide a military escort and a body of priestly attendants. This activity in itself provides another example of the narrowing of the gulf between king and commoner in the Twelfth Dynasty. How many other officials, of any period, embellished their tombs with colossi? It should also be noted that the nomarchs of this family dated their activities by their own years of office in exactly the same way as regnal years of kings are employed. His authority did not, however, stop there. In his tomb he also describes himself as 'Chief of the Nomes of Upper Egypt', implying a position of overriding power well beyond his own province.

Most instructive of all is the great biographical inscription of Khnumhotep II (Beni Hasan, Tomb 3), the most important text of its kind from any source in the Middle Kingdom which provides the history of the nomarch family of the Oryx Nome from the beginning to the middle of the Twelfth Dynasty (Lloyd 1992: 21–36; Simpson (ed.) 2003: 420–4). This nome had an unusual structure in that the section on the east side of the river operated as a sub-prefecture called 'The Mountain of Horus' with its capital at Menat-Khufu[23] which had its own governor drawn from the nomarch's close family and which tended to function with a degree of independence, the nomarch himself exercising direct control only over the western side of his province. Khnumhotep II himself never rose above the status of governor of this subprefecture, but the text reveals with great clarity the role of a number of major operational principles that were of general validity amongst nomarch families of this

---

[23] The name strongly suggests that it was, in origin, an Old Kingdom *ḥwt*-foundation.

period. In the first place, hereditary succession played a crucial part, but, at the same time, the text insists that all appointments required royal assent, and that Khnumhotep II enjoyed high favour with the king and at court which he claims derived from his personal qualities and was clearly considered vital to the family's continued success. The text also emphasizes that the crown insisted on the accurate delineation of the boundaries of Menat-Khufu and the nomes themselves, and these were confirmed by setting up numerous boundary stelae. Evidently kings were determined to establish exactly how far the authority of their provincial governors extended. Similarly, water, timber, and property rights were also defined on the basis of old records. Of particular interest is the evidence provided on the use by nomarchs of marriage as a strategy for building up and consolidating political alliances in Middle Egypt: Khnumhotep's mother married a major figure at court called Neheri, and, since Neheri is a common name of the nomarch family of the adjacent Fifteenth Nome, we can be confident that he was a member of that family; it belongs in the same order of things that Khnumhotep's eldest son Nakht was appointed governor of the adjacent Seventeenth (Cynopolitan) Nome. This means that the Fifteenth, Sixteenth, and Seventeenth Nomes of Upper Egypt constituted a major power block in Middle Egypt that had the potential to pose a serious threat to royal authority, however loud the protestations of dependence on royal favour in tomb inscriptions might be. We should add to this the fact that Khnumhotep's family also exercised other major functions: Nakht was appointed Head of Upper Egypt, an office that may well parallel Djehutyhotep's overarching authority in Upper Egypt, and Khnumhotep III, another son, was appointed 'Door of the Foreign Lands', a position that involved the orchestration of foreign trade relations and parallels the role of Khnumhotep II as 'Overseer of the Eastern Foreign Lands'.

Evidence of nomarchs disappears at most sites during the reign of Senwosret III, though they survived rather longer at Elephantine and Qau el-Kebir (Tenth Nome of Upper Egypt) (Lloyd 1992: 30; Willems 2010: 97). This phenomenon has given rise to much discussion, and it has frequently been claimed in older literature that it was the result of the suppression of the nomarchs by Senwosret III. That there was a systemic change is clear, but this does not appear to involve the suppression of the old provincial nobility. The career of Khnumhotep III, the son of our Khnumhotep II, illustrates this perfectly. Although he started as governor of Menat-Khufu, his later career unfolded in close association with the king, and he eventually achieved the rank of vizier. Not surprisingly, therefore, he was not buried at Beni Hasan but in a mastaba tomb in the necropolis at Dahshur near the pyramid of his royal master Senwosret III (Franke 1991; Allen 2008). This example would suggest that, except where it suited the king to do otherwise, the nomarch system was displaced by civil service appointments and the activities of the senior members of the nomarch families focused on the palace where their ambitions and inordinate self-esteem could be channelled in directions of the Pharaoh's own choosing. If we accept that the *Duties of the Vizier* is essentially a late Middle Kingdom document (Quirke 2004: 18–24), it is possible to provide a highly plausible reconstruction of the way this system worked (van den Boorn 1988: 326–9). It was based on units denoted by the term *sepat* (*spȝt*), the old word for 'nome', but now best translated as 'district'. These units, which may well have been based on the old nomes, contained urban elements that might be towns (*niwt*) or estates (*ḥwt*) and rural districts (*w*) and were administered at the highest level by a triumvirate of officials. The main urban settlement and its ramifications was controlled either by a 'town mayor', or a 'settlement-governor', and there were also an 'Overseer of Fields' and a 'district council-lor'. Where the line of demarcation was drawn between the latter two officials is unclear, but van den Boorn (1988: 328) may well be right in suggesting that the 'district counseller' was particularly concerned with irrigation and 'other rural duties of a "technical" nature'. The 'town mayor' or 'settlement-governor' presumably exercised overall authority in the *sepat* and will have been ultim-ately responsible, above all, for the administration of the local economy and ensuring that it met the fiscal requirements of central government, but it is quite clear that both the 'Overseer' and the 'Councillor' retained an obligation to report directly to the vizier. It is, of course, possible that this system had its origins in arrangements employed earlier during the Twelfth Dynasty in the nomes where nomarchs are not in evidence, and the position of Menat-Khufu with its *ḥȝty-ꜥ*-governor in the Oryx Nome provides an obvious parallel, but the uneven spread of the evidence for Middle Kingdom local government prevents a definitive decision on the matter. It is, however, quite clear that this system, once established, became the basis for local administration throughout the New Kingdom during which 'mayors' (*ḥȝtyw-ꜥ*) are the lynchpins of local administration.

Whatever the arrangements at nome- or subnome-level, it is clear that Middle Kingdom Pharaohs, like their Old Kingdom counterparts, eventually found it expedient to introduce administrative structures that combined nomes into larger units. In the late Middle Kingdom the nomes of the southern part of the country stretching from Elephantine to Abydos were grouped into a unit described as 'the Sector of the Head of the South' (*wꜥrt tp rs(y)*) whose administrative centre, with an impressive array of officials, lay at Thebes. The area to the north may well have constituted a similar unit based on the capital Itjtawy (at, or near, Lisht), but the evidence on that issue is unclear (Quirke 2004: 25, 116–18). 'Sectors of the South' and 'North' do occur in texts from Lahun, but they are clearly local subdivisions of larger administrative units and in no way comparable to 'the Sector of the Head of the South'.

Evidence for the post-New Kingdom Period is patchy. The Piye Stele reveals that *ḥȝtyw-ꜥ*-governors continued to exercise authority in the late eighth century, often over several districts at the same time, and that they were largely, if not completely, independent entities, i.e. the pendulum has once again swung in favour of the provincial-baron model for nome government, and that situation seems to be replicated in the Assyrian Period. However, the kings of the Twenty-sixth Dynasty swiftly reversed this situation (Perdu 2010: 141–2), and administration of provinces by royal officials became the norm for the rest of the Pharaonic Period (Helck 1974: 58), even during the Persian Occupation (Bresciani 1958: 138–9).

LAW AND ORDER

In all societies most behaviour is determined by a traditional and conventional code of conduct which is assimilated by its members through social interaction and responses to social imperatives. However, when norms are transgressed, mechanisms are needed to resolve the situation, and it is a major characteristic of state systems that they increasingly take over control of the enforcement of norms or the administration of justice from the familistic context (see p. 57) and vest this function in state institutions. Pharaonic Egypt provides excellent evidence of this process, but it would be a mistake to assume that the age-old right to achieve individual satisfaction against enemies by personal action, i.e. revenge, had disappeared from the land. The *Westcar Papyrus* presents us with the spectacle of Djedi wishing well to Prince Hardedef with a series of pieties including the words, 'May your *ka* vent its anger upon your enemy' (A. M. Blackman 1988: 9, 7. 25). This looks very much like personal vengeance. In the *Conflict of Horus and Seth* Seth threatens the Ennead of gods, 'I shall take my sceptre of 4,500 *nmst*[24] and kill one of you daily' (Gardiner 1932: 42), and elsewhere in the story we encounter other violent vengeful acts. Indeed, the whole of this narrative revolves around the issue of whether physical might should take precedence over law and custom and is surely a clear reflection, despite its fictional nature, that the delicate balance between these factors was a serious concern in Egyptian society. A particularly vicious example of the application of violence to a quarrel occurs in P.Rylands IX where the priests of el-Hiba are described as hiring hit-men to murder the sons of Horudja, an enterprise in which they were sadly all too successful (see below). Such data, together with the frequency with which beatings, official and otherwise, appear in our evidence on Egyptian life, indicate that violence lurked very close to the surface in Ancient Egyptian society and almost certainly led to the revenge, honour killings, and blood feuds still detectable

---

[24] The value of this measure of weight is unknown.

in traditional society in more modern Egypt.[25] Even at a more general level the dangers to life and limb beyond the town could be particularly acute, as Bagnall has rightly emphasized:

Life in rural areas in antiquity was hazardous to person and property. As one moved away from the centers of population, the risk of being robbed, assaulted, or killed increased. Both travellers and country residents were constantly beset by these problems. The extent and nature of the lawlessness in any area, naturally, depended in part on the degree to which it was thickly settled, had urban centers, and had a tradition of controlling violence.   (2006: pp. xviii, 67)

In Ancient Mesopotamia the development and publication of law codes became a major feature of the state system. In Egypt, on the other hand, there does not seem to have been any comprehensive, systematic legal code for most of its history,[26] and decisions were guided by a mix of custom and practice, the good sense of those hearing the case, and, at times, the relative capacity of the disputants to bribe the judge or judges. Furthermore, there were no professional legal officials until the Saite Period at the earliest, adjudication potentially forming part of the portfolio of any official of standing. The villages in which the majority of Ancient Egyptians lived probably saw little significantly aberrant behaviour, and even serious cases would usually have been resolved by taking the matter to respected members of the village community who would adjudicate on the matter, no doubt at times with voluble advice from anyone else who happened to be present. Village notables (*rmṯ ꜥꜣw*, lit. 'Great Men') who could be expected to discharge this role are mentioned in the New Kingdom inscription of Mose (Mes), though here they appear in the context of a formal state legal enquiry.[27] However, in general, the paucity of written evidence means that the workings of village justice are largely a matter of informed speculation, the one exception being the workmen's village of Deir el-Medina.

We should never forget that Deir el-Medina is a far from typical village settlement in a number of respects, but the method of conducting trials is not likely to have been significantly different from that observed elsewhere. We hear of a court (*knbt*) convened very much on an ad hoc basis and consisting of members who could include workmen, gang-foremen, and outside officials and varied from case to case. It dealt with a wide range of civil trials, but its competence did not extend to criminal matters, which were dealt with by outside agencies such as the vizier's court. Oaths and witnesses are a recurrent

---

[25] We even have a text from Deir el-Medina mentioning two murders perpetrated to cover the tracks of some of the tomb-robbers (McDowell 1999: 199).

[26] Classical traditions (e.g. Diodorus Siculus 1. 95) on the activities of royal law-givers in the Late Period should be treated with extreme caution (Lloyd 1988: 220).

[27] The Mose of this text is often called Mes after the form used in the classic discussion of the inscription by Gardiner (1905).

feature in the proceedings, and verdicts were delivered, as usual, on the basis of custom and practice which occasionally involved reference to royal decrees on specific issues.[28] It is clear that getting the decision of the court implemented could be a very difficult matter, but Deir el-Medina was certainly not unique in that respect. Penalties for misdemeanours, if they were exacted, could involve fines, beatings, confiscation of property, or terms of hard labour that might include work in the royal necropolis itself.

Secular methods were not the only option available at Deir el-Medina to deal with civil complaints. There was also the oracle of Amenhotep I, who was the equivalent of a patron-saint of the necropolis. When the statue of this long dead king was brought out on a bier and carried by his priests, it was possible to place before it questions written on papyrus or ostraca which were couched in such a way that they could be answered in the form of a Yes/No response. Confronted with one of these, the god's statue would move forward towards it (for assent) or backwards (for disagreement), propelled by the priests carrying the statue who were presumably considered to be inspired by the deceased king in their actions. Whilst the verdict gained in this way carried considerable weight, a disappointed suppliant might well find some difficulty in accepting it and cases of extreme recalcitrance are not unknown (McDowell 1999: 165–200).

The role of officials in the administration of justice is well documented. In Old Kingdom tomb biographies the tomb-owner frequently boasts: 'I never judged between two disputants . . . in a case where a son was deprived of his father's portion' (*Urk.* i. 123 ll. 3–4), and, since this kind of issue occurs frequently in our sources, it would appear that inheritance disputes were a common problem.[29] An official as a potential source of justice also appears in the *Tale of the Eloquent Peasant.* When the peasant was robbed and sought redress, he did not go to anything remotely like a modern police station but turned to a Chief Steward called Rensi for redress, who dealt with the matter initially by submitting it the officials (*srw*) in his entourage, though no immediate redress was forthcoming, and the peasant's importunate demands for justice led to his being given a thorough thrashing at one point in the narrative, a common ingredient in Egyptian administrative practice (Parkinson 1998: 60ff.). A text from the Kahun archive presents us with a particularly detailed account of the procedure followed in a case brought by a

---

[28] Royal decrees handing down rulings on particular issues (*wḏ(w) nsw*, *hpw* (of particular kings)) were not uncommon and could be expanded into comprehensive instructions on dealing with specific categories of offence, e.g. the Decree of Horemheb in the late Eighteenth Dynasty (Kruchten 1981).

[29] P.Berlin 9010 (probably late Old Kingdom) from Elephantine, despite its damaged condition, gives some insight into the practicalities of dealing with such matters (Strudwick 2005: 186–7).

man who had been swindled, and here too standard administrators play a major role:

It is the case that his son spoke: 'As for my father, he made a deed of conveyance with regard to his office of *Web*-priest in Charge of the Phyle of Sopdu, Lord of the East, with the Scribe in Charge of the Seal of East-Side Iyemyatib. To my father did he say, "I shall give to you the revenue [?], incidental income [?] and all your rights". So did he say. Then was my father questioned by the Overseer of Fields Mersu as proxy for The Member of the Official Body, saying, "Are you satisfied at being given the said revenue together with incidentals and all these rights accruing to you in exchange for your [office of] *Web*-priest in Charge of the Phyle?" Then did my father say, "I am satisfied". That which The Member of the Official Body said: "The two men shall be made to swear an oath saying, 'We are satisfied'". Then the two men were asked to swear an oath in the presence of the Count///////Overseer of Fields Mersu as proxy for The Member of the Official Body.'

List of witnesses in whose presence this was made: (List follows).

'Now my father died, and the problems in connection with the revenue had not been removed. Furthermore my father said to me when he was ill, "If you do not receive the revenue sworn to me by the Scribe in Charge of the Seal Iyemyatib, then shall you make a plea concerning it to an official who will hear it. Then the revenue shall be given to you". So did he say. I approached someone who might carry out . . . therein concerning the immediate payment of that which the Scribe in Charge of the Seal Iyemyatib had agreed.'   (Sethe 1928: 91–2)

The problem that had arisen here was that the office of *Web*-priest had been separated from its revenues, and the office has been handed over to Iyemyatib on the understanding that he allowed the income to continue to be paid to the father. Presumably such payments would cease on the old man's death, and the revenues would be reunited with the office. Iyemyatib did not keep his side of the bargain, and the son was anxious to recover the missing payments. The arrangements, as usual, were accompanied by an oath and agreed in the presence of witnesses. The officials involved were not dedicated legal officials but an Overseer of Fields and a Member of the Official Body, a title that seems to have been borne by anyone who formed part of the corps of officials in the palace.[30] The involvement of these major officials was obviously a matter of some importance to the father who made this contract.

Some civil disputes passed well beyond the local level for resolution. The case recorded in the tomb of Mose, the Treasury Scribe of Ptah, (Gardiner 1905; Kitchen 2000: 307–12) concerned a complex dispute over land rights and mentions the involvement of the highest courts in the land, the Great Court (*ḳnbt ʿꜢt*, kenbet aat) which was based in Heliopolis and chaired by the vizier and the Court of Memphis (*ḳnbt Mn-nfr*). We also hear of the Hall of

---

[30] See Quirke 1990: 56–7, for an excellent discussion of this title.

Pharaoh (ʿrʿyt nt pr-ʿꜣ), but its precise role in the affair is not clear. At one point a list of judges is provided, and, as we have come to expect, they are all officials with a wide range of duties, but none exercised exclusively legal functions; they were probably simply appointed ad hoc from officials who happened to be available to serve. The same holds true of the court which tried the harîm conspirators in the reign of Ramesses III (see p. 82) and the Great Court of Thebes which dealt with cases of tomb robbery at the end of the Twentieth Dynasty (Peet 1930: 42). Documentation features prominently in the Mose case, though some of it was clearly forged, and a particularly impressive aspect of this complex saga is the trouble that government officials took to resolve the matter, even visiting the village where the land dispute had arisen and invoking the assistance of local witnesses. A similar care in gathering evidence and establishing the truth appears again in the Tomb Robbery Papyri. The Mose inscription reveals that the punishment for bearing false witness in this case could have involved exile or cutting off the nose and ears of the guilty party, and a similar situation, supplemented by the death penalty, is envisaged in the Tomb Robbery texts, though such severe penalties would presumably have arisen only because these were cases which involved the Crown. The penalty for anyone found guilty of tomb robbery was death by impaling (Peet 1930: 26–7). It is likely, but undemonstrable, that all cases involving disfigurement or death needed the approval of the Pharaoh.

Papyrus Rylands IX from the Persian Period provides evidence of another dispute over rights of ownership with a long history, in this instance going right back to the beginning of the Saite Dynasty (Vittmann 1998). The focus of dispute was priestly rights to temple revenues in el-Hiba, and the entire narrative paints a grim picture of ecclesiastical violence and murder during a period when central government is supposed to have been strong, and again we have information on the officers involved. We encounter the terms *wp(t)y*, 'judge', and ʿ.wy (n) wpy(.t), 'place of judgement', which may well indicate the existence at this period of dedicated legal officials. In formal legal contexts we hear of complaints being brought before the vizier and also the Pharaoh, and of official actions involving bribery, torture, beatings, imprisonment, and execution. However, on a more positive note we are told of police attempts to control the situation involving a Chief of Ma,[31] who at one point mobilized fifty men to assist him, and a General operating in a policing role.

The policing function of officers described in P. Rylands IX prompts the question of how policing was conducted at earlier periods. Evidence there is, but it is not plentiful. Beginning in the Old Kingdom we encounter the *zꜣ (w) pr*, literally 'sons of the house', functioning as police or watchmen on behalf of officials who might need to apply force to recalcitrant subordinates

---

[31] For the Ma see p. 79.

(Yoyotte 1952; Jones 2000: 798), and from the Middle Kingdom onwards we hear of 'policemen' (*šnꜥw, šntw,*) and 'overseers of policemen' (*imyw-r šnꜥw/ šntw*) (Faulkner 1953: 41) whose duties embraced urban and desert areas as well as temples. The role of the 'district overseers' (*imyw-r w*) also probably included police functions (van den Boorn 1988: 50–3). From the Middle Kingdom onwards policing activities were discharged by the Nubian Medjay (Quirke 1990: 22), and they played a major role in the royal necropolises in Western Thebes during the New Kingdom. Indeed, Medjay eventually became so closely associated with policing that their name could be used generally as a term for police, irrespective of ethnic origin (*Wb.* ii. 186; Gardiner 1947: i. 82*–9*). We also hear of police called *sashau* (*sꜥšꜣw*) of whom Gardiner comments that they 'seem to have exercised in the towns, temples and fields much the same functions as the Medjay did in the desert and in the necropolises' (1947: i. 93*).The emphasis in all the activities of these officials was not so much on upholding the law but acting as security police or providing an element of forceful compulsion for officials such as tax collectors who might well find such an increment to their apparatus of persuasion a useful adjunct. The existence of these 'gendarmes' in no way precluded the mobilization of the army in a policing role whenever circumstances required, and there is good reason to believe that it functioned in just that way to impose the religious policy of Akhenaten at the end of the Eighteenth Dynasty (Redford 1984: 139, 152, 193; Reeves 2001: 154–5).

6

The Dialogue with Environment

None of the systems analysed in the previous chapters would have been possible without the underpinning of sound economic structures, i.e. the effective exploitation of physical context. One of the most impressive cultural achievements of the Ancient Egyptians was the efficiency with which they exploited their physical environment to meet their economic requirements, extracting the maximum benefit from it and circumventing whatever deficiencies it presented. Those needs might be practical, such as food and raw materials, or ritual, such as items required for cultic purposes, though Egyptian perceptions of such distinctions would differ very greatly from our own.

THE PHYSICAL ENVIRONMENT

The geographical area in which Egyptian civilization evolved falls into three main sections (see Fig. 1.1): the valley, which had been gouged out by the Nile over millions of years through bedrocks consisting of granite, sandstone, and limestone; the Delta to the north, originally a great bay of the sea that had slowly been filled in by depositions of silt from the river; and the Fayyum to the west of the valley, a depression in the desert occupied over a significant area by a lake of variable extent now called the Birket Karun. This lake owed its genesis to an offshoot of the Nile that had broken through from the east of the depression by piercing the limestone cliffs flanking the west side of the valley, the most recent manifestation of this offshoot being the current Bahr Yusuf (Butzer 1976; Wenke 2009: 38–49; Parcak 2010).

The geological and hydrographic features of this variegated and extraordinary landscape created opportunities but also imperatives that exercised a critical effect on the evolution of Egyptian civilization. The most obvious of these is the regime of the Nile itself. Before the modern dams at Aswan altered its natural behaviour, it began to rise in Egypt during July, reached high water in September/October, and had finally returned to its bed by January. This process conferred a number of benefits: in the first place it made possible an extremely rich agricultural economy by yielding an abundance of water in an environment that would otherwise have been largely desert, but water was not the end of the story; for the inundation also brought with it every year large quantities of rich mud washed off the lands to the far south, and this renewed the arable soil of Egypt without any need for artificial fertilizers.[1] The Egyptians designated the areas covered by this dark-brown mud, i.e. the Valley, the Delta, and the Fayyum, as 'The Black Land' (*Kmt*), which was the standard name for Egypt in Pharaonic times, and only this territory was regarded as Egypt proper. It provided approximately 22,400 sq. km of cultivable land during the New Kingdom, ample to support a population that probably never exceeded three million in Pharaonic times, though improvements in agricultural techniques during the Ptolemaic Period increased the amount of usable land to approximately 27,300 sq. km and permitted a population rise to about five million (Butzer 1976: 82–98). In contrast, the deserts to the west and east of the alluvium, frequently regarded as hostile territory, were designated 'The Red Land' (*Dšrt*) and were never considered to be part of Egypt proper. However, despite the bleak view the Egyptians often took of these areas, they were of considerable economic importance. The trade routes passing through the Western Desert, above all the Darb el-Arbayin ('The Road of Forty (Days)') running north from the Sudan parallel to the Nile, were a major economic asset tapped throughout Egyptian history by such well-placed cities as Asyut in Middle Egypt. In addition, much of the oasis area was brought under Egyptian control from as early as the Old Kingdom and constituted another source of wealth as well as providing a buffer zone against the nomadic tribes of the Libyan Desert. The desert to the east also had much to offer. Not only did it boast a rich store of raw materials such as gold, copper, and high-quality stone such as granite and greywacke, but it was also the site of several routes, such as the Wadi Hammamat, joining the Nile Valley to ports on the Red Sea through which the Egyptians could develop trade relations with the land of Punt (Somaliland, Eritrea, and the Sudan).

NUTRITIONAL RESOURCES

Since precipitation in Egypt is negligible, agriculture has to rely for nearly all its water on the Nile. Initially the waters of the river would simply have been exploited for agricultural purposes on an opportunistic basis without any attempt to control the river's natural regime, and this strategy would have yielded perfectly adequate returns for small communities, but these successes

[1] See p. 178 for the use of fertilizer in areas not covered by the inundation.

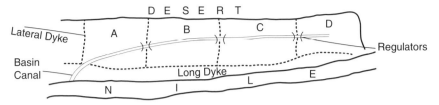

Fig. 6.1. The basin system of irrigation. Drawing by Lloyd.

would, in themselves, have eventually created a problem: once a society has become dependent on an agricultural economy as a major part of its subsistence strategy, the rise in population that inevitably follows creates increasing demands on food production, and the Egyptians would have experienced a growing need to manage the water regime of the river to increase productivity. Therefore, from at least the late Predynastic Period, but probably much earlier, they gradually developed a system of basin irrigation, complementing and enhancing the natural basins already in existence. This made it possible to generate a significantly greater return from the soil, thereby creating one of the most impressive and successful of their technological interventions in their environment (Butzer 1976: 39–56). Texts and representations are not generous in providing details on how this system was orchestrated, but the basin-system survived in Egypt into the early twentieth century (Willcocks and Craig 1913: 303–11), and the study of this technology, combined with such ancient data as survive, permits a broad reconstruction of ancient practice (Eyre 1994: 7). In the form that survived into modern times it involved constructing dykes parallel to the river banks, which were themselves higher than the land behind them,[2] with lateral dykes running off towards the desert to west or east (Fig. 6.1). To admit the floodwater into the basins and control its flow a canal was excavated from the river bank through a series of basins. This canal was sealed by a sluice designed to contain the floodwaters for as long as possible, but, once sufficient pressure had built up, the sluice would be opened and the water would pour through the canal and fill the furthest basin served by a particular system. The sluice gate of the furthest basin would then be closed and the next basin filled up until they had all been filled. The effect of this procedure was not only to guarantee the thorough watering of the surface of the basins and increase the area watered by increasing the lateral velocity of

---

[2] When the Nile flooded, the largest particles held in suspension were deposited first so that the river banks were raised to a level higher than the land behind, creating a convex profile. Since the Nile changed its bed frequently in antiquity, with a general tendency to move eastwards, this phenomenon left many old banks running along the valley which could be integrated into the man-made irrigation system.

the flood but also to ensure, as far as possible, an even spread of the mud held in suspension. A further advantage of the system was that it guaranteed an annual short-term throughput of water which ensured that the ever-present danger of salinization of the arable land was averted. Once the water was released back into the river (during October in the southern provinces in modern times), the farmers could sow their seed. The Ancient Egyptians frequently dispensed with preliminary ploughing, simply broadcasting the seed directly onto the alluvium, and the seeds were then covered over either by means of light ploughs are by releasing animals onto the ground to tread them in.

Whilst the Nile created Egypt,[3] it was far from being consistently benign. Ancient sources leave us in no doubt that dykes were seen not simply as a means of assisting the Egyptians in directing water where it was required but also as a means of protection from high Niles, and the Eloquent Peasant of the eponymous story can naturally use the dyke as a metaphor for protection when he tries to persuade a High Steward to assist him: 'You are trusted—and are become a misleader. You were appointed as a dyke for the pauper—beware lest he drown!' (Parkinson 1998: 69). Later in the same text the torrent of water that could pour from a breached dyke is compared to the torrent of words that the Peasant delivers to his listener: 'Now my body is full, my heart laden, and what comes forth from my body due to its state is the breach of a dyke, whose waters have flown out, as my mouth opens to speak' (p. 71). The problems created by a high Nile are portrayed graphically in a number of texts. A stele of Sobekhotep VIII of the Thirteenth Dynasty describes the effect on a temple: 'His Majesty went to the hall of this temple <in order to> see the great inundation. His Majesty came <to> the hall of the temple which was full of <water>. [Then His Majesty] waded there...' (Baines 1974: 40, modified). Even more impressive is the description in a text of the Twenty-second Dynasty at Karnak: 'The flood came on, in this whole land; it invaded the two shores as in the beginning. This land was in his power like the sea, there was no dyke of the people to withstand its fury. All the people were like birds upon its [...] ... All the temples of Thebes were like marshes' (BAR iv. §743). Low Niles could be even more disastrous. Human figures obviously suffering from severe malnutrition appear from time to time in Egyptian representations, the best known being those on the causeway of Unis at Saqqara (W. Smith 1981: 134; cf. p. 177 herein and Hawass and Verner 1996), and there is compelling climatological evidence that low Niles were a serious problem at the end of the Old Kingdom (Stanley et al. 2003; Parcak 2010:

---

[3] It has been stated on countless occasions, and will doubtless be stated on countless more, that the Greek historian Herodotus asserted that Egypt was 'the gift of the Nile'. He did not say that. The relevant Greek expression translates: 'Egypt, *as far as Greeks sail*... is a gift of the Nile' (2. 5. 1), i.e. it is the land between the Fayyum and the sea alone which was 'a gift of the Nile'.

8–10). Several texts of the First Intermediate Period mention the disastrous effects, the most famous being that in the tomb of Ankhtify of Moalla:

everybody died] of hunger on this sandbank of Apophis ... All of Upper Egypt was dying of hunger and people were eating their children, but I did not allow anybody to die of hunger in this nome ... I cared for the house of Elephantine and for the town of Iat-negen in these years after Hefat and Hor-mer had been satisfied ... The whole country has become like locusts, going upstream and downstream [in search of food], but never did I allow anybody in need to go from this nome to another one (i.e. for the same purpose).   (trans. Seidlmayer 2000: 129)

The stele of the butler Merer from the same area and period speaks in equally grim terms of economic crisis, though for him charity definitely began at home:

I buried the dead and nourished the living, wherever I went in this drought which had occurred. I closed off all their fields and mounds in town and countryside, not letting their water inundate for someone else, as does a worthy citizen so that his family may swim. When it happened that Upper Egyptian barley was given to the town, I transported it many times. I gave a heap of white Upper Egyptian barley and a heap of *ḥmi*-barley, and measured out for every man according to his wish.

(trans. Lichtheim 1975: 87)

Whilst we should be cautious in accepting the literal truth of such assertions and must allow for the conventional nature of Egyptian biographical texts and their claims that their subjects were paragons of benevolence, even the most minimalist interpretation must accept that famine created by the vagaries of the Nile was a crisis high on the level of official consciousness at this period, and the recurrence of the problem of drought in First Intermediate Period inscriptions would suggest that it was a not infrequent experience at that time.

It will be evident that the irrigation system, heavily dependent on the construction and proper working of a system of dykes, canals, and reservoirs, was not only highly labour-intensive but also required a substantial amount of organization at local level. It has sometimes been argued that the requirement for systematic direction created by the irrigation system was a major factor in creating a centralized government in Ancient Egypt, and there is no doubt that, from an early period, the Pharaoh was regarded as a major figure, if only at a symbolic level, in the running of the economy, and crown officials may well have exercised a general oversight of its workings (see p. 61), but the basin system was a technology that, by its very nature, had be to operated locally, and there was no role for central government in its detailed workings (Butzer 1976: 50–1).

In its fully developed form the Egyptian irrigation-based agricultural system was one of the most productive in the ancient world (cf. Hartmann 1923; Murray 2000: 505–36; Wenke 2009: 56–69; Moreno García 2008; Eyre 1999,

2010: 292–5). The cereal crops characteristic of Pharaonic agriculture were barley and emmer wheat which indisputably have their origins in the Near East and were then imported via the Delta and spread southwards to dominate the entire country (see p. 38). Once established, barley and emmer formed the basis of the Egyptian diet which relied heavily on bread and beer made from these crops. In addition, Egyptian agriculture produced flax on a large scale, and this crop provided the raw material for linen production, the standard Egyptian textile material, as well as yielding a source of oil. Whilst, however, these three crops are the most important products of Egyptian agriculture, we should not ignore the fact that food-production went well beyond these items. Orchards and vegetable plots were a standard feature of the landscape which exploited a simple, if effective, form of perennial irrigation (Eyre 1994). These market-garden operations were located in areas that were not affected by the inundation under normal circumstances, out on the margins of the cultivation where the deserts began, or on any high points in the alluvial area such as natural hills, the tops of dykes, or the high banks of extinct river courses. Agricultural activity in these locations concentrated on such crops as fruit trees, vines, lentils, pulses, onions, and melons and were watered from several sources including the Nile and its offshoots, canals, cisterns, wells, and natural ponds. Since all such water had to be delivered by hand, this brand of agriculture was extremely laborious, though this was slightly alleviated from the New Kingdom by the introduction of the *shaduf* from the Near East. A further labour commitment would have been the need to fertilize since these plots would not have benefited from the annual depositions of mud brought down by the Nile.

Another benefit to farming largely created by the Nile and vigorously exploited was the natural vegetation consisting of marsh-land and scrub which was available along the margins of the cultivation in the valley but in particular abundance in the Delta. This resource provided an excellent basis for stock-rearing of many different kinds which the Egyptians developed with great success, and even private individuals could boast of possessing large numbers of domestic animals, though it should be remembered that in animal husbandry, as in arable farming, Egyptian practice did not develop independently. Near Eastern influence is again easily detected: Egyptian short-horned cattle certainly emanated from Asia, as did the hump-backed cattle that appeared during the New Kingdom, and the same held true of domestic sheep and goats (see p. 38). Cattle rearing occupied pride of place, and there is ample evidence of substantial herds of cattle of several different kinds, tended by a class of herdsmen who were very much regarded as marginal members of Egyptian society and whose function it was to manage their charges to the best advantage on the basis of well-established practices. The fragmentary *Tale of the Herdsman* gives tantalizing glimpses of the sometimes stressful life of these individuals, putting into the mouth of one of their number:

> ... I went down <to> the pool,
> ... let the calves cross over (the water) and the herd spend the night
> on the edge of the grazing land,
> with the herders looking after them!
> Our skiff for the return!
> With the bulls and cows behind it,
> and the herders' sages reciting a water-spell.
>
> (trans. Parkinson 1998: 287–8)

Here the care exercised over the movement of the herds comes vividly to life and, in particular, the close proximity of water and the need for water transport as one of the tools of the trade. This environment had its dangers, creating crises that could require the assistance of ritual experts to circumvent, as the spell of the water sage in the same text reveals:

> I will not be driven from the water-meadow,
> Even in a year of a great Nile flood who issues the order to the earth's surface,
> when the pool cannot be told from the river!
> Be well within Your house!
> The cattle stay in their proper place.
> Come! Fear of You has perished,
> dread of You is driven away ...   (p. 288)

Here it is clear that a high Nile that brought the floodwaters further out than usual towards the cliffs in the valley or the desert margins in the Delta could create major problems for the pastoralists who habitually haunted these marginal areas. In addition the menace of crocodile attack could never be discounted, as is discretely suggested by scenes showing the passage of animals through water with crocodiles in attendance in such Old Kingdom tombs as those of Ti and Mereruka, and hippopotami must also at times have been a problem and can also feature in such contexts, as in the tomb of Pepiankh at Meir, but they do not achieve the prominence of their reptilian associates. The generally peaceful life of the herdsmen could also occasionally be enlivened by vicious conflicts between bulls within the herd which, not very surprisingly, made a deep impression on the Egyptians so that they are frequently represented in tombs and evidently acquired a religious significance (Lloyd 1978; Galán 1994). Other aspects of their mode of life excited equal interest in the artists, such as milking, impregnation, calving, separation of animals for butchery, and the careful fattening of the animals in stalls for special purposes such as temple and mortuary offerings which required considerable numbers of animals at all periods. Whilst, however, the meat offerings would then be distributed to priests and officers of many different kinds, the meat of cattle would very rarely have featured in the diet of poorer Egyptians.

Pride of place in stock-rearing lies firmly with cattle in Ancient Egypt, but there is ample evidence of other types of animal husbandry that must also have been practised in the main in the same marginal areas away from arable land. Scenes of goats attacking bushes or trees are a common phenomenon in tombs which sometimes show goatherds trying to suppress their activities with sticks (e.g. the tomb of Khunes at Zawiyet el-Maietin). They certainly provided meat, and in that capacity frequently feature as offerings. Their milk, however, was not apparently drunk, but it may have been made into cheese and is known to have been used as a medicament. Representations of herds of pigs appear for the first time in the New Kingdom (e.g. in the tombs of Renni at Elkab and Nebamun in Western Thebes), and in the Late Period a class of dedicated swineherds was a recognized part of Egyptian society, though the animals are known to have been farmed in prehistoric times. Despite the evidence that the pig could be regarded as ritually unclean, large herds are known to have been kept by temples in the New Kingdom, and there is ample archaeological evidence of their use as a source of meat. Another, rather unexpected use of the pig, doubtless ancillary, was their employment to tread seed into the Nile mud after it had been broadcast. Large flocks of sheep were also kept—and they too could be used to tread in seed corn—but their main function seems to have been to provide wool for clothing, despite the fact that wool was regarded as ritually unclean, in some periods at least. There is also plentiful representational evidence that the Egyptians maintained significant numbers of domesticated desert animals such as oryx and gazelles as a further food resource and even went so far as to investigate other rather unlikely alternatives such as hyenas, which are sometimes depicted being force-fed for the table, but oddities of this sort seem to be confined to the earlier periods of Egyptian history.

The Nile also harboured rich stocks of fish and fowl which were intensively exploited at all periods, and tomb iconography provides much information on these activities, particularly in the Old Kingdom. The practitioners of these forms of hunting, like herdsmen, were very much regarded as lying on the margins of civilized society but were very skilful at what they did. Fishing was always a major source of protein in Ancient Egypt, especially for the less wealthy, and it flourished the length and breadth of the river, particularly in the Delta and the Fayyum (Bates 1917; Brewer and Friedman 1989). Some idea of productivity may perhaps be deduced from the fact that in the nineteenth century in conditions not greatly different from those obtaining in Ancient Egypt there were over 6,000 boats employed in freshwater fishing. Fishermen employed a wide range of trapping strategies: those favouring the expertise of a solitary practitioner, such as hook and line and the harpoon, which can often acquire a sporting dimension, and those requiring less finely tuned skills such as the wicker fish trap and a variety of nets, such as cast nets and drag nets. Birds were caught in a variety of nets, including a sophisticated clapnet which is often represented and whose workings clearly fascinated the Egyptian artist who can expend great efforts to convey its operation. These strategies were often assisted by the use of tame birds as decoys, a capacity in which the heron features in a number of cases. Once caught, birds could be kept in pens before consumption, and they were not infrequently force-fed, a process that could make even such birds as cranes more palatable than they otherwise might have been (Lloyd, Spencer, and Ali el-Khouli 2008: 16–18).

Both fishing and fowling could also feature as sporting activities that would yield provisions for the table but were pursued by those with the leisure to do so largely for fun. Scenes in tombs of all periods can depict the owner engaged in these activities, though the artist always has a broader agenda than that of depicting the rich at play, and the scenes have only an intermittent purchase on reality (see p. 276). Much the most enlightening insight into these hunting expeditions is provided by a New Kingdom text describing the pleasures that can accrue from a hunting expedition to the Fayyum:

> A happy day, as we go down to the water-meadow,
> As we snare bi<rds and catch> many <fish> in Two-Waters,
> And the catcher and harpooner come to us,
> As we draw in the net<s full of> fowl;
> We moor our skiff at a thicket,
> And put offerings on the fire
> For Sobek, Lord of the Lake,
> The < . . . of> the Sovereign (l.<p.>h.!)
> My lord! My lord!
> Spend the night in the hide!
> Success will be given to the man who draws the net
> When it is dawn <on the> midmost <isle>.
> The Marsh-goddess has been kind to you;
> Your fishing rods have been kind to you.
> Every water-meadow is green, and you have fed on the countryside,
> If only I were in <the country>—
> <I would do> what my heart desires,
> as when the country was my town,
> when the top of the water-meadow was <my dwelling>;
> no <one could part me from> the people my heart desires and from my friends;
> I would spend the day in the place of <my> longing,
> <in the . . . and> the papyrus clumps.
> When it was dawn, I would have a snack,
> And be far away, walking in the place of my heart.   (trans. Parkinson 1998: 294)

This entire remarkable text is informed by the sophisticated, town-dwelling litterateur's nostalgia for the countryside and the freedom it brings, even ending, it would seem, with an indication of the opportunities it provides for leisurely dreaming, but the practicalities of the operation are not ignored.

The use of nets, fishing rods, and a hide to conceal the hunter are all mentioned, and, though the lord is assisted by experts, he is very much regarded as an active participant, even to the extent of lurking in the hide all night. For all that, the expedition is regarded as needing divine assistance to succeed.

The catalogue of food items available from the Nile is still not exhausted. Amongst the less obvious resources were the three types of lily (lotus) that can be identified in Ancient Egypt. The seeds of the widely available white and blue lily were used to make a very nutritious bread that could be eaten at the highest levels of society, and the rhizomes of these plants were also edible. The latter are known to have been consumed in Pharaonic times, but, unlike the bread, they are not the most desirable of food items and would probably have been confined to the lower classes. The rose lily was not native to Egypt but was certainly there by the mid-fifth century when it is mentioned by the Greek historian Herodotus (2. 92. 4–5). The seeds of this plant also were made into flour for breadmaking, and the root was also eaten. Even the papyrus, which grew in abundance in marshy areas, was a food resource, the lower end of the stem and the rhizomes both being exploited in this way.

ACQUISITION OF RAW MATERIALS

The Egyptians were considerably more fortunate than the contemporaneous populations of ancient Iraq in the geology of their country. The Nile Valley had been created by erosion through large deposits of stone which were often of high quality, and other valuable assets were also accessible in the deserts adjacent to Egypt or further south in the Nubian deserts. Above all, these materials were very close either to the Nile or to the contexts where they were needed. The technological systems developed to exploit these materials were far from sophisticated but were, nevertheless, highly effective and represent a significant achievement in the exploitation of the environment.

The first stage in any such operation involved the extraction of the material itself which might take place by an open-cast process or by mining. In granite quarries it might be necessary to remove a substandard surface layer using a fire to heat the rock and then pouring water on the hot surface to break it up. Once the target had been identified, it was often marked up by a foreman using red ochre, a process that, amongst other things, would assist in allocating workmen to specific sections of the job in hand. Blocks were then separated off by cutting channels across the top, if necessary, and down the back and sides. The tools used in these activities would be chisels of stone or metal, probably mason's picks, levers, or pounders of hard rock such as dolerite. Indeed the pounder was the only possible option when dealing with hard stone such as granite. The block would finally be separated from its base by the same means but apparently without the use of the wedges so beloved of earlier students of Egyptology. An alternative method of isolating and extracting blocks has recently been identified which involved the use of fire (Kelany et al. 2009). Once freed up, the block would not normally be given its finished form in case it were damaged in transit. It would simply be roughed out and then moved to the site for which it was intended, and here human muscle was very much at a premium. As appropriate, the block would be dragged onto a ramp or a roadway specially made up or cleared for the purpose, but there would have been a determined and well-calculated effort in all cases to get it to the nearest point where water transport could be used (see p. 274). In the case of quarries such as Gebel es-Silsila this was easy since the river was immediately adjacent, but in other cases canals might be constructed leading to the river from the quarry area, as seems to have been done in the granite quarries at Aswan. This transportation process is mentioned on several occasions in descriptions of expeditions to the Wadi Hammamat quarries: in the Montuhotep IV text previously discussed (see p. 80) 3,000 men were involved in transporting the lid of the stone sarcophagus from the quarry to Egypt, and the inscription of Regnal Year 38 of Senwosret I tells us that teams ranging from 500 to 2,000 were used to haul the relevant blocks. Representations fill out the picture somewhat: in the colossus representation in the tomb of Djehutyhotep at el-Bersha (see p. 274) 172 men are depicted dragging the colossus on a sledge. On the plinth of the statue stands a workman pouring water before the sledge, presumably as a lubricant which may well have been applied to a thin layer of mud at some stages in the process to make it more viscous (Lauer 1973: 132; Kemp 2000: 93). In attendance there are three workmen described as carrying 'dragging timbers' (*ḫ(w)t n stȝ*) which have sometimes been interpreted as rollers, but it is much more probable that they were used as fillers, where necessary, to even out the surface over which the colossus was being pulled (cf. Clarke and Engelbach 1930: 85). The use of sledges in this context is easily paralleled (Clarke and Engelbach 1930: 88–9; Partridge 1996: 131–7), and slipways of Nile mud reinforced laterally by wooden battens are also known to have been used (Vercoutter 1970: 204ff.). Once it had arrived at its destination, the block would be moved into position by the same means as those used in the quarry and with liberal use of ramps and brick or rubble fillings to circumvent the use of scaffolding, which does not seem to feature as a building device in Pharaonic times, though it is known to have been employed by sculptors in the manufacture of large-scale statues. In all cases where the movement of blocks was at issue there does not seem to have been any use of rollers at any time during the Pharaonic Period (Clarke and Engelbach 1930; Aston, Harrell, and Shaw 2000).

Egypt was also fortunate in its access to significant metal resources. Until well into the first millennium BC Egypt was reliant on access to supplies of copper for the production of copper or bronze tools and weapons. The Eastern Desert adjacent both to Egypt and Nubia contained rich deposits in such contexts as Abu Hamamid, Gebel el-Atawi, Abu Seyal, Umm Semiuki, and the Kuban area, and these were exploited vigorously. However, it is clear that requirements were not met entirely from such sources, and the Egyptians were fortunate in having relatively easy access to deposits in Sinai from at least as early as the First Dynasty (Mumford 2010: 344, 347–8), and we find them going even further afield to Timna in the Negev during the New Kingdom where evidence of tubular shafts can still be seen, equipped with footholds and giving access to the galleries from which the deposits were worked. Once extracted, the ore was reduced to fragments with the use of hammers and grinders and then smelted in furnaces, which by the end of the second millennium were becoming very sophisticated. However, rich though the deposits of the Eastern Desert, Sinai, and the Negev might be, we still find evidence of the Egyptians importing extra copper from abroad from such sources as Cyprus (J. Ogden 2000: 149–61).

The Egyptians also had access in Nubia and the Eastern Desert to rich gold resources that were of two types. Alluvial deposits, known as 'gold of the water', were available in Nubia and were relatively easily exploited by panning. The resultant material could be reduced by pounding, if necessary, and then smelted to produce the precious metal in a fit state for transport. The gold mines in Nubia in such sites as the Saras plain area and the Wadi Allaki or in the Eastern Desert of Egypt, e.g. the Wadi Baramiya and Wadi Hammamat, were a different matter. Here the gold was to be found in quartz rocks which had to be worked either by open-cast methods or by mining underground, though available evidence suggests that this process never involved mines of any depth. Once the ore was extracted it would then be crushed by pounding with stones, which survive in considerable quantity on ancient mining sites, and the crushed material would then be milled and washed before being smelted in crucibles (J. Ogden 2000: 161–6). The annual Nubian gold revenue accruing from these operations to the temple of Amon-re at Thebes in the Eighteenth Dynasty would have been capable of supporting in excess of 7,000 unskilled workmen for a year,[4] and that does not include gold that might have formed part of the tribute paid directly to the king (S. Smith 1995: 166–73). Therefore, this revenue constituted a significant proportion of the state's annual income whose loss at the end of the New Kingdom had severe economic effects.

I have already discussed the use of papyrus as a food substance, but that was only a small part of the potential of this enormously useful plant whose uses

---

[4] Based on the calculations of S. Smith (1995: 168–71) and using the 30:1 ratio of value between *deben* of gold and copper. If we use the 50:1 ratio, which might have been current in the Eighteenth Dynasty, the purchasing power of the gold would have been even greater.

provide a particularly impressive example of the ingenuity with which the Egyptians could exploit available assets (Leach and Tait 2000). Its value as a boat-building material is particularly well known and will be discussed in detail, but it had an extraordinary range of other uses. It could make up for the shortage of timber for building purposes, and there is evidence that some of the earliest religious buildings in Egypt were made entirely of this material, but throughout Pharaonic history many of the lower-class dwellings or shelters in the countryside could be built in whole or in part of papyrus. Making columns to support porches or internal roofing was straightforward since bundles of papyrus could easily be bound together and then fixed vertically in the ground and covered with a mud plaster. It could also be used as a roofing material either on its own or in association with wooden beams. Papyrus was also used in the manufacture of rope, sandals, mats, sails, and even boxes, but of particular importance was its use in the production of paper. In this respect the Egyptians were notably more fortunate than their contemporaries in Iraq who were forced throughout their ancient history to use as their main writing material clay tablets which needed baking in ovens, and indeed, despite its disadvantages, they succeeded in passing this technology on to most of their Near Eastern neighbours. However, whilst clay tablets have a major advantage over papyrus in terms of durability, they can hardly be claimed to be the most convenient of media. Certainly, the use of mud tablets is known in Pharaonic Egypt from the site of Ain Asil in the Dakhla Oasis (Strudwick 2005: 180–1), and for many purposes ostraca consisting of pieces of stone or pottery could be employed, but paper made from the pith of the papyrus was the preferred medium of the scribe who benefited enormously from its ready availability, its lightness, and its ease of storage.

In addition to their exploitation of Nile mud for agricultural purposes the Egyptians also developed a technology that enabled them to use it as a building material (Kemp 2000). Their technique of making sun-dried brick from Nile mud evolved in prehistoric times and could hardly have been simpler. First, the mud was dug out and mixed with water and chaff to act as a binding material. This compound was then kneaded by foot and the resulting mixture poured into rectangular forms set on the ground to give the bricks the requisite shape before being removed. The bricks were then left to harden up in the burning Egyptian sun to produce a building material ideally suited to the climatic conditions of the country and, therefore, used for the vast majority of building purposes from tombs to temples right down into modern times. Indeed, the process still takes place in rural areas of Egypt, despite the fact that it is illegal. For domestic housing the material was ideal, being cheap, easily available, and capable of creating houses that are warm in winter and cool in summer.

THE INSTITUTIONAL INFRASTRUCTURE FOR PRODUCTION AND DISTRIBUTION

How was all this economic activity organized? There has been much talk of Pharaonic Egypt as an example of a society that ran a storage-and-redistribution economic system focused on the palace. There is an element of truth in this, but such a model runs the risk of greatly oversimplifying the way economic activity unfolded on the ground. Whilst it is true that the palace was the major hub in a storage-and-redistribution network that covered all areas over which Egypt exercised control, it was far from being the only economic driver or even the only type of resource-generating mechanism to be found. We should rather think of the country at all periods as containing a patchwork of economic systems, sometimes large, sometimes small, but, wherever we look, it is evident that the systems are normally based on the model of a largely self-contained household economy (Eyre 1999, 2010: 304–6). Sometimes the household is a small, family-orientated and family-maintained unit; elsewhere we may be faced with much larger institutions that could take a variety of forms: estates run by the crown, used as payment for office or held in private hands; mortuary endowments, both royal and private; temple estates that become increasingly important, above all from the New Kingdom onwards; and finally the palace itself. I shall discuss the material bottom-up.

In the *Tale of the Two Brothers*, a fictional narrative dating to the New Kingdom, we are presented with a most vivid picture of agricultural life at the most basic level:

There were once two brothers . . . Anubis was the name of the elder, and Bata the name of the younger. As for Anubis, he had a house and a wife whilst his young brother was with him as though he were a son, it being he who made clothes for him, and he went behind his cattle to the fields. He it was who did the ploughing, and he it was who harvested for him, and he it was who did for him all the business in the fields . . . Now when many days had passed, his younger brother <looked after> his cattle according to his daily routine. And he [returned] to his house every evening, laden with all the plants of the field, with milk, with wood, and with every <good thing> of the countryside . . . Then he drank and ate and he <went to sleep in?> his stable amongst his cattle. Now when day dawned . . . he [i.e. the elder brother] gave him bread for the fields, and he drove his cattle to let them eat in the fields . . . Now at ploughing time his <elder> brother said to him: 'Get a team <of oxen> ready for us for ploughing; for the land has emerged [from the inundation] and is ready for ploughing. Also, you shall come to the field with seed; for we shall start ploughing tomorrow.'   (1, 1–2, 4)

Here the narrative is focused firmly at the household level because the narrative dynamic requires that. We can see very clearly the way in which a mixed-agriculture farm of the New Kingdom operated, and there can be little doubt that this picture held true for much of Egyptian history. Whether we are to regard Anubis as an independent farmer or as a share-cropper of some kind does not emerge, but there is no indication of control from above, and he seems to go his own way and make his own choices. A similar picture of independence of action emerges in the Middle Kingdom tale of the *Eloquent Peasant* where the peasant is presented as an independent decision-maker confronted with a problem of economic supply which he set about solving on a commercial basis using his own initiative without consulting any higher authority, and this picture of independence is subsequently carried through the entire narrative (Parkinson 1998: 58).

The early Twelfth Dynasty contracts of Hapydjefa present us with another form of land usage in which the nomarch hands out parcels of land as payment for services to rather lowly functionaries, e.g. an 'Overseer of Stone-masons', for whom farming would have been only part of their economic activity and who either worked it themselves, if they had time, or leased it out, probably on a share-cropping basis (Reisner 1918; Sethe 1928: 92–6). The rights to such land would not belong to specific individuals but lay with the office-holder and would pass, in due course, to anyone who discharged that office or even back to the original donor, depending on the circumstances prevailing at the time. From the same period the Hekanakhte Papers provide a wealth of information on the way in which a middle-ranking official organized his agricultural activities (Allen 2002). This body of documentation is by no means consistently clear because it is a set of administrative documents related to contexts with which all involved were familiar, and no one felt obliged to provide the explanatory material required by the modern reader, but the picture that emerges is of an Egyptian official who enjoyed the benefits both of an inherited estate and a perpetual endowment in his capacity as a mortuary priest and, in addition, leased land when circumstances required—indeed, at times he may even have leased out portions of his own land. The land holdings involved did not form a contiguous estate but were located in different parts of the country, the mortuary estate lying in the Thinite Nome, a considerable distance from Hekanakhte's base in the northern part of the country. On his personal property he grew barley, emmer, and flax (some of which was made into linen on the estate), and he also ran thirty-five head of cattle. Overall, the most impressive aspect of the documentation is the picture it gives of the initiative and flexibility in the owner's managerial approach to dealing with the land that, in the conditions created by essentially unpredictable inundations, required not only constant vigilance but also an ability to adapt to circumstances and ring the changes on what was grown and where, combined, at times, with a goodly allotment of strong nerves when making guesses, however well informed by experience, as to what the Nile's behaviour would require at any one time.

Finally, we move to the topmost stratum of Egyptian society. The earliest textual material to give information on the subject is that from the early

Fourth Dynasty tomb of Metjen (Gödecken 1976; Strudwick 2005: 192–4). Linguistic problems make it difficult to be sure of its detailed interpretation at many points, but it is possible to extract some information with confidence. In the first place, whilst we cannot assume that all land at this stage was under royal control, it is clear that there was a wide-ranging royal prerogative to allocate land by decree that embraced the entire kingdom, and it emerges that the crown was highly proactive in this respect. The existence of a central 'Office of Provisions' (*st-df3*) bears witness to the control of the palace in the distribution of wealth, and it is also evident that the crown had an interest in linen production, though whether this took the form of large-scale manufacture in the palace itself or that of a more generalized organizational function remains an open question. The mention of payment for land would suggest that something approaching private property might have existed (cf. Eyre 1997: 377), but the relevant passage in the text need not mean outright purchase and would be compatible with a system of renting land. We also hear of a group of individuals, apparently numerous, who are called 'king's men' (*nswtyw*) whose name obviously implies a close relationship with the palace. They appear to be people of some consequence since they not only enjoyed a right to use land but also the right of transfer. Whatever the precise status of a piece of real estate, the Metjen texts reveal a number of institutions through which agricultural activity might be organized. Whatever their nature, however, it is evident that agricultural units were frequently regarded not simply as land per se but also included the agricultural workers and 'small cattle' (*'wt*), a term which was meant to exclude the larger bovids. At the lowest level in the hierarchy of units stood the individual household where the titles to land could be various. At the next level we encounter villages or towns, which are covered by the term *niwt*. We also hear of 'estates' (*ḥwt*, sometimes *ḥwt '3(w)t*, 'great estates') which might contain a number of *niwt*, and these entities became a standard feature of Old Kingdom tomb iconography in which scenes frequently occur representing the owner's estates and towns bringing offerings to the deceased and also of the owner watching agricultural activities in his 'towns'.[5] A particularly interesting phenomenon is the 'foundations' (*grg(w)t*), which appear to have been a means by which the crown encouraged agricultural expansion and exploitation in certain areas, a process sometimes described in modern literature as 'colonization'. How far 'towns', 'estates', or 'foundations' were owned by the officials in question, held as units to administer on behalf of the crown, or simply allocated as 'salary' by the crown for services rendered cannot be determined. Finally, it should be noted that a mortuary installation of King Huni features in the text as an economic agent engaged in agricultural activity.

---

[5] Moreno García (1999: 76–88) rightly emphasizes that such representations should not be treated as historically accurate documents.

Some of the institutions occurring in the Metjen texts are encountered in later Old Kingdom contexts. In the Sixth Dynasty inscription of Weni we find that *ḥwt* and *niwt* are specifically mentioned as administrative units of major importance, and the phrase 'New Towns', which occurs from the Fifth Dynasty onwards, immediately recalls the *grg(w)t*-foundations of Metjen, probably serving a similar function as bases for the promotion of the crown's development of agricultural potential. The late Sixth Dynasty inscription of Harkhuf also mentions the *pr-šnꜥ*, 'storage and processing installation'. Organizations bearing this name occur frequently in Egyptian texts, but in this case it looks like a royal institution with overarching authority which should probably be regarded as a key driver in the network established by the crown to guarantee efficient economic exploitation of the country (see p. 160).

As already emerges in the Metjen texts, royal mortuary endowments set up to provide the economic basis for royal mortuary cults were important centres of Old Kingdom agricultural activity. The Dahshur decrees issued on behalf of the two pyramid towns of Snofru by Pepi I are invaluable in filling out the picture of their workings (*Urk.* i. 209–13; Strudwick 2005: 103–5), confirming that they had their own land and that a significant element in running it was a group of officials called *ḥntyw-š*. These men, who feature very prominently in the inscriptions on Old Kingdom cemeteries, were royal servants operating both during the life of the king and after his death who received land-holdings on the pyramid estate as their payment. The importance of these agricultural activities is revealed by the emphasis in one of the decrees on canals, pools, wells, sluices, and trees. Cattle are also an issue, and the importance of royal warrants in running the estates is also clear.

At a lower level, but in the same order of things, we find that non-royal mortuary endowments also functioned as a device for generating and managing economic resources during the Old and Middle Kingdoms. Like their royal counterparts they were intended to ensure support for the mortuary priest or priests charged with performing the rituals of maintenance for the dead in their mortuary chapels, but they would also provide a living to the agricultural workers who formed part of the endowment. The fullest record of the working of such an endowment is that contained in the Twelfth Dynasty contracts of Hapydjefa preserved in his tomb at Asyut (see p. 163). After indicating the function of the mortuary priest as the trustee of the endowment who was charged with guaranteeing that the provisions of the contracts were fulfilled, Hapydjefa defines the nature of the mortuary estate and the terms of its use in remarkably sophisticated terms:

Behold, I have endowed you with fields, people, cattle, gardens and everything like every official of Siut in order that you may carry out rituals for me with a beneficial heart. You shall stand up for all my arrangements which I have placed under your authority. Behold, it is before you in writing. These things shall pass to one of your sons whom you desire who shall carry out for me the office of mortuary priest from amongst your sons as a beneficiary without any right of alienation, without allowing him to divide it up to his children in accordance with this commandment which I have made to you.   (Sethe 1928: 92)

Clearly, the endowment was set up as a legal entity in its own right with tightly controlled conditions which included the provision that it was to remain intact in perpetuity. Evidently, however, if such endowments continued to be set up generation after generation, a large part, if not all, of the ancestral estate would be used up to sustain them to the serious economic detriment of the governor himself, and that problem, in itself, would have guaranteed that perpetual endowments were anything but perpetual. It should be noted that there is no mention anywhere of the need for a royal affidavit ratifying the arrangements, and Hapydjefa is depicted as acting as a free agent able to make dispositions as he thought fit.

Not the least of the merits of this fascinating body of texts is the fact that it allows us a brief glimpse into the land-holding system that prevailed amongst nomarchs during the early Twelfth Dynasty, in Middle Egypt at least. It is evident that Hapydjefa had access to two types of holdings: the 'Ancestral Estate' (*pr it.f*) and 'the Estate of the Count'(*pr-ḥȝt(y)-ˁ*) which had a 'storage and processing installation' (*šnˁ(w)*) empowered to receive taxes and other dues, including temple offerings in kind.[6] The 'Estate of the Count' was held by the tenant of the office of nomarch who enjoyed the usufruct of it but not the right of disposition. As such, it functioned as a 'salary' to reimburse the holder of the office in question, though the contracts reveal that Hapydjefa, quite illegally, tried to use some of the income as part of his mortuary endowment. The 'Ancestral Estate' was a very different matter in that it belonged to the individual nomarch as his personal property, and he had the right of unimpeded disposition. This situation is far from unparalleled. Even in the Old Kingdom, despite all the evidence for pervasive royal control, we find indications of high-ranking officials making disposition of land without any reference to other authorities. In the Fifth Dynasty tomb chapel of Nykaankh in the Tehna mountain (Middle Egypt) the tomb-owner features setting up a mortuary endowment as though he owned the land on which it was based, and there is no mention of any need for a royal warrant (*Urk*. i. 161–3: Strudwick 2005: 195–9). The text also states that the beneficiaries of the endowment are to act 'under the authority of my eldest son, just as they do for their personal property', a statement that reinforces the suspicion that de facto personal property was a known phenomenon at the time. Similarly, in the Middle Kingdom we find Montjuwosru, a steward of Senwosret I,

---

[6] I assume that the term *pr-ḏt* which is also used as the counterpart to *pr-ḥȝt(y)-ˁ* refers to this entity.

enthusiastically cataloguing his wealth which he claims consisted of cattle, small cattle, donkeys, sheep, barley, emmer wheat, textiles, ships, and vineyards, and the wording of the context strongly suggests that he regarded all this as his personal wealth (Sethe 1928: 79–80; Lichtheim 1988: 104–5).

All this, of course, raises the question of how exactly such de facto private land holdings came into existence in the first place. One possible explanation would be that some estates had originally been tied to particular offices but that such links had simply dissolved through the passage of time and had not been reasserted by the crown. In other cases it may well be that gifts like those made to Metjen became, for practical purposes, estates of the family and passed unimpeded from one generation to another. That is certainly the situation that emerges in the Nineteenth Dynasty Inscription of Mose (Mes) in his tomb at Saqqara where we are informed that an estate was given as a reward to a ship's captain called Neshi by King Ahmose at the beginning of the Eighteenth Dynasty and then passed by inheritance through about ten generations (Gardiner 1905). Whilst it emerges explicitly in the text that there was a central government record of ownership of the land, there is no question in the documentation of the crown's having retained even a residual claim over it. The Edfu Donation Text and the Hauswalt Papyri of the Ptolemaic Period present a similar picture (Manning 2007a: 74–83). The Donation Text reveals that the temple of Horus the Behdetite at Edfu owned land in four contiguous nomes, though the bulk inevitably lay in the Edfu Nome. The text refers both to temple land and royal land, but it is absolutely clear that such land was not closely controlled by either the palace or the temple; rather this terminology serves to indicate the institution that had the right to any payments or services from the tenants whenever these fell due. The land-holders who farmed the land clearly had a right of disposition which would usually have taken the form of automatic inheritance by members of the family in what Manning well describes as 'a largely informal, family based land-tenure regime', but other forms of disposition such as sale, marriage contract, or will were all possible. In a situation like this we may not have absolute ownership in the modern sense because dues were required, but the freedom to dispose of land in so many different ways without there being any indication of a requirement to inform or gain the approval of the titular head entirely justifies us in describing the status of the tenants as that of 'virtual' owners. It is suspected by many scholars that such ownership was much more widespread in Ancient Egypt than we have been inclined to recognize, and we should also bear in mind that, with the passage of time, it is perfectly possible that even the titular ownership of a temple or the crown may have fallen into abeyance and been forgotten, and in such situations private ownership in the fullest sense could have arisen. I have a very strong suspicion that this was not a rare phenomenon.

Temples could also function as economic agents and became increasingly important in this capacity. The late Old Kingdom inscription Coptos G, for all its difficulties, shows the crown allocating land to the temple of Min with considerable care (*Urk.* i. 293–5; Strudwick 2005: 114–15), and other decrees from the same corpus leave us in no doubt of the temple's role as an economic agent. Information on the workings of the temple of Wepwawet at Siut shows the same dimension, but the composition of the temple staff does not suggest that this was a large part of its activities. The temple had the services of an 'Overseer of the Store' which received, amongst other things, quantities of charcoal, a highly valuable commodity in the timber-poor conditions of Egypt, and there is an interesting distinction between the 'Scribe of the Temple' and the 'Scribe of the Altar' which is best explained by regarding the former as the temple administrator and the latter as the member of staff responsible for recording offerings and ensuring that they reverted in due course and quickly to anyone entitled to a percentage, but we get no sense from the surviving documentation that the temple was a big player in economic terms. The New Kingdom is a different matter altogether. The abundant evidence from this period provides a much fuller picture of the role of temples in generating, storing, and dispensing resources, though the written material is often damaged and locally focused and frequently not as easy to interpret as we should like.

It has been calculated that the temples of Egypt owned, or had the use of, at least one-third of the land of Egypt in the early Twentieth Dynasty. The *Great Harris Papyrus* dating to the end of the reign of Ramesses III and the beginning of that of Ramesses IV describes benefactions made by Ramesses III to the temples of Egypt, particularly to the three major state deities Amon-re of Thebes, Ptah of Memphis, and Re of Heliopolis (Grandet 1994). For our purposes it makes no difference whether these donations were all the work of Ramesses himself or in some, perhaps many, cases simply a confirmation of what had been allocated by previous rulers. It is the end result described in the text that matters. The following extract from the benefactions to Ramesses III's mortuary temple at Medinet Habu (which functioned as an appendage of the great temple of Amon-re at Karnak) is typical:

I filled its treasury with the products of the lands of Egypt: gold, silver, and every costly stone by the hundred-thousand. Its granaries overflowed with barley and corn, and, as for its fields and its herds, their numbers were like the sands of the shore. I taxed Upper Egypt for it as well as Lower Egypt, and Nubia and Djahi <came> to it bearing their dues, it being filled with captives, which you gave to me from the Nine Bows, and with conscripts which I trained by the ten-thousand ... I multiplied the divine offerings presented before you consisting of bread, wine, beer, fat geese, young oxen, short-horned cattle, bulls in large numbers, oryxes, and gazelles which were offered in his [i.e. the god's] slaughter house.   (4. 3–8)

The detailed information in this and parallel sections of the papyrus demonstrates that the resources donated in perpetuity by the crown made the temples into institutions with a far-reaching role as generators of resource in their own right: through the lands they possessed in great quantity in various parts of the country they produced grain, garden produce, wine, and olives; they enjoyed the benefits of large herds of livestock and owned fattening stalls for cattle; they had workshops producing goods for the temple and other users, as is well illustrated in the paintings in the tomb of the Eighteenth Dynasty vizier Rekhmire in Western Thebes; there were huntsmen to acquire oryxes from the desert, a classic offering, as well as specialist farmers such as bee-keepers; and they possessed their own shipping to transport resources to the temples, both from Egypt and abroad. In addition to generating resources directly the temples were also recipients of income on a massive scale in the form of benefactions, taxes, and offerings from many sources, including towns that were specifically allocated to them for this purpose. All this economic activity meant that there was a constant stream of produce, commodities, and raw materials flowing into temple institutions which required the establishment of massive storage installations where the material could be 'banked' and which are variously described as granaries, storehouses, and treasuries, the scale of which is spectacularly illustrated by the huge and well-preserved storage area at the Ramesseum in Western Thebes. The resources accumulated in this way would be partly consumed by the huge staff needed to service temple ritual, and within this context it should always be borne in mind that the offerings made in the daily rituals and also in great public festivals were not a wasted asset but were distributed to those entitled to share in the 'reversion of offerings' (*wdb-ḥt*) as part of their income which might either be stored, consumed, or used up by the direct recipients or employed by them as a means of purchasing services or resources from third parties. A further expenditure met from these massive 'banks' was defraying the costs of running the temple estates in all their aspects, and they were also used to provide means to maintain and expand temple buildings or build completely new sanctuaries.

Whilst the *Great Harris Papyrus* provides a very detailed picture of the composition of the temple estates in question, it is rather less fulsome on the administrative infrastructure for running them. At the top of the structure it mentions 'officials' (*srw*), high priests, stewards, and a general, and these worked through lower-ranking personnel such as scribes, overseers, inspectors (*rwdw*), and deputies (*idnw*) who would monitor and direct the activities of production workers such as shepherds, conscript labourers, prisoners of war, and slaves. Although it is not mentioned in this text, we know that it was also possible at this period for land to be worked by convicted criminals. It is evident that, with the weakening of the authority of the crown both within Egypt and without, it became increasingly necessary for temples and temple officials to become much more proactive in their economic activities. This emerges with particular clarity in the *The Story of Wenamun* written at the end of the Twentieth Dynasty. Although this is a work of fiction (see p. 250), the context in which the action unfolds must be modelled on the way in which things were done at the time of its composition. It describes an expedition on which Wenamun, an 'Elder of the Portal' of the temple of Amon-re at Thebes, was sent by the temple to obtain timber from the Lebanon for the great barque of Amon-re called *Amon-user-hat*. He was supplied with a significant quantity of highly valuable trade goods to exchange for this wood, but, although royal figures are mentioned in the text, essentially Wenamun is depicted as acting on behalf of the temple as an independent entity without the royal figures in any way acting as initiators; they are facilitators only. Pharaoh's power has mightily declined since the glory days described in the *Great Harris Papyrus*!

The *Wilbour Papyrus* fills out considerably the detail of the organizational structure of these temples (Gardiner 1941–8; Katary 1989). This document, dating to Regnal Year 4 of Ramesses V and, therefore, only a little later than the *Harris Papyrus*, covers a stretch of land in Middle Egypt about 140 km in length and deals with the administration of about 2,800 plots of land in that area in which a large number of temples are mentioned as landowners. It is particularly revealing on the personnel responsible for individual plots, mentioning various categories of priest, stewards, deputies (some of them military), scribes, a stable master, soldiers, and even women. Many of the small-holders seem to have operated as virtual landowners and would not necessarily have farmed the land themselves but could have leased it out to be cultivated by agricultural workers who are defined as 'field-workers, cultivators' (*iḥwtyw*).

The palace itself functioned as a major economic hub, both receiving and dispensing resources. It is clear that crown land existed from an early period in great quantity all over the country, and these lands could be exploited either directly by the palace itself or, much more frequently, through intermediaries who would channel the benefits to the palace, as appropriate, and this income was further enhanced by tax revenues. The palace was liberally supplied with storage facilities, workshops, and processing installations to service these economic activities and ensure that all its requirements were met in full (see p. 139). However, evidence of indirect exploitation of crown real estate is plentiful, revealing that the favoured policy of the palace was to delegate the task of cultivation. Whenever it was in a position of strength, it maintained and exercised a very wide-ranging right of disposition of land throughout the country, and large quantities of real estate were frequently handed over by the king as gifts, rewards, or remuneration for services rendered. The extent to which such territories remained ultimately royal property held on lease by a tenant remains an open question and probably varied from one period to another. In the New Kingdom, as already indicated, huge quantities of land were handed over to the temples which then became the agents of the king in its economic exploitation to create what has been aptly described as the 'essential unity of Temple and Crown' (Katary 1989: 183), but the *Wilbour Papyrus* speaks of secular royal land holdings such as 'Landing-Places of Pharaoh', 'Fields of Pharaoh', 'Treasuries of Pharaoh', Harîm and Queens' installations, *mint*-land, and *ḥȝ-tȝ* land, all of which are clearly crown lands administered by agents but farmed by cultivators (*iḥwtyw*) who paid surprisingly low rents and exercised a high degree of independence. This situation also appears in the Edfu Donation Text previously discussed (Katary 1989: 4).

The most visible examples of the direct involvement of the palace in economic activities are the expeditions which it sent outside Egypt to access high-prestige items and raw materials for elite consumption, and we are fortunate in possessing some very revealing texts describing such enterprises. The Palermo Stone's records for the Old Kingdom mention the proceeds of expeditions to the Lebanon (pine and cedar), Sinai (probably copper), and Punt (myrrh, electrum, malachite, and possibly unguent) (*Urk.* i. 236, 246; Strudwick 2005: 66, 72), but by far the best-documented royal venture of this kind is the great maritime expedition sent to Punt by Hatshepsut which brought back plants, myrrh in the form of gum and trees, ebony, ivory, gold, spices, frankincense, baboons, long-tailed monkeys, and serfs (*Urk.* iv. 328; Desroches Noblecourt 2002: 191–238; Fabre 2005). Information on royal activities in mines and quarries is voluminous since it was standard practice to leave inscriptional records of their work which sometimes provide considerable detail on the organization of the expeditions. An Eleventh Dynasty inscription in the Wadi Hammamat dating to the second year of Montuhotep IV informs us that the initial expeditionary force sent into the wadi to obtain greywacke for the king's sarcophagus was 10,000 strong and under the direction of no less a person than Amenemhet, the vizier himself. These workmen were all drawn from areas located within striking distance of the entrance to the wadi, but subsequently another force of 3,000 men, this time from Lower Egypt, was brought in to drag the stone destined for the lid of the sarcophagus to the river. It says much for the speed with which the quarrymen could work that they were able to extract this particular stone in twelve days (De Buck 1970: 74–5; Lichtheim 1975: 113–15).

The composition and the overall organization of the expedition are described in some detail in the vizier's own typically idealized and self-glorificatory text in these terms:

His Majesty commanded that I should come forth to this august desert land, an expeditionary force being with me [consisting of] men from the choice of the entire land, stone masons, craftsmen, quarrymen, sculptors, scribes of forms, metal-workers, callers, gold-workers, seal-bearers of the Great House, every seal office of the Treasury and every office of the royal house being united behind me. As a river did I make the desert land, and its upper wadis as a road of water. I brought for him an eternal memorial [consisting of] a lord of life which would endure for eternity. Never had its like gone down from this desert since the time of the god. Without loss to it did the expeditionary force go down. No man perished. No contingent turned back. Not a donkey died.   (De Buck 1970: 76)

The staff list is intriguing. It mentions the technical experts responsible for extracting and preparing the stone for transport (stonemasons, craftsmen, quarrymen) and to ensure that the metal tools used were in good order, gold workers to carry out the ancillary function of the expedition by exploiting the Wadi Hammamat gold mines, sculptors and scribes of forms to create the epigraphic record on site, and administrators, particularly treasury officials. However, the list makes no explicit mention of the large force of men who would provide the muscle to move the stone, once it had been excavated, only obliquely referring to their involvement through the mention of the 'callers' (*mdw*) whose function it was through chants and other forms of instruction to control the pulling action of large forces of labour engaged in dragging large blocks of material to the Nile. To the vizier only the higher-profile members of his team are worth mentioning! During the next dynasty we get considerably more detail on staffing in the account of the great expedition of Regnal Year 38 of Senwosret I to the same area. This boasted a total establishment well in excess of 18,000 men, including a labour force of 17,000, and many different categories of staff are mentioned. There is agreement with the Amenemhet text in mentioning administrative officers, stone-cutters, and sailors, but a conspicuous difference occurs in the mentioning of the commissariat staff (fishermen, sandal-makers (we hear of resinated sandals), brewers, and bakers),[7] soldiers (to protect against marauding Bedouin and perhaps to deal with any internal disorder that might arise), and pathfinders with local knowledge. This time the human muscle is recognized when the text speaks of the individual stones being dragged by teams varying from 500 to as much as 2,000 men (Goyon 1957: 17–19).

One of the major problems in running such expeditions was the problem of water supply. In the case of the Montuhotep IV and Amenemhet texts there is much emphasis on success in dealing with this problem which was solved, at least partially, by the discovery of a well that was allegedly completely unknown. The importance of wells is also mentioned in the expedition of Henenu conducted during the reign of Montuhotep III, but he also provided waterskins with two jugs of water per day, presumably as a contingency in case supplies were not forthcoming (Couyat and Montet 1912: 114). Such a disastrous eventuality could occur, as is conspicuously stated in the Redesiya

---

[7] The role of the fishermen in this context is puzzling. Perhaps the answer is that expanses of fish-bearing water were still extant in the area. Alternatively, the fishermen may only have been operational when the expedition was close to Nile on the way into and out of the desert.

Inscription of Sety I and the Kuban Inscription of Ramesses II, both referring to the Eastern Desert.

The great Hammamat Inscription of Regnal 3 of Ramesses IV paints an even fuller picture of the organization of an expedition, but one which, in its essentials, reflects the same conditions as earlier texts (*KRI* vi. 12–14; Peden 1994*b*: 86–90). As usual, the operation is stated to have been set up by the king himself. It fell into two phases: first, an exploration was conducted by two scribes and the high priest of Min at Coptos to identify suitable stone for the mortuary service, presumably of the king himself; secondly a large-scale expedition was sent out consisting of over 9,000 men under the leadership of the High Priest of Amun. The team that was taken fell into six groups: high-level administrators, both civil and military; a large military contingent, which was presumably there both for protection and to participate in the work; a group of quarrymen and stonemasons, which is surprisingly small but must reflect the fact that experts in the relevant fields were simply not needed in large quantity; draughtsmen and sculptors to produce the epigraphic record of the expedition; members of a supply train that brought provisions in carts from Egypt; and finally priests supplied with offerings from Thebes whose function was to perform rituals to thank and appease the deities of the quarry area without whose good will failure was guaranteed. The last element is given particular prominence in this text, possibly because at this period the issue had assumed a particular importance, but it is simply a logical extension of the attitudes and activities described in the Hammamat inscriptions of Montuhotep IV.

THE COMMUNICATION NETWORK

The physical configuration of the Nile Valley meant that the Nile was the only major highway running through the valley from Aswan to the apex of the Delta. At that point the river divided into branches which flowed through the Delta to the sea, varying considerably in number from one period to another, though currently only two exist. This hydrographic profile, in association with man-made canals, created relatively easy access by water to all parts of the country and provided the network of communication channels that was essential for the effective working of an economic system dependent on the easy transport of goods and produce to and from the many storage and distribution centres located throughout the country (Partridge 1996, 2010; Eyre 2010: 292).

The ability to exploit this network was dependent on the development of satisfactory shipping, and this is something at which the Ancient Egyptians excelled. In most societies, until relatively recently, the ship has been the most elaborate tool available and can be taken as the yardstick of the skill with which that society has come to terms with its physical environment. The entire history of Pharaonic shipbuilding strikingly illustrates the extreme skill of the Egyptians in exploiting the resources of their environment and circumventing its deficiencies. The major problem they had to confront was the shortage of good shipbuilding timber within Egypt itself, native species such as acacia and tamarisk being incapable of yielding lengthy planks for this purpose. One solution, which was inexpensive and widely adopted, was to avoid the use of timber altogether and exploit the possibilities of something the Egyptians had available in great quantity along the margins of the cultivation and in marshy areas throughout the country, i.e. papyrus, a plant of the sedge family, which could easily be used for the construction of viable rafts and boats and was certainly employed for that purpose from prehistoric times onwards. The technique involved constructing a raft by making several bundles of papyrus and binding them tightly together with ropes that could themselves consist of papyrus (Fig. 6.2). The upper surface of the raft could be covered with a bottom board of timber to provide a robust platform, but that would have been difficult to obtain for many Egyptians and was by no means obligatory. Rafts constructed in this way would eventually become waterlogged and start to sink, but it was a simple matter to propel the vessel to a neighbouring clump of papyrus and repair it by making and tying on extra bundles. Not surprisingly, rafts of this type were a standard mode of water transport for fishermen, bird-catchers, or sportsmen throughout Egyptian history, though we should, perhaps, be a little cautious in taking too literally the representations of elite Egyptians using such rafts for hunting purposes in the marshes (see p. 276). They could, however, be made more complicated; for it is clear from terracotta and stone models of Naqada I and II date that rafts could be turned into more boat-like structures by using bundles of papyrus to build up the sides and create a hollow interior for accommodating cargo and passengers. Whether simple or elaborate, the propulsion of these rafts was achieved by the use of punting poles or paddles.

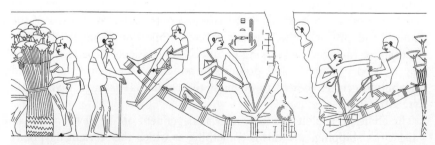

Fig. 6.2. Making a papyrus raft. After Blackman 1915: pl. IV.

Even in prehistoric times the Egyptians had moved on to the construction of plank boats, though such vessels consistently display the influence of the tradition of papyrus-raft building in the overall shape of the hull throughout Egyptian history. We are fortunate that a number of these vessels have survived in a good state of preservation, the oldest being the fourteen plank boats discovered adjacent to the mortuary enclosure of Khasekhemwy (Shunet ez-Zebib) at Abydos which probably date to the later First Dynasty. They measure, on average, 18–19 m in length, and the only example to be partially excavated at the time of writing is constructed of thick planks bound together by leather straps passing through mortises. They could have held about thirty oarsmen, but their draft was so shallow that the freeboard would have been very limited (O'Connor 2009: 185–94). There is ample evidence from later sources on the way in which plank boats were constructed without the benefit of long planks of timber. As is well illustrated by representations such as that of a fishing-boat from the tomb of Ipuy at Thebes (probably Twentieth Dynasty) (Fig. 6.3) the Egyptians developed a system whereby short planks were fitted together, joined end-to-end and edge-to-edge, to create an appearance that Herodotus (2. 96. 1) aptly describes as resembling brickwork. The boat discovered next to the pyramid of Khufu illustrates how that was done (Fig. 6.4). This large vessel (length 43.4 m; beam 5.9 m) has a shell-built hull made up of short planks of cedar joined end-to-end and fitted edge-to-edge by means of mortise-and-tenon joints and a system of rope bindings.[8] The joins are sealed off by battens kept in place by the rope binding. Twelve passive

Fig. 6.3. Tomb of Ipuy. Scene showing the brick-like style used in building wooden boats. Facsimile of a scene in his tomb at Thebes, Paris, Collège de France.

---

[8] Later European shipbuilders built up wooden ships from a skeleton consisting of a keel and ribs around which the planking was subsequently wrapped. The Egyptian method is the exact opposite. Since the Khufu boat is made of cedar, it would have been possible for the shipwrights to use long planks, but they worked to their traditional model and reduced the timber to the standard short planks!

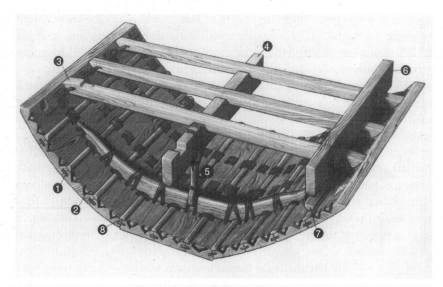

Fig. 6.4. The structure of the hull of the Khufu boat: 1. Mortise and tenon system joining planks; 2. Slots for rope bindings; 3. Cross thwarts; 4. Hogging beam; 5. Stanchions supporting the hogging beam and lashed to a passive frame; 6. Side shelf; 7. Lower shelf; 8. Battens sealing joints in planks. After Landström 1970: 29.

frames were then inserted and bound in place to assist in maintaining the shape of the hull, and in the centre of the hull vertical fixtures were inserted to support a hogging-beam running the length of the vessel. At right angles to the beam cross-thwarts are fixed and secured by means of ropes, and these, in turn, support the deck planking. If the hulls of such vessels needed to be strengthened either to carry unusually heavy loads or to face the rigours of maritime sailing, this could be done by the addition of rope truss girdles running round the hull and by the addition of a hogging truss as indicated in the ships depicted in the mortuary complex of Sahure at Abusir (Fig. 6.5). Propulsion could be achieved by using sails, oars, paddles, a towing-agent (human or another vessel), or the current of the river.[9] Sail technology provides yet another example of the Egyptians' ingenuity in making the most of their environmental resources. They could certainly be made of linen (Vogelsang-Eastwood 2000: 292), but this was the expensive option, and a much cheaper alternative, certainly widely employed, was to make them out of papyrus matting (Herodotus 2. 96. 2; Lloyd 1976: 38).

Ships constructed on these principles were more than capable of meeting Egyptian requirements. Vessels carrying general cargo are frequently depicted

---

[9] If the current were exploited, the sailors would have to ensure that the vessel moved faster than the current; otherwise it would have no steerage way. For an intriguing description of one way in which this could be done see Herodotus 2. 96. 3–5 with Lloyd 1976: 389–90.

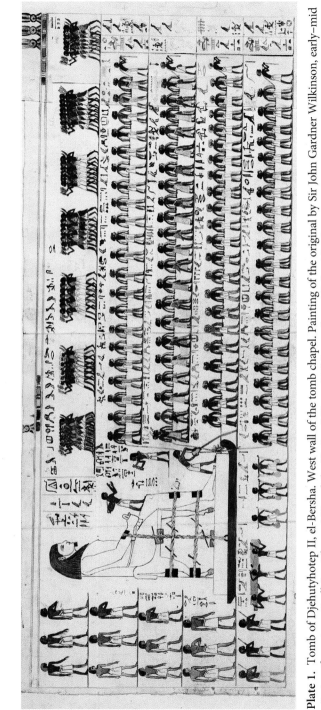

Plate 1. Tomb of Djehutyhotep II, el-Bersha. West wall of the tomb chapel. Painting of the original by Sir John Gardner Wilkinson, early–mid nineteenth century. Bodleian Library MS and the National Trust. Wilkinson dep.a.17, fos. 12–13.

Plate 2a. Tomb of Paheri, Elkab. West wall of the chapel, south end.

Plate 2b. Tomb of Paheri, Elkab. West wall of the chapel, north end.

Plate 3a. Nebamun hunting in the marshes, from the tomb of Nebamun, Western Thebes.

Plate 3b. Banquet scene from the tomb of Nebamun, Western Thebes.

Plate 4. Tomb of Sennedjem, Deir el-Medina. East wall.

Fig. 6.5. A seagoing ship represented in the mortuary complex of Sahure. The cable hogging truss runs around the prow and then along the centre-line of the ship, supported on stanchions, and around the stern. Tension on the cable was achieved by inserting a Spanish windlass (stick) through the cable and turning until the requisite stiffness was achieved. The windlass was then lashed to the mast to stop it unwinding. After Vinson 1994: 13.

(Landström 1970: 60–2, 134–9), and from the Old Kingdom onwards large items such as columns for temples or sarcophagi commonly feature. The transport of two granite obelisks from Aswan to Karnak in the reign of Hatshepsut is a spectacular example of what could be achieved. This activity is represented in her mortuary temple at Deir el-Bahri, and, although there are problems in the interpretation of these scenes, particularly in establishing which obelisks were involved, we are indisputably confronted with a colossal achievement. If we assume that the obelisks in question are the smaller of the two possible groups, each measured 29.5 m and weighed 374 metric tons. Using the known height of the one surviving specimen and information on an obelisk barge from the tomb of Ineni, we can calculate the length of the barge on which they were placed as *c*.63 m and the beam as *c*.21 m. Given the huge weight to be transported, the barge was strengthened laterally by three sets of cross-thwarts passing through the shell of the hull, and longitudinal integrity was guaranteed by a series of five hogging trusses. There is no indication of internal supports for the decking, but there must have been massive internal bracing to take the weight of the obelisks. The barge was steered by two sets of steering oars, one on each side of the stern, and propulsion was achieved by using thirty oared tugs on the common 'butty'-boat principle still used in England in the nineteenth century in canal navigation.[10] If the obelisks were the pair of larger specimens allegedly *c*.57 m high that are known to have been set up in the temple by Hatshepsut, the size of the barge would need to be recalculated on that basis, and that would make it a truly spectacular piece of shipbuilding expertise, but it would be prudent to doubt whether the second set really were as large as the 108 cubits claimed in the Northampton stele

---

[10] The 'butty' boat in an English context was an unpowered barge or boat towed by another barge and requiring someone on board only to steer it.

(Habachi 1957: 99; 1984: 59–72; Landström 1970: 128–33). How these monstrous obelisks were manoeuvred onto the barge is a matter of speculation, but the Roman writer Pliny the Elder gives the following description of the process as he understood it:

a canal was dug from the river Nile to the spot where the obelisk lay; and two broad vessels, laden with blocks of similar stone a foot square, the cargo of each amounting to double the size, and consequently double the weight, of the obelisk, were brought beneath it; the extremities of the obelisk remaining supported by the opposite sides of the canal. The blocks of stone were then removed, and the vessels, being thus gradually lightened, received their burden.   (*Historia Naturalis* 36. 14)

It must be conceded that this account is not entirely clear on detail, but the elements in this method are compatible with Egyptian practice and ring true, not least because of their simplicity, though the number of barges used must have varied according to circumstances and the size of the obelisks carried.

Transport by land was altogether more arduous and time-consuming than that by water and was avoided wherever possible. Roads within the alluvial area would have been rare and generally followed the tops of dykes or river banks well clear of the waters of a normal inundation (Partridge 1996: 79–82; 2010: 380–2). Frequently they would have consisted of no more than insignificant and well-beaten mud pathways, a situation which persisted in the countryside well into modern times.[11] Out in the desert areas there were long-established routes running between key points, sometimes provided with watering stations and forts for protection, but these routes were usually little more than long-established tracks recognized as being the most convenient means of travelling between two points. However, specially constructed roads serving quarries and mines are well represented in the archaeological record (Aston, Harrell, and Shaw 2000: 18–20, 32, 51, 93; Shaw 2006, 2010). When land travel had to be done, the donkey was the standard beast of burden throughout Pharaonic history (Partridge 1996: 95–9; 2010 383–4). In the Eleventh Dynasty Hammamat inscription of Henenu we are informed that on his expedition through the Eastern Desert he used donkeys to carry sandals and probably much else besides, and the vizier Amenemhet makes the improbable boast that no donkey died on his expedition into the same area, a certain indication that significant losses could be expected with these animals (see p. 196). Donkeys are also mentioned in the great inscription of Regnal Year 3 of Ramesses IV dealing with a large-scale expedition into the Wadi

---

[11] Clarke and Engelbach, writing in the early twentieth century, comment: 'It must be remembered . . . that, even to-day, the *fellāḥ* makes very little use of carts, and many villages in Egypt cannot be approached even on a bicycle. Until quite recently there was no road between successive capitals of provinces in Upper Egypt' (1930: 88).

Hammamat to obtain greywacke, but by then, although porters and donkeys are mentioned, wheeled transport was also available:

There was transported for them supplies from Egypt, in 10 wagons, with 6 span of oxen per wagon, pulling [them] from Egypt as far as the mountain of *bekhen*-stone. <There were> numerous <port>ers who were laden with loaves of bread, meat, and cakes beyond number. There were brought the offerings to satisfy the gods of heaven and earth from the Southern City, they having been purified in a great purification, and they being on the shoulders <4 *groups lost*> they being placed upon asses so that they might be pure together.   (*KRI* vi. 14)

However, donkeys and wheeled carts were only practical for relatively light burdens, and throughout Egyptian history the only means available to move large bodies of material overland was to drag them, using either manpower or oxen (see p. 195). Given the relatively high levels of manpower available to the Egyptians and their mental attunement to pre-modern timescales, this was a perfectly acceptable proposition, but it was inevitably a very slow and arduous process.[12]

---

[12] It is sometimes claimed that no fewer than 900 men died on the Ramesses IV expedition (e.g. Peden 1994*b*: 89). However, the relevant passage in the inscription looks deeply corrupt, and the claim that the 900 in question had died is based on a highly speculative late nineteenth-century guess at its possible meaning by Spiegelberg (Lloyd 2013: forthcoming).

7

The Conceptualized Environment

We are all accustomed to opening general books about Ancient Egypt and finding that the first substantial discussion is a description of the physical environment in which Egyptian civilization evolved. There is a sound logic in this since Egypt is a particularly good example of a civilization whose potential for and directions of development were determined to a remarkable degree by its physical context. That said, however, we very frequently ignore the important fact that the world which the Egyptians inhabited was not simply a physical world. To an even greater degree they lived their lives within a conceptualized version of that physical environment, and in this respect they were no exception amongst the nations of the earth.

It is a fundamental requirement for all societies that they should be able to form a mental picture of the world within which they operate; for without the ability to generate a mental picture which imposes a conceptual order on the world of experience the world must remain a meaningless chaos where nothing fits, and nothing is predictable. It would be impossible to negotiate terms with such a world, and human beings would simply not be able to devise the mental and physical strategies necessary to their survival. If such concepts are to be of any value, they must, of course, be shared concepts and form the basis of the entire conceptual apparatus governing the actions of the entire community, i.e. they must be social artefacts. However, this conceptual universe cannot be definitive. The concepts that form the apparatus for creating this world picture are constantly in need of testing against the world of experience and constantly in need of restating and reaffirmation. From time to time they will need redefining and, very occasionally, they will need to be radically modified under pressure from new conceptual worlds that may even require the abandonment of older views. Egypt is an excellent example of a society which, in the end, abandoned a conceptual world that had stood it in good stead for well in excess of three millennia.

THE PHYSICAL STRUCTURE OF THE COSMOS

The Egyptian conceptual model of the physical structure of the universe was formulated along two axes, the vertical and the horizontal. The vertical axis consisted of three superimposed levels: heaven, earth, and the underworld. The horizontal axis was conceptualized as three concentric zones the innermost of which was formed by Pharaoh's residence, a status often denoted by its designation as the *khenu* (*ḥnw*), 'the inside, the innermost'. The next zone was made up of Egypt proper which was habitually divided conceptually into two sections. This division might take the form of a longitudinal line of demarcation along the course of the Nile, and in that mode of thought the Egyptians frequently described Egypt as 'The Two Banks'; alternatively, and much more frequently, the division might be made horizontally at the apex of the Delta, and in that case Egypt was described as 'The Two Lands'. Whichever option was invoked, Egypt was envisaged as a unity in duality, and in both cases Egypt, just like Pharaoh's residence, could be described as *khenu*, the implication being that Egypt, like the palace, was the centre of the universe. Beyond this zone came the third and final zone which consisted of everything else on the horizontal plane, and that was always regarded as the province of the alien, 'the other', something either to be avoided or brought actually or conceptually into the Egyptian orbit and under Egyptian control. The East was often ideologically tamed by transmutation into 'God's Land' (*tꜣ nṯr*), the location of the daily appearance of the sun-god, but the West was a different matter altogether, the focus of ambiguous and often negative attitudes associated with death and chaotic forces. This cosmos was not believed to function on anything like a defined set of mechanical laws. It was a world of infinite possibilities where events might fall at any point on a spectrum that ran from the normal at one end to the extremely unusual at the other. In such a cosmos miracles could not happen, only marvels that arrest attention not because they break a cosmic law of physics but because they have rarely, if ever, occurred before.

THE CONCEPT OF TIME

The conceptualization of space will inevitably be accompanied by a conceptualization of time. Time itself has no objective reality. It is a social construct by means of which human beings conceptualize the relationships between events and between events and themselves. Such structures may be articulated in the form of cycles, linear sequences, or a combination of both. In Ancient Egypt events were located at the highest level within a cosmic framework demarcated by two fixed points: the creation of the ordered universe, on the one hand, and its ultimate dissolution, on the other (see p. 229). Whether the Egyptians expected this cycle to be renewed never seems to emerge clearly in the textual record, though the conceptual material was certainly available inasmuch as Nun, the primeval ocean from which all things came and to which all things would return, was believed to contain the potentiality of all things. Cyclical recreation was, therefore, a distinct *theoretical* possibility.[1]

Within the cosmic framework the evolution of events was perceived to have consisted essentially of two major blocks of time. The first was the phase immediately initiated by the creation when the gods ruled on earth, a period that the Egyptians frequently denote as the *rek netjer* (*rk nṯr*), 'the time of the god', or the *paut ta* (*pꜣwt tꜣ*), 'the primeval time of the earth'. They were followed as rulers by the *akhu* (*ꜣḫw*) or demigods (Greek *hēmitheoi*) who mediated the change to the second major phase. This consisted of a long series of rulers who occupied a liminal position between the human and divine, i.e. human Pharaohs who functioned as incarnations of Horus, the last divine ruler of Egypt. However, whilst there is this marked linear dimension to Egyptian perceptions of 'human' time, the sequence of reigns has a clear cyclical dimension; for every king dies and becomes an Osiris to be succeeded by a new king who functions as an incarnation of Horus and so on ad infinitum so that at the beginning of each reign the year count begins again at Year 1. The cyclical dimension in the perception of time was denoted by the term *neheh* (*nḥḥ*) and the linear by the term *djet* (*ḏt*) both of which are conventionally translated, *faute de mieux*, as 'eternity' but both of which would be terminated by the ultimate dissolution of the cosmos.

Human and, where appropriate, divine time was divided into smaller blocks, the largest being the year (*rnpt*). In the Civil Calendar used for all official business this consisted of three equal seasons designated *akhet* (*ꜣḫt*), 'inundation', *peret* (*prt*), 'emergence (from the water of the land)', and *shomu* (*šmw*), probably 'low water' (cf. Gardiner 1957: 203). Each season was divided into four months of thirty days to yield a total of 360 days which were supplemented by five additional days to give 365 which approximated to, but did not quite equal, the length of the astronomical year (the time it takes the earth to pass from point x on its course round the sun back to the same point). Each day was divided into 24 hours (*wnwt*), 12 allocated to daylight and 12 to the night, but these were of flexible length to take account of differences in the length of day and night arising from seasonal changes.

Whilst the Civil Calendar had high relevance for priests and administrators, it was of very limited use to anyone engaged in agricultural production since it was shorter than the astronomical year, and the calendrical seasons under the

---

[1] It is conceivable that the possibility of a new cosmic cycle is mentioned in the *Book of the Celestial Cow* (Piankoff 1955: 29), but the relevant passage is not explicit.

Civil Calendar would, therefore, frequently be at variance with the natural phenomena after which they were named. However, the Civil Calendar had its origins in the concept of a lunar year based on twelve lunar months, and this continued to be employed where harmony with the seasons and celestial phenomena was critical (Spalinger 2001). Clearly, the perception of time for the vast majority of Egyptians would have been dominated by the annual cycle of seasonal variations, above all the regime of the Nile, and any associated astronomical phenomena for the simple reason that these events were the most important factors impinging on their lives.

At all levels of society, to a greater or lesser degree, there were perceptions of past, present, and future time, and the Egyptian language at every period provided structures that made it possible to allocate phenomena or events to a specific time-frame. Nevertheless, the use of abstract nouns to denote 'past', 'present', and 'future' as entities in themselves is of extreme rarity. The Egyptians were interested in allocating events to these timescales, but they were not very interested in thinking of the past, present, and future as global blocks of time. However, the sophistication of such perceptions would have differed greatly from one level of society to another. In traditional African communities overwhelmingly what matters is the present and the immediate past, the future being of little concern because it has not yet happened and does not affect the individual to any significant degree, if at all. Mbiti (1969: 17) comments as follows:

For them [i.e. Africans], time is simply a composition of events which have occurred, those which are taking place now and those which are immediately to occur... The most significant consequence of this is that, according to traditional concepts, time is a two dimensional phenomenon, with a long *past*, a *present* and virtually *no future*... The future is virtually absent because events which lie in it have not taken place, they have not been realized and cannot, therefore, constitute time... people set their minds not on future things, but chiefly on what has taken place.

Since the conditions of life for the Ancient Egyptian peasantry would not have been greatly different from those in such societies, we could hardly be far wrong if we assumed that most Egyptians located themselves in time in very much the same way. However, at the elite level concepts were considerably more elaborate. The past, above all, was fully populated with the concepts and events described above and regarded as a source from which the Egyptians could read off patterns of ideal behaviour and prototypes for the future, perceptions that meant, as in Ancient Greece and Rome, that progress in the modern sense was impossible; the best one could expect was the re-establishment of an ideal past. A return to the best of the past is, therefore, the message of prophetic texts such as the *Prophecy of Neferty*, but, beyond that, even at a sophisticated level of society, there is no great interest in the future, though leaving a good name to future generations was certainly a matter of concern.

THE INHABITANTS OF THE COSMOS

To the Egyptians the cosmos teemed with entities that formed elements in a carefully articulated hierarchy of dimensions of being (see Fig. 7.1). In ascending order the main elements were *remetj* (*rmṯ*), 'mankind', the *mutu* (*mwtw*), 'the dead', the *akhu* (*ꜣḫw*), 'the luminous ones, the transfigured dead', and the *netjeru* (*nṯrw*), 'the gods' (*Wb.* ii. 167 l. 2). The boundaries between these categories were permeable, and the relationship between them was regarded ultimately as a continuum of being in which the differences were those of the degree to which individual categories possessed, or had access to, specific attributes, so that the further up the hierarchy a group of beings was located the greater their power and capacities became. This means that it was perfectly possible to migrate from the lowest to the highest stratum, and the Egyptians believed that this did happen, though very few were ever believed to have achieved such elevation.

Remetj

The Egyptians were well aware that mankind consisted of a wide variety of societies with a wide range of cultures and some variation in physical characteristics of which their artists were supremely conscious. Surviving creation myths rarely address the question of the origins of humanity in its totality. According to one such myth mankind was created by Re-Atum from his tears (see p. 234), an idea based on the similarity of sound between the Egyptian words for 'mankind' (*rmṯ*) and 'tears' (*rmyt*), but, although this concept would

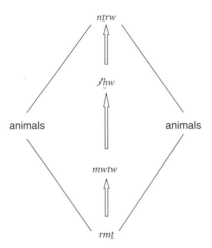

Fig. 7.1. The Continuum of Being. Drawing by Lloyd.

seem to a modern observer to have considerable symbolic potential, the Egyptians do not seem to have pursued it. However, the idea that man came into existence through the agency of the creator god was firmly rooted in Egyptian consciousness, though the focus of attention in such statements seems to hover precariously between the concept of mankind as a global phenomenon and mankind as simply the Egyptians themselves. *The Instruction for Merikare*, whilst making no explicit reference to the tear myth, states unequivocally and at some length that mankind 'are his (i.e. the creator's) images, who came forth from his limbs', that they were 'cattle of god' (i.e. they were under his care as were cattle under a herdsman), and that the creator had set in place a whole series of benefactions, physical and social, which made it possible for them to lead secure and happy lives (*Merikare* 130–8; Parkinson 1998: 226–7).

Whilst the Egyptians were certainly capable of thinking of mankind as a collection of differing peoples, their self-perception in relation to neighbours was marked by a strong sense of superiority. They are perfectly capable of using the word 'man' (*rmṯ*) in the sense of 'Egyptian', i.e. everyone else was subhuman (*Wb.* ii. 423 l. 4). However, it is important to realize that this mode of thought was not, in the strict sense, racial in content; it was not a reaction to physical characteristics but to cultural differences such as language, religious practices, and diet. It was, therefore, perfectly possible for a foreigner to become 'Egyptian' by adopting fully the culture of Egypt in all its forms, and throughout Egyptian history this took place on countless occasions.

Man as Individual

The Egyptians expressed their concept and experience of man by treating him as an amalgam of discrete elements all of which were essential to his being as a personal entity. The loss of any one of these elements gravely imperilled his continued existence as an individual. They were the *ba* (*bꜣ*), *ka* (*kꜣ*), *ren* (*rn*), *shuyet* (*šwyt*), *ib* (*ib*) or *haty* (*ḥꜣty*), and *khet* (*ḫt*) or *khat* (*ḫꜣt* or *ḥꜣt*). Defining the precise meaning of the first two has been the subject of much debate, the interpretation of the *ba* being particularly controversial. Not infrequently it has been translated into English as 'soul', but this rendering is seriously misleading in that it ignores the fact that the Egyptians did not think in terms of body and spirit in anything like Christian, Jewish, or Islamic modes of thought; in their conceptual world all things were material and perceived as concrete. What the *ba*-concept does is to encapsulate the notion that all living entities possess a 'vital power', a dynamic and active force that enables them to move and affect, in some degree, everything and everyone around them. This notion fits perfectly with its standard iconography as a human-headed bird which is highly mobile and even capable of leaving the body for a short time after death. The *ka*, on the other hand, is 'vital essence', the element that makes the difference between life and death. It came into existence at conception, stayed with the individual throughout life, and left the body at death to precede the deceased into the realm of the resurrected dead where the owner would rejoin it and resume existence as a living being. Iconographically, this concept is aptly expressed by representing the *ka* as the double of its owner. The other concepts are more tangible, though frequently widely at variance with modern Western thought-patterns. Unlike us, the Egyptians treated 'the name' as an essential part of the personality. It might be altered according to context or even reflect changes in the ruling monarch, but it remained an integral part of his being.[2] Indeed, it was so embedded in his personality that knowledge of it even gave power over its owner, whether the owner was human or divine, and for that reason some gods were regarded as having secret names, their *real* names which alone encapsulated their being. The crucial importance of the name is reflected in its constant repetition in mortuary contexts such as tomb walls and grave goods, and its destruction would bring about complete personal annihilation. The *shuyet*, 'the shadow', was also treated as a physical entity regarded as an integral part of the person and is sometimes represented in attendance on the individual as a black silhouette of his form. This idea is even more foreign to modern Western thinking than the concept of the name, but the conviction of the importance and significance of an individual's shadow is far from unique and is well represented both in folklore and the anthropological record, e.g. in Western tradition vampires are alleged not to cast shadows. With the concept of the *ib*, 'the heart', we are on rather more familiar ground in that it was considered to be the seat of the emotional being, but it was also regarded as the location of the intellect, the Egyptians having no understanding of the function of the brain, and in textual material it features prominently as the Egyptian equivalent of 'mind'. The *ḥt*, 'the body', was uncompromisingly regarded as an essential part of the personality, another concept at variance with modern thinking for which 'the person' is generally regarded as something interior to the body and not necessarily dependent for its existence upon it.[3] The Egyptian 'body' was inhabited by, or inseparably linked to, all the entities just discussed, but the best-informed Egyptians also show awareness of many of its anatomical elements, though their understanding of bodily processes was very limited. However, their knowledge-base does display some impressive features such as the recognition that the body is full of 'vessels' (*mtw*) which were

---

[2] In the Old Kingdom we hear of the *ren nefer* (*rn nfr*), 'young name', which was borne by an individual as a familiar name, and the *ren aa* (*rn ꜥꜣ*), 'big name', which was his official name (James 1953: 12). An example of a change in name reflecting a change of reign is provided by the tomb of Meru at Saqqara who started as Tetisonb but changed to Pepisonb at some stage after the accession of Pepi I (Lloyd, Spencer, and el-Khouli 1990: 6).

[3] For detailed discussions of these concepts see Lloyd 1989; Goelet 1994; J. Taylor 2001: 10–32.

thought to play an important role in its mechanics. At a less scientific level the body was believed to be subject to attack from malevolent forces which brought on sickness and had to be removed by the actions of an appropriate *heka*-master (for which see p. 233), and the concept of demonic possession was a standard feature of the Egyptian aetiology of disease (Nunn 1996: 103–4).

The elements of the individual just described feature prominently in the textual record and are standard for all periods, but, from time to time, other features are mentioned that reflect perceptions of yet other aspects of person. One of these is the concept, first clearly identifiable in the New Kingdom,[4] that individuals have a personal 'fate'. Among the entities due to receive offerings in the Eighteenth Dynasty tomb of Amenemhet is his 'fate' (*sha*, *šȝ*). The biography of Ahmose, son of Abana, speaks of a rebel being taken by 'his fate' (*šȝ w.f*) (*Urk.* iv. 5, 17), and the *Instruction of Any* expresses the same idea: 'It is the god who judges the righteous. His fate comes and takes him away' (Lichtheim 2006: 141). The *Tale of the Doomed Prince* is gratifyingly explicit on how it was thought to work. We are told that the fate of the newly born prince was defined at his birth by the Seven Hathors,[5] but the text also reveals that it was believed to be possible to avoid fate with divine help, i.e. the Egyptian concept of fate was far from the rigidly deterministic view of the Ancient Greeks for whom its decrees were unbreakable. We hear of yet another entity in the great funerary stele of Paheri in the statement: 'You shall spend eternity in sweetness of heart in the praises of the god who is within you' (*Urk.* iv. 117 ll. 11–12). This passage, which seems to be unique, clearly reflects the idea that individuals harbour within them something very much like our concept of conscience. We also encounter the idea, again in the New Kingdom, that the individual can enjoy the personal protection of his own guardian deity, an entity resembling our notion of the guardian angel. When the Doomed Prince's wife saves him from a snake, one of the creatures fated to kill him, she comments: 'Look, *your god* has given one of your fates into your hand. He will protect <you ˈfrom the others alsoˈ>' (Lichtheim 2006: 202). The text immediately following these words shows that, in this case, the god in question is Re but, at the same time, implies that any god of recognized power might be perceived as functioning in this way. We should also remember that in the tomb of Amenemhet already mentioned the owner is regarded

---

[4] The basics of this idea are already present in the Middle Kingdom. In the *Story of Sinuhe* Sinuhe asks before his encounter with the champion of Retjenu: 'Is there a god who does not know what he has ordained?' (Lichtheim 2006: 227). However, there does not seem to be any reference to the notion of a personal fate before the New Kingdom. In general see Quaegebeur 1975.

[5] The number is not used in the text but is given in other contexts. Seven is a significant number in Ancient Egypt indicating wholeness, perfection, and potency (Pinch 1994: 37, 56, 83; R. Wilkinson 1994: 135–7).

as possessing his own Meskhenet, Renenet, and Khnum, classic birth deities responsible for bringing him into being and creating his physical form. This, of course, is the Egyptian formulation for the notion that all beings share in the attentions of these divine beings.

Man in Society

Human societies are constructs of the human mind. They can take many different forms, depending on practical and ideological constraints, but in all cases their building blocks are the nuclear family consisting of the basic breeding group of mother, father, and offspring. Fundamentally, the nuclear family is biologically determined, even though its internal relations can be conceptualized and operated in very different ways, but nuclear families rarely function in isolation because of their limited manpower resources and usually bond together into extended families consisting of several related nuclear groups. The nuclear and extended families are the only kinship-based institutions that certainly survived into Pharaonic times, and there is a very good case to be made for the survival of clans, but the tribes which we can be sure existed during the Prehistoric Period have simply disappeared. We can only assume that they were slowly eroded under the impetus of the growing power of the evolving state system that found the centrifugal pressures inherent in such institutions an intolerable obstacle to the establishment of a unitary state.

Both nuclear and extended families are highly visible in surviving documentation (Frood 2010), and setting up a household of one's own was evidently seen as a major priority. The Egyptian words denoting families and their members tell us much about their conceptual basis. There are several terms that can be translated as 'family'. The word *abt* (*ꜣbt*) occurs from the Old Kingdom onwards (Franke 1983: 277–88) and is contrasted with *hau* (*ḥꜣw*), 'neighbours', in the Middle Kingdom stele of Montjuwoser who claims, 'I was one beloved of his neighbours and attached to his family' (Sethe 1928: 79 ll. 12–13).[6] This broad formulation looks like an overarching description of his social landscape and suggests that *ꜣbt* is intended here to cover all his relations, i.e. the extended family. The term *wehyt* (*wḥyt*) is not so straightforward. It is certainly used in the sense of 'kindred', but it is also employed to refer to Bedouin tribes and in the sense of 'village' (Gardiner 1947: ii. 205*: cf. Franke 1983: 204–10). This range of application implies a recognition that kinship was perceived to be a defining characteristic of Bedouin society, a phenomenon also illustrated by the word *mehut* (*mhwt*) which shows an equal capacity to shift between application to the family and Bedouin tribes, but the case of *wehyt* takes us further, showing that there was a conceptual link, at some stage in

---

[6] The distinction here would be the same as that in the English expression 'kith and kin' where 'kith' is an old word for friends and acquaintances.

history, at least, between kinship and the village. This is hardly surprising. Evidence from Deir el-Medina demonstrates that kinship links were a pervasive ingredient of the social structure of the village (Bierbrier 1982: 76; McDowell 1999: 51–2), and a high degree of intermarriage must always have occurred in village communities the length and breadth of the land, not least because many of them were relatively isolated, and inter-village mobility would have been very restricted. In many cases this situation would certainly have been aggravated by the fierce hostility between neighbouring villages which continued to blight the Egyptian countryside well into modern times (W. Blackman 1927: 129–34).[7] It seems perfectly possible that the term *wehyt* was used to refer to a group of linked extended families, i.e. a clan.

The kinship terminology used within families surprises and confuses in about equal measure. The system involved the extension of the terminology of the nuclear family (*iot* (*it*), 'father', *mut* (*mwt*), 'mother', *sa* (*s3*), 'son', *sat* (*s3t*), 'daughter', *sen* (*sn*), 'brother', *senet* (*snt*), 'sister') to cover more distant relationships, e.g. grandparents and more remote ascendants could all be designated 'father' or 'mother'; grandsons could be designated 'sons' and granddaughters were probably denoted as 'daughters', nephews and nieces could become 'brothers' or 'sisters', and cousins could also become 'brothers' or 'sisters', as appropriate. A father-in-law, son-in-law (probably), and daughter-in-law could also be designated by the simple terminology 'father', 'son', or 'daughter' respectively, and a brother-in-law could be designated simply as a 'brother' (Robins 1979: 197–217; Bierbrier 1980: 100–7; Franke 1983; Whale 1989; Hagen 2007; Frood 2010).[8] Whilst it was possible for the Egyptians to define more precisely a particular blood relationship, when required, they normally preferred the minimalist approach. This may, in part, have arisen from the fact that the family units in question were relatively small and relatively static in location so that everyone knew what the actual degrees of affinity were, but it may also have been the case that the simple terminology helped to maintain family solidarity by its straightforward insistence on the closeness of the relationships.

Egyptian texts frequently highlight the importance of good relations within the family, none more so than ideal biographies where a tomb owner will claim that he was:

---

[7] Juvenal (15. 33–92) comments on the bitter hostility between the towns of Ombos and Tentyra in the Roman Period. This is enough to justify the assumption that the modern evidence reflects a behavioural pattern going right back to the Pharaonic Period and even beyond.

[8] This flexibility in terminology also appears in the bifurcate-merging or Iroquois system of kinship widely exemplified in the anthropological record (Bohannan 1969: 64–7), though there is no sign in the Egyptian evidence of the subtleties relating to marriage regulations that form part of that system. It is by no means out of the question that Egyptian practice is the remnant of this much more elaborate kinship strategy which may have prevailed in the Prehistoric Period.

> One beloved of his father,
> Praised by his mother,
> One beloved by all his siblings.   (*Urk.* i. 122, 3–5)

Texts particularly focus on wives, sons, and mothers and the obligations that the husband has to them. In Pharaonic Egypt marriage was an entirely private matter, i.e. two people set up house together, and that was that. There was no formal religious dimension nor was the state interested in the event in any shape or form. However, a marriage might raise issues connected with property rights, and in such cases legal documentation might be drawn up to guarantee that the interests of relevant parties were assured. For most of Egyptian history such documentation would have taken the form of an *imt-pr* (*imet-per*), literally 'that which is in the house', but best translated 'deed of conveyance', a type of document of wide application which could also function as something approaching a marriage contract. The following Middle Kingdom text from Kahun may well be such a document:

Regnal year 2, month 2 of *akhet*, day 18. The deed of conveyance made by the *Web-priest-in-control-of-the-phyle* of Sopdu, Lord of the East, Wahu:

I am making a deed of conveyance for my wife, a woman of East-Side, Shefet, daughter of Sitsopdu, who is called Teti, in respect of everything given to me by my brother, the trusty seal-bearer of the controller-of-works Ankhren, with reference to all chattels in their several places, and in respect of everything which he gave to me. It is she who shall give it to whomsoever she prefers of the children she has borne me. I (also) give to her the four head of Asiatics given to me by my brother the trusty seal-bearer of the controller-of-works Ankhren. It is she who shall give them to whomsoever she prefers of her children.

As for my tomb, I shall be buried in it together with my wife, and no person shall be allowed to interfere with it. Furthermore, as for the house which was built for me by my brothers the trusty seal-bearer Ankhren, my wife shall live in it, and no-one shall be permitted to expel her from it. It is the deputy Gebu who shall act as guardian to my son.

List of witnesses in whose presence this was made: (List follows).

(Sethe 1928: 20–1)

This impressive text is a carefully formulated legal document identifying very precisely all relevant parties, as appropriate, by their full names, parentage, origin, or provenance and listing the witnesses in whose presence it was made. It was clearly intended to forestall problems that might arise on Wahu's death, possibly in connection with an earlier marriage, and it, therefore, has features that could also make it serve the accessory role of a last will and testament. It is particularly important to note that, as throughout the Pharaonic Period, the woman has exactly the same rights over property as a man, and, in particular, she has complete freedom of disposition over whatever goods and chattels she may hold in her own right. Of course, in the vast majority of marriages nothing like this document would ever have been needed because the parties to it would have owned next to nothing. Property rights could also become an issue in the event of a divorce. Here again we find that practice was remarkably informal, though it is likely that neighbours and relations would have taken a keen interest in such events and expressed their views in various ways, if there was a feeling that the treatment of either party was unfair. However, there was a convention relating to property in cases of divorce. If any property had been acquired jointly by the pair during their marriage, this had to be divided up in a ratio of 2:1 in favour of the husband, though the woman's rights in this respect were severely threatened if she had been guilty of some such misdemeanour as adultery (McDowell 1999: 32).

The favourable impression on marital relations presented by the Wahu deed is confirmed by *Instruction* texts. The Middle Kingdom *Instruction of Ptahhotep* writes:

> Love your wife with proper ardour.
> Fill her belly, clothe her back!
> Perfume is a restorative for her limbs.
> Make her joyful as long as you live!
> She is a field, good for her lord.   (trans. Parkinson 1998: 257)

The later *Instruction of Any* is insistent on showing respect to a good wife:

> Do not control your wife in her house,
> When you know she is efficient;
> Don't say to her: 'Where is it? Go get it!'
> When she has put it in the right place.
> Let your eye observe in silence,
> Then you recognize her skill;
> It is joy when your hand is with her,
> There are many who do not know this.   (trans. Lichtheim 2006: 143)

Particularly amusing is the comment in *Ptahhotep* that reveals a distinct preference for the svelte in female beauty as well as a perfectly comprehensible predilection for a quiet domestic life:

> If you take to wife a plump woman,
> someone light-hearted, well known to her town,
> who is volatile, to whom the moment is fair,
> do not reject her! Let her eat!
> The light-hearted woman provides fresh water.   (trans. Parkinson 1998: 261)

However, the wife is not a dominant entity in *Instruction* texts. It is sons who are the main focus since the very *raison-d'être* of such texts is to present a father advising his son on how to lead a successful life, both official and private. In this respect the father is presented as helping to fulfil one of the most important roles of the family in any society, i.e. to serve as the society in miniature and thereby to inculcate its fundamental values both by example and precept; for it was within the family, in the first instance and above all, that an Egyptian learned how to be an Egyptian. These social values are presented most clearly and fully by *Instruction* texts, but they would have been endorsed well beyond the charmed circle of the literate elite who could read them. These texts present the duty of the son to his father as to listen, learn, and obey, but the son's obligations pass beyond that to embrace a duty of care to other members of his family, and the obligation to care for a mother is most movingly expressed in the *Instruction of Any*:

> Double the food your mother gave you,
> Support her as she supported you;
> She had a heavy load in you,
> But she did not abandon you.
> When you were born after your months,
> She was yet yoked <to you>,
> Her breast in your mouth for three years.
> As you grew and your excrement disgusted,
> She was not disgusted, saying: 'What shall I do!'
> When she sent you to school,
> And you were taught to write,
> She kept watching over you daily,
> With bread and beer in her house.
> When as a youth you take a wife,
> And you are settled in your house,
> Pay attention to your offspring,
> Bring him up as did your mother.
> Do not give her cause to blame you,
> Lest she raise her hands to god,
> And he hears her cries.   (trans. Lichtheim 2006: 141)[9]

Herodotus provides an interesting gloss on the obligation to care for parents when he comments in his fifth-century BC account of Egypt: 'supporting parents is not a (legal) necessity incumbent on sons, if they do not wish to, but it is absolutely incumbent on daughters, even if they do not wish to' (2. 35. 4). This certainly held true for the period when Herodotus was writing, but evidence from Deir el-Medina shows that, in the New Kingdom at least, women were not legally bound in this way, though parents who felt that filial obligations had not been discharged could, and did, cut ungrateful female offspring out of their wills (McDowell 1999: 39).

---

[9] The great respect shown to the mother in traditional Egyptian villages in modern times was highlighted by Winifred Blackman (1927: 45) and is still very much in evidence.

A common way of ensuring that a son supported a father was the use of the institution of the 'staff of old age' (*medu iau, mdw iȝw*) exemplified in the following text which provides another case of the use of the ubiquitous *imt-pr*:

Regnal year 39, month 4 of *akhet*, day 19. The deed of conveyance made by the controller-of-the-phyle Mery, son of Inyotef, who is called Kebi, on behalf of his son Inyotef, son of Mery, who is called Ioseneb:

I give my office of controller-of-the-phyle to my son Inyotef, son of Mery, who is called Ioseneb, so as to be a staff of old age because I am old. Let him be appointed forthwith.[10]   (Sethe 1928: 90)

This part of the text is designed to do two things. In the first place it is activating Mery's equivalent of a pension fund by ensuring that his son is legally obliged to support him as a 'staff of old age', and, secondly, it ensures that the son has the financial resources to do so by handing over Mery's priestly office (and the attendant income). It should be noted that the office is treated as property on exactly the same terms as real estate.

Up to this point the family has been discussed in terms of its synchronous members, but, to the Egyptians, the family was not simply its living representatives but a corporation of the living, the transfigured dead, and putative or actual descendants. These diachronic dimensions were of great importance. In the first place, the reputations and achievements of family ancestors lived on in the present and contributed mightily to the prestige of their descendants. In his great biographical inscription at Beni Hasan Khnumhotep II is at great pains to describe the achievements of recent ancestors going back to the beginning of the Twelfth Dynasty both as an affirmation and enhancement of his family's status and as a validation of his own position (Lloyd 1992). This interest in defining genealogical links becomes noticeably more marked during the New Kingdom (Pirelli 1998), and the Late Period provides a spectacular example in the form of the early fifth-century inscription of the Overseer of Works Khnumibre in the Wadi Hammamat which presents us with a list, in part demonstrably fictitious, of ancestors going right back to the New Kingdom (Posener 1936: 98–105). A more practical way of using one's ancestors was the ancestor cult on which Deir el-Medina is particularly enlightening, though there is evidence of it elsewhere in Egypt and Nubia. This cult, which could form part of household religious practice, focused on recently deceased ancestors and was concerned partly to enlist their aid but also to ward them off, if they were believed to be exercising a malign influence on the living, an eventuality that the Egyptians clearly felt was very likely to arise (F. Friedman 1994: 111–17; Borghouts 1994: 124; cf. McDowell 1999: 106–7). The concept

---

[10] Priests in an Egyptian temple of any size were divided into four 'watches' (*sȝw*) which the Greeks called 'phylae'. They served in rotation one month at a time and were headed by a controller.

of the family as a continuum passing into the future is also very much in evidence. Khnumhotep reveals that his family's success had continued into the next generation, and in the reign of Ramesses II Roma, High Priest of Amun at Karnak, could boast:

> He (sc. Amun) placed my children in my presence as an entire future generation;
> they are priests shouldering his image.
> I was high priest as the gift of Amun,
> my (eldest) son established at my side as second priest,
> my second son as *Sem*-priest
> in the royal (mortuary) temple on the west of Thebes,
> the son of my son is fourth priest
> shouldering Amun, lord of the gods,
> the son of my son as god's father
> and lector priest, pure of hands, of the Hidden-of-Name.   (Frood 2007: 51)

This text demonstrates that Roma and his family had effectively acquired a stranglehold over the most senior offices in the most important temple in the kingdom.

In Egypt, as elsewhere, the extended family offered considerable opportunities at all levels of society. These included a significant enhancement of manpower and an insurance policy for a nuclear family in the event of disaster. It was also an institution that could be exploited for political purposes. Here again the biography of Khnumhotep II is invaluable since its detailed account of the history of the nomarchs of the Sixteenth (Oryx) Nome in the first half of the Twelfth Dynasty reveals that his family succeeded in creating a power bloc welding together the Fifteenth, Sixteenth, and Seventeenth Nomes by the careful use of intermarriage as a political stratagem, thereby creating a large extended family embracing a significant part of Middle Egypt. We can be certain that similar strategic alliances were the norm at all levels of society whenever a family, nuclear or extended, had a perceived need to strengthen its political or social position.

The examples just discussed almost inevitably come from the elite strata of Egyptian society that was capable of leaving a written record of their status and achievements, but there is no reason to assume that the situation that they adumbrate was fundamentally any different at the lower levels where the silent majority functioned. In particular, we should always remember that, whatever stratum is at issue, the family, nuclear or extended, was never simply the sum of its human parts, living and deceased. A crucially important factor in creating its corporate identity and solidarity was its status within the community. *Instruction* texts emphasize the importance of acquiring a good reputation specifically in relation to individuals, as we should expect, given their agenda, but the status and prestige, i.e. honour, of the entire family was of the highest importance and something to be jealously guarded and maintained.

At all levels that status would have been created by such factors as ancestry, office (particularly proximity to the king and priestly functions), wealth, piety, family monuments, generosity, powers of patronage, and the reputation of its members as conspicuous exemplars of the moral code. Assaults on family prestige or honour would have been a very serious matter and would doubtless have given rise to a vigorous response, in some cases generating the long-term feuding between families that we are justified in suspecting occurred as readily in antiquity as it has in more modern times.

Social Norms

The bedrock of the Egyptian moral and behavioural system was the concept of *maat* which encapsulated the idea that at the creation of the world a moral and physical order came into existence that was definitive and, therefore, incapable of improvement. Society might fall away from the moral imperatives of *maat* for many reasons, but all men had an absolute obligation to try to meet its requirements. Those who were perceived to have done so were *maaw* (*mȝʿw*), 'righteous men', and the yardstick of this status was success in one's life which was regarded as the result of divine approbation. In the words of *Ptahhotep* (32) such men were those 'who have listened to the gods'. The standard, though not sole, opposite of *maat* was *isfet* (*isft, Wb.* i. 129 l. 9). Its perpetrators might be called *isfetiu* (*isftyw*), but other words were available. Whatever their designation, those who failed to adhere to the requirements of *maat* could sooner or later expect divine retribution for their iniquities (H. Bonnet 1952: 430–4; Lichtheim 1992, 1997).

This theoretical moral thinking gave rise to a well-defined concept of acceptable behaviour which is articulated in considerable detail in the biographies common in tombs throughout Egyptian history and further expounded by *Instruction* texts, though there are clear differences of emphasis and focus as thinking evolved over time (Strudwick 2005: 261–378; Frood 2007; Ch. 8 of this volume). The biographies insist on the owner's success as a family member and on his benevolence, generosity, and care for those less fortunate than himself. They also emphasize the importance of the use of appropriate language in social relations, the avoidance of denigrating individuals to a superior, fairness in passing judgement in legal disputes, and increasingly the requirement to fulfil religious obligations. Whatever their date, these texts frequently affirm that this moral system was policed by divine agency, an issue that assumes a notable increase in importance during the New Kingdom. Of course, it may well have been the case that some of those claiming in biographies to be paragons of all the virtues were, in fact, double-dyed scoundrels, but the point remains that there was a code—and an admirable code—to which the Egyptians were expected to adhere.

To the *Instructions* the ethical model was the *seger* (*sgr*), 'the quiet man', who is modest, self-reliant, fulfils family obligations, practises hospitality, recognizes his place in society, respects authority, observes the rules of social etiquette, is fair in discharging official functions, acknowledges and respects the will of god and fulfils religious duties. Above all the 'quiet man' shows self-control in all that he does. Those who observe this code would acquire a good name in the present and in future: 'no good character is reproached; an evil character is blamed' (*Any* 6. 11ff.); 'His remembrance is in the mouth of the living, those on earth and those who will be' (*Ptahhotep* 562–3). The opposite of the 'quiet man' is often denoted in *Instruction* texts by words or expressions based on heat or fire, e.g. at *Ptahhotep* 378 such a person is described as *ta ib* (*tꜣ ib*), 'hot of heart'. This phrase and its parallels are most revealing. The Roman historian Ammianus Marcellinus (22. 16. 23) describes the Ancient Egyptians thus: 'Now Egyptians are . . . excitable in every movement, argumentative, and most insistent in their demands.' Winifred Blackman (1927: 23–4) makes it clear that this character trait was still alive and well amongst their modern descendants, describing a case that might well have had more than a few parallels, when she states that the Egyptian peasant had many admirable qualities but:

At the same time they are very emotional, highly strung, most inflammable . . . and nearly always conspicuously lacking in self-control.

Thus a man normally of a quiet, gentle, and peaceful disposition may on the spur of the moment commit some brutal murder. One year when I was staying in a small out-of-the-way village in Upper Egypt a man killed a neighbour in a terrible way because he had stolen some onions from his (the murderer's) field. The moment after he had committed the crime he was weeping over the body of the victim!

These two sources strongly suggest that *Instruction* texts, far from simply endorsing a virtue widely practised, were targeting a serious and endemic problem of social behaviour in insisting on the virtues of self-control and forbearance, and they justify the suspicion that explosive outbursts of fiery temper were a common feature of social relations in Pharaonic Egypt.[11] Calm, measured, and dutiful adherence to the requirements of *maat* was probably more honoured in the breach than in the observance!

The *Mutu*

The Egyptians' concept of the individual had far-reaching consequences for their concept of death and the dead. Once the individual had died be became

---

[11] Modern Egyptians have inherited this trait. Anyone familiar with Egypt will almost certainly have encountered it in some context or other.

one of the *mutu*, 'the dead', a being in a transitional state between life and elevation to the status of an *akh*, one of the blessed dead, though it was by no means a foregone conclusion that he would achieve that goal. If he did not, his fate was utter destruction! This blessed state could only be reached through the restoration of life to the deceased by funerary ritual and the successful negotiation of the trials impeding his journey to the domain of the resurrected dead, described by various terms such as *Duat* (*dwȝt*), 'the Underworld', the *Sekhet Iaru* (*sḫt iȝrw*), 'The Field of Reeds', or the *Sekhet Hetepu* (*sḫt ḥtpw*), 'The Field of Offerings'. Given the Egyptians' concept of the constitution of an individual during his earthly existence and their conviction that the deceased must retain his individuality fully in the afterlife, it was an inescapable consequence that they developed the belief that all the constituent elements of the personality must be preserved after death. This they tried to ensure by developing a mortuary apparatus that was believed capable of initiating and promoting that desirable end. This apparatus, a sequence of ritual activity of such finely grained detail that it virtually compelled belief, had two interlocking aspects, the material and the ritual, but many, if not all, its dimensions, fall under both headings and cannot easily be treated separately.

Devices that can be described as material, at least in the sense that they were built or manufactured, formed a crucial part of the mortuary apparatus for post-mortem survival. The most important and elaborate was the tomb. At the socio-political level this operated as an instrument of conspicuous display projecting a powerful image of the lofty status of the tomb owner and his family for all eternity, but in cultic terms it functioned as a ritual device for guaranteeing the preservation of all the elements of a person that were regarded as essential to resurrection. There were two main types, the mastaba and the rock tomb, which both show the same basic elements, a superstructure and a substructure (Fig. 7.2) (Spencer 1982; Grajetski 2003; Dodson 2008, 2010*b*). The superstructure of the mastaba normally took the form of an oblong box-like structure of mud-brick, stone, or a mixture of the two which was built up from ground level and might be completely solid, apart from tomb shafts, or equipped with built-in chambers that, at the highest level of society, could be numerous, e.g. the tombs of Mereruka, Kagemni, and Ti at Saqqara. The main functions of the superstructure were, first, to assist in the preservation of the essential elements of the personality; second, at the earliest periods, to serve as a repository for grave goods thought to be needed by the resurrected dead; and, third, to provide the context for the mortuary cult, the rituals of maintenance that were of crucial importance to the survival of the resurrected dead. The focus of this cult was the mortuary chapel or 'mansion of the *ka*' (*ḥwt-kȝ*), the name itself indicating that its function was the maintenance of the life-force of the tomb owner. This chapel was a liminal area where the mortuary priest could confront the *ka* of the deceased which gained access to the chamber through a false door before which lay an offering

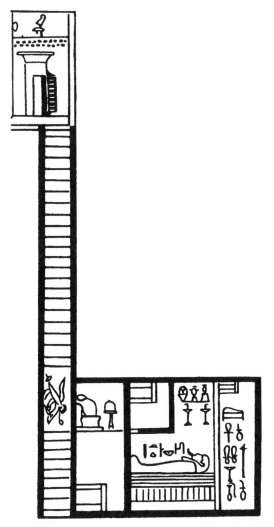

Fig. 7.2. The structure of an Egyptian tomb as depicted in the Eighteenth Dynasty funerary papyrus of Nebked, Musée du Louvre. Drawing after Naville 1886: i. pl. IV.

table where the priest (the 'servant of the *ka*', *ḥm-kɜ*) could present food and other items deemed essential to survival beyond the grave. However, there was more to this structure than that. The mortuary chapel and its associated chambers were copiously decorated with canonical offering scenes and representations of daily and official life which in many cases can be seen, at one level, as commemorative and as an argument that such a great man deserves mortuary service from posterity, but they also, and probably more importantly, acted as magical substitutes to guarantee the ritual service for ever and also to ensure that the resurrected tomb owner would continue to enjoy beyond the grave the life enjoyed on earth (see p. 211). Since these scenes contained representations of the deceased, sometimes in large numbers, they also provided body substitutes in case of damage to the corpse, and, since the name of the tomb owner was also copiously recorded, the scenes helped in the preservation of this all-important ingredient of the person. Statues of the deceased also functioned in the same way, sometimes in the Old Kingdom being placed in the chapel within a special enclosed chamber called by Egypt-ologists a 'serdab' equipped with openings for the owner to look out through. The reserve heads of the Fourth Dynasty may also have served a similar purpose, though there has been much debate as to their precise role (Lacovara 1997*b*; Roehrig 1999). Another artefact that could serve very much the same function as the decoration in tombs is the stele, of stone or wood, which might be part of the apparatus of the tomb but could also feature in other mortuary contexts such as the commemorative complex surrounding the alleged tomb of Osiris at Abydos. These artefacts commonly provide representations of the deceased with names and titles, and sometimes his family is also represented.

An important New Kingdom development of the mastaba superstructure was the temple tomb which became a standard high-status type for the rest of Egyptian history, exemplified, amongst others, by the Eighteenth Dynasty Memphite tomb of Horemheb and the Late Period tomb of Petosiris at Tuna el-Gebel. In this design the mastaba superstructure was stripped of everything except the tomb chapel which was then architecturally reformu-lated on the model of a New Kingdom temple, though its mortuary function was stridently marked in the New Kingdom by the presence of a small pyramid on the temple building proper (Spencer 1982: 238–42; J. Taylor 2001: 153).

The rock tomb appears throughout the Nile Valley at all periods of Phar-aonic history, excellent examples being found at Meir, Beni Hasan, el-Bersha, Thebes, and Aswan. The main difference from the mastaba lies in the super-structure which is not free-standing but excavated into the face of one of the cliffs lining the valley. Apart from that, what we have said of the ingredients of the mastaba holds true also for the rock tomb.

The substructure of both types of tomb was formed by a tomb chamber, sometimes more than one, linked to the superstructure by a vertical shaft or sloping passage-way which would be filled up after deposition of the corpse. A tomb chamber usually consisted of one room, though occasionally more elaborate substructures are exemplified. Normally it was not decorated and could be very roughly finished, but there are some spectacular exceptions to this rule (Kanawati 2010). Whatever its character, the most important single element in the tomb chamber was the body whose preservation and triumph-ant resurrection the Egyptians attempted to guarantee by a series of ritual devices. First, and most obviously, the body was mummified to prevent decomposition, though the technology for this process took some time to reach fruition, attempts in the Old and Middle Kingdoms looking a great deal better on the outside than they do internally. It was not until the New Kingdom that the technology reached its peak of effectiveness, though this was not maintained and reached its nadir in the Graeco-Roman Period (Lucas and Harris 1962: 248–50; Andrews 1998; J. Taylor 2001). However, mummification was not simply a matter of technology. In its developed form the full process took seventy days, much more than was required to carry out the physical treatment of the body. This timescale was necessitated because the actions of the embalmers were accompanied in the developed system by an elaborate series of rites that formed part of a ritual sequence designed to convert the deceased into an Osiris, a counterpart of the god Osiris whose death, mummification, and resurrection provided the prototype for the treatment of ordinary mortals.[12]

When transferred to the tomb, the mummy was frequently equipped with a mask, another ritual device for preserving the head, and was placed in a coffin that served two functions: first, and most obviously, it provided physical protection for the body, but, whatever its form, it was also a potent ritual object that played a major part in assisting in the resurrection and maintenance of the deceased. Earlier coffins were box-shaped and were often heavily inscribed inside and out with ritual texts such as offering lists (intended to guarantee that offerings would always be available) and the *Coffin Texts*, which provided incantations and the information that would enable the resurrected deceased to circumvent the many dangers that the afterlife presented. In all this material the name of the owner would feature prominently. The Second Intermediate Period saw the beginnings of a radical change in coffin design with the development of the independent anthropoid type, which could function as a stand-alone container rather than as an extended mask within a rectangular coffin as had previously been the case. This continued to serve the coffin's protective function, a point sometimes reinforced by an image of the protective mother-goddess Nut on the inner side of the lid, but such coffins offered much less room for inscriptions, though ritual texts and images are commonly applied to them, and opportunities for repeating the name are usually well exploited. However, the new design offered other possibilities. Its physical shape meant that it could function as yet another body substitute, and it could also be treated ritually as the equivalent of the body. Therefore, since

---

[12] In older literature the claim is often made that the deceased *became* Osiris himself. This view, which was always intrinsically improbable, has been effectively demolished by Mark Smith (2008). For most of Egyptian history both males and females could achieve this status, despite the gender problem, but about 400 BC the Gordian knot was cut, and a deceased female could be regarded as becoming a Hathor or an Osiris-Hathor rather than an Osiris *tout court* (Riggs 2005: 41–8). This change reflected the enormously important role that Hathor always played in mortuary religion.

gold was believed to be the flesh of the gods, the coffin could be covered in whole or in part by gold or it could simply be painted yellow, which would be regarded as a perfectly adequate substitute; in addition, the hair could be painted blue to imitate lapis-lazuli, if the real thing were not available, and this recreated the hair of the gods which was alleged to be of that substance. In this way the coffin became directly a ritual device for converting the deceased into a divine being, which is exactly what the resurrected dead became. Finally, in the most elaborate burials the coffin would be deposited in a wooden or stone sarcophagus of rectangular form which might be totally devoid of decoration but could be covered in ritual texts and images and serve very much the same functions as the coffin.

The *Akhu*

Up to this point the main focus for the discussion of the mortuary cult has been on things material. However, elaborate ritual sequences formed a central part of the system designed to bring the deceased back to life and keep them there, i.e. to convert them to *akh*s, 'luminous ones', members of the resurrected and transfigured dead. The key rituals were those performed by the mortuary priest whose relationship to the deceased was conceptualized from the Middle Kingdom onwards as replicating the relationship between Horus and his father Osiris. As a ritual-Horus the mortuary priest became the son who championed and supported his ritual-father Osiris, the deceased replicating the career of Osiris who functioned as the archetype for all the resurrected dead (see p. 225). These and related rituals would normally have consisted of two aspects, a manual rite, i.e. what the priest did, and an oral rite, i.e. the words of power associated with the manual rite and often based on a mythological prototype.

We have already mentioned the ritual activity associated with mummification, but there was much more that was regarded as essential to the resurrection and maintenance of the deceased. The west wall of the tomb chapel of Paheri at Elkab depicts the transportation of the coffin to the tomb in a bier placed on a sledge pulled by oxen (Tylor and Griffith 1894: pl. 5). It is accompanied by officials burning incense, itself a divinizing process, and a number of priests either dragging along grave goods or reciting incantations. The dance of the *muu* is also being performed, probably enacting a ritual of welcome by divine guides to the afterlife, as well as the dragging of the *tekenu* on its sledge. The significance of the latter is obscure, but the facts that a human head or even a torso is sometimes shown emerging from this enigmatic object and that it can be replaced by a complete dormant human body suggest that the outer skin always contained a living being who played a role of some importance in the funerary rituals conducted at the tomb (cf. Reeder 1994).

Once at the tomb the major rite performed was the ritual of the Opening of the Mouth. This was designed originally to activate statues and bring them to life but was later also transferred to the treatment of coffins and mummies, which, for ritual purposes, amounted to the same thing. Its function in the mortuary cult was the all-important restoration of bodily functions to the deceased such as speech, sight, hearing, and smell so that the inanimate corpse was converted once more into a living being (Roth 1992, 1993). From this point it enjoyed the corporeal attributes needed to take the deceased through the journey to the afterlife and maintain them there in the fullness of their earthly being, but at this point in the ritual sequence there was still some way to go; for it was necessary to circumvent a series of dangers and undergo a series of trials until the deceased reached 'The Hall of the Two Truths' where the judgement of the dead was conducted before a divine tribunal. Once successfully through this last trial, he entered the land of the blessed dead as an *akh* to enjoy a triumphant afterlife which is described in detail in the great stele in the tomb of Paheri and depicted in mortuary iconography as an ideal version of the agricultural life of Egypt where needs would be the same as they had been during life, though we can be quite confident that such scenes should be interpreted as code for 'ideal existence'. It is abundantly clear that no deceased Egyptian expected or wanted to carry out agricultural labour beyond the grave and, indeed, he often took worker images (shabtis) with him to ensure that, if the call for labour ever came, he could activate them to do it for him.[13]

To achieve successful translation to the land of the blessed dead the deceased not only had the benefit of the rituals performed in the mortuary chapel but also of a large body of incantations designed to ensure that he had all the ritual power needed to protect and supply him with everything he required. At one level this could take the form of incantations inscribed in tombs, in particular, the *hotep-di-nesu* formula. This ubiquitous text could vary considerably in length and elaboration, but essentially, from the Middle Kingdom onwards, it took the form: 'A boon which the king gives to Osiris, the Great God, Lord of Abydos, that he may give invocation offerings of bread, beer, cattle, fowl, jars of alabaster, garments, and all things good and pure from which a god lives to the *ka* of *x*.' This utterance was regarded as embodying words of enormous power, and their very presence on a monument was enough to bring into being the relevant offerings for the deceased in the afterlife, but it is a common occurrence to find texts in prominent positions asking the living to recite this and related formulae as an additional form of back-up. Inscriptions were, however, only part of the repertoire. They were supplemented from the Middle Kingdom onwards by collections of

---

[13] Spell 5 of the *Book of the Dead* bears the title: 'Spell for not doing work in the realm of the dead' (Faulkner 1985: 36). The worker-figures took the form of small figures headed by a foreman (shabtis) which could be activated by reciting ch. 6 of the *Book of the Dead*.

incantations such as the *Coffin Texts* and the *Book of the Dead* which could be inscribed or deposited on papyrus rolls in close proximity to the deceased for easy access, as required. Here again, their very presence was sufficient for them to be effective without any formal need for recitation, though the latter was evidently regarded as the preferable option.

What *exactly* the *akh*, so carefully produced and protected by these measures, was really thought to be is an intriguing question. It is evident that the tomb was supposed to continue for eternity as the repository of the essential elements of a person. It is equally clear that it was regarded as the main context for communicating with and supplying the dead with offerings and ritual support, including the *sakhu*-rituals (*s3ḥw*), the rituals of rejuvenation that were periodically required in order to recharge the deceased with the *akh*-dimension required for their transfigured lives in glory beyond the grave. Nevertheless, it is evident that the tomb was very far from being the only context where the *akh* could operate, and it is clear from many mortuary texts that its capacity for migration was considerable. The best interpretation would be that the *akh* was the post-mortem dimension of being of the living person, the counterpart of the living person endowed with all the components of the latter but with the crucial addition of a large dose of divinity which is marked both by the designation 'luminous one' and by the acquisition of the beard of divinity. However, like the gods themselves (see p. 229), this entity was not absolutely or unconditionally immortal. Its continued existence was always dependent on a continual supply of ritual and material support administered in so many ways through the mortuary cult. It should also be borne in mind that *akhu* were not consistently regarded as benign entities. They could erupt into the world of the living with malign intent, and spells are extant that were designed to ward off their potential malevolence (Szpakowska 2003: 168).

The *nṯrw*, 'Gods'

The concept of 'god' is ubiquitous in human culture, but the content of that concept can vary considerably from one society to another. An Egyptian *netjer* is very different from an Ancient Greek *theos*, and both differ from the concept denoted by a modern monotheist's use of the word 'God'. In the first place, in seeking to understand the Ancient Egyptian concept of deity, we need to shed our notion that an essential part of the nature of godhead is that god is transcendental. Whether we are Christians, Jews, or Muslims, it is an essential tenet of faith for most believers that God created the universe but exists apart from it. He is from everlasting to everlasting. While some believers have adopted a pantheistic position and argued that the physical essence of God permeates everything, this is not canonical doctrine, and, since transcendentalism is the orthodox position for all these monotheistic faiths, it has been necessary for their adherents to argue that there must be intermediaries between man and God in the form of prophets, messiahs, saints, angels, and, if we turn to early Christian and related texts, we also have to deal with such entities as Thrones and Dominations. The Egyptians took quite a different view. For them no god is from everlasting to everlasting. The gods came into existence as part of a process of cosmic creation which was formulated in a variety of different ways depending on the cult centre in question, the pre-eminent version being that of Heliopolis. A section in *Coffin Text* 80 is based on this doctrine and places in the mouth of the creator god Re-Atum a graphic description of his solitary state in the primeval waters of Nun before the cosmos came into existence:

I was alone with Nun in lassitude, and I could find no place on which to stand or sit, when Heliopolis had not yet been founded that I might dwell in it, when my seat (?) had not yet been put together that I might sit on it; before I had made Nut that she might be above me, before the first generation had been born, before the Primeval Ennead had come into being that they might dwell with me.   (33–4)[14]

Subsequently Re-Atum took his place on the primeval hill and set about the creation of a pair of deities, Shu (Air) and Tefnut (Moisture), who, in turn, generated Nut and Geb who were separated by Shu to become the sky and earth respectively (Fig. 7.3). Nut and Geb, in turn, generated two pairs of

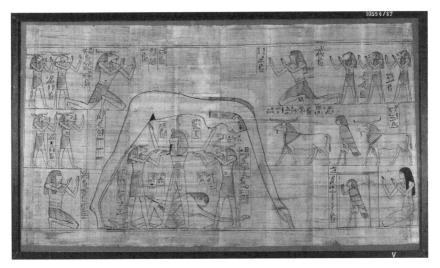

Fig. 7.3. The structure of the cosmos according to the Greenfield Papyrus.

---

[14] Cf. the account of creation in P.Bremner-Rhind (Faulkner 1937: 172) and that in *The Book of the Celestial Cow* (Piankoff 1955 (1977): 27–34).

deities, Osiris and Isis, Seth and Nephthys under whom the fundamental order of the universe as historical Egyptians knew it was ultimately established after a long struggle between Horus, the son of Osiris, and Seth. However, this world of order was always under threat from the forces of chaos, quintessentially represented by the god Seth and the serpent Apophis. The latter was perceived as a particular danger, and P.Bremner-Rhind contains a book for overthrowing this malevolent spirit which is entitled, 'The Book of the Felling of Apophis, the foe of Re and the foe of King Wenennefer, justified, which is performed daily in the temple of Amon-re, Lord of the Thrones of the Two Lands, who dwells in Karnak' (Faulkner 1937: 166), but the Egyptians clearly believed, though they were disinclined to trumpet the matter, that the cosmic order would eventually come to an end. Chapter 175 of the *Book of the Dead* strikingly portrays its demise at the hands of Atum to which even the gods are not exempt when the god forecasts: 'I will send the Elders and destroy all that I have made; the earth shall return to the Primeval Water, to the flood, as at its origin' (Kákosy 1963; cf. Lesko 2006).

The Egyptians also considered that the gods were not transcendental but immanent, i.e. they interpenetrated all things and could, therefore, be encountered anywhere. This idea is well illustrated in the *Westcar Papyrus* where we find the goddesses Isis, Nephthys, Meskhenet, and Heket in association with the god Khnum wandering through the Egyptian countryside as an itinerant dancing troupe passing from one district to another giving public performances (Parkinson 1998: 116–19). It only slowly and indirectly emerges in the course of the narrative that there was something uncanny about them, but the text serves to illustrate that an Ancient Egyptian could never know when he might run into a deity or what form that deity might take. However, whilst the divine might manifest itself anywhere, the Egyptians were no strangers to the widespread concept of 'sacred space', i.e. the conviction that there were locations where the divine could manifest itself with particular potency and efficacy (Lloyd 2013). The numerous temple sites, which had been a focus of cult for centuries, if not millennia, are obvious examples, but topographical features such as the Qorn in the western cliffs at Thebes, the *akhet* (concave-shaped) declivity in the horizon east of el-Amarna, or even caves provide further examples. The first two must have achieved this status because of their shape, the Qorn resembling a pyramid and the second serving as an image of the birthplace of the sun. Caves, on the other hand, were probably thought to give access to divine power within the earth and sometimes gave rise to the phenomenon of the *speos* temple, i.e. a temple excavated into a cliff, exemplified at Speos Artemidos in Middle Egypt and Abu Simbel in Nubia.[15] Yet other

---

[15] Note that an inscription in the South Chapel at Abu Simbel describes the mountain in which the temple was excavated as 'the Pure Mountain', i.e. it is in the maximum state of ritual purity (Kitchen 1996*b*: 495).

contexts where the concept of sacred space is in evidence are quarries and mines in such areas as Sinai, Gebel es-Silsila, Aswan, and the Wadi Hammamat. One of the texts in the copious material surviving in the latter site develops the concept of its status as sacred space in some detail, describing it as 'this august and primeval mountain, pre-eminent of place in the land of the horizon-dwellers, the god's palace endowed with life, the divine bird-pool of Horus, in which this god is content, his pure place of enjoyment which is upon the desert lands, the god's land' (Couyat and Montet 1912: 98). This quarry area was regarded as being particularly associated with the god Min-Hor, and the vocabulary used here to describe his abode is heavily loaded with religious associations: the mountain is *shepsy* (*špsy*), 'august', a term frequently used of gods and things divine; it is *paty* (*pȝty*), 'primeval', which immediately associates it with the time and forces of creation; this notion is then strengthened by the reference to the 'horizon-dwellers' who are particularly associated with the sun-god and his demiurgic powers; by claiming that the mountain is 'the god's palace' it is asserted to be the place where the god Min-Hor lives, and it is also stated to be a source of life, one of the great gifts of the gods; it is also described as the 'divine bird-pool of Horus', and, since Horus here is identical with Min, this claim means that the mountain is the birthplace of the god and, therefore, like all divine birth sites, of potent sacrality; finally, the mountain is affirmed to be *ta netjer* (*tȝ nṯr*), 'God's Land', and, therefore, a place under the direct control of divinity, a zone with a particularly heavy charge of divine presence and activity. It is of a piece with this body of concepts that materials provided to man by the gods in such areas were not regarded as inert substances but were believed themselves to be sacred and capable of imparting that sacrality to mankind. Thus, the greywacke stone cut from the cliffs in the Wadi Hammamat was regarded as having life-giving powers that made it ideal for use as a sarcophagus for a king whose corpse could assimilate divinizing power from it, and the same held true of gold, the colour and substance of the gods' flesh, which could function in the same way when used for masks or coffins.

A character sketch of the Egyptian gods does not stop at birth, immanence, and ultimate mortality. In the hierarchy of being previously tabulated they were distinguished from other orders not so much by a fundamental difference of essence as by the degree to which they possessed certain qualities or powers. In numerous ritual contexts the Egyptians associated the gods with three major attributes: *ankh* (*ꜥnḫ*), 'life', *djed* (*ḏd*), 'stability, long-lastingness', and *was* (*wȝs*), 'power', which they are frequently shown imparting to the Pharaoh in representations on temple walls as a reward for cult attention. Less iconographically prominent attributes, but no less important, were *bau* (*bȝw*), 'power', and *kau* (*kȝw*), 'life force', both being plurals of attributes that humans and *akhu* possessed but which the gods enjoyed to a much higher degree. Indeed, the gods, like the Pharaoh, were believed to have fourteen *kas*, the number being a symbolic figure not to be taken literally but indicating superabundance (see p. 212). The gods also possessed *menkhu* (*mnḫw*), 'efficient power', a most interesting concept that has not, perhaps, been given the attention it deserves. Basically, the adjective *menekh* (*mnḫ*) means 'efficient, that which does the job it was intended for'. Hence, when it is used of the king in the common phrase *nṯr mnḫ*, it is an affirmation that the king is doing what a king ought to do, i.e. he is operating according to *maat*, 'the cosmic order' in fulfilling the king's cosmicizing role. Similarly, when a deity is said to possess or employ *mnḫw* a claim is being made that the deity possesses cosmicizing power and is using it in the maintenance of cosmic order. The gods also possessed *heka* (*ḥkȝ*), often translated, *faute de mieux*, as 'magic', but this rendering trivializes and misrepresents the status of the concept in Egyptian thought-patterns (Ritner 1993). Basically, it indicates knowledge of words and actions of power that can be activated to change the world around the *heka*-master. The gods enjoyed this capacity ex officio and, therefore, had the potential to change the world around them at will. Knowledge of *heka* was not exclusive to the gods; human beings were able to acquire it by study and instruction at the hands of a living master, but it was not an innate human quality. However, whether human or divine, the proper role of *heka* was considered to be cosmicizing, and its employment for nefarious or criminal purposes was regarded as highly reprehensible (Lloyd 2006: 77–8). Two other innate qualities of the gods were Hu (*ḥw*), 'authoritative utterance' and Sia (*siȝ*), 'perception'. These seem originally to have been the prerogative of the creator god who mentally conceived of the entities which he was to create through Sia and then brought them into being by his utterance, but it is evident that, at least as early as the *Coffin Texts*, the two capacities had become generalized attributes of divinity so that the deceased could claim: 'My soul gives me power over authoritative utterance, and I have absorbed the perception of every god, taking away the power of the luminous ones' (*Coffin Texts*: ch. 469 l. 391).

Another capacity of the Egyptian gods was mutability of form. One of the best known of all the iconographic features of Egyptian deities is their ability to appear either entirely anthropomorphically, entirely in animal form, or as a mixture of the two. Probably the vast majority of Egyptians believed in the physical possibility of such variations in manifestation, but it may well be that a more sophisticated attitude prevailed at a higher level in society for which these iconographic variations may well have been regarded as a visual language whereby a completely anthropomorphic representation asserted that the gods, for all their power, have a psychological make-up and behavioural pattern that is essentially human. A completely zoomorphic image, on the other hand, could be seen as a way of conveying the idea that the gods possessed uncanny powers shared with the animal world. The use of a mixed format could then provide a means for the Egyptians to insist on the mixed nature of their deities' capabilities. However, though there is likely to be some truth in this symbolic interpretation, it is quite clear that the gods were believed to possess the ability to change their form ad hoc as and when they chose. In *The Conflict of Horus and Seth* Isis turns herself from a beautiful young goddess into an old crone and a bird to achieve her ends, and both Horus and Seth are described as assuming the form of hippopotami. Such feats these deities were able to achieve because of their innate *heka*-power, but such changes of form were only possible for mortals or the transfigured dead by the application of *heka* expertise which they had acquired by study or by purchasing appropriate texts such as the *Coffin Texts* and *The Book of the Dead*.

Up to this point discussion has focused on the features that set the gods apart from human beings either in capacities or the degree to which divine capabilities exceeded those of human beings, but it is a common feature of all religious systems that the adherents of those systems work on the basis that the psychological make-up and behaviour of their gods is in large measure that of human beings, and this is reflected in a great deal of ritual activity that can be aimed at meeting the same basic physical needs as human beings have but can also take the form of defending, praising, flattering, threatening, or compelling the deity very much as the worshipper would when dealing with individuals in a purely human context. The Ancient Egyptians were no exception to this general phenomenon.

An extremely important part of this anthropomorphizing process was the marked Egyptian tendency to conceptualize divine behaviour in terms of that of human authority figures, above all the king or, in the case of goddesses, of queens, i.e. the gods are very frequently regarded as being royal beings operating in a royal context and having royal attributes. A very clear example of this trait is provided by the *Myth of the Destruction of Mankind* which forms part of *The Book of the Celestial Cow*:

Now it came to pass <in the time of the Majesty of> Re, the god who came into being of himself, after he held the kingship of men and gods together. Then did mankind plot against him, when His Majesty (life, prosperity, health) had grown old, his bones being of silver, his flesh of gold, and his hair of real lapis lazuli. Then did His Majesty perceive the plotting of mankind against him, and did His Majesty (life, prosperity, health) say to those who were in his entourage: 'Pray, summon to me my Eye, and Shu, Tefnut, Geb, Nut, and the fathers and mothers who were with me when I was in Nun, and also furthermore to my god Nun; and he shall bring his courtiers with him. You shall bring them quietly. Let mankind not see and let them not lose heart. You shall come with them to the Palace, in order that they may give [me] their counsel since[16] I came from Nun to the place where I came into being.'

---

[16] The text is problematic. The reading in the Sety I version is *drt(y)w*, 'ancestors', which makes no sense. The Ramesses II text is damaged at this point; that in the tomb of Ramesses III retains *dr* but is defective after that group (Maystre 1941: 61). Presumably the original text read

Then these gods were brought, and the gods were placed on his two sides, bowing to the ground before His Majesty, that he might make his speech in the presence of the eldest father who made mankind, the king of the Lapwing Folk. Then did they say to His Majesty, 'Speak to us, that we may hear it.' Then did Re say to Nun: 'O eldest god from whom I came into being, and ancestor gods, look, as for mankind, which issued from my Eye,[17] they have plotted against me. Tell me what you will do about it. As for me, behold, I search. I have not slain them until I have heard what you will say concerning it.'

Then spoke the Majesty of Nun: 'My son Re, god greater than his maker, mightier than those who created him, stay on your throne! Great is fear of you. Your Eye is on those who conspire against you.' Then did the Majesty of Re say, 'Look, they have fled to the desert, their hearts being fearful of that which I say to them.' Then did they say to His Majesty, 'Cause your Eye to go that it may smite them for you, those who meditate evil! No Eye is superior to it for smiting them for you. Let it go down as Hathor!'

Then, indeed, did this goddess return after slaying mankind in the desert, and the Majesty of this god said, 'Welcome in peace, Hathor. O Eye, has that which I came for been done?'[18] Then this goddess said, 'I swear, I have achieved mastery over mankind, and it was sweet to my heart.' Then said the Majesty of Re, 'I shall have power over them as king by diminishing them.' (This is the coming into being of Sekhmet.)[19]

The bread paste of the night for her who would wade in their blood as far as Hnes.

Re then said, 'Summon to me, I beseech you, swift and speedy messengers that they may run like a body's shadow!' Then were these messengers brought immediately, and the Majesty of this god said, 'Let them travel to Elephantine and bring me red ochre in great quantity!' Then was the red ochre brought to him, and the Majesty of this great god set the Side-Lock Wearer in Heliopolis to grinding this ochre, whilst maidservants were crushing barley for beer. Then was the red ochre put into the bread paste, and it was like the blood of men; and seven thousand *hebny*-jars of beer were made. Then, indeed, did the Majesty of the King of Upper and Lower Egypt Re come together with these gods to see this beer.

Now when the day dawned for the goddess to slay mankind in their time of travelling south, the Majesty of Re said, 'How good it is! I shall protect mankind with it!' Then did Re say, 'Bear some of it to the place where she said she would plan to slay mankind'. Then did the Majesty of the King of Upper and Lower Egypt Re rise early in the beauty of the night to cause this sleeping draught to be poured out. Then

the preposition/conjunction *ḏr*, and this was subsequently corrupted into the related word for 'ancestors'. If we interpret *ḏr* in the rare sense 'since, because' (cf. Gardiner 1957: 232 §176. 2), the clause would be insisting on the affinity between Re and the deities being summoned and, thereby, justifying his dependence on them.

[17] See p. 209. The myth that mankind arose from the tears of the sun-god emerges with particular clarity in *The Book of Overthrowing Apophis* (Faulkner 1937: 172).

[18] This section of the text is damaged in all versions (Maystre 1941: 66). I assume that the *n* of *irt n* in the Sety I text is corrupt and that the original reading was the word for Eye.

[19] This gloss is one of several inserted into the text that purport to explain the origins of aspects of Egyptian religion, i.e. we are dealing with a string of aetiological myths.

were fields flooded to a depth of three palms[20] with the liquid through the might of the Majesty of this god. Then this goddess came in the morning, and in flood did she find them, and her face was pleased by it. She drank, and it pleased her heart. Then did she come in a state of drunkenness without perceiving mankind. Then the Majesty of Re said to this goddess, 'Welcome in peace, o charming one!' [This means the appearance of beautiful women in Imu.]   (Maystre 1941: 58–73)

It should be noted that the terminology of kingship is used frequently here of Re (*ḥm*, 'Majesty', *nsyt*, 'kingship', *ꜥnḫ wḏ snb*, 'life, prosperity, health', *nsw*, 'king', *ꜥnḫ.k n.i*, lit. 'As surely as you live for me'[21]), and Nun is seen in the same light (*nsw rḥyt*, 'king of the Lapwing-folk'[22]); Re has a court (*šnyt*), as does Nun; the courtiers bow to Re as to a king (*dhn tꜣ*); Re has a palace (*ḥwt ꜥ ꜣt*); there is a hint of *Königsnovelle* (another feature of texts dealing with royal action: see p. 153); and there is a reference to messengers (*ipwtyw*), an integral part of the Egyptian state's communication system. What has happened here is that the human order, above all the order of the Egyptian state, has been transposed on to the divine level, i.e. man has created god in his own image.[23]

For practical purposes of everyday life the most important ramification of the Egyptian perception of the gods as figures of power and authority was the conviction that they could be expected to display the same qualities as authority figures within the world of human activity. These could, of course, be negative, but overwhelmingly Egyptian texts that relate to issues of the gods and daily life emphasize two things. In the first place, as authority figures, the gods were expected to police and maintain the moral order, and man is, therefore, ultimately dependent on their good will. This thinking emerges with particular clarity in the *Instruction Texts*. In *Ptahhotep* we read:

> It is god's command which comes to pass.
> Plan to live in the midst of calm.
> Of itself will come what they [i.e. the gods] vouchsafe.   (6. 9–10)

In a similar vein the New Kingdom *Instruction of Any* insists:

> It is the god who judges the righteous.
> His fate comes and takes him away.
> Offer to your god,

---

[20] This is the standard interpretation. Only the text of Sety I is fully preserved at this point, and the translation of his text should run, 'Then were fields of three palms flooding with liquid,' a somewhat oblique way of describing the depth of the flood, unless the phrase 'of three palms' was a technical term for a particular category of land.

[21] A formula used in swearing oaths based explicitly or implicitly on the name of a ruler.

[22] 'Lapwing-folk' is a term used commonly to refer to the subjects of the king in general but also, more narrowly, in the sense of commoners (Gardiner 1947: i. 98*–112*).

[23] Such texts provide excellent examples of the Durkheimian principle, '. . . the god and the society are one and the same' (1912 (1995): 208).

Beware of offending him.
...
Let your eye watch out for his wrath,
And kiss the ground in his name.
He gives power in a million forms,
He who magnifies him is magnified.
God of this earth is the sun in the sky,
While his images are on earth.   (trans. Lichtheim 2006: 141)

The second ramification of the perception of the gods as authority figures is this: there was a deeply rooted tradition in Ancient Egyptian society, as there still is in its modern counterpart, that the 'haves' had an absolute obligation to assist the 'have-nots', particularly in times of anxiety and trouble, an idea most obviously and movingly expressed in the ideal biographies that appear in Egyptian tombs. The gods and goddesses of the pantheon, therefore, became a source of comfort and support to which the Egyptians could turn in times of trouble. Numerous texts bring out this concept with striking clarity, e.g. the personal piety documentation from Deir el-Medina (McDowell 199: 98–9) and Ramesside letters. A particularly impressive example of the latter is P. Leiden I 369 (late Twentieth Dynasty) in which the well-known Scribe of the Necropolis Djehutymose begins a missive to several colleagues with the words: 'I tell Arsaphes, Lord of Herakleopolis, Thoth, Lord of Hermopolis, and every god and goddess by whom I pass to give you life, prosperity, and health, a long lifetime, and a good old age; and to give you favour before gods and men' (trans.Wente 1967: 18). Later in the same text the homesick scribe continues with a request to the letter's recipients in his own interest:

Please tell Amun to bring me back. Indeed I was ill when I arrived north, and I am not at all in my [normal] condition. Do not set your minds to anything else. As soon as my letter reaches you, you shall go to the open court of Amun of the Thrones of the Two Lands taking the children along with you and coax him and tell him to save me.

The transposition of the Egyptian socio-political order and behavioural pattern into the world of the divine affects more than the conversion of gods into Pharaohs or equivalents of other human authority figures. The Egyptians experienced the world in which they lived as a context where a continued tension existed between the forces of order and chaos that periodically broke out into open conflict and disruption. That dimension is also something that is transposed into the world of the gods which is far from being a peaceful place and is represented as a forum where conflict could easily break out. Certainly the gods, as a whole, are frequently presented as positive forces that actively patrol the moral system and punish human transgression, but *The Conflict of Horus and Seth* makes it abundantly clear that divine beings who embodied violence and other negative forces could be a major problem to the peace of the gods themselves, and *The Book of the Celestial Cow* and *The Book of*

Overthrowing Apophis powerfully illustrate the Egyptian conviction that warding off the onset of cosmic chaos is a recurrent necessity.

At a more general level the humanizing of the gods on the basis of the Egyptian concept of what a human being is means that they live and behave very much as human beings do and have very much the same needs. This emerges vividly in the highly anthropomorphized *Conflict of Horus and Seth* in which the deities in question have their own tents, the Ennead eats bread in the All-Lord's pavilion, Hathor milks a gazelle, and Seth shows a marked predilection for eating lettuces. They also send letters, cheat one another, display jealousies, fears, and anger, and are afflicted with periodic bouts of sexual enthusiasm. This last point is, of course, of particular importance since the Egyptians' marked tendency to equate creation with procreation meant that sexual congress, or at least sexual activity, functioned as a major element in creation myths.

To a modern student a particularly surprising aspect of the concept of deity in Ancient Egypt is the conviction that the gods were dependent on human activity for survival. Neither Greeks nor Romans nor any of the great modern religions would countenance such an idea for one moment, but the Egyptians were quite convinced that the gods 'long-lastingness' was not absolute but conditional on the fulfilment of strict requirements focused on the temple. Here again the conceptualization of the gods in essentially human terms came powerfully into play: the temple was regarded as the god's dwelling as well as a source of creative and cosmicizing power (see p. 258). This power-source could be tapped by the performance of rituals of maintenance for the cult statue/deity which had two dimensions. At the most obvious level they took the form of offering foods and other physical necessities, such as cosmetics and items of clothing, a process modelled on what would be required by the king or any high-ranking Egyptian. However, overlaid on this activity was the notion that the offerings were also equivalent to the enemies of the deity and needed to be ritually slain to preserve him or her from their malevolence so that we frequently encounter scenes in which the offerings are being smitten with a mace or even slain in the god's presence. Strictly it was Pharaoh, an incarnate god and hence the perfect intermediary between man and deity, who was responsible for carrying out the cult, and in theory and iconographically it always was, but, in practice, he could not discharge this function in every temple every day throughout the country, and it was necessary to employ substitutes. The 'Pharaoh substitute' was the high priest who was ritually converted into Pharaoh every day in order to perform this function, but it was only in his capacity as a substitute that he could validly carry out this function (A. M. Blackman 1918*a*, 1918*b*, 1919, 1921; Fairman 1954; Wilson 2010). The terminology used to describe the high priest again betrays the conceptualization of the offering ritual as equivalent to service in a palace or elite mansion; for he is normally known as the *hem netjer tepy* (ḥm nṯr tpy), 'first god's servant', the term used for 'servant' being a standard term for servants in secular contexts. He was assisted in a temple of any size by a corps of lesser 'servants' as well as by lower-ranking priests, above all the *web*-priests (*wꜥbw*) whose major function was safeguarding ritual purity within the temple. Provided that these rituals were performed, the gods would continue to flourish, and the cosmic order would be maintained, but, if they were omitted, the entire cosmic structure could shake apart. For this reason it was common practice to decorate temple walls with depictions of key ritual activities that were due to take place in them, the representations having the capacity to function as the equivalent of priestly action if that were not, in fact, forthcoming. If served in the appropriate manner, the deity, in return, would impart to the king life, stability, and power, and through him support the Egyptian people as a whole so that, in effect, the temple functioned as a powerhouse from which Pharaoh, but only Pharaoh, was able to draw divine support for himself and the kingdom. Clearly, this symbiotic relationship gave the king a status far beyond that of a mere ruler of men and located him at the very centre of the universe itself, in the process enormously strengthening his position in the organizational structure of the kingdom.

It is a natural, though not inevitable, consequence of the concept of the immanence and omnipresence of the divine that Egyptian gods were thought to be capable of communicating with men directly in a variety of different ways. Oracles become increasingly common in our evidence from the New Kingdom onwards both in the lives of ordinary people and in appointments to major religious offices, and the appointment of Nebwenenef as High Priest of Amun in Regnal Year 1 of Ramesses II is an excellent example of the way in which this practice could be used to serve the royal agenda (Kitchen 2000: 202).[24] Dreams are another common medium of communication at all levels of society (Szpakowska 2003) and again a political dimension can appear as in the case of the Dream Stele of Tuthmose IV (Szpakowska 2003: 50–2). The gods can also use portents as a means of indicating their will, and in this context a particularly interesting device is the *biayet* (*biꜣyt*), 'wonder', which is sent to kings (see p. 70). Two classic examples appear in the Hammamat inscriptions of Montuhotep IV. In the inscription of day 3 we read of a gazelle which gave birth on the stone that was to be used for the lid of the sarcophagus. The text of day 23 describes another *biayet*, this time the discovery of a well where none had ever been seen before. Since a *biayet* is a divine signal that the king is doing what the gods approve, both narratives function as divine endorsement of the actions of the ruler, a point worth making in the case of Montuhotep IV since his claim to the throne was evidently open to question. The lines of communication could, of course, run the other way, and

---

[24] The oracle is not mentioned in so many words, but it must be the basis for the process described.

Egyptians were certainly able to communicate with their divinities through such familiar media as offerings and prayers.

Up to this point we have focused attention on the great gods of the Egyptian cosmos, but the term *netjeru* cannot be confined to them. The word 'demons' frequently occurs in modern discussions of Egyptian religious belief and practice, but its use is so redolent of Christian thinking that it is often seriously misleading in that it always evokes the notion of malevolent beings, more or less anthropomorphized and usually grotesque, who are at odds with the will of God and pursue their own malicious agenda. The Pharaonic Egyptians had no concept of such beings and, therefore, had no generic term for 'demon'. What they did have was a concept of a large and variegated corpus of divine entities inhabiting the world of the *netjeru* who were not regarded as the equivalent of the great gods but, nevertheless, shared in their divine status (H. Bonnet 1952: 146; Meeks 1971). It is these entities that have been designated 'demons' in modern literature, but the term is not apposite. Although some of them can act in a destructive and malicious fashion, they may also function in many ways as agents of the higher gods or, at least, render assistance to gods and even men, as required. In the *Tale of the Doomed Prince* the eponymous Prince received aid from a *Nakht* (*nḫt*), 'Power', who is nameless but clearly enjoys divine status. In the *Westcar Papyrus* one of the portals of the Underworld is said to be guarded by a being with the name *Hebesu-bag* (*ḥbs(w)-bȝg*), 'He who shrouds the Tired One', guardianship being a typical function of such figures. The Underworld, not surprisingly, was believed to be populated by a large group of beings of this sort, often with ominous names such as 'Backward-facing One who comes from the Abyss', whose role in maintaining the divine order is clear, even though, at the same time, their iconography and epithets strongly suggest that they are ultimately reifications of the Egyptians' fears and anxieties relating to death and the dead. In a word, there were no demons in the Ancient Egyptian conceptual world, only lesser divinities, often of bizarre appearance, who were thought to function frequently as agents, beneficent or otherwise, of the greater gods.

Finally, we must address the issue of the status of animals in the cosmic order. As argued above, the Egyptian universe was conceived of as a continuum of being, and within this context animals played a crucial role. At one level they were a constant part of the daily life of the Egyptians and belonged to the same level of being as they did. Such a perception was greatly facilitated by the fact that the Egyptian perception of the animals around them was not that they were inferior to humans but rather that they were a different and at least equal order of being. However, the perception of difference went much further in that many animals—and an increasing number of them, perhaps, as time went on—were perceived as possessing mysterious, uncanny, and ultimately godlike powers which the Egyptians wished to exploit or ward off and which enabled them to locate animals in the category of gods as well as in the world of men. This situation, in itself, would be sufficient to trigger cult activity in relation to animals and to encourage the use of animal forms in religious iconography, but I suspect that animals also served another function, if only at a subliminal level: as entities that could be located in the sphere of the human and the divine, they could also serve to knit the order of beings in the universe into one continuum and could, therefore, be seen as playing a major part in maintaining the integrity of the very fabric of the cosmos itself.

8

Affirmation of a Conceptual World

Up to this point I have focused on socio-political structures and their ideological underpinning. However, like all societies, the postulates on which
Egyptian civilization was based required continual restatement and reassertion
if they were to retain their validity in the eyes of society. This could be done in
a variety of contexts, not least through the recurrent practice of war which has
already been analysed (see Ch. 4), but in the following discussion I propose to
concentrate on three major areas in which this process is particularly at issue:
ceremonies, text, and visual media.

CEREMONIES

Confucius had no doubt of the critical role of ceremonies in maintaining social
cohesion: 'ceremonies . . . are the bond that holds the multitudes together, and,
if the bond be removed, those multitudes fall into confusion' (1967, Li Qi 16),
but his comments have a relevance well beyond Imperial China. Ceremonies
consist of ritualized schemes of action normally combining a manual dimension with verbal formulae that define the action's rationale. They are usually
repeated on a regular basis, but in some cases they are tied to specific events
whose occurrence is unpredictable, such as coronations, births, or funerals. In
religious contexts, ancient or modern, they may be regarded as possessing
such potency that they are capable of bringing about changes in a conceptual
or physical environment. Alternatively, their main focus may be political or
social, even though a religious dimension is frequently incorporated. However,
whatever their explicit function, their most important, if subliminal, role is to
act as a means by which a society or social group can assert a corporate
commitment to religious systems, ideologies, specific aims, values, or the
socio-political order.

In Pharaonic Egypt the most important context for ceremonial activity was
religious festivals, some of irregular occurrence, others taking place annually at
fixed points during the year (Schott 1950; Altenmüller *LÄ* ii. 171–91). These

were very numerous, though many of those connected with temples were probably small-scale affairs in which only priests would have participated. Since the underlying ritual strategies tend to be the same for all, it will be sufficient to pick out some typical examples to illustrate their workings and focus.

Inevitably, the central importance of kingship led to the intense ceremonial ritualization of the institution so that its ideological substrate could be continually restated and reaffirmed. The most regular ceremonial assertion of the king's key position in the cosmic order was the ceremonies of the temple cult itself; for in theory, whatever the practicalities might be, it was always the king who performed this critically important ritual function (see p. 237). All priestly assistants participating in these daily cult acts were constantly reaffirming a commitment to a crucially important aspect of royal ideology and the state system that went with it, but these activities were closely confined to the priestly elite. However, the need for more public ceremonial events was amply met. We have already discussed the coronation rituals and the *Heb-sed* festivals, which served at the highest level as state ceremonial sequences that rulers were required to undergo in order to validate or revalidate their position (see p. 68), but they did not stand alone. The spectacular Beautiful Festival of Opet held at Thebes in the second month of *Akhet* was an annual royal festival in which the king always participated and which, in its most developed form, lasted up to twenty-seven days. To the accompaniment of enthusiastic rejoicing, statues of the Theban triad (Amon-re, his wife Mut, and his son Khonsu) were transported from the Karnak temple to Luxor which was dedicated to an aspect of Amun (Amenemopet) resident in the Opet or Harîm suite at the extreme southern end of the temple. On arrival the sacred barks were deposited in bark shrines located behind the main offering chamber, and a series of rituals was then performed which focused on the regeneration of the royal *ka*, i.e. the king (see p. 67), and that of the Theban triad and Amun of Luxor.[1] These rites may have included a sacred marriage enacted in the Birth Room located to the east of the main shrine, but they certainly involved a re-enactment of elements of the coronation ritual as the conclusion to the process whereby the king was restored to the maximum state of efficacy that he had enjoyed at his original coronation. In the same way the cosmicizing power of the divine participants, particularly that of the two manifestations of Amun, was recharged and raised to maximum efficiency. Whilst these rituals took place within the most sacred parts of the temple and were seen by very few, the processions by land and water were great public events in which all could participate so that in-group identity was strongly reinforced, and corporate commitment to the ideology of kingship reaffirmed. They also allowed

---

[1] The use of the term *nefer* to describe the festival is an explicit statement that invigoration is the key issue (see p. 211).

widespread rejoicing at the regeneration of cosmic energy at large; for Amun, as creator god, was intimately linked to the processes of cosmic birth and generation. Through the recharging of his power and that of his agent the king, the cosmos could continue its orderly progress for yet another year (Wolf 1931; Epigraphic Survey 1994; Bell 1997: 157–80).

The Festival of Khoiak, celebrated annually at Abydos, in later times from the 18th to the 30th of the last month of the season of *Akhet*, did not require the physical presence of the king. It consisted of an elaborate ritual sequence, partly public and partly confined to the priests, which took the form of the re-enactment of the death, burial, and resurrection of Osiris into which fertility rituals focusing on the sowing and sprouting of corn (identified with Osiris) were later integrated (Lloyd 1976: 277–9). Through the latter ritual sequence, technically, if not actually carried out by the king, the Egyptians were asserting direct royal agency in maintaining the annual cycle of the growth of corn and thereby the well-being of Egypt itself. In the death–resurrection cycle two aspects were at play. At one level, it was directly relevant to all Egyptians because it restated the most important part of the mythological prototype for, and guarantee of, the post-mortem destiny of all men, but it had a particular relevance to the king since the death and resurrection of Osiris was the death and resurrection of his father. Therefore, the position of Osiris as king of the resurrected dead and that of Pharaoh as ruler of men were annually being restated and reaffirmed. One consequence of this was that, when coronations took place, they were held at the beginning of the first month of the season of *Peret*, immediately after the end of *Akhet* so that the resurrection of Osiris as king of the resurrected dead is directly linked to the formal accession of the new Pharaoh.

Festivals in which the dead had an interest were of wide currency and great importance to the Egyptians. Therefore, they are frequently listed with greater or less completeness in tomb inscriptions, a typical example occurring in a passage in the biography of Khnumhotep II at Beni Hasan:

I commanded a mortuary offering in every festival of the necropolis, [to wit] in the first-of-the-year festival, the opening-of-the-year festival, the great year festival, the lesser year festival, the last-day-of-the-year festival, and the great festival, the great year festival, in the great fire festival, in the lesser fire festival, in the feast of the five epagomenal days, in the *sḏt-šʿ* festival, the twelve month festivals and the twelve half-month festivals, and every festival of one who is upon earth or rejuvenated in the necropolis.   (De Buck 1970: 69)

All these events were public celebrations widely observed and, to that extent, they played an important socializing role in all communities, but they feature in mortuary texts because they provided a means by which the resurrected dead could continue to participate in events which they enjoyed so much whilst living and thereby provided repeated opportunities to reaffirm the concept of the family as a corporation of the living and the dead. This social awareness of the abiding presence of the dead and the obligation of the living to serve them is exemplified at an even higher level in the Beautiful Festival of the Valley (*ḥb nfr n int*)[2] in which a statue of the god Amon-re, later accompanied by those of his wife Mut and son Khonsu, was taken in a great procession from Karnak to the temple of Hatshepsut at Deir el-Bahri from which the god subsequently visited the royal mortuary temples lining the margins of the cultivation which were all equipped with special installations designed to receive him. These events were celebrated by large numbers of the populace who visited the tombs of their ancestors where a nocturnal vigil was held, followed by feasts which were copiously fuelled with alcohol and accompanied with dancing and music, all of which was designed to induce an ecstatic state of trance in which the dead and the living were thought to enter into communion.[3] The deceased were also recharged with life-giving potency by being presented with bouquets of the god and other floral gifts whose fragrance was believed to impart regenerative power to the recipients (Schott 1953; Bell 1997: 136–7).

TEXT

Text takes many different forms in Ancient Egypt, but I propose to focus in this section on narrative. Even that category, however, is not homogeneous since it embraces such disparate material as ritual texts, stories, and accounts of historical events, but, whatever their precise nature, such texts have the potential to reflect, evaluate, and confirm the values and ideology of the Egyptian socio-political system. It would pass well beyond the compass of this study if I were to attempt a systematic analysis of all available examples, an enterprise that requires a book in its own right. I shall, therefore, focus on some typical examples, beginning with ritual narrative.[4]

---

[2] For the significance of the word *nefer* see p. 211.

[3] This phenomenon was not confined to festivals of the dead and has many counterparts in Egyptian cult. There was even a Festival of Drunkenness celebrated in honour of Hathor at Dendera (Lloyd 1976: 276). Whilst music, dance, and alcohol would undoubtedly have assisted in inducing a trance-like state where a sense of oneness with divine beings might arise, we can be confident that the Egyptians could very easily turn a holy day into a holiday, a phenomenon not without parallel in many other societies.

[4] Good surveys of Egyptian literature in general and the issues it raises will be found in Loprieno 1996; Parkinson 2002: Lloyd (ed.) 2010c: 663–731.

Ritual Text

I shall take as my example from the large group of possibilities a text that we have already encountered, i.e. *The Book of the Celestial Cow* (see p. 233) which first appears in the tomb of Tutankhamun and then recurs in royal tombs of the Nineteenth and Twentieth Dynasties. It consists both of texts and representations and falls into four sections: the account of the destruction of mankind, a description of the withdrawal of the sun god Re into heaven, Re's subsequent organization of the underworld and strengthening of the structure of the universe, and an account of the power of magic (*heka*, *ḥkȝ*), a major instrument of divine action. Recurrent features are statements that particular sections have a specific function and also instructions on the manual rites which are to accompany the recitation of sections of text, presumably as part of the king's funerary ceremonies. Clearly, when considered *in toto*, one function of the text is to present a view of divine and human history in terms of both cosmogony and cosmology. Within that broader framework *The Destruction of Mankind* not only explains the relationship between the creator and mankind but also provides a model for royal action on earth; for, since Re and his actions are blueprints for the actions of the king himself, the moral, or morals, of the narrative are directly relevant to the human sphere: sedition will be punished, and with divine approval, and the king should operate fairly, where appropriate through consultation, and also with mercy. Both content and context make it clear that this text serves ultimately as an instrument of *heka* (see p. 233). It is, therefore, more than text. It is nothing less than a cosmicizing device, a vital dynamic creative force that can bring into being and maintain in being the very situation it describes. However, crucial though this dimension undoubtedly was, the text is also a restatement and reaffirmation of a canonical worldview and thereby serves as one small element in the copious and elaborate textual apparatus for supporting the Ancient Egyptian concept of the structure and workings of the cosmos. This would have been accessible only to those who could read it and anyone who happened to be in earshot when the texts were recited, but ultimately it was precisely such elite figures who were responsible for maintaining the integrity of Pharaonic culture.

Stories

Stories are a widespread form of expression in the Middle East (without casting the net any wider), the most famous example by far being the Arabic *Thousand and One Nights*. The cultural context in which they are delivered is very frequently oral in character, e.g. there are professional storytellers who earn their living by relating these tales. Such a context brings with it certain characteristics such as fluidity in detail and repetition of words, phrases, and even whole passages. The surviving Egyptian stories are obviously at least one step beyond that stage because they have survived in written form.

Egyptian stories show considerable variety both in origin, subject matter, form, style, attitudes, and points of emphasis. They clearly draw on a variety of sources: oral tradition, faded myth, propaganda (pre-eminently propaganda of kingship), wisdom texts, tomb biographies, royal inscriptions, official reports, and encomia of the king, to name but a few, and that provides many opportunities for intertextualities which the Egyptians exploited to the full. They are also characterized by great skill in storytelling, sophisticated structure, and close attention to stylistic effect. They frequently contain a strong escapist element that can include fantasy and reversals of fortune, and they show a marked tendency to the didactic in that they are frequently implicitly, if not explicitly, reaffirmations of the moral order under and through which the Ancient Egyptians operated. Numerous examples have survived in whole or in part, and it is not necessary for my purposes to survey them all. I shall confine myself to the discussion of a selection from the major periods of literary production up to the Macedonian conquest.

The Middle Kingdom has left us a number of examples. The *Tale of the Eloquent Peasant* describes the experience of a peasant from the Wadi Natrun called Khuenanup who had set out for Egypt to obtain food for his family and was illegally deprived of his donkey by an official called Nemtynakht (Parkinson 1998: 54–88). When he failed to gain redress from him for this offence, he went to the High Steward Rensi, son of Meru, to obtain compensation. This sets up a situation where the peasant finds himself delivering nine highly rhetorical appeals for justice before Rensi who was so enthused by their eloquence that he informed the king who ordered him to have them written down. These were ultimately presented to the king who was highly impressed and told Rensi to resolve the dispute. The thief Nemtynakht was then punished with total loss of property which was handed over to the peasant. This carefully constructed tale is dominated by the nine appeals to Rensi which are composed in highly wrought and allusive language that was designed, in itself, to give pleasure to the audience, but their most important dimension is their marked social and moral slant, which is concerned to make statements about the way government should be conducted and the way the governed should react. There is a recognition that the administration could be corrupt, and officials could show an arrogant disdain for the less powerful. Officials need to keep an eye on magistrates, but a high standard of official probity is advocated throughout. Pharaoh is presented as being on the side of the victim of injustice, and he also shows solicitude for the family of Khuenanup. Paternalistic concern for the unfortunate is strongly emphasized. Indeed, kindness is recommended as an official virtue throughout the narrative. Whilst clients are asserted to have claims on their lord, deference to authority is implicitly expected, and the peasant, despite variations in emotional register, is present-ed as thoroughly reasonable and usually polite. There is recurrent emphasis on the need for law-abiding behaviour and non-deviation from what is proper, a stance to be achieved by strict adherence to the requirements of *maat* the rewards for which are described in highly figurative language in this passage:

> If you go down to the lake of *maat*,
> You will sail on it with a fair wind;
> The bunt will not be stripped from your sail, nor will your boat be held back;
> Nor will misfortune befall your mast, nor will your yards snap;
> You will not founder [?], touching on land;
> Nor will the flood sweep you away;
> You will not taste the river's evil, nor will you look on the face of fear.
> But caught fish will come to you,
> And you will take fatted fowl.   (R54–62)

Within that context the ideal of behaviour is presented, as usual, as the 'silent' man (see p. 221), and the entire narrative puts over the point that persistence in an appropriate manner will bring success. This moral system is policed by the gods; righteous conduct determines whether someone lives eternally; and evil is ultimately punished.

The story of the *Shipwrecked Sailor* provides an account of the adventures of a sailor who had been sent on an expedition by sea to Sinai (Parkinson 1998: 89–101). On the way his ship is assailed by a great storm and sinks. He survives and is cast up on an island that contains an abundance of everything needed to sustain life. Suddenly he is confronted by a great serpent which is clearly divine and has the power of speech. They engage in a long conversation in which the serpent makes appropriate comments on the moral qualities needed to survive tribulations, and he also recounts a disaster that had happened to his family. Eventually a ship arrives and the sailor boards it, laden with all the good things the island can provide, and he returns to Egypt to great acclaim in the royal court. We are informed that after his departure the island will disappear.

The agendas of this text are multifarious. Registers of reality in Egyptian texts can vary considerably, and this one lies very much at the marvellous end of the spectrum, playing to the taste for imaginative excitement, wish-fulfilment, and escapism which is part of the stock-in-trade of Egyptian narrative fiction. This is not to deny that there is an element of historicity in the context; for expeditions to Sinai on the Red Sea were frequent events, and, since expedition texts are a common phenomenon, there are clear opportun-ities for intertextual references which are undoubtedly exploited, but the ship and crew used by the sailor are extraordinary, and the island with its excep-tional riches, its capacity for disappearance, and its divine serpent passes well beyond the bounds of normal experience. The island and serpent draw their preternatural dimension from a source that was probably exploited on some scale in Egyptian narrative fiction, i.e. faded myth; for there can be no doubt whatsoever that the island is, in origin, the island of creation and that the serpent was originally the creator god himself. However, the marvellous is not everything in this text. It is also intended to get the Egyptian adrenalin going with a sequence of exciting episodes, which would doubtless have been made more exciting by many an accomplished oral narrator. Even more important is the didactic dimension, a recurrent feature that again offers opportunities for intertextuality, in this case with the very rich literary genre of *seboyet* or *Instruction* texts. However, this element goes well beyond casual comment and forms part of the very structure of the tale itself: the sailor is trying to teach his leader how to cope with adversity. The serpent does likewise to the sailor, firmly insisting: 'if you are brave and strong of heart, you will fill your embrace with your children, you will kiss your wife, and you will see your home. It is better than anything else' (132–4). Thus, the Egyptian tale is insisting on the value of those most Egyptian of virtues, patience and forbearance, as a means of coping with the vicissitudes of human existence. Yet firm and emphatic though this advice may be, we are presented in the last lines of the tale with the unexpected spectacle of the expedition leader refusing to accept it. All the efforts of the sailor come to nought so that, in the end, there is an element of subversion in this text. One may teach the traditional wisdom, whose intrinsic value few Egyptians would have doubted, but people do not necessarily listen!

The *Westcar Papyrus* consists of a lengthy narrative sequence set in the reign of the Fourth Dynasty king Khufu. The first part consists mainly of accounts of the achievements of a series of deceased *heka*-masters which are narrated by sons of Khufu to entertain him. These conclude with Hardedef, one of Khufu's sons, suggesting that a living *heka*-master called Djedi should be brought to the palace in order to show his skill before the king, and Hardedef is promptly sent off to bring him. On his arrival Djedi performs appropriately astonishing feats and is then used as the means of introducing the second part of the text which contains a narrative of the divine origins of the three early kings of the Fifth Dynasty (Parkinson 1998: 102–27). There is much grist to our mill in all this. The power of *heka* and its masters is repeatedly displayed; the courteous interchange between Hardedef and Djedi exemplifies the importance of good manners in social relations; the doctrine of the theogamy, which held that kings were the sons of Re, is powerfully affirmed, and the role of *biayet* as an indication of divine approval is explicitly stated (see p. 70); descriptions of the palace and its activities present the appropriate image of the splendour of kingship; the classic agenda of royal action is invoked on several occasions as a statement of what kings are for, though Djedi insists that there are limits to what it is proper for a king to do; royal generosity, one of the lynchpins of royal power, is described on several occasions; the accessibility of the Pharaoh is taken for granted; the concept of the immanence of the gods is clearly asserted; the idea that men are the cattle of Re is affirmed in Djedi's description of them as 'the august cattle' (*ta aut shepset*; *tꜣ ꜥwt špst*, 8, 17); the picture of Redjedet fulfilling her role as a *nebet per* ('Mistress of the House') provides a model of wifely diligence in the household; there is a clear conviction that retribution will befall antisocial behaviour; and the punning on the names of the Fifth Dynasty kings springs from the widely held Egyptian conviction that similarities of sound indicate important inner relationships between the entities to which they refer.

The *Story of Sinuhe* is rightly regarded as the finest surviving example of Egyptian narrative literature. In the interests of verisimilitude it is cast super-ficially in the form of a tomb biography and given a genuine historical context. Within this framework the writer locates an account of the career of an Egyptian courtier called Sinuhe who flees Egypt in panic on the assassination of Amenemhet I and makes his way with some difficulty to Syria-Palestine where his luck turns, and he becomes a major figure in one of the local tribal communities, on one occasion fighting a successful duel with an Asiatic champion. Despite his successes in Asia he is anxious to return to Egypt to end his days there. This aspiration comes to the attention of King Senwosret I who summons him to return. This Sinuhe does, and he is reinstated in his erstwhile high position and granted all the equipment for a prestigious traditional burial (Parkinson 1998: 21–53). However, this interesting and entertaining narrative is far from being an end in itself. Rather, it is used by the author to present a vision of the role of Pharaoh in relation to his subjects and to human well-being in general, a focus reinforced by an intertextual dimension that incorporates literary genres such as praises of the king and royal edicts. The message is essentially that proximity to the king brings with it fullness of life and prosperity, absence means, at best, a half-life. The return to Egypt and Pharaoh's good will brings deliverance not only from a foreign mode of life but from death itself (cf. Baines 1982).[5] In addition, the text reaffirms concepts of the role of the gods and fate in human affairs and the crucial importance of a proper burial according to traditional Egyptian rites. It also recognizes the psychological dimension in human actions that are not regarded simply as an exterior phenomenon but as springing from the state of mind of the individual himself.

The New Kingdom *Conflict of Horus and Seth* is a tale of extraordinary interest. It is based on the final episode of the myth of Osiris which deals with

---

[5] The critical role of the king in guaranteeing the basics of Egyptian life and the proper functioning of the realm were recurrent themes of Egyptian literature, e.g. in the Middle Kingdom *Admonitions* (Parkinson 1998: 166–99) argues at length that, if kingship does not function properly, political, economic, and social collapse is the inevitable result, and the *Loyalist Teaching* (Parkinson 1998: 235–45) is equally fulsome on the critical position of the king whilst adding complementary injunctions on the proper behaviour of officials.

the conflict of Horus and Seth fought out to determine who should succeed Osiris as king on earth. The narrative takes the form of a series of contests that range from legal debates to contests of physical strength and battles of wits, interspersed with instances of divine trickery (Simpson (ed.) 2003: 91–103). The central issue is whether 'right' (*maat*) should take precedence over 'power' (*user; wsr*), i.e., in this case, whether the strength and power of Seth should guarantee his success or whether the hereditary principle (the proper legal procedure) should give victory to Horus. After much struggling Seth concedes defeat when Atum uses force against him to get him to accept the verdict, and he is given a position of honour with Pre-Harakhty which enables him to use his formidable power on behalf of Pre himself. The relevance of all this as a paradigm for attitudes to power and decision-making in a human context is self-evident, in particular, the emphasis on debate, arbitration, and the search for compromise which yields an acceptable conclusion by concessions to all parties and the implication that, whilst it is appropriate for the proper authority to use compulsion to fulfil the requirements of *maat*, it is not acceptable for decisions to be determined by brute force. Failure to act in accordance with *maat* can lead to its erosion as emphasized in the striking comment of Osiris when criticizing the actions of the Ennead in dealing with the dispute: '*Maat* has been caused to sink into the netherworld' (15. 4). Whilst this is the main thrust of the narrative, that is not an end of the matter. It also affirms Egyptian concepts of the nature of the gods and divine action: their psychological make-up is that of human beings; they are partisan, tricksters, prone to violence, and highly sexually active. They can also display mutability of form.

The Misfortunes of Wenamun (Simpson (ed.) 2003: 116–24) is widely regarded as the masterpiece of Late Egyptian narrative fiction. Not all commentators have been convinced that the text should be characterized in that way and have preferred to think of it as a genuine official report, but it is now generally conceded that the content of the text cannot be reconciled with that view (Baines 1999). The furthest we could go in that direction would be to argue that it is a heavily fictionalized account of a genuine report. The story exemplifies the common folk- or narrative-motif of the journey and takes the form of an account of a foreign expedition undertaken by an Egyptian official called Wenamun, 'the Elder of the Portal of the Temple of Amun' at Thebes. The purpose is to obtain timber for a sacred barque of the god from the Lebanon, and the story revolves around his confrontations with a series of obstacles and his ultimately successful responses to them: first, he has to gain the assistance of a dynast called Smendes, based at Tanis, who eventually provides a ship and supplies for the journey to Syria. He then encounters his first misfortune when a crew member steals a significant part of his bartering goods whilst he was staying in a Tjeker port called Dor. He tries to get redress from the local prince, and, when this fails, he leaves and on his way to Byblos robs a Tjeker ship of a quantity of silver and refuses to hand it back until his own resources are returned. He then establishes himself at Byblos in a tent on the seashore. After a series of vicissitudes Wenamun succeeds in getting the timber he requires and is about to leave with it when Tjeker ships arrive demanding his arrest for the theft of the silver. This the king of Byblos is not prepared to do, and he embarks on a compromise solution that involves Wenamun being given a head start before the Tjeker are allowed to pursue. Yet another misfortune ensues in that he is driven off-course to Cyprus where he is just saved from a lynch mob by the intervention of the local princess. Sadly at this point our one manuscript breaks off, and we do not know for sure what the outcome was, though the probability must be, given the marked Egyptian predilection for happy endings, that he eventually got back safe and sound.

Despite the fact that the tale paints a sad picture of the decline of Egypt's status in the Near East in the late New Kingdom, it does at one point indulge in some pro-Egyptian propaganda when the prince of Byblos comments to Wenamun: 'Indeed, Amun founded all lands. He founded them after he had previously founded the land of Egypt from which you have come. Furthermore, craftsmanship came forth from it to reach the place where I am and learning came forth from there to reach the place where I am' (2. 20–1). Of course, this piece of Egyptian self-congratulation loses nothing of its force by being voiced not by Wenamun but by a foreign potentate. This, however, is not the main thrust of the narrative. The story does not make its main point obviously, in the ways that we found, for example, in *The Shipwrecked Sailor*. The reader is not presented with a glaring moral lesson, but must read it off through sensitive consideration of the text. If we look carefully at Wenamun's words and actions, he emerges certainly as persistent, determined, and resilient, but he is also impatient, high-handed, hot-headed, brash, arrogant, and insensitive, and it is these deficiencies that time and time again get him into trouble. In other words, he is his own worst enemy, and the tale presents us with an object lesson, oblique and implicit though it may be, on the desirability of circumspection, self-restraint, and moderation, those cardinal virtues so ardently advocated in Egyptian wisdom texts.

Instruction Texts

Instruction texts are the most explicit written medium through which the Egyptians expressed and affirmed their vision of a moral universe, and their importance in that respect is reflected by the fact that they form one of largest literary genres surviving from Ancient Egypt and appear at every period from the Middle Kingdom onwards. It is, of course, possible that they existed at an earlier stage in Egyptian history, but there is, as yet, no evidence that this was the case. Such texts as the *Instruction of Kagemni* and the *Instruction of Ptahhotep* are located by their authors in the Old Kingdom for prestige purposes, but their linguistic character demonstrates that they belong very firmly in the Middle Kingdom, and there is no reason to believe that they are updated versions of older texts. Whichever texts we examine it is as well to remember that they all present a certain amount of linguistic difficulty which often arises from textual corruption. Consequently it is frequently the case that modern translations will show significant differences from each other at particular points.

I shall begin with the Middle Kingdom *Instruction of Ptahhotep* which survives in one complete copy and several partial versions (Parkinson 1998: 246–72). The timespan of these copies makes it clear that the text retained its popularity into the New Kingdom. Its purpose is made quite evident at the very beginning where it is stated to be addressed to the reader (or listener):

> So that I may tell him the words of those who heard,
> The counsels of the ancestors,
> Who listened to the gods
> So that the like is done for you,
> Strife is driven from the people,
> And the Two Banks serve you!
> Then did the majesty of this god say:
> 'Instruct him, then, in the sayings of the past
> Before you retire
> So that he becomes a model for the children of the nobles.
> Obedience entering into him and all honesty.
> Speak to him.
> No man is born wise.'   (5. 3–6)

The instruction dimension is then reinforced by the observation that the text consists of 'the maxims of excellent discourse . . . in instructing the ignorant in knowledge and in the method of excellent discourse, a thing beneficial to him who will hear and a misery to him who will neglect them' (5. 6–8). These introductory comments are very revealing: they show that the moral system is a traditional one to be found in the ways of the ancestors and embodied in the sayings of the past, but all this derives ultimately from the gods; it is clearly stated that the king himself can benefit from such instruction and that listening to it can guarantee harmony within the kingdom; the text takes a position on the nurture-versus-nature discussion of the origin of moral and intellectual qualities in that it insists that wisdom is an acquired characteristic; there is an emphasis on obedience; and reference to 'excellent discourse' shows a very Egyptian interest in eloquence as something that is both intellectually and aesthetically pleasing.

The main body of the text consists of thirty-seven maxims. The maxims themselves do not present us with any attempt to provide a carefully thought out system of conduct based on establishing basic principles as might be the case in an ancient Greek work on ethics nor is there any compelling overriding logic behind the order in which the advice is given, the governing factor being much more akin to a stream-of-consciousness approach. They present the reader/listener, instead, with a series of real-world situations and severely practical advice on the best way to deal with them. The maxims are, therefore, often couched in the form of conditional clauses that present a specific problem and its solution. However, such clauses are periodically interleaved with straightforward imperatives to provide some measure of variety.

Despite the loose format of the instruction section of *Ptahhotep* a very clear world-view appears and a coherent recommended code of conduct.

General principles of behaviour: keep a balanced attitude to life, alternating work with play; conceit and arrogance are deplored on the grounds that no one ever achieves complete mastery of anything, and even the untutored can achieve excellence ('Fine speech is more hidden than malachite. Yet it may be found among serving maids at the grindstones' (5. 10)—in this case the scribe is conceding that nature rather than nurture can be the source of personal qualities); avoid avarice with its capacity for creating alienation; when dealing with your fellow men you should recognize difference of rank and orchestrate your conduct accordingly—above all you should practise self-control, and this will, in the end, bring success; strive to attain a high reputation, and perform beneficent acts; generosity and kindness are strongly recommended; do not steal, and avoid dissension; above all follow the principles of *maat* which are unalterable, and punishment for injustice is inevitable; avoid improper sexual liaisons ('Beware of approaching the women' (9. 9)); cultivate friends, treating them with tact and restraint even in difficult circumstances since they can be very useful and even function as an insurance policy; if you are uncertain of the truth of something, do not repeat it because the consequences may be quite unforeseen; finally, if you punish, ensure that the punishment is just, firm, and a genuine deterrent.

The family: whilst some offspring can be a problem, ultimately the make-up of the unsatisfactory offspring is the doing of the gods, and they will deal with them, but a good son should be nurtured; be generous in your support of your wife ('Do not take her to court but keep her from power and restrain her. When she looks, it is her eye which is her storm wind.[6] Thus you will keep her in your house' (10. 10–12)); if you marry a flighty wife, and she gets out of

[6] i.e. if looks could kill, they would, but they are harmless, and you can put up with them.

hand, 'Do not drive her away; indeed, let her eat. The joyful spirit brings fair water'[7] (15. 7).

Social etiquette: the all-important principle is to know your place, whatever that may be; build up support by gaining people's trust.

Official behaviour: in administrative tasks be careful to observe your rank and act on that basis, and, if you end up a leader, strive to excel and take the long-term view, avoiding generating hostility ('Be calm when you listen to the speech of a suppliant. Do not prevent him from purging his body of that which he had planned to say. A man in distress wants to pour out his heart more than he wants to get what he came for' (9. 3–5)); speak only when you have something worth saying; make sure that you have the requisite knowledge; issue orders only as appropriate; do not throw your weight around but, at the same time, use the authority you have; tread carefully with superiors, respect them, and strive to be of use to them; try to create harmony and be even-handed.

Determinants of the world order: the concept of fate occurs on several occasions, but overwhelmingly the text is marked by the conviction that the gods police the moral order, ensuring success, failure, and retribution, and ultimately all things are in their hands—'It is only what god commands which comes to pass' (6. 10).

The text then concludes with an epilogue that is particularly concerned to emphasize the virtues of listening to advice and obeying it and the benefits that accrue therefrom.

The New Kingdom saw the continued popularity of this genre of text. I shall concentrate on the *Instruction of Any* which, despite its many and obvious corruptions, is particularly interesting because in some measure it subverts the very genre to which it belongs. Although the beginning is lost, it is clear that we have the same basic structure as our preceding text: an introduction and conclusion that constitute the 'frame' and a body of maxims that form the substance of the text. How detailed the frame was we cannot tell from what survives but the basic situation is that the scribe Any of the Palace of Nefertari addresses a string of maxims to his son Khonsuhotep. It will be noted that the status of the putative writer is well below that of putative writers of the Middle Kingdom examples, and this may well have been typical of New Kingdom instruction texts. The instruction then concludes with an epilogue that takes the form of a vigorous argument with his son about the value of the advice that the latter has been given.

The maxims cover the same range of issues as the *Instruction of Ptahhotep*, but the detail, points of emphasis, and tone can be very different. As usual, the writer insists on the practical nature of the advice:

---

[7] The word ʿkȝȝ is unique. The determinative indicates a connection with water, and the root suggests something positive, as does the context. My translation seems a reasonable guess.

Behold, I give you these useful counsels,
For you to consider in your heart;
Do it, and you will be happy,
All evils will be far from you.[8]

General principles of behaviour: there is insistence at the beginning of the text on the need to discharge ritual obligations to the gods, and such issues recur— be self-effacing in the temple, and discharge your mortuary obligations to your parents, actions that will win the favour of the gods; they will also reward those who live a prudent life. This heavy emphasis on religious issues is very typical of the period when the text was written. There is a stern warning against the dangers that can arise through sexual liaisons ('Beware of a woman who is a stranger, one not known in her town. Don't stare at her when she goes by. Do not know her carnally. A deep water whose course is unknown, such is a woman away from her husband. "I am pretty", she tells you daily, when she has no witnesses. She is ready to ensnare you, a great deadly crime when it is heard'); be careful in relations with men of rank, and bear in mind how important rank is ('A woman is asked about her husband. A man is asked about his rank'), knowing your place at all times; keep on the right side of authority; show circumspection in controversy; avoid excessive drinking be- cause it can lead to humiliation; above all things ensure that you organize your life appropriately in all its aspects; set up your mortuary endowment, and accept death when it comes; be careful in your choice of associates; look after your resources ('Keep your eye on what you own lest you end as a beggar'), and be self-reliant; do not put too much hope on receiving an inheritance because you may not get it; look after your mother and model your behaviour in the family on the way she treated you; avoid expressions of communal *Angst* because you might get caught up in things that are not your concern. It is clear that social approval is of crucial importance to the writer.

The family: insistence on setting up a family is of prime concern to the author and begins the sequence of maxims; deal fairly with your wife.

Social etiquette: domestic privacy should be respected; make distinctions in the way in which you behave to specific categories of people; observe the rules of hospitality, not least because it is an insurance policy ('You don't know your end at all. Should you come to be in want, another may do good to you').

Behaviour as an official: be circumspect in dealing with superiors; old age should be respected ('Do not sit when another is standing, one who is older than you'); learning is all-important in promotion and should be cultivated ('One will do all you say if you are versed in writings . . . Whatever office a scribe is given, he should consult the writings . . . The scribe is chosen for his hand. His office has no children').

---

[8] All translations from this text after Lichtheim 2006: 135–46 (courtesy University of Cali- fornia Press).

Determinants of the world order: the gods police the moral order ('Do not rush to attack your attacker. Leave him to the god. Report him daily to the god, tomorrow being like today, and you will see what the god does, when he injures him who injured you,' or again, 'It is the god who judges the righteous. His fate[9] comes and takes him away').

The epilogue is a most remarkable document in that it goes some way towards subverting the entire instruction genre to the extent that it does at least question the value of Any's advice. The argument rages around the nature/nurture issue, which we have already encountered, though in a less inflamed context, and the son's comments may not be entirely devoid of sarcasm, though the obscurity of some of the language makes it impossible to be sure. The son's opening gambit takes the form of a claim that he simply cannot follow his father's advice since his character is determined by nature and cannot, therefore, be changed. The father vigorously protests against this by quoting a series of examples, several from the natural world, where learning can and does take place. In a distinctly obscure and probably corrupt response the son seems to argue that, if there is to be such a change, it requires innate virtues that derive from the gods. The father's response is to reiterate that change can clearly be wrought. The final exchange, if I read it aright, involves the son replying that people are ruled by basic requirements rather than fine sentiments, i.e. his father's advice is a waste of time, given human nature.

Any is by no means the only piece that questions canonical attitudes. From the Middle Kingdom onwards we encounter texts that express doubts about the validity of traditional ideas, particularly in relation to the efficacy of the mortuary cult. In *The Dialogue of a Man with his Soul* (Parkinson 1998: 151–65) we find the Man presenting an image of death and the blessings it brings:

> Death is in my eyes today
> Like the scent of myrrh,
> Like sitting under an awning on a windy day.
> Death is in my eyes today
> Like the scent of the lotus,
> Like sitting on the shore of drunkenness.[10]   (132–6)

The Soul, on the other hand, takes an altogether bleaker view:

> If you call burial to mind, it is heartbreak;
> It is bringing tears, a harbinger of misery;
> It is taking a man from his home,
> Casting him on the high ground.
> You will not come up again to see the sun.
> As for those who built in granite,

---

[9] i.e. the offender's fate.   [10] i.e. almost drunk.

Who constructed pavilions in beauteous pyramids consisting of beauteous works,
So that the builders might become gods,
Their offering stones are no more, like the deceased
Who died on the shore and lacked a survivor.   (56–64)

Doubts about the fate of the dead are powerfully expressed in the *Harper Song* (Simpson (ed.) 2003: 332–3), and the advice is given that, in the face of such uncertainties, men should adopt a *carpe diem* philosophy. *The Book of the Dead* is equally dubious about the land of the dead which is described as devoid of water and air and being 'deep, dark, and unsearchable' (ch. 175), and a text in P.Chester Beatty IV goes considerably further: 'Man decays, his corpse is dust.' For this author the best guarantee of immortality is the production of a book that preserves the author's name for posterity much more effectively than a tomb-chapel or a stele (Lichtheim 2006: 177).

VISUAL MEDIA

The present section is not intended in any way to function as a general survey of Egyptian visual arts in all their aspects. I am concerned here simply with the role they played in defining and confirming the Egyptians' concept of the physical and conceptual world that they inhabited.[11]

Whilst there can be no doubt that Egyptian visual arts exemplify a degree of expressionism, a keen sense of the aesthetic and decorative, and even, at times, individual artistic initiative, there is equally no doubt from context alone that the main driver in large-scale artistic production was pragmatic: it was intended to serve as a means of describing, formulating, and maintaining a world order. For the Egyptians, as for anyone else, the creation of images, be they large or small, was part of a process whereby conceptual entities, which are intrinsically somewhat amorphous, could be objectivized and given a visual format that imparted to them a much sharper definition. This, in turn, made them more tangible and, therefore, more tractable. In early societies this often goes a step further to the point where the representation acquires an objective reality of its own and can be treated as the equivalent of the entity depicted. Representation, therefore, becomes not only a means of giving definition to the world of experience but also a device for physically manipulating it. The mental transmutation of the representation into the represented provides a starting point for ritual activities designed to maintain and control the perceived world. The representations of wild animals on a cave

---

[11] Studies of Egyptian art are legion. Excellent surveys will be found in Groenewegen-Frankfort 1951: bk. 1; Schäfer 1974; Aldred 1980; W. Smith 1981; Gombrich 1995: 55–73; Robins 2008; Lloyd (ed.) 2010c: 779–1007.

wall or of priests or kings on a temple surface became more than representations; the representations *were* what they represented and guaranteed their continued presence and, indeed, a measure of human control and even mastery over them; a statuette of an enemy became the enemy and could be damaged with every expectation that this damage would affect the person depicted.

One of the most important developments in any society's representational strategies is the establishment of a visual code or vocabulary capable of conveying the concepts with which that society is concerned. Such codes are often of great sophistication and require great care in interpretation, and of no society is this more true than that of Ancient Egypt. To enable us to establish the nature of the code prevailing in Pharaonic Egypt and its role in conveying and maintaining a conceptual universe it is useful to make a distinction between the royal and the private context.

The Royal Context

The largest and most typical creative artefacts of the Ancient Egyptians are cult temples and royal mortuary installations, and both have ultimately the same function: to formulate and guarantee the cosmic order.

Cult Temples

Cult temples can be identified from the Prehistoric Period well into the latest phase of Pharaonic culture under the Roman Empire, but nearly all those surviving in a good state of preservation date from the New Kingdom and later. Temple building and renovation were always a cardinal function of the Pharaonic office, and temples were always the most spectacular recurrent statements by the Egyptians of what their universe was considered to be and the central role of the king in maintaining it. The temple was the Egyptians' main instrument whereby the order of the universe was maintained and also the most important medium for expressing the content of that order (Quirke 1997; Shafer 1997; Wilson 2010). Therefore, their foundation was a major state event involving elaborate ceremonies in which the king and his wife were expected to play the major role (the ritual of *pedj-shes* (*pḏ šs*), 'The Stretching of the Cord'), though doubtless, in practice, ritual substitutes could be invoked, if that were necessary.

Given their role as guarantors of order, it is not in the least surprising that all major temples show a marked tendency in architectural design towards balance and symmetry. In their developed form they are normally constructed around a median line which runs through the main entrance to the *sanctum*, and structures to the right and left of that line are usually direct counterparts of each other.[12] Furthermore, the design vocabulary of all chambers is dominated by horizontal and vertical lines, curvilinear elements always being conspicuous by their absence. Furthermore, the breadth of buildings always prevails over their height, a characteristic accentuated by the inward sloping batter frequently applied to outer walls (Fig. 8.1). This feature is, of course, quite at variance with the architectural language of medieval cathedrals which are intended to make quite different statements. The ultimate effect of these design principles is to create an overwhelming sense of order, solidity, and permanence and, *ipso facto*, to provide an appropriate instrument for imposing those qualities on the chaos that was perceived to be continually threatening the Egyptian cosmos and occasionally getting very close to destroying it.

The conceptual principles that determined the detailed design of these buildings have two dimensions. In the first place, they were considered to be the dwelling places of deities, and, as such, a major aspect of the architectural vocabulary is that the temple was a house. It was frequently called a *per netjer* (*pr nṯr*), 'house of the god', or *hut netjer* (*ḥwt nṯr*), 'mansion of the god', and initially this was expressed in physical terms by giving it the structure of one of the simplest Egyptian house forms consisting of a chamber often preceded by a porch supported on columns and enclosed by a courtyard which was surrounded by fencing and might contain a standard defining the divine owner. This archetype had a major effect on the temple's subsequent architectural evolution. The *sanctum* or holy-of-holies (*set weret, st wrt*, 'great place') in the classic design is the descendant of the solitary chamber of earlier practice; the porch could be developed into one or more hypostyle halls; and the courtyard evolved into one or several columned courts as well as the *temenos* or sacred enclosure surrounded by a massive wall. Within this complex the deity was believed to reside in the cult statue housed in a shrine in the *sanctum*. The cardinal importance of this element is emphasized by making it the apex of four main structural planes: the floor of the temple rises steadily towards it, the roof descends steadily from above towards it, and the left and right sides of the inner section of the temple converge towards it. The one aspect of the temple-house concept that is untypical of the houses of lesser beings was that, in their fully developed form, temples were built largely or completely of stone rather than mud-brick; for the gods needed a much greater degree of permanence than could possibly be provided by brick.

Important though the house-concept undoubtedly was, it is only, at best, half the picture. The temple was also believed to be a source of creative power, a cosmos in its own right (Baines 1997), and this idea was usually conceptualized by insisting that the *sanctum* was constructed on the primeval hill. In

---

[12] Amongst other prescriptions, *The Book of the Temple* laid down principles to be followed in the design of temples (Quack 2000). The extant copies are late, but this manual, or texts like it, were probably available at earlier periods.

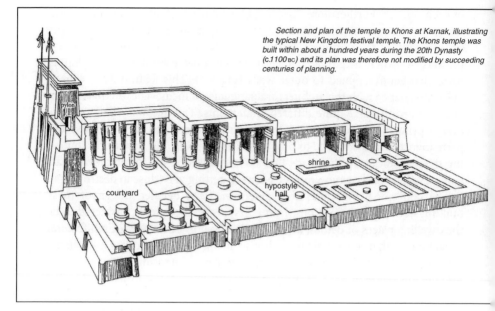

Section and plan of the temple to Khons at Karnak, illustrating the typical New Kingdom festival temple. The Khons temple was built within about a hundred years during the 20th Dynasty (c.1100 BC) and its plan was therefore not modified by succeeding centuries of planning.

Fig. 8.1. The structure of the Egyptian temple. After Quirke and Spencer (eds) 1992: 161 no. 124.

architectural terms this was expressed by structuring access in the form of ascending planes or steps ending in the *sanctum* at the highest point. In some cases the hill concept is also expressed by constructing a plinth along the base of the outer wall of the main structure. The concept of the temple as a powerhouse of creative energy is also articulated through the common use of plant forms for columns and the decoration of the lowest sections of inner walls with images of sprouting vegetation, and the depiction of stars on the ceilings further projects the image of the temple as cosmos. A rather less obvious feature is that the temple becomes progressively more gloomy the further one penetrates into it until the *sanctum* is completely bathed in darkness, only dissipated by the light brought in by the officiants as part of the daily rituals of maintenance. These bursts of light signified and, at the same time, brought into being the reactivation of the deity's demiurgic power for yet another day.

Another major feature of the classic temple was the pylons. These not only gave access to the buildings but also can be regarded as truncated pyramids, primeval hills in their own right, whose potent demiurgic force protected the temples at their most vulnerable points. They also supported poles on their outer surface whose tops were embellished with streamers, at one level marking the presence of sacred space but at another injecting the divine power within them into the buildings themselves. Both could be supplemented in this protective role by royal colossi and avenues of sphinxes, images of lions with the heads of gods that functioned as protective agents guarding the route to the main gates; for it has long been recognized that statues in temples and the images on temple walls were regarded by the Egyptians not simply as representations but as images that were capable of *becoming* what they represented (Blackman and Fairman 1946). Therefore, divine images such as colossi and sphinxes *are* what they represent and are capable of bringing to bear all the divine power instinct within them.

In addition to numerous sculptures in the round, temples were copiously adorned with scenes sculpted in brightly painted relief over all available surfaces. These were allocated space on a standard principle: scenes on the more public walls were dedicated to Pharaoh in his martial role or as a mighty hunter whilst images became progressively more cultic in character the closer one proceeded to the *sanctum*. They functioned at various levels: the many scenes of Pharaoh defeating the enemies of Egypt certainly had a commemorative dimension and provided ample scope for the predilection for self-glorification of such rulers as Ramesses II, but they also stridently conveyed to observers, both human and divine, that the ruler in question had fulfilled the central function of the Pharaonic office, i.e. the destruction of the forces of chaos. That the gods were indeed regarded as an audience is well illustrated by an inscription in the Akhmenu temple at Karnak in which Tuthmose III states clearly why he has recorded a list of plants and animals brought from Syria: 'My Majesty did this in order to cause that they should be in the presence of my father Amun in his great mansion of Akhmenu for ever and ever' (*Urk.* iii. 776). That a more than human audience was envisaged is also demonstrated by the fact that there are numerous scenes and texts in temples that cannot be seen clearly from the ground and, at least at one level, must have been addressed to a divine audience. However, as with sculpture in the round, there is a crucially important further dimension to all temple decoration: scenes of Pharaoh on temple walls destroying the foes of Egypt or hunting wild animals, all embodiments of the forces of chaos, *are* Pharaoh defeating these forces, and representations of the king performing temple rituals *are* Pharaoh doing precisely that. The representations are vital dynamic entities in their own right, and, as long as they exist, they will guarantee the performance of what they depict. These images, therefore, have a critical role to perform as part of the overall strategy underpinning the temple as a guarantor of the continued existence of an ordered universe.

The visual vocabulary of temple sculpture, in relief or in the round, is an organic outcome of function. Of this the engaged colossi of Ramesses II protecting the entrance of the great Abu Simbel temple are paradigmatic (Fig. 8.2). The overall composition of the temple façade exhibits the canonical principles of balance and antithesis setting a mood of order and stability that is strongly reinforced by the repetition of the royal image in two groups of two in exactly the same format and on exactly the same plane. A standard element of

Fig. 8.2. The colossi of Ramesses II at Abu Simbel.

the Egyptian visual code is the use of relative size as a means of indicating relative importance, and this requirement is amply fulfilled by the four 20 m high colossi dwarfing the images of the members of the royal family beside and between the king's legs. The visual language of the design of the colossi is essentially cubist, i.e. it works with an underlying matrix of horizontal and vertical lines, a feature that contributes powerfully to the generation of a sense of immutability. The figures are also frontally posed: the eyes look straight ahead in aloof and focused concentration on more than mortal concerns, disdaining all incidental distractions, and the figures are placed firmly on a base without any deviation from the vertical; they are also perfectly balanced so that a line drawn down the middle of a statue from top to bottom would separate it into two essentially equal masses of material. This visual language, *in toto*, succeeds perfectly in creating potent images of the overwhelming majesty, superhuman power, permanence, and unassailable godlike quiet confidence of the divine king whose temple this is and which he is more than capable of maintaining.

The same imperatives applied to the relief sculptures that covered the temple walls. The massive tableau representing the defeat of the Sea Peoples on the north wall of the temple of Ramesses III at Medinet Habu is an excellent example (Fig. 8.3). The surface has been articulated into three registers that

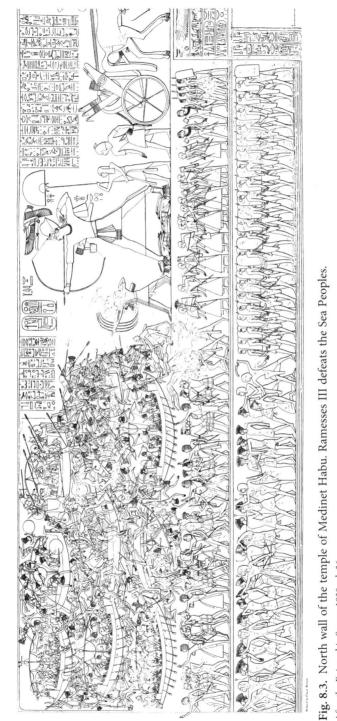

Fig. 8.3. North wall of the temple of Medinet Habu. Ramesses III defeats the Sea Peoples.

After the Epigraphic Survey 1930: pl. 36.

should be read from top to bottom. The largest at the top is divided into two linked main images, that to the right depicting the king in action against the Sea Peoples whilst standing on representations of the Nine Bows, the traditional enemies of Egypt. Behind him are depicted his chariot and pair, its attendants, and a fan-bearer ensuring the king's comfort by providing him with shade whilst he rains down arrows on his enemies. The vulture of the Upper Egyptian protective goddess Nekhbet hovers above the king's head and the presence of her Lower Egyptian counterpart Wadjet is indicated by text. Before the king four archers are depicted firing into the enemy. This image of the masterful royal warrior dominates the whole tableau. It is probably self-evident that this image sequence is replete with symbolic elements that take it a long way from being anything remotely like a snapshot of a historical event. To the left of the royal image sequence and occupying much the same volume of space is a representation of the defeat of the Sea Peoples in a naval battle which, at first sight, seems devoid of register divisions, but closer inspection reveals that the ships are disposed in three superimposed rows of three that can be regarded as the equivalent of subregisters. The king's arrows are shown hitting this force on the right-hand side. The lower two registers depict the successful aftermath of the conflict with the Egyptian troops leading off prisoners from the defeated forces.

As with royal sculpture in the round the overall intention of this tableau is to generate a sense of order, stability, immutability, and the overwhelming power and majesty of Pharaoh guaranteeing the triumph of *maat*. Majesty and power, as usual, are conveyed by the use of relative scale: the king is much larger than anyone else, and in this instance his chariot enjoys the same privilege. The register system and the verticality of the columns of hieroglyphs contribute greatly to a sense of order as does the standard practice whereby all standing figures are anchored to the ground lines that form the bases of the registers. Egyptian soldiers progress in mathematically precise ranks that even the Brigade of Guards could not achieve, and the archers in the top register lay down their volley fire with preternatural coordination. Even the Egyptians directing the columns of prisoners are distributed over the surface with commendable regularity. The iconography of the human figures, which follows standard practice, reflects the same imperative. The sense of order is in no way compromised by the chaotic tumult of the battle scene; for it is ultimately meant to convey the innately chaotic affinities of the enemies of Pharaoh that can be defeated only by the Egyptians entering into that chaos and subduing it.

The principles on which all figures are depicted are well illustrated by the representation of Amenhotep I from the tomb of Kynebu now in the British Museum (Fig. 8.4). The design is clearly based on horizontal and vertical lines. The vertical band to the right is echoed in the line of the stem of the lotus plant that the king is carrying in his left hand and also by the rigidly vertical stance

Fig. 8.4. Representation of the deceased Amenhotep I from the Twentieth Dynasty tomb of Kynebu.

of the figure. Two altars placed in front of the king also assert the verticality of the composition.[13] The horizontal dimension appears in the ground line which is echoed by the line of the garment immediately above, by the line of the kilt, the shoulder line, the lines of the fillet on the head, and the line of the horns on the crown. The figure is located firmly on the ground line; it is

---

[13] A drawing by Robert Hay in the British Library and the discovery of new fragments on site make it possible to place the British Museum image fully in its overall context on the tomb wall (Bács and Parkinson 2011).

analytically treated so that each element is isolated and depicted diagrammatically from what the Egyptians considered its most typical point of view that best represented what it was. Therefore, the figure has two right feet, the legs are represented in profile; the kilt is portrayed in a mixture of profile and frontality; the upper body is shown frontally; the head is depicted in profile but the eye and eyebrow are essentially frontal; the fillet is twisted round so that we can see clearly the tie at the back; and the head of the uraeus is in profile whereas its upper body is presented frontally. All colouring is flat with no suggestion of the three-dimensional, a convention clearly designed to anchor the figure firmly to the surface with no sense that it is emerging from it. The figure is there for eternity. It should also be noted that, typically, there is no sense of individuality in the facial representation. In itself this figure could be anyone.

The Kynebu scene gives no sense of movement, despite the fact that the right leg is advanced, and that, again, is a standard feature of the artistic vocabulary. The same holds true of the king in the Sea Peoples tableau; the image is not allowed to become unbalanced, standing firmly on its base, and the same principle determines the representation of the archers before him and the Egyptian troops in the other two registers. This is a freeze-frame image of the triumph of Egypt and its king intended for eternity. The Sea People prisoners, on the other hand, are not depicted in such orderly groups, and in several cases they break the rule whereby heads are represented in profile and look out at the viewer, an artistic device used also in other contexts, e.g. representation of dancing girls and of the god Bes, to indicate that the entities in question belong to or have very close affinities with the world of chaos (see p. 279).

Royal Mortuary Installations

Royal mortuary complexes of all periods were of critical importance as ritual devices guaranteeing the resurrection of the king and his post-mortem cultic support, but they were also strident assertions by and for the living of the eternal overwhelming power, wealth, and cosmic centrality of the Pharaonic office. I have already discussed the conceptualization, structure, and decoration of these monuments in an earlier chapter (see p. 72), and these issues need no rehearsing here, but it is necessary to highlight a number of points for the purposes of the current discussion.

Size was a critical dimension in the construction of these installations and formed an intrinsic part of their architectural vocabulary; the monuments were always as big as a king could make them, and their building presupposed and confirmed a massive corporate commitment to royal ideology. The great increase in the size of substructures in the tombs of the Valley of the Kings provided massive scope for an increase in the quantity and wealth of grave goods whose accumulation and deposition bore the same implications. The tomb of Tutankhamun demonstrates, if that were needed, that sculptures in the round were a numerous component of this apparatus, and here the iconographic principles described in the previous section prevailed with the same conceptual basis. Thereby they were fitted to function eternally as instruments of resurrection, provide substitute bodies, guard the tomb's contents, and ensure that the king continued to enjoy activities that were pleasurable during life (cf. Reeves 1990*b*).[14] Although ultimately in the same tradition as the *Pyramid Texts* of earlier periods, the extensive insertion of painted and relief-sculpture images on the walls and ceilings of tombs in the Valley of the Kings is a major departure from previous royal practice. However, novel though the tableaux are, they exploit the same visual code as temple decoration, not surprisingly, since their purpose was fundamentally the same, i.e. the maintenance of the cosmic order, though in this case the focus is on a specific aspect, the safe passage of the sun-god Amon-re at night through the underworld and the resurrection of the dead during this nocturnal journey, a process in which the resurrection of the deceased ruler formed a crucial part (see p. 72). The fact that these scenes would be locked away from view once the tomb was sealed strikingly illustrates the principle that ultimately all that was necessary was for the images to exist to fulfil their purpose. As long as they were there, the processes they depict would continue to be replicated for eternity. The tomb of Ramesses V/VI (KV9) is typical of the iconographic scheme employed during the Twentieth Dynasty, containing extracts from standard mortuary texts such as the *Book of Gates*, the *Book of the Celestial Cow*, the *Book of the Dead*, and the *Book of Night* all of which show the complementary mix of text and image that we encountered in the temple context and all of which were regarded as potent agents in enabling the tomb to fulfil its cosmicizing role. In the post-New Kingdom period this iconography was much abbreviated, as illustrated by the royal tombs at Tanis, but its visual language and function remained quite unimpaired.

The Iconographic Code Adapted

Whilst the iconographic strategy described in the preceding paragraphs is overwhelmingly the strategy employed for Pharaonic royal imagery throughout its history, there are exceptions. Some of the statues of Senwosret III and Amenemhet III show distinctly untypical treatment of the face, though the other standard aspects of royal imagery are all present (see p. 76). In these representations we find a radical departure from the aloof serenity characteristic of standard iconography and its replacement by startlingly individualistic physiognomies depicting the king in a much more human manner. This may

[14] Statuary in the tomb of Tutankhamun continues to show some Amarna features (as we shall see), but these elements do not affect the basic code.

well be the result of the narrowing of the gap between the king and his subjects for which there is good evidence in the Middle Kingdom (see p. 163), and some commentators have regarded these images as an attempt to depict the personal toll taken on rulers by the burden of kingship (Aldred 1980: 126). This may well be true, but second-guessing Egyptian intentions in such contexts is no straightforward matter, and the somewhat brutal dimensions of these faces may well have been intended to convey a sense of something much less benign, i.e. the ruthless power available to the king in fulfilling his cosmic mission (cf. Robins 2008: 112–13).

The novelties in Amarna artistic projections of the state and royal self-perception were far more pervasive and radical than anything seen earlier. Traditional Egyptian architecture and iconography were designed to serve the requirements of traditional Egyptian religious and political thinking. It follows, therefore, that, if major changes were made to such thinking, these would lead to radical changes in architecture and iconography. When Akhenaten elevated the Aten, embodied in the solar disc, to the status of the sole valid object of cult[15] and installed himself as the pre-eminent intermediary between his subjects and the Aten (see p. 78),[16] significant changes in artistic expression were inevitable, but the break with the past was far from complete nor, indeed, was a complete break necessary since the Amarna religious system had its roots firmly in earlier belief and practice (see p. 94). Therefore, many traditional artistic traditions survived: the architectural dimension of the city of Akhetaten as a theatre for displays of Pharaonic majesty parallels the architectural development of Thebes under Amenhotep III; features of the design of Akhenaten's tomb in the Royal Wadi at Amarna closely follow earlier Eighteenth Dynasty practice; balance, antithesis, and symmetry still prevail in architectural design; statues in the round are still frontally posed and look straight ahead far into the distance; in relief sculpture scenes are still composed in registers; relative size still defines relative importance, and colossi were an established part of the sculptural repertoire; images of figures and other elements, such as buildings, are still composed in the traditional analytical mode combining different simultaneous viewpoints in the same image; figures are distributed over surfaces of relief and painting in a symmetrical and orderly manner; symbolism continues to play a major role, above all in the pervasive presence of the image of the Aten in close association with the royal family in tableaux of royal action; even when figures are supposed to be

[15] We should not forget that Akhenaten's theological thinking underwent a clear evolution that increased his insistence on the henotheistic dimensions of his god (W. Smith 1981: 303).

[16] Scenes representing Akhenaten, Nefertiti, and daughters worshipping the Aten (e.g. Robins 2008: 172) are paradigmatic. Akhenaten is the key figure, Nefertiti the chief assistant, and the daughters, who can be shown waving the systrum typical of priestesses, the sole additional worshippers, i.e. the king's immediate family alone share in his status as unique worshippers of the god.

moving across a surface, there is still little sense of movement, and the overall impression is that the viewer is faced with a freeze-frame scene; finally, text and image still constantly complement each other in the traditional manner.

Whilst, however, we must concede the many antecedents of Amarna image strategy, there is no escaping the fact that there are also radical changes: the architecture of Akhenaten's four temples at Karnak was quite at variance with standard practice since all were based on the open-court principle of the ancient Heliopolitan solar cult and were devoid of divine images as the focus of worship—the sun's disc in the heavens itself served that purpose—and that practice was continued in the temples subsequently built at el-Amarna; in temple scenes there is much greater emphasis on offerings than previously or later; in early images of the royal family heads are elongated vertically and horizontally, faces can become gaunt and even brutal, lips protrude, breasts are emphasized, stomachs swell out, hips and thighs are prominently delineated, and artists show much interest in bodily anatomy, all features that have their influence generally in the representation of non-royal figures (Fig. 8.5).[17] The origin and function of these iconographic traits have given rise to much discussion. The most recent analysis of the remains from Tomb 55 in the Valley of the Kings (generally held to be either Smenkhkare or Akhenaten) and those of Tutankhamun give no indication of any of the anatomical anomalies suggested by iconography (Hawass et al. 2010),[18] and, if these results are valid, we are left with no alternative but to regard these traits as essentially an artistic convention. Decoding their symbolic significance is impossible with any certainty, but a plausible guess would be that the markedly female dimensions imparted to representations of Akhenaten were designed to convey the notion that he embodied both male and female dimensions of deity within his divine person (cf. Robins 2008: 150), and the distortion of the head and face may also have started with Akhenaten as a means of asserting his unique status. All these features could then have been applied to other members of the royal family by a process of assimilation. Such an insistence on unique status would be very much of a piece with the novel and frequent representations of non-royal figures bent at the waist in postures of extreme obeisance before the king, an iconographic device that has no parallel in representations of other rulers. However, whilst this element of exclusivity is certainly present, it is very much at variance with the informal and naturalistic treatment of family behaviour that constitutes so marked a characteristic of Amarna royal iconography. Yet another departure is the

---

[17] This style is manifested above all in work from the early part of the reign and later undergoes considerable modification (W. Smith 1981: 335).

[18] This study opts for the identification of the body in Tomb 55 with Akhenaten, but this remains open to question since the age of the person to whom the bones belonged is still open to debate. The validity and rigour of the DNA results of the Hawass study are also questionable (Marchant 2011).

Fig. 8.5. Akhenaten and family represented in Amarna style. Egyptian Museum, Cairo. H. 105 cm.

persistent foregrounding of Queen Nefertiti in state imagery.[19] Certainly this has a clear antecedent in the high status of Tiyi in the previous reign, but the treatment of Nefertiti far surpasses anything seen previously: on *talatat* blocks she appears almost twice as often as Akhenaten; she can be represented engaged in activities that are almost always elsewhere activities of the king, e.g. smiting scenes, and female captives can be associated with her; and

---

[19] For her role as a member of the Atenist triad see p. 94.

Nefertiti is depicted with the king when he performs ritual acts with a frequency and prominence that has no earlier counterpart. Indeed, in the *Hutbenben* temple built at Karnak about Regnal Year 4 there is no sign of Akhenaten in the extant representations; Nefertiti is the sole worshipper, though her daughter Meketaten also appears (Redford 1984; Gohary 1992: pls. 1–2; Reeves 2001; Robins 2008).

As indicated above, royal mortuary practice was a crucial element in the propaganda of kingship, and it could not escape this revolution. Whilst Akhenaten's tomb and mortuary equipment present much that is familiar, there are novel features directly springing from the new religious thinking: the orientation to the east of the entrance and passage leading to the royal burial chamber facing the rising sun is significant and was probably designed to facilitate the daily reunification of the king with the sun-god;[20] the old underworld books are completely abandoned and replaced by scenes that depict either Akhenaten and members of his family worshipping the Aten or scenes of mourning associated with the death of his daughter Meketaten, all of which show the mixture of old and new in execution that has already been noted. It is evident from the prevalence of scenes of adoration of the Aten that the mortuary dimension of the king's fate was considered to be eternity in association with the god or, indeed, complete absorption into his being. On the other hand, the mourning scenes, which have no parallel elsewhere in royal tombs, eternalize the devotion of the family towards one of its beloved members, a purpose they achieve with a remarkable degree of frankness in depicting the extremes of royal grief (Martin 1989).[21]

The Private Context

The main non-royal context to be considered is the private tomb and its associated buildings which have much to say on the Egyptian vision of

---

[20] It has also been suggested that the intention was that the solar power within the tomb would burst forth from the burial chamber upon the city of Akhetaten (Reeves 2001: 127–8). The orientation of the entrance suits this idea less well, but that is not to deny that the tomb was intended to play a crucial part in the cultic role of the city.

[21] There is a scene of mourners on the north wall of Akhenaten's burial chamber that was almost certainly connected to his burial (cf. Martin 1989: 26). The decoration in other Amarna or sub-Amarna royal tombs provides plentiful evidence of a swift return to the old ways, though Amarna influence on the iconography of figures remains strong. Other non-traditional features also occur: the tomb of Tutankhamun (KV62) continues to some degree the Amarna interest in post-mortem events involving the living in the depiction of his funeral in the burial chamber, and the tomb of Ay (KV23) contains a scene of the king hunting in the marshes that has no known parallel in any royal tomb, though it is extremely common in non-royal contexts (see p. 276). The decoration of the tomb of Horemheb in the Valley of the Kings (KV57) shows a decisive, though not complete, return to the traditional style, though his earlier Memphite tomb continues to show Amarna influences (W. Smith 1981: 340–50; Martin 1989: 24–8, 79, 94; Robins 2008: 162).

themselves and their physical and conceptual worlds, though the parameters within which this process operated were always severely limited by custom and practice, and the degree of elaboration varied greatly according to wealth and status. As stated previously (see p. 222), tombs are polyvalent artefacts serving both as a means of conspicuous display for the individual and his family and also as a ritual device whereby the post-mortem survival of the deceased could be guaranteed. Architectural vocabulary, sculpture, and painting were all crucial instruments in achieving these aims. Architecture has already been discussed in some detail and needs no further comment here (see p. 222ff.), but sculpture and painting require detailed analysis.

Sculpture in the Round

Sculpture in the round played as important a part in the mortuary cult of private individuals as it did in the temple cult and tombs of kings, and very much the same iconographic principles applied. One example, amongst the very best, will suffice to make this point, i.e. the famous statue of Sheikh el-Beled (Fig. 8.6). This composite statue made of sycamore, probably of Fifth Dynasty date, depicts a chief lector priest called Kaaper and derives from his tomb chapel at Saqqara. Its funerary function is, therefore, indisputable: it was a ritual device to guarantee the preservation of the body, a means of projecting his image on to the consciousness of the living, and, at the same time, an implicit appeal for the presentation of funerary offerings in perpetuity.

The visual language directly reflects the statue's funerary role. It is essentially cubist, i.e. it is the three-dimensional equivalent of the horizontal and vertical compositional matrix of painting and relief sculpture. The figure is also frontally posed and designed to stand firmly on a base without any deviation from the vertical. It is perfectly balanced so that a line drawn down the middle of the statue would separate it into two essentially equal masses of material. All this, together with the figure's corpulence, generates a powerful image of solidity, permanence, stability, wealth, and unassailable confidence. On the other hand, the left leg is advanced to create some sense of movement, a desirable capacity in the afterlife.

The head is modelled with great skill and creates a strong impression of individuality and even of benevolence. How far these features are an accurate portrayal cannot be determined. They may well be, but current thinking on 'realism' in such sculptures regards it as a symbolic device for conveying the essence of the ideal official (cf. Robins 2008: no. 292). The eyes of the figure look straight ahead in aloof and focused concentration, disdaining all incidental distractions, in all probability a reflection of the image of a person of rank that prevailed in daily life and that would be expected to endure for eternity. The well-covered body, which shows attention to modelling (though the waist is much too high), serves to represent the subject in what was to the

Fig. 8.6. Fifth Dynasty sycamore-wood statue of Kaaper (Sheikh el-Beled), Egyptian Museum, Cairo. H. 112 cm.

Egyptians the prime of life, the stage of existence on earth that they would wish to perpetuate. The sculptor has also taken care to ensure that Kaaper's rank endures by adding the standard indices of status, the wand of office in his left hand and a slot for a handkerchief, now missing, in the right hand.

Painting and Relief Sculpture

The walls of private tomb chapels were often copiously decorated throughout Pharaonic history; burial chambers can also receive this treatment, but they are usually devoid of any decoration and frequently quite roughly finished. The decoration in burial chambers, sealed from view after interment, could only have served a magico-religious function, but that in tomb chapels is located in contexts that remained accessible and served several purposes.

However, whatever their context, they are all statements and reaffirmations of the Egyptian vision of their world, conceptual and physical. The following examples will illustrate how these images were formulated to serve this purpose.

The Twelfth Dynasty colossus scene in the tomb of nomarch Djehutyhotep II at el-Bersha depicts the dragging of a colossal statue of the owner from the travertine quarries at Hatnub to his tomb (see Plate 1).[22] Its subject matter is unique amongst known tomb scenes, but the visual strategies it displays are not. It cannot plausibly be argued that this scene is designed to recreate the event depicted beyond the grave, though it could function in a more general sense as part of an attempt to guarantee by depiction the privileged status of the nomarch for eternity. The prime motive here is surely commemorative, the desire to record a spectacular event in Djehutyhotep's career that displayed his wealth, power, and privileged position. Indeed, there is no other known case of a colossus being produced for a private person at any other time in Egyptian history. Therefore, the scene becomes a claim for recognition and a claim of a right to mortuary service from posterity.

The tableau consists of a mixture of representation and text in which the texts complement the images either by describing who is being represented, their attitude to the events, the functions they are performing, or the comments they are making. Colouring is of the simplest, the colossus kept white to reflect the colour of travertine, though the base block should have been reddish in colour to reflect the fact that it was made of sandstone; the workmen are all depicted with reddish skin, the colour being applied without any hint of shading, and there is no attempt to suggest anything but the two-dimensional. In terms of composition the artist is working with a large rectangular surface that is then divided into a large number of smaller rectangles, i.e. the design is dominated by horizontal and vertical lines either delineated physically on the wall or notionally present. To the left, where we should normally find a figure of the tomb owner watching the events before him, we find the colossus on its sledge being dragged to the right. Note that the colossus is shown completely in profile, a fact that demonstrates that such a mode of representation is entirely within the capabilities of Egyptian artists despite the fact that it is normally not employed. Much attention is devoted to the bindings of the statue, and there are also representations of the caller, a figure pouring water on the surface in front of the sledge, and a mortuary priest who is said to be offering incense. We must, however, beware of treating these elements in the scene as a realistic representation. It is indisputable that, although the colossus is represented as being complete in exactly the form that it would take at its

---

[22] This tomb was systematically published by Newberry (1893). His plate 15 depicts the colossus scene in the damaged state in which he found it. The image that I have used (Plate 1) is an older copy by J. Gardner Wilkinson now housed in the Bodleian Library, Oxford.

destination, this cannot be correct. The dangers at this stage of damage to a completed statue would be far too great. The statue would have been roughed out in the quarry and brought in that rough state to the site to be finished there. We are, therefore, confronted with a scene that is not a representation of one stage in the operation but a combination of at least two.

The surface to the right of the colossus is divided into five registers by horizontal lines which function as ground lines to which the figures are firmly anchored, a design principle fundamental to Pharaonic painting and relief sculpture that we have already encountered. That rectilinear dimension is confirmed to the far right by the addition of four boxes containing visually identical texts identifying the group to the left. The top group consists of seven rows of men who are escorting the statue, all showing an identical stance and marching with the precision of guardsmen. All rows are slewed to their left so that all the members are represented, i.e. we have again moved away from representation of the feature as seen from one consistent angle. In this case a diagrammatic dimension has intervened because the artist wishes to make it clear what the detail was. The four rows below depict the gangs dragging the colossus along, and here again we move away from representation since they have been tipped up and represented one on top of the other instead of walking side-by-side so that it is made clear diagrammatically exactly what is going on. It will be noted that only the leaders at the front are given a positioning that reflects to some degree the effort of pulling whereas the other workmen are usually statuesquely vertical with only the vaguest hint that hard physical labour is at issue. At bottom left there are two other square groupings each containing three individuals. Overall, there are some concessions to variety in the composition: the escort at the top is moving in the opposite direction to the figures below and their pose is quite different; there is also some variation in their dress, as is the case with the workmen below who also show distinctions in their headdress and the direction in which their heads are turned. These features certainly display an artistic awareness of the need to avoid monotony and over-regimentation, but overwhelmingly the artistic vocabulary has created a scene which is dominated by a sense of order, discipline, control, and, above all, something frozen immutably in time. This dimension could not be more appropriate. Since the tomb is a ritual device intended to function for eternity, all the visual language used in it springs organically from that concept and must give expression to it.

The west wall of Paheri's tomb chapel at Elkab shows much the same foci, techniques, and principles (see Plate 2a and 2b). The wall is treated as a long rectangular surface divided into smaller rectangular blocks focusing, from right to left, on funerary rites, private life, and official activities. There is the usual mixture of text and representation, and the entire sequence is explicitly locked into the mortuary context by the prayers for offerings and blessings beyond the grave which run across the top of the entire sequence. The composition works throughout with rectangular blocks, the largest forming registers, and within the registers subsidiary ground lines are employed to anchor additional elements firmly in position. All the design principles previously identified in the Djehutyhotep scene are in evidence, and it is particularly noticeable that in the left-hand section of the wall, although many agricultural activities are depicted, some of which would have involved considerable physical labour, there is no great sense of movement, and even the pigs at bottom left have organized themselves into the neatest of rows (see Plate 2a). The iconographic vocabulary again effectively creates the impression of individuals and events frozen in time and eternalized.

There is no doubt that the purpose of the left-hand group of scenes and those in the centre of the wall is pre-eminently to guarantee that the deceased will continue to enjoy his privileged existence beyond the grave, but the situation with the scenes to the right is rather more complicated. This section of the wall is dominated by a representation of Paheri's funeral rituals and the grave goods involved, but at bottom right the deceased is represented praying to Osiris in the underworld (see Plate 2b). The latter scene can be interpreted like the others on the wall as a scene designed to bring about beyond the grave what is depicted in the tomb, but it would not be plausible to apply that principle baldly to the rest of this section of the wall and argue that Paheri wished to recreate his funeral in the afterlife.[23] There would seem to be several possible explanations: the ritual scenes may have been intended as an insurance policy in case the key funerary rituals were not carried out or were not carried out properly; they could be regarded as a case of conspicuous display asserting to everyone who entered the chapel that Paheri was a member of the elite with all the resources needed to benefit from an elite funeral; yet another possibility would be that, as a member of the elite, it was incumbent on him to ensure that he received an elite funeral, and this scene shows him discharging his social obligation to the full in this respect; alternatively, all of these motivations may be at issue at one and the same time. However, whatever the truth of the matter, it is clear that, yet again, we have a tableau that shifts its ground so that events that would be expected to take place at different points in time have been amalgamated into one global composition.

The fowling scene from the Eighteenth Dynasty tomb of Nebamun, now in the British Museum, presents us with a canonical motif in tomb decoration (see Plate 3a).[24] The combination of text and representation is standard and serves to reinforce the subject matter of the images and also to provide a

---

[23] The tomb of Paheri is far from unique in showing such a scene. Stages in the funeral are a frequent element of tomb decoration.

[24] The decoration of this tomb is discussed in detail by Parkinson 2008. The two scenes in my treatment are illustrated, described, and analysed at his pp. 122–32 (fowling) and 70–91 (banquet).

context where the names and titles of the figures depicted can be used to reinforce their identity. The text behind the owner indicates, however, that the event is located in the *set neheh* (*st nḥḥ*), 'the place of eternity', a location reflected by the cone worn by his wife and the elaborate bouquet that she carries.[25] It is of a piece with this that the fowling activity itself is not simply a reflection of something that might happen in the secular world. It is also a cosmicizing process since the wild creatures being knocked down belong to the world of disorder, and their submission brings with it the continuation of the ordered universe and, by the same token, a guarantee of the survival of the deceased beyond the grave. There is no attempt whatsoever to represent the activity as it would have happened in reality. On the contrary, the owner is dressed in the height of fashion more suitable for a party than for sporting activity, and his wife is wearing the most elegant of party-going outfits. Furthermore, the relative scale of the elements in the picture is anything but natural, e.g. the raft is much too small and the wife is diminutive. Yet again scale is used to mark out the relative importance of the ingredients in the scene. It should also be noted that there is no effort in the representation of any of the human figures to create a sense of individuality; visually they could be anyone, and they can only be identified, if at all, by inscriptions that tell us who they are.

The analysis thus far makes it immediately evident that we are confronted with a scene that has at least three dimensions: it is an abstract and idealized evocation of a sporting activity traditionally associated with the Egyptian elite, however infrequently it may have taken place in reality; it represents at a symbolic level and also actualizes the triumph of order and life; and it is concerned to represent and also guarantee the continued existence of the family in the best possible form in the afterlife. This familistic dimension may even be reflected in the presence of the splendid tabby cat. Although this creature has often been described as a retriever that picks up the smitten birds, that suggestion is in the highest degree improbable since it is impossible to train cats to do this kind of thing. A much better explanation is that it is there because it was an important part of the family whose presence the owner of the tomb wished to continue to enjoy beyond the grave. The solar affinities of the cat in Egyptian mythology are certainly also relevant.

This is far from the end of the matter. Let us now turn to the scene's design. The careful observer will quickly note that the artistic vision underpinning the representation is dominated by horizontal and vertical lines. The use of the

---

[25] It has long been claimed that the cone was a piece of scented unguent worn during parties, but Padgham (2012) has argued that it is entirely symbolic, indicating that the *ba* of the deceased wearer is in receipt of funerary offerings that enable him or her to return to the world of the living. The bouquet should be regarded as an example of the bouquets that feature prominently in the Festival of the Valley (see p. 244). Cf., however, *Ancient Egypt* (2013).

ground line is very conspicuous: the surface of the water that supports the papyrus raft is given a severely horizontal dimension, and this is reinforced by the treatment of the raft, the upper surface of which is strictly parallel to the water surface; the owner is also firmly anchored to a wooden bottom-board, as is his wife and the goose at the front, whilst the daughter is seated squarely on the same feature. This linear design principle does not exclude counterpoint with curves, as, for example, with the curved lines of the papyrus clump, but overwhelmingly the visual vocabulary is rectilinear and is clearly intended to convey an invincible impression of unshakeable stability, immutability, and order. This impression is reinforced by the stance of the owner who stands bolt upright, echoing the vertical lines delimiting the inscriptions behind him, and also his stance on the raft which fixes him four-square on the bottom board in a position quite unnatural for anyone engaged in hurling a throw-stick. Again, stability is the issue. Equally his wife and daughter show no inclination to bend to the right or left. This sense of order is further conveyed by the design of the papyrus plants to the left which are forced into a quite unnatural order consisting of two neat parallel rows, and the artist has even arranged the umbels of the lower row to fit snugly exactly below the joins between the umbels of the top row. It belongs in the same order of things that the artist shows no interest at any point in the use of shading. Colour has been added in a uniform density across all figures, and this again enhances the sense of immutability; even surfaces in the scene do not change the quality of their colour as they would in the world of experience to reflect transient phenomena such as the position of objects or light conditions; for transience is exactly the opposite of what this tradition of representation is all about.

The tomb of Nebamun has further riches to offer. The banquet scene from the same tomb is a most remarkable tableau. At the most obvious level its function is to guarantee the continuation of partying beyond the grave, amongst other things, in association with the Festival of the Valley, and it will be noted that virtually everyone displays the cone that probably defines the figures as the *ba* forms of the resurrected deceased participants (see n. 25). It would follow that anyone without the cone is to be regarded as belonging to the world of the living. It should also be noted that there is a clear sexual dimension to the scene that should not be underplayed (see Plate 3b). To the Egyptians creation presupposed procreation, and these cosmic processes are inseparably linked to rebirth and resurrection. Iconographically, traditional elements are certainly present: the ground line is retained as well as the linear disposition of the figures across the surface, the flat colouring, and the analytical treatment of the two women to the right, a treatment that is also evident to some degree in the portrayal of the two dancers. There are, however, remarkable departures from the norm. In the first place, the two central figures are depicted looking straight out of the scene, thereby breaking the rule that human figures should be represented in profile. This breaking of the visual code is highly significant since such cases only occur when the Egyptian is trying to make the point that the individuals involved belong to, or border on, the world of disorder and chaos, e.g. the enemies of Egypt can be depicted in this way as can the god Bes and other deities associated with joy, revelry, and merrymaking (cf. p. 266). These women and what they do belong on the frontiers of order and propriety, and the artist is making that point by departing from the visual code. It should also be noted that the figures overlap, creating a sense of depth, and show variation in their poses in a manner quite different from the ordered disposition of their betters in the scene above, and the treatment of the hair of the two central figures conveys a strong sense of movement and activity as well as enhancing sexual allure. The sweeping curvilinear treatment of the lines of their linen garments accentuates this sense of movement. The two dancers, like the serving girl above, are almost completely naked, at one level a sign of social status but also an element that contributes to the erotic character of the scene, a dimension not diminished by the fact that they do wear some items of clothing even if they conceal nothing. The juxtaposition of the battery of wine jars to the right also contributes to the sense of the revelry that formed part of the Festival of the Valley, undoubtedly the major point of reference of this scene. It is also noteworthy that there is a real attempt in the case of the two dancers to create a sense of movement.

The previous examples all originate from tomb chapels, but the well-known scene from the tomb of Sennedjem at Deir el-Medina appears on the east side of the family burial vault, which remained permanently accessible to receive serial interments (see Plate 4).[26] This remarkable composition occupies the entire surface of the wall and presents a most powerful projection of the current conceptualization of the cosmos and post-mortem existence. Since the ceiling is vaulted, the available surface is reminiscent of that of a round-topped stele and is treated in the same way, the tympanum at the top forming one major element and the rectangular element below, the other. The bottom of the tympanum is the ground line to which the main features of this element are anchored, and the overall design is an excellent example of balanced antithetical composition. The notional vertical centre line is dominated by a seated figure of Re-Harakhty in a barque, and he is being summoned forth at dawn over the horizon by two baboons at either end of the composition that face him and each other. Their identical colouring and appearance powerfully reinforce the sense of antithetical balance. Visually the scene insists on the order and stability of the heavenly sphere, but ideologically the emphasis is firmly on resurrection, the reappearance of the sun in the morning prefiguring the resurrection of the dead and guaranteeing the continued existence of the ordered universe. The references to Re-Harakhty, Atum, and Khopri in the textual material point very much in the same direction.

.   [26] Shedid (1994) provides a detailed illustrated account of this tomb.

The scenes in the rest of this section are inspired by 'The Chapter of the Field of Offerings', ch. 110 of the *Book of the Dead*, but that is not the whole story.[27] There is an image of Sennedjem's son performing the ritual of the Opening of the Mouth on his father's mummy/mummy case, and another son is represented boating. These two events would have taken place before the tomb owner appeared in the Underworld and demonstrate that, yet again, the scene overall is focusing on activities that belong to different timescales. In the case of the figures engaged in agricultural activity there is some attempt to portray the physical labour involved in that the figures are given appropriate stances. We can assert with some confidence that neither Sennedjem nor his wife ever engaged in such work during life, but the scenes form part of a spell to guarantee food for the deceased and his wife beyond the grave. Two elements are particularly noteworthy in the subject matter: in the first place, the boating scene is a reworking of the traditional motif depicting *the deceased* boating in the Underworld, and the barque of Wennefer has been reduced to a very insignificant position in the scene. Both innovations indicate that Sennedjem is pre-eminently concerned in these scenes with his own fate and that of his family, and that everything else is very much of secondary importance.

In compositional terms we should expect to find here a series of registers running the whole width of the wall, and that pattern clearly lies at the back of the tableau, but in this case the artist has treated the design with great originality, breaking up the lowest register by introducing water channels and also by abandoning the right angle at the right-hand lower corner and inserting an irregularly shaped island. These innovations create an intriguing tension between the standard template and the artist's vision of its potential for development. The tympanum and the lower section of the scene are linked by a feature consisting of black and white squares symbolic of heaven and the underworld, asserting and confirming the unity of the cosmos.

The composition of the lower scene makes full use of secondary and primary ground lines to anchor elements of the representation, and this principle is pursued fully in the last register where all the plants are fixed firmly to ground lines formed by the edges of watercourses. However, the composition is particularly distinguished by careful, though not rigid, attention to symmetry. A sense of a notional vertical centre line picking up the position of the sun-god is created by the block of gods in the centre of the first register and the figure of Sennedjem ploughing in the third. In the first register the block of two figures to the left is balanced by the square to the right, and the same holds true of the second and third registers. However, in the third register the tree in front of the oxen actually breaks into the adjacent block,

---

[27] Illustrations of this chapter are common. That in the papyrus of Any has many of the features found here, including the use of water to provide a frame and demarcate registers, but it is greatly inferior in composition and execution (Faulkner 1994: pl. 34).

slightly impairing its rectilinear design, and it may be regarded as a visual prolepsis of what occurs in the lower register. This sense of balance is strengthened overall by the verticality of the block sequences to right and left. The last register breaks the pattern of those above, except that the island element at bottom right echoes to some degree the shape of the blocks above. The concern with symmetry also extends to detail: the right-hand block in register 1 shows three symmetrically arranged oblong pools which form a register spatially identical with those below, and symmetrical arrangement of the pools is even more evident in registers 3 and 4; the trees along the top end of the canal are distributed in such a way that the four heavily laden date palms are disposed at equal intervals; and the plants at the bottom show a strikingly symmetrical arrangement by groups of three. Although the island at bottom right is irregular in form, symmetry again shows up on the treatment of the serpent heads at either end of the barque of Wennefer.

Up to this point I have discussed tombs that give expression to traditional mortuary concepts, but the topic cannot be concluded without discussing the effects of the Amarna revolution on non-royal funerary practice. What I have already said about the tomb of Akhenaten has clear parallels in the non-royal context. The tomb of Huya in the northern group of private tombs in the eastern cliff face at Amarna illustrates the point perfectly (N. Davies 1905). There is nothing startling about the architecture itself, and it is evident that the old concept of the tomb as a ritual device for guaranteeing the resurrection of the deceased still holds good. Traditional design principles continue to dominate the way in which scenes are arranged on walls; we continue to find the old synergy between text and image; and the old progression whereby scenes become more cultic the closer one approaches the cult image at the rear of the tomb chapel still prevails. Despite the distinctive features of the Amarna treatment of the human form, graphic elements are disposed within tableaux according to traditional principles with particularly heavy use of relative scale to emphasize the overwhelmingly superior status of the king and his family. The old conception of the components of a human being shows no change, and the *ba*, *ka*, and name continue to feature in texts. There is also much that is traditional in the thinking and terminology of the prayers within the tomb, the influence of the *hotep-di-nesu* formula (see p. 227) being very marked. The subject matter of the decoration and the main thrust of the ritual texts are focused above all else on emphasizing the central importance of Akhenaten and his family to Huya during life and also beyond the grave. All the decoration of the outer chamber is concerned to make this point to a degree that does not have the remotest parallel in private tombs of any other period. Most of the tableaux in the outer hall are commemorative, conveying the role of Huya in events of the reign or his great favour with the king, though the two scenes on the lintel of the doorway into the inner hall depicting Akhenaten and family to the left and Amenhotep III, Tiyi, and their daughter Baketaten to the right do not feature Huya in any way but serve an emblematic function in emphasizing their key role in Huya's official and conceptual world (N. Davies 1905: pl. 18).

The great departure in all this iconographic and inscriptional material lies in the almost complete elimination of the traditional concepts of the Osirian mortuary cult. The underworld has gone; the world of light is all-important. Under the new dispensation the deceased hopes to come forth from the tomb and enjoy the blessings of the Aten every day, as is well illustrated by a text at the entrance to his tomb in which Huya prays to the Aten:

May you cause me to be eternally in the place of favour in my mansion of justification. As for my *ba*, may it come forth <to see> your rays and receive nourishment from its offerings. May I be summoned by name and come at the voice. May I partake of the offerings which issue <from the presence, that I might eat *shenes*-loaves, *bit*-pastry, offering loaves, jugs <of beer>>, roast meat, meals, cool water, wine, milk, everything which issues <from the Mansion of the Aten in Akhet-Aten>.　(pl. 2)[28]

And the mediator who guarantees these blessings from the Aten is to be Akhenaten himself, as indicated by a highly revealing text in the shrine:

Receiving offerings of the king's giving, consisting of bread and beer, and food at every place of yours, that your <name> may endure upon your tomb, and that each generation, when it comes into being, should invoke you, and that your *ba* (?) should live in your tomb, without your name being sought in your mansion, every mouth <making or saying> for you a 'boon which the king gives'.　(pl. 20, east thickness)

---

[28] The text in N. de Garis Davies's publication records what was visible when he worked on the tomb, but his translation (1905: 17) and that of Murnane (1995: 131, 66.1) reflect restorations based on other sources.

9

Dialogue and Transition

The final millennium BC saw Egypt conquered and occupied by a series of foreign invaders, Libyans, Nubians, Assyrians, Persians, and Macedonians, but until the fourth century, whatever the short-term consequences, none of these events exercised a radical and permanent effect on the institutional structure or civilization of Pharaonic Egypt. The invasion of the country by Alexander the Great in 332 BC was quite a different matter; for it inaugurated a thousand years of intimate contact between the Egyptian and Classical worlds, both physical and conceptual, which, despite the many signs of the continued brilliance and vitality during the Ptolemaic and early Roman Periods, led ultimately to the complete erosion of Pharaonic civilization and the transmutation of native Egyptian culture into something quite new. Not the least of Egypt's claims to the attention of historians is that this process of cultural attrition is copiously documented and provides the clearest possible picture of the gradual, deadly abrasion of a great civilization to the point where nothing but vestigial remains were left. It is the purpose of this chapter to plot this process through the last two major periods of Egypt's ancient history (Fig. 9.1).

THE PTOLEMAIC PERIOD

Kingship

Alexander's conquest brought no immediate change in the theory or practice of Pharaonic kingship. As far as the Egyptians were concerned, he replaced the Persian kings as Pharaoh of Egypt, and he was given a titulary of the traditional kind and presented as fulfilling the traditional royal agenda. A Karnak inscription gives perfect expression to this position:

The renewal of a monument performed by the King of Upper and Lower Egypt Meryamun Setepuenre, the son of Re, Lord of Diadems, Alexandros, may he live for ever, after he found it built under the Majesty of the Horus Strong Bull Khaemwaset,

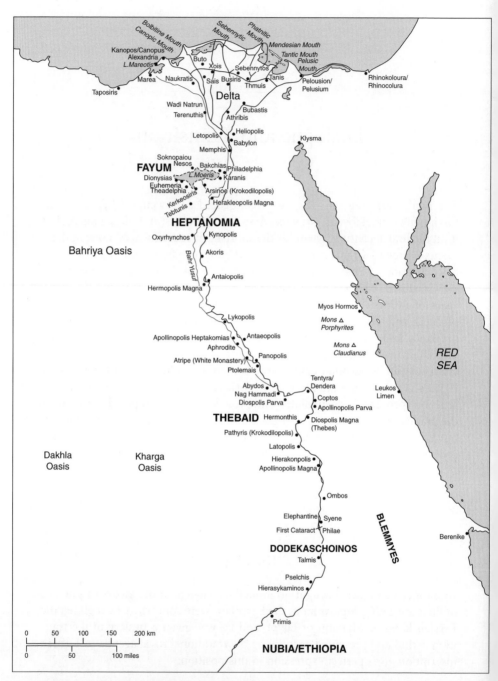

Fig. 9.1. Main sites of Graeco-Roman Egypt. After Lloyd (ed.) 2010*c*: map 2.

the Lord of the Two Lands, Menkheperre, son of Re, Tuthmose, beautiful [or uniter][1] of appearances, beloved of Amon-re, lord of heaven, king of the gods, creator of that which exists ... (Sethe 1904: 7 no. 3; Barguet 1962: 194–5)

It is doubtful whether Alexander even knew of this event, but the important point for my purposes is that the local priests were prepared to endorse the new king in this way and package him in the traditional format. According to the *Alexander Romance* (1. 34), a source of decidedly erratic historical value, he was even formally crowned king of Egypt at Memphis. At present the first Ptolemaic ruler demonstrably crowned in this way is Ptolemy V, but it is in the highest degree probable that most, if not all, Ptolemaic kings underwent this ritual. On Alexander's death in 323 his half-brother Philip Arrhidaeus succeeded, and he too was elevated to the status of Pharaoh and credited with canonical royal building achievements, above all the construction in the great Karnak temple of a new *sanctum* in which his pious activities are still vividly in evidence. He was later associated in kingship with Alexander's posthumous son Alexander IV (II of Egypt) to create a dual monarchy, and he too was invested with the status of Pharaoh in the fullest sense.

The Egyptian treatment of Philip and Alexander IV met the technical requirements of the Egyptian state system, but the realities of power during their reigns lay far beyond such formal procedures in the turbulent events attendant upon the dissolution of Alexander's empire into its main constituent geographical segments which quickly assumed the status of kingdoms under the control of erstwhile generals of Alexander the Great. As a result of these struggles Ptolemy, son of Lagus, emerged as ruler of Egypt, Libya, and southern Syria, and in 306 he assumed the title of king, inaugurating the Ptolemaic Dynasty that lasted until the Roman conquest in 30 BC.

The nature of kingship under the Ptolemies was a complex affair in that it involved the cohabitation of three very different concepts of the office reflecting the need to address three different constituencies. In the first place, the Ptolemies were required to function and project themselves within the framework of Macedonian kingship. Kings within this system enjoyed an element of divine status, since the Macedonian royal house claimed descent from Zeus, but acclamation by the army was an essential prerequisite, though this function very speedily devolved upon the Graeco-Macedonian citizenry of Alexandria, the Ptolemaic capital, whose taste for murderous mob violence created recurrent instability within, if not beyond, the city (Lloyd 2000c: 418–19). The Macedonian kingship system was also characterized by a marked predilection for internecine strife between its male members and the very high level of de facto power traditionally wielded by royal women,

---

[1] The reading of the sign before *kheperu* is problematic. Legrain read *sm3(w)* (uniter) and Lepsius *nfr* (beautiful).

Alexander's redoubtable mother Olympias being only the best-known example, and this feature became a recurrent issue in Ptolemaic Egypt, the most conspicuous representative of this phenomenon by far being the formidable Cleopatra VII who dominated the history of the last years of the dynasty. This trait found its most extreme expression in the institution of full brother–sister marriage, which first appears in the reign of Ptolemy II Philadelphus and subsequently became a regular phenomenon. Inevitably its origin has given rise to much debate, and it is frequently stated that it followed Egyptian practice within the royal house (Carney 1987: 420–39). However, there is no certain case of marriage between full siblings in Pharaonic royal families, though the marriage of half-siblings was common, and it should be remembered that the practice is exemplified in royal families elsewhere in the Mediterranean world before the establishment of the Ptolemaic dynasty, Hecatomnid Caria and Achaemenid Persia being cases in point. We should also remember that the Ptolemaic royal house claimed descent from Zeus who had himself married his sister Hera, but, whatever the origins or formal justification for the practice may have been, it is in the highest degree probable that the underlying motive was political, above all, to ensure that the ambitions and power of queens imbued with the ethos of Macedonian royal politics were channelled in directions that the king could control, and *that*, in the murderous cut-and-thrust of Ptolemaic royal politics, was no small matter. There is, therefore, no strong reason to look for an Egyptian prototype at all, but, nevertheless, the pervasive assimilation of the Ptolemaic queen to Isis the sister-wife of Osiris, the identification in Graeco-Macedonian circles of Osiris with Dionysus, and the close link between the Ptolemaic royal house and Dionysus all presented the Ptolemies with a convenient mythological prototype for the practice that would not have lacked appeal to the indigenous Egyptian population. The titles borne by Arsinoe II strikingly reflect her enhanced position, insisting that she is the daughter of numerous deities and that she is 'hereditary lord', 'ruler', 'great ruler of Egypt', 'lady of diadems', 'female king of the two lands', and, most remarkably of all 'Female Horus', and it is evident that this precedent, once set, was followed by later queens, particularly Cleopatra III and VII (Troy 1986: register A, P4; Ashton 2003).

For the Egyptians (pre-eminently, if not exclusively, the Egyptian elite) a much more important issue ideologically was the Ptolemaic attitude to the traditional concept of the Egyptian state, i.e. to the Pharaonic office, since this was the only conceptual framework within which Egyptians could locate what we should describe as political and military action. Here the Ptolemies speedily realized what needed to be done, and they embraced the Egyptian concept of divine kingship to very good effect and with ever greater enthusiasm as they increasingly recognized, in the face of shifting power dynamics within and without the kingdom, that maintaining the allegiance of the Egyptian priesthood was of crucial importance to their survival. The *Demotic Chronicle* presents us with an Egyptian source of the early Ptolemaic Period which, despite many obscurities, reflects the continued importance to the elite of key aspects of the traditional concept of Egyptian kingship and which any prospective ruler would be expected to recognize (Felber 2002). The text insists on the crucial role of coronation rituals in validating accession which the Ptolemies surely recognized, though the evidence is not as full as we should wish (cf. p. 68); the king's obligations in maintaining the temples are very much to the fore, obligations that the Ptolemies fully discharged (cf. p. 69); and the king's duty in defending the kingdom from its enemies is also paramount, a duty that the Ptolemies discharged with enthusiasm, though, in practice, their military operations were more often designed to serve Ptolemaic interests than those of their Egyptian subjects at large (cf. p. 97ff.). The *Chronicle* is far from unique in emphasizing this royal agenda, and other textual material of the period, such as the Satrap Stele, shows precisely the same points of emphasis in descriptions of royal action. However, the *Chronicle* does provide a concept that is novel, if currently available evidence is typical, in so far as it explicitly concedes that kings may be fallible, an area where earlier texts normally refuse to go, insisting that kings can act in contravention of divine law, and that such actions may bring upon them condign divine retribution (J. Johnson 1983: 66–72).[2]

There was yet a third concept of kingship of great importance within the kingdom in the form of a Hellenistic ruler-cult developed by the Ptolemies themselves. This had its origins in Greek political thinking and played a major role in Ptolemaic political ideology, particularly in providing a conceptual validation for their position that was acceptable to the considerable Greek constituency created by large-scale immigration into the country. This institution took the form of a cult based on the concept of a *hiera oikia* (sacred household), which included all Ptolemaic rulers and their wives, living or dead. Not the least of the merits of this invention was the fact that it presented opportunities for convergence with traditional Egyptian attitudes to kingship which were certainly exploited. The Greek epithets applied to Ptolemaic kings such as *Sōtēr*, 'Saviour', *Eurgetēs*, 'Benefactor', and *Epiphanēs*, 'Manifest', all part of the apparatus of Hellenistic kingship doctrine, were entirely compatible with Egyptian concepts and taken over into priestly usage without any difficulty. In addition, cult statues of rulers were set up in Egyptian temples to share in the benefits of ritual activity, a practice that, as far as we know, had not been practised in Egypt's recent past but was not without earlier parallels and

---

[2] Earlier cases of rulers regarded as delinquent were, where possible, simply erased from the record, e.g. the omission of Hatshepsut and the Amarna Pharaohs from the Abydos king list. When this option was not available, a rogue monarch was passed over as quickly as possible, sometimes with a distinct element of distaste, e.g. Akhenaten is designated as 'the enemy (ḫrw) of Akhetaten' in the inscription of Mose/Mes (Gardiner 1905: 54) when the requirement to date an event in his reign could not be avoided.

certainly not inconsistent with Egyptian religious thinking (Manning, 2010: 73–116; Lloyd: 2010*b*: 92–3).

Clearly, despite some novelties at the margins, the Egyptian concept of kingship remained intact at the ideological level under the Ptolemies, but their efforts to present themselves as Pharaohs could not prevent serious and increasing Egyptian unrest generated principally by economic hardship arising from the operation of an administrative system that was often experienced as oppressive, corrupt, and unjust (e.g. Austin 2006: no. 321). This perception was aggravated by nationalist resentment at foreign rule, the ambitions of local elites, and the pressures of sectional interests such as those of the Egyptian military class, though these factors were not consistently at issue and operated to different degrees in different contexts (Lloyd 2000*c*: 419–20). The first Egyptian revolt occurred in 245 during the reign of Ptolemy III and was followed, after a long interval, by a series of uprisings: a revolt fomented by members of the Egyptian *Machimoi* class broke out in the north soon after 217; in 206 an independent kingdom was established in the Thebaid under the Pharaohs Wenennefer and Ankhwennefer that lasted until 186; about 165 there was widespread trouble including the revolt of Dionysius Petosarapis; and in 131 the revolt of Hariese occurred in Thebes, a particularly noteworthy event since he briefly established himself as the last known Pharaoh of Egyptian extraction. It is within this context of unrest that we must locate the intriguing *Oracle of the Potter*, which only survives in Greek from the Roman Period but was almost certainly composed in Demotic *c.*130 BC. This text is violently hostile to the Greeks whose arrival in Egypt is prophesied as bringing disaster. It foretells their end as well as the destruction of Alexandria, deliverance from Greek control being attributed to an Egyptian ruler who would inaugurate a new Golden Age (Lloyd 1982: 50–4). In all this, however, we are not confronted with the erosion of Egyptian political ideology. Three concepts of kingship there certainly were, but they operated side by side. There was a certain amount of cross-fertilization, but, if anything, Egyptian concepts had more influence on those of the Ptolemies than the other way round.

Force and the State

Ptolemaic military institutions and objectives show nothing like the same convenient spirit of mutual accommodation that we find at the ideological level; for the agenda and systems were unequivocally Macedonian. The wars that followed the death of Alexander in 323 resulted in the emergence of the three major Hellenistic kingdoms of Ptolemaic Egypt, the Seleucid Empire, centred on Syria and Mesopotamia but with significant ramifications beyond, and a Macedonian kingdom whose tentacles and aspirations spread well beyond the Macedonian homeland (Fig. 9.2). Given that the rulers of all three kingdoms were not infrequently hard, ruthless, and very capable men, it comes as no surprise that the history of relations was characterized by vicious conflicts supported by self-serving and unstable alliances as they each jockeyed to carve out the largest possible slice of the available real estate at the expense of their rivals. Whilst, however, the initial aim may have been to retain and expand their separate kingdoms, we are justified in suspecting that several of the Hellenistic kings harboured dreams (or was it fantasies?) of going much further, i.e. the recreation of the great empire of Alexander himself.

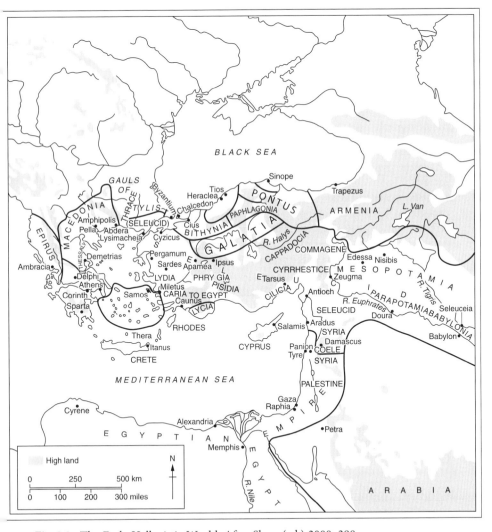

Fig. 9.2. The Early Hellenistic World. After Shaw (ed.) 2000: 398.

Polybius leaves us in no doubt of the military successes of the first three rulers of the Ptolemaic dynasty:

they threatened the kings of Syria by land and by sea, as they were masters of Coele Syria and Cyprus; their sphere of control included the dynasts in Asia and also the islands, as they were masters of the most important cities, strongholds and harbours along the whole coast from Pamphylia to the Hellespont and the region of Lysimacheia. They kept watch on affairs in Thrace and Macedonia through their control of Aenus and Maronea and of even more distant cities. In this way, having extended their reach so far and having shielded themselves at a great distance with these possessions, they never worried about their rule in Egypt.   (5. 34)

We can see clearly from this assessment that some points of interest replicate traditional areas of concern in Pharaonic times, and it is indisputable that there was an imperative to respond to the traditional external preoccupations of Egyptian kings both for economic reasons and to maintain the credibility of the Ptolemies as latter-day Pharaohs. The Adulis inscription from the reign of Ptolemy III is particularly revealing not only because of its very Egyptian character but because it picks up a number of elements of traditional Egyptian historiography:

King Ptolemy . . . having taken over from his father the kingdom of Egypt, Libya, Syria, Phoenicia, Cyprus, Lycia, Caria and the Cyclades islands, marched out into Asia with a force of infantry and cavalry, a fleet and *elephants from the Troglodytes and Ethiopia, which his father and he himself were the first to hunt from these places*, and [which] they brought to Egypt and equipped for use in war. Having secured control of all the territory within the Euphrates and of Cilicia, Pamphylia, Ionia, the Hellespont, Thrace, and of all the forces in those places and of the Indian elephants, and having reduced to his obedience all the rulers in the provinces, he crossed the river Euphrates, and having subdued Mesopotamia, Babylonia, Susiana, Persis, Media and all the remaining territory as far as Bactria, and *having sought out all the sacred objects that were removed from Egypt by the Persians and having brought them back to Egypt* together with the rest of the treasure from the provinces, he sent his force across the dug out rivers . . .[3]

(*OGIS* 54, trans. Austin 2006: no. 268)

However, much of this Ptolemaic activity passed well outside what would have been expected of an Egyptian Pharaoh, even in the Late Period, and that is far from surprising since the main focus of these Ptolemaic rulers was very different. The Ptolemies, like Alexander in his Egyptian policy, had their gaze fixed overwhelmingly on the world to the north and north-west, and their overriding concern was to make their mark in the traditional areas of Greek and Macedonian political and military activity, i.e. the Aegean area and

---

[3] The italicized elements have direct Egyptian parallels: elephant hunting is ascribed to a number of rulers of the Eighteenth Dynasty (e.g. the Gebel Barkal Stele, Der Manuelian 2006: 413), and the issue of the return of objects taken by the Persians arises in a number of Egyptian texts.

the Eastern Mediterranean. Realizing these military ambitions came at a price, and a very heavy one at that, for success depended on a first-class military establishment. Appian, a native of Alexandria, leaves us in no doubt of the prodigious size of the Ptolemaic military establishment:

The kings of my country alone had an army consisting of 200,000 foot, 40,000 horse, 300 war elephants, and 2,000 armed chariots, and arms in reserve for 300,000 soldiers more. This was their force for land service. For naval service they had 2,000 barges propelled by poles, and other smaller craft, 1,500 galleys ranging from *hēmiolia* to *pentērēs*, and galley furniture for twice as many ships, 800 vessels provided with cabins, gilded on stem and stern for the pomp of war, with which the kings themselves were wont to go to naval combats; and money in their treasuries to the amount of 740,000 Egyptian talents. Such was the state of preparedness for war shown by the royal accounts as recorded and left by the king of Egypt second in succession after Alexander, who was the most formidable of these rulers in his preparations...

(*History of Rome*, Preface 10)

The figures recorded in this passage are certainly exaggerated, but they can still be safely taken to convey the impression made on ancient observers by the enormous size of Ptolemaic forces and the huge economic infrastructure that supported them. The statement also indicates that their composition was markedly different from that of the pre-conquest military establishment. Like all Hellenistic armies that of the Ptolemies continued the tactical doctrine and composition of the army of Alexander the Great as modified in the light of experience (Chaniotis 2005; Sekunda 2006: 17–20; Fischer-Bovet 2011). The main field force consisted of a phalanx of heavy infantry (at the Battle of Raphia in 217 probably *c*.25,000 strong) and heavy cavalry that formed an elite striking force. This was supplemented by Hypaspists (an elite infantry guards unit, *c*.2,000 at Raphia), light cavalry (scouts and skirmishers), light infantry (at Raphia there were 3,000 Cretans and 6,000 Thracians and Galatians), war elephants (73 at Raphia which were a subspecies of the African forest elephant greatly inferior militarily to the Indian elephants of the Seleucids), engineers, and artillery. This imported military system was quite at variance with that with which the *Machimoi*, the Egyptian warrior class, were familiar, and this meant that the armies of the Ptolemies were drawn initially from Graeco-Macedonian sources, supplemented by substantial corps of mercenaries. It is only in 217 that we find Egyptian troops being trained to fight in the Macedonian style when it was proving increasingly difficult to get enough troops of Graeco-Macedonian origin.[4]

The navy displayed a similarly advanced profile, though the move to a Graeco-Phoenician mode of warfare had already been made during the

---

[4] This military organization was modified along Roman lines in the 160s (Sekunda 2006: 17–83).

Pharaonic Period. The Ptolemaic navy was designed to function in two ways: in the first place, it was required to maintain command of the sea, which was crucial if the Ptolemies were to have access to the Mediterranean, the Aegean, and the adjacent coastal areas; and, secondly, it served as a propaganda device, in particular by providing a means of projecting an image of power and wealth to the outside world. To achieve these aims the navy required the most up-to-date equipment and systems available. Therefore, its major units consisted of the most modern warships in existence, i.e. polyremes, equipped with artillery, the main type being the 'five' (*pentērēs*, quinquereme), though there were larger and more powerful ships in the inventory. Similarly, the navy was trained to employ state-of-the-art tactics based on concentration of force at one point in the enemy's line, tactics which were essentially those employed in general field actions on land (Grainger 2011: 53–66).

The maintenance of such a large and competitive military created a manpower and fiscal problem destined to have far-reaching consequences. Initially, the Ptolemies did not use Egyptian personnel to meet their military requirements, not least because Macedonian warfare was a highly specialized business, and they preferred to employ troops of Graeco-Macedonian origin who were familiar with it. Potentially, this situation could have committed the state to a massive and unsustainable capital outlay, but the problem was sidestepped neatly through the establishment of a system whereby troops were paid for their services by giving them land allotments (*klēroi*) within Egypt that they could exploit as they saw fit; in return they would serve in the army as required. The largest concentration of these settlers, known as *klērouchoi*, 'allotment-holders', was located in the Fayyum, but there were other settlements throughout the country. Initially *klēroi* were allocated only to non-Egyptian troops, but by the end of the third century there were not enough foreign soldiers to meet requirements, and Ptolemy IV was forced to train up members of the *Machimoi* to serve in his Macedonian-style phalanx, in which they were very successful, and they too became eligible for land allotments, though not on as generous a scale as those given to Graeco-Macedonian troops. Apart from meeting the manpower requirements of the military establishment these arrangements guaranteed a military presence, and oversight, throughout the entire country and functioned as a significant instrument of state control. Not surprisingly the members of this large military establishment constituted one of the elite strata of Ptolemaic society, but there was nothing new in that; for there were clear Pharaonic precedents for this policy (see p. 115). However, the long-term effects of this development had no precedent. Whilst it is true that cultural interchange between settlers and Egyptians was by no means one-sided, particularly in religion, the presence of a large number of Greek-speaking soldiers permanently settled in the country provided one of the media through which Hellenic culture could radiate out to the country at large, a process that led slowly but inexorably to the erosion and ultimate obliteration of its native Egyptian counterpart.

Governance

After the conquest of Egypt Alexander's top priority was to get on with the war against Persia, but he did make arrangements for running the country in his absence. These arrangements were characterized by a clear determination to respect Egyptian practice and a keen awareness of the wealth of his new conquest. It was divided into two halves, each controlled by an Egyptian official, and, when one of these declined to act, the other was given oversight of both parts. Provincial administration based on the nomes was retained, but military control of the province was kept firmly in the hands of Greek and Macedonian officers, and the taxation of Egypt and Libya was assigned, un-wisely in the event, to Cleomenes of Naucratis who eventually ended up as governor of the province before being executed by Ptolemy, son of Lagus, who acquired Egypt after Alexander's death. Of great long-term importance was the foundation, at the western end of the Nile Delta, of Alexandria, which was destined to become the capital of Egypt, though it was never quite regarded by Greeks or Romans as part of Egypt itself.[5] The location of this city gave a clear signal that the focus of Graeco-Macedonian Egypt was going to be the Medi-terranean area both for trade and military purposes, the latter being clearly expressed by the Egyptian name for the place: 'The Fortress of the King of Upper and Lower Egypt Merikaamun-setepuenre, son of Re, Alexander'.[6]

The lead given by Alexander was closely followed in the developed Ptolem-aic system. The king, based in his palace in Alexandria, was technically the head of the administration in all its aspects, but his freedom of action was far from absolute. He was confronted with a number of powerful constituencies of which he had to take account and whose support was crucial to maintaining his position. The most immediate of these was the ever-present royal court which could restrict his freedom of movement in many ways (Herman 1997). It consisted of the royal family, both legitimate and otherwise, and below that of a wide range of personnel holding titles that must initially have followed traditional Macedonian practice, including the king's *hetairoi*, 'companions', *philoi*, 'friends', *sōmatophylakes*, 'bodyguards', and *basilikoi paides*, 'royal pages' (Hammond 1989: 53–8, 140–8, 282), but the system clearly evolved, and a well-defined hierarchy of titles is visible from the reign of Ptolemy V,

---

[5] Both Greeks and Romans regarded it explicitly as a separate entity, in Greek *Alexandreia pros Aigyptoi*, in Latin *Alexandria ad Aegyptum*, both of which translate as 'Alexandria by Egypt' (Turner 1984: 145).

[6] Lloyd 2010: 87.

though it is not always possible to determine whether these titles were simply honorific or genuinely related to offices actually discharged (Mooren 1975; Turner 1984: 163; Bowman 1990: 29). The most important factor in determining the power of court members was royal favour, the loss of which could be catastrophic and the pursuit of which was conducted with ferocious and sometimes lethal determination as ambitious courtiers and their supporters strove for position and status with every means at their disposal. Within this noxious environment the king worked through the major group of courtiers, his *philoi*, who formed a corps from which he could draw his agents, military or civilian, as required for domestic or foreign duties. The most prominent functioned as chief minister, a position that was anything but secure, as the careers of Sosibius and Agathocles in the reigns of Ptolemy IV and V vividly demonstrate. At the point of transition between these two rulers we find the royal bodyguard playing a key role in dynastic politics (Polybius 15. 25–32), but it is impossible to establish on present evidence how far the Praetorian Guard syndrome was a recurrent factor in palace upheavals, though it must surely have been an endemic problem. This machinery was run almost entirely by Greeks[7] with minimal participation of native Egyptians. Certainly the Egyptians would have found much here that was reminiscent of the old Pharaonic court, particularly the centrality of the palace in the governmental system and the title of 'companion' (see p. 137ff.), but there was no disguising the facts that the governance of Egypt lay firmly in the hands of a foreign occupying power, and that the agenda of these foreign rulers was ultimately not Egyptian.

The imperatives of the civil administration of the kingdom were a further factor in defining the parameters within which the king had to operate. Perceptions of this system have undergone radical reassessment in recent years, and the old concept of Ptolemaic government as a monolithic centralist machine has rightly given way to a much more nuanced perception in which the crown was certainly concerned to exercise control but with a keen awareness of the complexity of its task and the need to work, as far as possible, by and through existing systems (Manning 2003, 2010). The most important driver in all this was the requirement to maximize the state's revenues from every possible source, above all, to meet the huge expense of servicing Ptolemaic military ambitions as well as the costs generated by the need to present the kingdom to the Graeco-Macedonian world as the epitome of wealth, splendour, and cultural pre-eminence (Monson 2012: 159–208, 227–36). This administrative system was controlled by the *dioikētēs* (lit. administrator) who resembled the Pharaonic vizier and whose chief administrative task was the supervision and orchestration of local government. He was in charge of all financial matters, above all the collection of taxes, for which he had the

---

[7] Macedonians quickly became a very minor element (Fraser 1972: 53, 69, 80, 88, 101, 129).

assistance of an army of *epimelētai*, (stewards) and *eklogistai* (accountants). The tax burden imposed by this system was extremely onerous, and there is little doubt that it was notably heavier than that which prevailed under the Romans (Monson 2012: 159–208).

The local-government system through which the *dioikētēs* worked was not identical throughout the country since it needed to take account of local conditions, nor is it identical throughout the Ptolemaic Period, but, in essentials, it tends to show the same structural elements. There were three major local administrative units in descending order of size and importance: the *nomos* (nome), *toparchy* (district, locality), and *kōmē* (village). The number of nomes, roughly equivalent to English counties, was variable but normally about forty. Their administration was elaborate and involved a number of officials. Initially they were governed by a *nomarchos/nomarchēs* (nomarch), but his power was gradually restricted as that of the *stratēgos* (general), increased. To begin with these officials were Greek or Macedonian officers established in the nomes as commanders of the local garrison, but they eventually became the major officials of the nome, assuming the role of local governor. Beneath the governor we find the *oikonomoi* ((financial) administrators) who were carefully shadowed by an *antigrapheus* (lit. countersigner), whose countersignature was required for every act. There was also a *basilikos grammateus* (royal scribe) who was responsible for collecting information for taxation purposes, and, as in Pharaonic times, each nome had a public record office (*chreōphylakia*) in which all public documentation would be stored. We also encounter the *epistatēs* (overseer), who could deputize for the *stratēgos* in his legal capacity, the *epistatēs tōn phylakōn* (Head of the Guard), the local chief of police, and the *architektōn* (Minister of Works), who was responsible for the irrigation system that was the foundation of the Egyptian economy. Below this level each nome was divided into a number of *toparchies* administered by toparchs assisted by a *topogrammateus* (district scribe). In turn the *toparchies* were divided into *kōmai*, the smallest unit in the system, administered by a komarch assisted by a *kōmogrammateus* (village scribe). These officials were charged particularly with keeping an accurate land register (Turner 1984: 144–67; Manning 2003: 52–3, 137). The Ptolemies, like their predecessors, found some difficulty in maintaining their authority in the southern part of the country. Consequently, from the end of the third century the nomes south of Lycopolis (i.e. Asyut) were formed into one large administrative area known as the Thebaid placed under the overall control of a *stratēgos tēs Thebaidos* (Governor of the Thebaid). Throughout the country we find members of the Ptolemaic police force, particularly the *phylakitai*, which was divided up into several smaller groups manned chiefly by native Egyptians and officered, in the main, by Greeks or Macedonians (Thompson 1997; Clarysse and Thompson 2006: 2, 165–77). They combined policing functions with a role as ad hoc agents of the government in a wide range of contexts including the enforcement of the decisions of courts of law. They were essentially a paramilitary body, and, as such, they might receive land allotments in addition to salary payments. They were probably inspired by Pharaonic precedents (see p. 171), but their level of organization and pervasive presence in the kingdom both surpass anything currently known from pre-Ptolemaic times.

Much of this was, in essence, a continuation of the old ways, but, whilst Demotic continued in use for administrative documentation, it steadily gave ground to Greek, the language of the higher echelons and a mark of elite status, but it was not the only novelty. The overriding imperative to maximize revenues led to the introduction of new fiscal systems, a process in which the introduction of a census of the whole country played a major role (Clarysse and Thompson 2006: 10–35). Coinage was no novelty in Egypt, but its use was massively extended in the Ptolemaic Period so that numerous taxes were no longer paid in kind but had to be paid in coin, which also had the merit, since coins bore the image of the ruler, of regularly hammering home the overriding authority of the state. However, whatever the merits of this development, it had the decided demerit that manipulation of the currency system was relatively easy and could, and did, give rise to massive hardship. Coinage did not come alone, but brought with it the establishment of a banking organization that provided repositories for tax revenues and, in the process, removed that function from the temples in many instances. Tax-farming, an entirely novel institution in Egypt, was also established, designed to guarantee a regular income stream for the state but, like such institutions everywhere, a ready breeding ground for financial corruption that was certainly exploited to the full. One unequivocally positive development in the taxation system was the widespread introduction of the practice of issuing written tax receipts, considerably restricting the scope for making illegal extra demands on taxpayers. Overall, it may safely be said that, wherever the Ptolemaic administration saw opportunities to maximize state income in any sector of economic life, those possibilities were exploited to the full, and with a significant degree of innovation wherever that promised efficient delivery of revenues.

Theoretically the king was the fount of all law, and, as such, he issued decrees on specific legal issues, very much on the same lines as his Egyptian predecessors. He was also the ultimate court of appeal, and it was open to all subjects, whatever their ethnicity, to submit *enteuxeis* (petitions), for his consideration (Guéraud 1931–2). The system of legal administration below that level provides a further, and striking, example of the desire to accommodate a plurality of existing systems whilst attempting to ensure some measure of state supervision, but the detailed workings of the system evolved over time and are, in any case, not always easy to establish. The largest constituency by far was the native Egyptians who continued in most cases to deal with legal disputes by traditional informal methods (see p. 168), but, if the state system was invoked, they retained the right to be judged on the basis of traditional Egyptian legal practice administered by *laokritai* (judges of the people), drawn from the priestly class. It is clear, however, that such cases might take place with a Greek *eisagōgeus* (registrar) in attendance to mark the state's abiding interest in such matters. Greeks, on the other hand, would be judged by the relevant city law, if they were based in Alexandria, Naucratis, or Ptolemais Hermiou, whilst those outside these settlements were dealt with under customary Greek law. In both cases the courts were designated by the traditional Greek title *dikastēria*. There was also the court of *chrēmatistai* described by Manning as 'a court that represented royal authority' and heard cases as and when required. However, whatever the formal details of legal administration were at any given time, we should not forget that in Ptolemaic Egypt there was all too often a large gap between theory and practice, and it is clear that Egyptians could, and did, have recourse at times, for whatever reason, to Greek officials with legal competence, sidestepping the traditional Egyptian mechanisms (Manning 2010: 165–201).

A constituency with which the Ptolemies were particularly careful to maintain good relations was the priesthood, who were not simply the key figures in the Egyptian elite but a major element in the elite stratum of the kingdom as a whole (Clarysse and Thompson 2006: 177–87; Monson 2012: 212–18). The high priests of Memphis enjoyed a particularly close relationship with the Ptolemaic government (Thompson 2012), but the Ptolemies cast their net much more widely amongst the ecclesiastical community and exercised a wide-ranging oversight of their activities, particularly at the financial level. The temples did gradually see the erosion of some of their ancient functions in the taxation system and legal administration, but they retained their position as major centres of economic activity, and the Ptolemaic Period saw the construction, reconstruction, or modification of many temple buildings. Indeed, many of the finest surviving examples of Egyptian religious architecture date to this period. It is quite clear that temples were able to raise substantial local funding for this purpose, even from local temples, but it would appear that the state kept a watchful eye on these activities (D. Arnold 1999; Manning 2010: 118). Nevertheless, there is no doubt that generous central funding was made available, as required, and that nothing of consequence was done in this sphere of activity without royal approval. The priesthood was more than satisfied with its treatment, as is amply demonstrated by the fulsome expressions of gratitude for royal generosity contained in records of the national priestly synods held at Memphis (e.g. the Canopus Decree and the Rosetta Stone, Austin 2006: nos. 271, 283), events that were clearly designed, amongst other things, to ensure that the crown kept its finger firmly on the priestly pulse.

The priests were not the only segment of the Egyptian elite with which the Ptolemies needed to maintain a working relationship—indeed, given the inveterate pluralism of the upper echelons of Egyptian society, priestly office would often be only one of a series of functions that an individual might discharge. There is clear evidence of the continued operation of great and ambitious elite families during the last years of Egyptian independence, and we should take careful note of the Satrap Stele's reference to 'the grandees of Lower Egypt'. These families continued to exist, and their power could not have been negligible so that the Ptolemies needed to tread very carefully. Not surprisingly, there is evidence to suggest that the eldest son of Nectanebo II, the last native king of Egypt, held high status in the early Ptolemaic Period, and we find Senenshepsu and Usermaatre featuring as high-ranking figures with court functions in the very early Ptolemaic Period. Similarly, during the early 160s we find an Egyptian called Dionysius Petosarapis occupying the high court position as a *philos* (friend), at Alexandria and being described by one Greek commentator as 'the most influential man at court', though his attempt to enhance his position by rebellion came to nothing (Diodorus Siculus 31. 15a). Furthermore, Egyptians seem to be operating as nomarchs (provincial governors) in the mid-third century BC (Lloyd 2002: 117–36). Dedicated pragmatists such as Ptolemy I and II would not have failed to recognize the value of keeping such men on their side and will have turned the phenomenon very much to their advantage.

Dialogue with the Environment

The Ptolemies devoted great attention to the exploitation of the physical context of their kingdom. The most important aspect of this policy was the agricultural system, but it must be emphasized that the possibilities for innovation in this respect were severely limited. The regime of the Nile imposed its own imperatives which could differ considerably from one part of the country to another, and the Egyptians had long since developed the most appropriate methods for dealing with it. The best the Ptolemies could normally do was to ensure, by careful official oversight, that the old systems worked at maximum efficiency. Irrigation was of cardinal importance here, and within each nome the *oikonomos* and *architektōn* (works superintendent), were required to ensure that embankments and water channels were properly maintained. The instructions to an *oikonomos* preserved in *P.Tebt.* 703 give a fascinating glimpse of what was required, e.g.:

(You must inspect)...the water-ducts which run through [the] fields, whether the intakes into them have the prescribed depth and whether there is sufficient space in them; the peasants are used to [leading] water from these to the land each of them sows. Similarly with the canals mentioned from which the intakes go into the above-mentioned water-ducts, (you must inspect) whether they are solidly made and whether the entries from the river are kept as clean as possible <and> whether in general they are in good condition.   (Austin 2006: no. 319)

One activity to which particular attention was devoted was land reclamation, the main focus being the Fayyum where much effort was expended on providing land allotments for military personnel (see p. 292; Manning 2007*b*). This policy will certainly have benefited greatly from the traditional expertise of the Egyptians in hydraulic engineering and brought a considerable increase in agricultural production in the area, but claims that new imported technology played a significant role in the process should be treated with considerable caution for the Ptolemaic Period (Manning 2010: 157–8). Maritime trade was also a major concern. The main focus for this was highly valuable luxury items, including incense and spices from Arabia, though the need to access essential raw materials such as high-quality timber was as important to the Ptolemies as it had been under their Egyptian predecessors. To the north both the Mediterranean and Aegean offered rich commercial pickings which were vigorously exploited, and much effort was expended on developing trade in the Red Sea and Indian Ocean for which the old Persian canal joining the Bitter Lakes to Egypt via the Wadi Tumilat was reopened, and an impressive series of ports on the west coast of the Red Sea was founded or reactivated, such as Berenice (south of Ras Benas) and Myos Hormos (Qoseir el-Qadim), the scope of these activities far surpassing anything that had taken place earlier. In this Red Sea activity one novel priority was the acquisition of African elephants for service in the Ptolemy's 'tank' corps (see p. 291), and special ships called *elephantagoi* (elephant-carriers) were designed to facilitate the transport of these creatures. All such developments were facilitated by well-organized lines of communication between the Nile and the Red Sea punctuated by strategically placed water stations (*hydreumata*) and were paralleled by systematic and highly successful exploitation of the resources of the Eastern Desert itself which was rich in gold and other resources (Sidebotham, Hense, and Nouwens 2008; Manning 2011). The Ptolemies were also successful in maintaining control of trade passing north from Central Africa through Libya both by means of their political and military control of Cyrenaica and their domination of the Western Oases which formed part of the ancient desert trade route running parallel to the Nile to Siwa and beyond (cf. Hölbl 2001: 18, 28–9, 55–7, 204).

Affirmation

In affirming and reaffirming image, status, and ideology the Ptolemies had to address two main constituencies, the Graeco-Macedonian and the Egyptian. The former included immigrants settled in the country as well as rivals and associates in the wider Hellenistic world. In this broad context the overriding concern was to make the Ptolemaic dynasty the great wonder of the age, eclipsing all rivals in the Greek-speaking world. This the Ptolemies attempted to achieve, at one level, by the lavish scale of their military establishment, particularly their fleet which served as, amongst other things, a propaganda device to project throughout the Eastern Mediterranean a potent image of the wealth and power of the kingdom. Above all there was an emphatic focus on generating an impression of the kingdom as the epitome of *lamprotēs* (splendour), and numerous opportunities were created or seized to project this dimension of Ptolemaic Egypt. Alexandria itself was exploited as a device for this purpose with spectacular and world-renowned structures such as the palace quarter, the lighthouse, the library, and the museum, and it was also deployed as a theatre for great ceremonial events such as the Great Procession of Ptolemy II in 270 BC which was carefully designed to project a vision of the kingdom as an exotic land of enormous wealth and might, as well as affirming the divine affinities of the dynasty and its association with Alexander the Great (Rice 1983). The establishment of the *Ptolemaieia* festival at Alexandria by the same ruler had the same propagandist role, and attendance was encouraged from all the states over which the Ptolemies exercised control or influence. Poets such as Theocritus were encouraged to produce works celebrating the dynasty in the most lavish terms (e.g. Austin 2006: no. 255), and in the visual arts sculptures were produced for Greek consumption depicting members of the royal family in typically Hellenistic style, though sculptures combining Greek and Egyptian styles were common, probably produced for Greek consumption to reflect the dual nature of the culture of Ptolemaic Egypt (cf. Ashton 2001). The establishment of cults throughout the country in honour of members of the royal house was a means of constant restatement of the power and status of the royal house in Greek-speaking contexts, as were the *Basileia* and public celebrations of the king's birthday.

For the Egyptians all the traditional means of cultural restatement and affirmation continue to operate and show no break with earlier practice, though differences of emphasis certainly occur. Temples and the temple cult flourished mightily under the Ptolemies. According to Kurth (1997: 152) more than a hundred temples are known from this period, and Dieter Arnold claims that over fifty large and medium-sized temples were built, in addition to numerous additions made to already existing temple structures (1999: 144). Despite some modifications in building techniques, architectural design, and styles of decoration, the ancient concept of the temple remained intact (see p. 258) and received particularly full restatement and development through copious inscriptions incised wherever a surface was available, though the hieroglyphic script used at this period is much more elaborate and difficult than anything employed earlier (Finnestad 1997; D. Arnold 1999: 143–224; Robins 2008: 235–41). Similarly, the ritual activities carried out in temples and in the many festivals continue to serve as powerful devices for restating and reasserting the Egyptians' conceptualization of their world (Coppens 2009). The mortuary cult continues the old conceptual traditions: the elite taste for chapel-tombs persisted, as did a predilection, when resources permitted, for spectacularly large stone sarcophagi (Spencer 1982: 190–2). An outstandingly fine example of a chapel-tomb from the very beginning of the period is that of Petosiris at Tuna el-Gebel, which is particularly remarkable for the evidence it provides of the influence of a Greek artistic vision in the less ritually important sections of the building. There would be a slow and persistent increase in such penetration throughout the Ptolemaic Period, but the native culture proved remarkably resilient in dealing with this threat.

Visual media generated in Egyptian milieux function in much the same way and take much the same form as those produced in the pre-Ptolemaic Period, with some significant modifications. In the royal context examples of sculpture in the round of kings and queens were still produced in the traditional style and to a very high standard (cf. Ashton 2001: 13–24), and the relief sculptures on temple walls follow the traditional pattern and make the same statements, though there is a greater tendency to emphasize their erotic loading, and the iconographic presentation of kingship shows an enhanced interest in the king's family and the cultic involvement of the queen as compared to the norm at earlier periods (Finnestad 1997: 229). Statues of the elite, some of the highest quality, continue to be produced in traditional formats and lie firmly within Pharaonic tradition, and the same holds true of relief and painting commissioned for the higher segments of Egyptian society (Robins 2008: 231–51).

The continued vitality of traditional culture is also manifest in the large body of textual material surviving from the Ptolemaic Period. I have already discussed the huge corpus of hieroglyphic inscriptions relating to the temple cult, but they are far from exhausting the texts preserved in the ancient script, though very few were capable of reading it, and the increasingly arcane development of hieroglyphic must have ensured that this select band steadily decreased in size throughout the Graeco-Roman Period. When we turn to literature preserved on papyrus we are handicapped by the fact that we cannot be sure which texts were composed during the Ptolemaic Period, which were composed earlier, and which were products of the Roman Period. The best that can done for my purposes is to consider texts that have been preserved in Ptolemaic manuscripts, whatever their origins, and that, at least, gives a clear indication of what was being copied and what was considered to be relevant at that period. I shall concentrate on two texts, *The Tale of Setne Khaemwese and Naneferkaptah (Setne I)* (Simpson (ed.) 2003: 453–69) and *The Instruction of Chasheshonqy/Onkhsheshonqy* (Simpson (ed.) 2003: 497–529; Ryholt 2010: 717–18).

The first of these texts is preserved in a papyrus of the early Ptolemaic Period, and, whilst it is rather longer than earlier tales, it lies firmly within the Pharaonic tradition of narrative literature. Its episodic composition and taste for verbatim verbal repetition are easily paralleled earlier, and the subject matter with its historical points of reference, focus on feats of *heka*, and taste for descriptions of wealth and splendour irresistibly recalls such texts as the Middle Kingdom *Westcar Papyrus*. The text's conceptual world is also in all respects traditionally Egyptian: the Pharaoh's role is presented as being of central importance, fearsome divine retribution is the reward for Nanefer-kaptah's impiety in purloining a book of *heka* written by Thoth himself, and Setne's lapse into sexually obsessive behaviour leads him into a situation of downright farce and potential personal disaster from which he is rescued only by the timely intervention of Pharaoh himself. The implicit warning to maintain self-control at all times chimes well with the exhortations against sexual dalliance proffered by earlier *Instruction* texts. Unlike the *Tale of Setne and Si-Osiri (Setne II)* preserved from the Roman Period, there is no trace in this narrative of the penetration of Greek motifs or ideas, a feature that probably reflects its earlier date.

The *Instruction of Chasheshonqy* survives in a number of copies from the Ptolemaic and Roman Periods, though it is perfectly possible that it was composed at an earlier stage. Its format is essentially the same as that of the *Instruction* texts analysed in Ch. 8. We begin with a frame-tale that provides the context for the delivery of the instruction; this is followed by a long series of maxims; and the text may well have concluded with an epilogue taking us back to the frame, though nothing of this has been preserved, if it ever existed. The frame itself is more elaborate than usual, consisting of an account of an abortive conspiracy against Pharaoh that lands the God's Father Chashe-shonqy in gaol. Presumably this section of the tale is itself intended to be didactic, preaching the lesson that nothing can be concealed from Pharaoh, and his vengeance is swift and sure. Whilst it may be argued that Pharaoh has been generous in simply imprisoning Chasheshonqy rather than executing him, Chasheshonqy begins his text with a complaint that he has been treated unjustly for being unwilling to kill the chief conspirator, and that his fate exemplifies the anger of Re which has been turned against Egypt and brought in its train a reversal of the proper order of things. This theme of reversal of the proper order is an old one, but its introduction here is rather perplexing. It is presumably meant to form part of the justification for instructing his son in the proper way to live but, at the same time, forms part of a wider agenda in which the state of the land itself is criticized. Without the complete text we cannot tell for sure, but it very much looks as though the agenda of this instruction is more complex than usual and combines the wisdom-text genre with that of reversal texts such as *Admonitions* which may have a specific historical reference point but may, on the other hand, simply be providing an elaborate justification for the instruction itself, i.e. the moral may be that, if we are to avoid both general and specific misfortune, the enunciated principles must be observed. This interpretation is strengthened by the fact that Pharaoh gives instructions that he should be informed daily of the maxims that have been written on that day, i.e. he needs the instruction too.

The maxims are presented in a very different format from that appearing in the previously discussed texts. They are composed as staccato one-liners, usually in the imperative, and are often grouped into sequences with the same grammatical structure, a device that imparts a distinctly incantatory dimension to sections of the text—chanting the material would be easy and very effective. Occasionally, however, the format changes so that the injunction dimension disappears, e.g. at 10, 11ff., we are presented with a series of wishes for desirable outcomes in a variety of different contexts.

When we turn to details of content we are immediately on familiar ground. The focus is very much on the individual, and there is much on general principles of behaviour. The recurrent mindset is hard-headed practicality that insists on self-reliance, the need to look after one's own interests, and the necessity for constant caution in all one's dealings. You should strive to gain a good name, beware of too much drinking, maintain good bodily health, keep control of your tongue, and work constantly and cautiously to guarantee your economic success and well-being; ensure that you live within your means and are careful in borrowing and lending, choose your friends carefully, treat your children on terms of equality ('Do not prefer one to another of your children. You do not know the one who will be charitable to you among them'), speak the truth, and be a loyal supporter of your community; avoid illicit sexual activity, and, above all, follow the precepts of wisdom, learning to recognize the order of the world and integrating with it.

Given the focus on the individual's well-being, it is hardly surprising that the family looms very large in the text: you should look after your parents because such behaviour will bring rewards, and you should be careful when taking a wife. In line with this latter advice there are a number of passages that show a great suspicion of women bordering on misogyny, e.g. 'Let your wife look at your property. Do not trust her with it'; 'Do not open your heart to your wife. What you have said to her belongs to the street'; 'Do not rejoice over the beauty of your wife; her heart is set just on her sexual gratification'. It is, however, recognized that a wife can have a higher social ranking than her husband, and in such cases the husband should defer to her. Care is also required when dealing with other relations: it is not a good idea to live with your parents-in-law; be generous to your brothers; do not let your son marry a woman from another town because he will be taken from you by this arrangement; and make sure your daughter gets a prudent husband, not a rich one. The general principle is also enunciated that you should treat others as you would like them to treat you.

Behaviour in official contexts does not feature as prominently as in some earlier instruction texts, but the advice is clear and within traditional parameters: respect superiors, and serve your master zealously, bearing in mind that just administration brings prosperity; deal conscientiously with the Pharaoh's business, and never talk about it when drinking alcohol. Above all, learn how to serve him in the proper manner. Thinking on the determinants of the world order is firmly in line with earlier teaching. There is an insistence that all things are ultimately in the hands of god/fate, and one should bear in mind that god operates on a basis of reciprocity. The gods are all-knowing and will ensure retribution, and that retribution can be visited not only on the perpetrator but on the entire family and people associated with it. However, ultimately life is unpredictable, and no-one should be called happy until he is dead. It must be conceded that some of the latter comments have their parallels in Greek thinking, but there is no need to argue for Greek influence since these ideas are present implicitly or explicitly in earlier Egyptian texts.

A clear picture emerges from the preceding survey of the effects of interaction between the Greek-speaking elite and the Egyptian population. The main concern of the Ptolemies was to make their mark in the most compelling manner in the Graeco-Macedonian world of the Aegean and Eastern Mediterranean. The early shift of the capital from Memphis to Alexandria was a clear indication of this preoccupation, and it is highly significant that, throughout antiquity, that city was never regarded as being part of Egypt. It was always the main base of an occupying power. Ptolemaic governance of Egypt and foreign dependencies was based essentially on the principle that the country was the milch cow to fund the dynasty's military and cultural ambitions. The structure of central administration evolved from a classic Macedonian format, though there were fortuitous parallels with Pharaonic systems. Local government was not radically altered. Both law and economy took account of local systems and worked with them, wherever possible, but administration was organized to ensure close governmental supervision. The language of higher administration and the governing elite was Greek, and there is clear evidence of the extension of its use at the expense of Egyptian. The Greek-speaking army was radically different from that of Pharaonic times in composition, tactics, and equipment, and constituted a major item in the royal budget, which was met by settling troops within the country and calling them up as required. This Greek-speaking stratum in Egypt's society provided a further channel for the gradual extension of the use of Greek and the establishment of the perception that it was the elite language, a phenomenon that was ultimately to have catastrophic consequences for native Egyptian culture. However, whilst the Ptolemies were determined to maximize revenues and presided over a taxation system that was both heavy and not infrequently corrupt, they recognized the importance of keeping on the right side of local Egyptian elites, above all the priests, whose interests and support were sedulously promoted. Textual material in temples and more secular contexts provides copious evidence that the Pharaonic conceptual world remained intact and was still susceptible to creative exploration and restatement, though it should be noted that the larger number of surviving copies of the *Book of the Dead* in the hieroglyphic script from this period are riddled with errors, which indicates that the grip of many scribes on this writing system had become very precarious. The visual arts likewise followed Pharaonic norms and continued to serve traditional functions, though attempts were made, with varying success, to integrate Greek and Egyptian artistic visions in the interests of political and cultural propaganda. Overall, our verdict must be that despite the strong focus of the Ptolemies on their standing in the Mediterranean world, the Ptolemaic Period was one of the great periods in Egyptian civilization, but the seeds of cultural dissolution were already in place, and some signs of the recession of Egyptian culture were already beginning to manifest themselves.

ROMAN EGYPT

Octavian's victory over the remnants of the Ptolemaic Dynasty brought Egypt abruptly into the Roman Empire in 30 BC and, at the same time, inaugurated the last phase of Pharaonic civilization. It is only the history of Roman Egypt in so far as it relates to the erosion of this culture that concerns me here, and that means that there is no need to proceed any later than the fifth century AD at which point only vestigial remains of Pharaonic culture survived.

Governance

To the Greek geographer Strabo, writing from first-hand experience during the early decades of Roman rule, the conquest of Egypt was an unequivocally good thing, bringing the restoration of good governance after the 'drunken violence' of the later Ptolemies (17. 1. 11–12), but the establishment of benign rule was rather far from Roman intentions, and it is clear, in any case, that Strabo is presenting altogether too rosy a picture of the effects of the change of masters on the population of the country, not least, perhaps, because of his personal acquaintance with the second governor Aelius Gallus.

The key issue for the Romans in Egypt was the country's extraordinary wealth, which gave it enormous economic and strategic power, and this brought with it two effects: in the first place, the emperors were determined to ensure that the resources of Egypt stayed firmly at the disposal of the emperor *and nobody else*. The bitter experience of the last years of the Republic when Egypt became the intended or actual power-base of major Roman commanders ensured that Augustus[8] took great care that no member of the senatorial aristocracy had an opportunity to emulate the precedent of Mark Antony in making a power-base out of this prodigiously wealthy province. Governors were, therefore, appointed from the equestrian rather than the senatorial class,[9] whose support for the emperor was always equivocal, and they held the title of Prefect (*Praefectus*), unique for the governor of an imperial province. Strabo had a high regard for the prefects of whom he knew, describing them as *sōphrones andres* (prudent men), but here again he is evidently presenting an overly positive view since neither of the first two could be described as men of impeccable political or military judgement. In addition Augustus placed an absolute embargo on senators even visiting the country without imperial permission.

In discussing the day-to-day practicalities of administration Strabo rightly insists that the prefects were the counterparts of Ptolemaic kings, operating from Alexandria very much as they did, and this would certainly have been the perception of many of their subjects. However, the system was not perceived in this way by the native Egyptian elite who were still steeped in the millennial traditions of Egyptian civilization. The only system of government compatible with Pharaonic state ideology was kingship, and to the native Egyptian elite the head of the state was the emperor himself, even though very few emperors ever set foot in the country. This situation is, therefore, an exact counterpart to the position of Egypt during the Persian Period when the satrap (governor) functioned exactly like the Roman *praefectus*, and the Great King of Persia, an equally absentee landlord, was accorded the status of Pharaoh. Consequently, during the Roman Period we find that in ritual scenes sculpted on the walls of temples Roman emperors are depicted in all respects as Pharaohs and carry out the critical religious functions that had been incumbent on the Pharaoh since the beginning of Egyptian history, the last emperor whose names appear in hieroglyphs in an Egyptian temple being Decius in the middle of the third century. These administrative arrangements were remarkably successful for a surprisingly long time in keeping the ambitions of enterprising provincial officials at bay: Vespasian was formally declared emperor in Alexandria in AD 69, no doubt with a shrewd awareness on his part of the military value of Egypt, but we do not hear of any further claimant to the imperial office emerging in Egypt before Avidius Cassius in AD 175, and we have to wait

---

[8] Octavian was awarded the title 'Augustus' in 27 BC and from that point on is generally designated by that name.

[9] The equestrian order consisted of those members of the Roman elite who, under the rules established in Augustus' reign, possessed a property qualification between 100,000 and 250,000 *denarii*. To get some sense of the value of these sums it should be borne in mind that, in the time of Augustus, the pay of a legionary soldier amounted to 225 *denarii* a year.

until 297–8 for the next pretender in the form of Lucius Domitius Domitianus, if we discount the problematic case of the prefect Marcus Julius Aemilianus in the 260s, and none of these claimants succeeded in getting anywhere near the throne of the Caesars. This relative lack of internal candidates did not, of course, prevent powerful figures in Egypt from supporting their favoured aspirants from other neighbouring provinces as and when occasion arose (Bowman 1990: 37–45; Capponi 2010: 180–98).

Immediately below the Prefect we find the Romans initially continuing, in the main, the old Ptolemaic administrative structure. His immediate subordinates were the *dikaiodotēs* and the *idiologos*. The former, a Roman invention, exercised authority over the administration of law that continued with all the old complexities of the Ptolemaic system already observed. However, his duties were further complicated by the additional need to administer Roman civil law that governed relations between Roman citizens and inevitably acquired ever greater prominence with the gradual extension of Roman citizenship within the country (Rowlandson 2010: 248–54). The *idiologos*, or 'private account', is described by Strabo as enquiring 'into all properties that are without owners and that ought to fall to Caesar'. These two officers were assisted by the *oikonomoi*, officials of considerable power and importance, who were no novelty, and the freedmen of Caesar, who most definitely were, being another element of the Roman imperial system grafted onto the old Ptolemaic structure and clearly intended, like the office of prefect, to guarantee the emperor's knowledge and oversight of this potentially very dangerous segment of the empire. In the administration of Alexandria we continue to meet the old Ptolemaic officials: the *exēgetēs* (interpreter), who had wide supervisory powers, the *hypomnēmatographos* (recorder), the *archidikastēs* (chief justice), and the *nykterinos stratēgos* (night commander).

For purposes of local government the broad outline of the Ptolemaic system was preserved for several centuries, but the Roman conquest brought with it significant modifications that had far-reaching consequences. A social system was quickly established whereby the population was divided into sharply defined categories in descending order of power and privilege. The object of this structure is perfectly described by Bowman and Rathbone (1992: 114), 'the Romans aimed to demarcate a privileged urban-based "Hellenic" élite, through whom and with whom they could rule and exploit the native population'. At the top were Roman citizens, Greeks, and Jews resident in the *poleis* (i.e. cities of Greek type with Greek institutions, initially Alexandria, Naucratis, and Ptolemais, with Antinoopolis being added in 130). Below them came 'the Egyptians', who were designated by this term *irrespective* of their ethnic origin. The majority would inevitably be ethnic Egyptians, but the group also included anyone who did not fall into the first category in the social hierarchy. The 'Egyptians' were further divided into those who lived in nome capitals (*mētropoleis*), the elite being the Hellenized products of the

Greek gymnasium culture,[10] and those who lived in villages. This structure was used as the basis for levying the completely new Roman-style poll-tax (*tributum capitis*): only 'the Egyptians' resident in the villages were liable to pay the full sum; the inhabitants of *mētropoleis* paid at a reduced rate; and the fortunate members of the upper stratum in this social order were completely exempt (Alston 2002: 20, 186–7).[11]

The new social structure worked in the *chōra*[12] within a system of provincial administration whose framework was inherited from the Ptolemies. The country was divided into about thirty–forty nomes, or provinces, each with its governor (*stratēgos*, lit. 'General') who, despite his name, had no military power under the Romans and resided in the nome capital (*mētropolis*). However, the Romans largely abandoned the old system whereby the *stratēgoi* were drawn from the local elite, often with strong priestly connections, and established the practice of confining these offices to prominent Alexandrians. Between the prefect and the *stratēgoi* we continue to find the *epistratēgoi* whose numbers could vary—there may at times have been as many as four—and they were always, like the prefects, of equestrian rank. It is self-evident that these arrangements served yet once more to strengthen central control over the machinery of government in Egypt. However, as early as the beginning of the first century AD we see the beginnings of the Romanization of society and administration in nome capitals that entailed a significant devolution of administrative functions from central government. The progressive transmutation of these settlements during the second century from traditional Egyptian urban communities into Romanized municipalities of the type widely current elsewhere in the empire made it possible for the Emperor Septimius Severus in AD 200 to complete the long process of administrative evolution by granting nome capitals Roman-style town councils and officials exercising wide-ranging administrative functions, above all in the collection of taxes, and orchestrating much of their public service through the liturgic system.[13] At the end of the third century Diocletian modified the nome-

---

[10] Attendance at a *gymnasion* was a mark of high status in a Greek city. In Egyptian *mētropoleis* membership was an unequivocal mark of 'Greekness', at least in terms of cultural commitment, and a jealously guarded privilege. In such communities 'the *gymnasium* men' (*hoi apo gymnasiou*) were the social, economic, and political elite.

[11] The Ptolemies had operated a poll-tax called the salt-tax, but it functioned quite differently from the Roman system (Monson 2012: 265–6).

[12] This term was used to designate Egypt proper to the exclusion of Alexandria, which was never regarded as part of Egypt in the strict sense (see p. 293).

[13] Liturgies were a time-honoured institution in the Classical world whereby wealthy members of a state or city undertook to defray the costs of public service from their own pockets. These benefactions might be conferred by state or civic officers as part of their duties, but they could be discharged as acts of public generosity by private individuals. The reward was the enhancement of individual or family prestige within the community, but the liturgic system could lead to financial disaster for those discharging it. Not surprisingly, therefore, some metropolites went to considerable lengths to avoid the burden of a liturgic office, though private

based system still further by dividing Egypt into rather larger units in the interests of administrative efficiency, and further modifications in the same spirit were subsequently made to this scheme down to the end of Roman/ Byzantine rule in the country (Bowman 1990: 68–88; Bowman and Rathbone 1992; Bowman 2000: 182–7; Alston 2002: 186–207, 272–81; Rowlandson 2010).

Economic Organization and Exploitation

A major consequence of Egypt's wealth for the Romans, as for the Ptolemies, was their determination to extract the maximum economic return from the province. Therefore, one of the earliest administrative tasks which they under-took was to carry out a census of the entire country to establish a basis for levying the poll-tax. However, this tax and the wide range of smaller fiscal imposts such as sales taxes, market dues, and import levies paled into insignificance compared with the returns from the corn levy, by far the most important single element in the taxation system. Therefore agriculture, in particular wheat production, was of cardinal importance. However, the potential for radical change in this activity was severely limited by the imperatives of the irrigation system, and we are confronted essentially with a continuation of Ptolemaic practice (see p. 298), though there is evidence of greater use of technological innovations such as the Archimedes screw, the *sakkiya* (water-wheel) for raising water, and the practice of crop-rotation (Rowlandson 1996: index, 380; Rathbone 2007: 700–5), and it has been plausibly argued that the use of such methods was indirectly encouraged by the vast increase in private land taxed at a highly favourable rate that was typical of the period (Monson 2012). The best the Roman authorities could do was to ensure that the system they had inherited functioned as efficiently as possible, and in this they were highly successful, so that in most years it produced a substantial grain surplus the tax on which, paid in kind, was used, amongst other things, to feed hungry mouths in Rome (Bowman 1990: 101–6) to which Egypt exported an annual quantity of grain equivalent to one-third of the city's total consumption—the foundation of Constantinople as the capital of the Eastern Empire in 324 brought with it the redirection thither of a significant proportion of this output, though the increased importance of North Africa as a source of grain had already led to a decline of Egypt's

---

acts of euergetism on behalf of the community were common. One of the characteristic features of Roman government was the conversion of many local government functions into compulsory liturgies, which were clearly highly burdensome to many and therefore avoided wherever possible (Bowman and Rathbone 1992: 111, 113, 120, 122–3, 126; P. Parsons 2007: 169–70; Monson 2012: 236–46).

importance in this respect.[14] To facilitate the levying of this tax the Romans simplified the old Ptolemaic subdivisions of the agricultural land by dividing it into two categories, public land and private land, with two different levels of fiscal obligation very much to the advantage of those who held private land (Rowlandson 1996; Monson 2012). Available evidence makes it clear that there was a marked tendency for private land to assimilate public land, a matter of considerable administrative convenience for the state and great economic benefit to the wealthy who were able to accumulate thereby very substantial holdings of real estate.

Older literature has shown a marked inclination to characterize the economic administration of Roman Egypt, particularly the taxation system, in the bleakest terms, and there is certainly evidence that might support this view. The Emperor Tiberius rebuked an overzealous governor with the words: 'I want my sheep shorn, not shaven' (Cassius Dio 57. 10. 1), but this may well have been an isolated case. Some taxpayers, enmeshed in actual or impending economic ruin, certainly did gave up the unequal struggle and fled their domicile to take up refuge in the marshes, the deserts, or even in the anonymity of great population centres such as Alexandria, whilst others took to a life of brigandage, but we should never forget that many Egyptian peasants had always lived permanently very much on the brink of disaster, and even a small mishap could tip them over the line into destitution. Certainly, from the second century we encounter a number of armed revolts—there was a massive uprising in AD 152, and another in the form of the revolt of the *Boukoloi* (lit. Herdsmen) which raged from 172–5 and may well have been connected in some way with the great plague that ravaged Egypt from 167 to *c*.179. Interestingly enough, the *Boukoloi* were led by an Egyptian priest, and it has plausibly been suggested that this fact may well reflect a nationalist dimension to the rebellion. Later outbreaks see the Emperor Galerius destroying the Upper Egyptian town of Coptos in 293/4 and the Emperor Diocletian putting down the usurpation of Lucius Domitius Domitianus in 298 and taking the city of Alexandria. These resentments also had their literary dimensions in the form of such anti-imperial texts as the *Acts of the Pagan Martyrs* (Musurillo 1954) and the more generally subversive *Oracle of the Potter* in which 'the Egyptians' eloquently express their indignation at and contempt for the ruling power (see p. 288). However, there is no reason to believe that all these uprisings had the same cause or even that the taxation system was a prime mover of any of them. Indeed, available evidence makes it clear that the tax burden was not unduly heavy and perfectly manageable under normal circumstances (Bowman 1990: 94).

---

[14] The wheat grown at this period was no longer the emmer wheat of the Pharaonic Period but the *durum triticum* favoured in the Greek and Roman world. This shift had begun during the Ptolemaic Period (Bowman 1990: 101; Rowlandson 1996: 20).

Whilst the fiscal exploitation of the population was of prime concern to the Roman authorities, measures were also taken to ensure the efficient development of all other possible sources of revenue: the highly lucrative trade with India through the Red Sea ports developed by the Ptolemies (see p. 299) was enthusiastically promoted, and the Romans continued their policy of vigorous exploitation of the resources of the Eastern Desert, showing particular enthusiasm for highly prized stones such as the porphyry of Mons Porphyrites and the speckled grey granodiorite of Mons Claudianus, both quarried from well-organized bases that still survive in an excellent state of preservation. Trade up the Nile into Nubia was also a focus of interest, and surviving military installations in the Western Desert leave us in no doubt of the Roman awareness of the commercial potential of that area and their determination to milk it to the full (Jackson 2002).

Military Organization

It is very much of a piece with the Romans' iron-grip imperial policy that they took great care in organizing the military control of Egypt, which was targeted not only at defence from external enemies but also at enforcing Rome's will within and guaranteeing its security as a major economic asset. Three legions were maintained in Egypt initially, but this number was reduced to two in AD 23. Strabo claims that one was stationed in Alexandria itself (17. 1. 12), but this may well be shorthand for Nicopolis, just outside the city, which quickly became the military headquarters of Egypt and the base for any legions established in the country. There were an additional three cohorts in Alexandria, three at the First Cataract in Syene, and three distributed throughout the country. There were also three squadrons (*alae*) of cavalry carefully distributed at critical points. In the course of the long Roman occupation these dispositions underwent some changes, but Strabo's narrative gives a clear picture of the Roman perception of the strategic requirements of the province. In addition to the Nile Valley the army was also employed to guard the trade routes and other economically important assets in the Western and Eastern Deserts where the remains of numerous military installations are still to be seen, frequently in a remarkable state of preservation. There was also a fleet known as the *classis Alexandrina* based at Alexandria. This was a standard component of the Roman navy and was required to guarantee Roman control of the eastern Mediterranean, a particularly important function of which must have been ensuring that there was no interruption in the supply of Egyptian corn to Rome.

From the very beginning of the Roman occupation we find these troops being used in support of the civil authority. Cornelius Gallus, the first prefect of Egypt, employed them to put down a revolt in Heroonpolis and also one in

the Thebaid which Strabo claims was caused by the taxation system, probably
the introduction of the Roman poll-tax. Petronius, the third prefect, had to
use them to put down a riot in Alexandria itself of which Strabo graphically
writes that he, 'when the huge Alexandrian population rushed against him
hurling stones, resisted them with his body-guard alone, and, having killed
some of them, put a stop to the rest' (17. 1. 53). Another source of civil unrest
not infrequently requiring military intervention was the hostility between
Greeks and Jews, which is particularly in evidence in the Alexandrian attack
on the Jews in 38. This problem simmered on for many years until it came to a
head in the great and bloody Jewish revolt of 115–17. This episode saw some
particularly vicious fighting with heavy casualties and effectively removed the
Jews as a significant element of the population of Egypt. A further source of
unrest consisted of clashes between rival religious groups amongst the native
Egyptian population over such matters as the treatment of animals held sacred
by some but not by others. Yet another phenomenon requiring the use of
armed force was the spread of Christianity in Egypt which gave rise to the
persecution by Decius in 250 and the even more notorious great persecution
under Diocletian which began in 303.

An altogether sterner test of the army's mettle was provided by the invasion
of southern Egypt by Nubians ruled by Queen Candace who had been
encouraged by the absence of the prefect Aelius Gallus on a campaign against
the Arabians *c.*25 BC. They succeeded in capturing Syene, Elephantine, and
Philae, but Petronius defeated them completely and mounted a major assault
on the Nubian kingdom, capturing Napata and razing it to the ground. He
then established a permanent base in Nubia which was subsequently attacked
by Candace. The conflict was eventually brought to a conclusion by diplomacy
conducted before Augustus himself, rather to the advantage of the Nubians.
After this Egypt's southern border seems to have remained inviolate until the
mid third century when nomadic incursions of the south by the Blemmyes
became a problem that would continue until the fifth century AD, despite the
efforts of Diocletian to set up a firm frontier at the First Cataract reinforced by
a policy of buying off the Blemmyes and setting up the Nobades in the
Dodecaschoenus as a buffer zone. The western frontier was much less problematic, but nevertheless the movements of nomads in that area constituted a
threat that could not be ignored and military precautions were certainly taken.
As so often in Egyptian history it was the eastern frontier that offered the most
dangerous threats, giving rise to the short-lived conquest and occupation of
Egypt by the Palmyrenes in 270–2, very much a portent of things to come in
the form of the Sassanid and Arab invasions of the seventh century (Alston
1995; Jackson 2002; Pollard 2010: 452–65).

The army's role in dedicated military operations is far from an end to the
matter. Soldiers on active service and time-expired veterans who were settled
in the country formed an integral part of Egyptian society, and, as they were all

Greek-speakers, they made a significant contribution to guaranteeing the status of Greek as the language of those who controlled the country. I can do no better than quote Richard Alston's (1995: 159) excellent summary of their effect:

Soldiers and veterans were in continual contact with civilian Egyptians. Soldiers worked with Egyptian civilians in manning the extensive security system of the province. They supervised the collection of taxes. They worked with local police in the nomes. They traded with civilians and probably received many supplies from civilian contractors. They married and the resultant children lived in Graeco-Egyptian settlements. There was no great cultural, social or economic division and it is unsurprising, viewed from this level, that the soldiers integrated.

Erosion and Transformation

The key issue for us in this historical evolution is its effect on Pharaonic culture. How far can we plot and account for its decline and supersession? For the first century and a half of the Roman Period the history of Egyptian civilization is very much a continuation of that of the Ptolemaic Dynasty, and we can still point to high achievement in traditional architecture, sculpture, and literature. The Roman conquest in 30 BC did not impair in any way the Egyptian ideology of kingship which remained alive and well, in religious contexts at least, well into the fourth century AD. The Egyptians simply repeated the policy applied in previous such cases by installing the Roman emperors as Pharaohs, and the latter are depicted in this capacity in many Egyptian temples such as Dendera, Kom Ombo, Philae, and Esna which boasts the latest known cartouche of a Roman emperor in any Egyptian temple, that of Decius who reigned 249–51. The Ptolemaic ruler cult, in turn, was replaced by the Roman imperial cult, and sometimes assimilated elements of Egyptian religious practice, as demonstrated by the letter of Claudius to the Alexandrians in 41 AD (Hunt and Edgar 1934: 78–89). However, the decline of Egyptian temple cult and the rapid spread of Christianity inevitably led to the disappearance of both.

For all the positives of the beginning of the Roman Period it is an age of gradual erosion for Pharaonic culture. One highly visible indicator of this process is the history of the use of scripts. A small guild of five hieroglyph cutters is known to have existed in Oxyrhynchus during the second century AD (Frankfurter 1998: 248), and it is highly likely that small groups of such craftsmen would have been found in settlements throughout Egypt at this time, but we cannot extrapolate from this the existence of a large number of scribes or priests capable of producing hieroglyphic drafts or reading texts in that script. This was an accomplishment probably always confined to small groups of highly educated scribes and priests, and even these exiguous numbers must have been sinking fast. However, the closure of pagan temples under the emperor Theodosius (379–95) will have almost completely wiped out the demand for such men. The only shrine exempt from this policy was Philae where the last datable hieroglyphic inscription occurs in AD 394, and that was executed with such incompetence that it can only be deciphered with the aid of a contiguous Demotic text.[15] We may reasonably assume that an increasingly limited capacity to read and write such material lasted well into the fifth century in isolated cases, but the loss of that ability was probably total by the end of the century and with it the loss of access to a vast store of material that expressed the very essence of Egyptian civilization. The history of the Demotic script under the Romans reveals an even more vivid picture of decline. To begin with its position looks secure. In the early Roman Period it is widely current, and the first century yields literary texts of considerable importance (Ryholt 2010), but subsequently its use declines rapidly until it disappears completely a little after AD 450, again at Philae. With this process we see the closing down of the other major means of access to the vast written tradition of Pharaonic culture.

In Egyptian-speaking milieux the decline in the use of ancient scripts was compensated in two ways, a process that, in itself, accelerated the loss of access to traditional Egyptian textual material. In the first place, since Greek was the language of the administration of the country[16] and also of the army, knowledge of this language and its script became common amongst Egyptians, and a significant number of educated Egyptians would have been at home in both, sometimes to the level where they were reading Greek literature as avidly as their own (Fowden 1993: 16; Frankfurter 1998: 250; Ryholt 2010: 710). Such a context helps to explain clear evidence of literary interchange in the early Roman Period whereby we find the penetration of elements of Greek literature into Demotic texts and the appearance of what are essentially Egyptian texts in Greek.[17]

A further substitute for the ancient writing systems was provided by the rise of the Coptic script. As early as the second century AD attempts to write Egyptian texts in the Greek alphabet supplemented by some Demotic signs reflect a desire to facilitate access to this material by using a more tractable

---

[15] The pagan temple cult was finally closed down about 537 under the emperor Justinian.

[16] In the reign of Diocletian Latin replaced Greek as the language of the upper reaches of the administration, but this will have done little to alter the massive prevalence of Greek outside that charmed circle. There is also evidence of what Peter Parsons calls 'a new popularity' of Latin in the fourth century (2007: 173, 209–10).

[17] Excellent examples of the first are the penetration of Greek mythological material in the text of *Setne II* (Simpson (ed.) 2003: 470–89) and the tale of *Egyptians and Amazons* in the Petubastis Cycle (Lichtheim 1980: 151–6) whilst the *Potter's Oracle* (see p. 310) and the Greek version of the Tefnut legend (West 1969) exemplify the second.

script than Demotic, but, at the same time, it betrays a dangerous willingness to turn away from an important aspect of Egyptian culture. At the end of the third century we see that trend boosted considerably with the development of this alphabetic script for the production of Christian literature in the native language. This development, in turn, betrays a growing shift on the part of the Egyptian-speaking population away from Pharaonic religious belief and practice and, therefore, from the most important single expression of Pharaonic culture.

The history of the priesthood, the major repository of Egyptian high culture, inevitably reflects the picture presented by the history of Egyptian scripts. To begin with priests were very numerous—Tebtunis had no fewer than fifty in the second century AD—but they were much less powerful and wealthy than they had been and certainly suffered a decline in status (Frankfurter 1998: 27–30; Monson 2012: 219–27). A particularly remarkable example of the Roman determination to keep them under control occurs in the reign of Augustus who placed them all under the supervision of a civil administrator known as 'the High Priest of Alexandria and all Egypt'. In the fourth century Egyptian priests were still part of the landscape but were visibly declining in numbers, and the persecution of pagans in the later fourth century will have encouraged this process. The decline of the priesthood is accompanied by a decline in the temples themselves whose economic resources the Romans significantly reduced. There was little new construction after *c*.AD 150, and as early as *c*.300 we find the Luxor temple being turned into a military camp. In this case the massive decline of the ancient city of Thebes, vividly described by Strabo (17. 1. 46), will have played a part, but instances of temples being abandoned or being turned into churches are increasingly in evidence from the third century onwards, a process that may well have been encouraged by a slow erosion of local financial support for traditional temples through the diversion of the funds of the elite into liturgies and other civic activities (see p. 308). We still find some Egyptian temples and priests functioning in the fifth century, but this is very much the final phase in the decline of Pharaonic religion (Frankfurter 1998; Alston 2002).

The decline of allegiance to Egyptian culture was strongly encouraged by the simple fact that Greek culture was the culture of the rulers of the land and had been since the end of the fourth century BC. This foreign culture, therefore, came to enjoy enormous prestige amongst Egyptian-speakers. Such a situation is fraught with peril. If people are presented century after century with such a perception, they will eventually accept that the best policy is to adhere to the elite culture, and they will wish to assimilate as much of it as possible, inevitably to the detriment of their own. Not surprisingly, as the *mētropoleis* increasingly acquired the appearance of Roman cities (see p. 308), their culture became ever more assertively Graeco-Roman. Certainly, although they retained elements of the Pharaonic past, above all the temples to the

Egyptian gods and an enthusiastic commitment to Egyptian mortuary religion (Riggs 2005), there can be no doubt that, as far as possible, the native Egyptian inhabitants of such places bought into the elite culture. This phenomenon is even identifiable in smaller settlements where wealth and success tend to manifest themselves in the acquisition of a Greek veneer, and this process would have been greatly helped by the fact that there were certainly numerous people of mixed ethnic origin for whom multiculturalism was a relatively easy option. Indeed, there is evidence that the precedent set by Manetho in the early Ptolemaic Period had its counterparts in Roman times since in the first-century the Egyptian Chaeremon could present himself as a priest of a native cult or a Stoic philosopher, and Apollonides of Memphis falls into a similar category. There is also evidence that in the second century Heraiscus, one of the stalwarts of the Second Sophistic, was buried in the Egyptian manner, which raises the possibility, at least, that he was of Egyptian extraction, and the same may held true of Ammonius (Fowden 1993: 52–7, 167, 183–5). Such figures, like the sixth-century Dioscorus of Aphrodito and Patermouthis of Syene, who were equally at home in Greek or Egyptian culture (MacCoull 1988; Alston 2002: 316–17; Dijkstra 2008), moved effortlessly between the two and must surely have been numerous. The cross-cultural activities of such men will have been the prototypes for such legendary counterparts as Petosiris and Nechepso, and it seems more than likely that it was people of this sort who were ultimately responsible for the heavily Hellenized version of the Isis myth that we encounter in Plutarch and the development of the highly eclectic Hermetic corpus whose influence has survived right down to modern times (Fowden 1993).

The final critical blow to traditional Egyptian culture was the advent of Christianity. The history of its arrival in Egypt is shrouded in legend. There is a tradition, current as early as the fourth century, that the Alexandrian church was founded by St Mark, but there is no evidence of the existence of Christianity in Egypt during the first century AD, and this claim should be treated with extreme caution. We are on firmer ground during the second century when we hear of a school for teaching Christian doctrine c.180 (the Catechetical School of Pantaenus). In the following century we are informed that Egyptian Christians suffered greatly in the persecution of Severus in 202. However, most of this early wave of Christians would have been Greek. The first Patriarch of Alexandria to interest himself in the native Egyptian population was Dionysius (247–64), and from the middle of the century the Christianization of the native Egyptian population speeded up considerably. According to Eusebius the country was largely Christian by the end of the century, despite the ravages of the persecution of Diocletian (see p. 25), and there is no doubt that by the end of the fourth century Christianity was numerically the most important religion in Egypt to the extent that the history of Egypt during that period is essentially the history of clashes between rival theological groupings on matters of Christological doctrine. Indeed, we are informed by Rufinus (*Historia Monachorum* 5) that the city of Oxyrhynchus was full of monks in the 370s, and conversions amongst the poorer members of the population were spectacularly successful—we even have a probable case of a senior ecclesiastic in the late fourth century whose father had been a high priest, i.e. apostasy was far from confined to the lower orders and saw conversions amongst the old traditional temple elite.

It is possible to perceive a number of reasons for the capacity of Christianity to supplant the old Egyptian belief system. Undoubtedly the most important factor for its ultimate success in Egypt, as elsewhere, was its establishment as the religion of the Roman Empire. This development, combined with the ruthless fanaticism with which Egyptian Christians persecuted pagans, made paganism not only problematic but physically highly dangerous. The steadiness of the Christian martyrs during the period of persecution must also have made a deep impression on all who saw it, even if most observers would have been somewhat reluctant to emulate their example. However, we should remember that Christianity was already widespread in Egypt well before it became the established religion of the Empire, and that the success of the new faith was far from dependent on such external factors as Constantine's conversion; for there were a number of dimensions within Christianity itself that made it deeply attractive. The events surrounding Christ's life, firmly rooted as they were in a historical context, provided a powerful inducement to faith, and Christianity offered a conceptual system marked by simplicity, clarity, and certainty as compared with the labyrinthine complexities of so much of Pharaonic religion. There was also a great deal in Christianity with which the Egyptians were already familiar from their own ancient religious system. Isis was easily subsumed by the Virgin Mary; the trinities of Egyptian gods made the Trinity of Christian doctrine an easily acceptable tenet; the concept of Christ as man-god would cause little difficulty to Egyptians with a tradition of the Pharaoh as man-god; Osiris as a dying and resurrected god, the prototype for all the resurrected dead, provided more than a fleeting parallel to the risen Christ; and it should be quite clear from my earlier discussion of *Instruction* Texts that the Ancient Egyptian moral universe had many points of similarity with that of Christianity. Finally, it is impossible to overemphasize the fact that Christianity in Egypt, despite bringing much that was new, proved highly successful in taking over slots that paganism had occupied for millennia, e.g. the old *heka*-masters (see p. 233), whether priests or lay experts, had played a crucial role in bringing help and comfort to Egyptians at all levels in the social hierarchy. This function still needed discharging, and the Church, far from confining itself to raging against the iniquities of such practices, proved quite capable of taking them over so that monks and Christian priests now provided their equivalent to the needy population. The old temple cult may have disappeared, but that did not mean the disappearance of Egyptian cults at lower levels in society, and it should not be ignored that some Pharaonic religious practices have survived in the villages of Egypt right down into modern times (W. Blackman 1927: 280–316; Frankfurter 1998; P. Parsons 2007: 207–10). It should also be recognized that Christianity offered replacements for the role of temples as the repositories and exponents of a conceptual world by substituting them with monasteries and churches, not least through the common practice of simply converting old temples, in part or *in toto*, to function in such roles, and it is no coincidence that the stone-built fifth-century White Monastery at Sohag bears a striking visual resemblance to an Egyptian temple, including a cavetto cornice. The Egyptian perception clearly persisted that, despite a sea-change in religious allegiance, the ancient cult sites retained their status as sacred space powerfully charged with the numinous. We should, therefore, regard the triumph of Christianity not simply as the annihilation of the Pharaonic system but rather as a process marked by a great deal of adjustment to and assimilation of the ancient corpus of belief and practice. In a very real sense we are, at the deepest level, confronted as much with reformulation as with conversion.

I should finally emphasize that the assimilation of the Christian faith was not confined to the assimilation of a new corpus of belief. It also had a radical effect on the visual arts. The Pharaonic artistic tradition had been irredeemably linked to the Pharaonic conceptual system, and the shift to a new conceptualization of the world and man's position within it severed that link almost completely, not least because a replacement was ready to hand. Alongside Christian belief the Egyptians took over the artistic vocabulary of the Christian Eastern Mediterranean, developing their own provincial version of that tradition that is still universally current in Coptic iconography. Certainly some remnants of the Pharaonic survived, such as the use of the *ankh* sign as a substitute for the Christian cross, the depiction of rider saints with the head of Horus, and the transference of the iconography of Isis and her infant son Horus to representations of Mary and the Christ Child, but these are rare survivals in an artistic tradition that is overwhelmingly late classical in character. Sadly, the quality of much of this work is mediocre at best compared with international standards and falls well below the achievements of Pharaonic tradition, which could claim to have produced some of the finest works of art ever created by the hand of man.

APPENDIX
Transliteration of Egyptian Titles

'Acquaintance of the King' (*rḫ nsw*)

'Administrators of the Harîm in the Suite' (*rwdw nw pr-ḫnr ḥr šms*)

'Army Leader' (*ḥꜣwty n mšꜥ r-ḏrw*)

'Captain of Archers of Nubia' (*ḥry pḏt n Kꜣš*)

'Captain of Police' (*ḥry sꜥšꜣt*)

'Chancellor of the God' (*ḫtmty nṯr*)

'Chantress of Amun' (*ḥst ḫnw n ʾImn*)

'Chief of Secrets of the King's House' (*ḥry sštꜣ n pr-nsw*)

'Chief of the Nomes of Upper Egypt' (*ḥry-tp spꜣ(w)t Šmꜥw*)

'Commander of Coptos' (*ṯsw n Gbtiw*)

'Commander-in-Chief of the Army' (*imy-r mšꜥ wr*)

'Commander-in-Chief of the Expeditionary Force of the Oryx Nome' (*imy-r mšꜥ wr
n Mḥt*)

'Controller of Archers' (*ḫrp tmꜣ*)

'Controller of the Two Thrones in the Two Houses' (*ḫrp nsty m prwy*)

'Count' (*ḥꜣt(i)-ꜥ* or *ḥꜣty-ꜥ*)

'Deputy of the Harîm in the Suite' (*idnw n pr ḫnr ḥr šms*)

'District Councillor' (*ḳnbty n w*)

'Door of the Foreign Lands' (*r-ꜥꜣ ḫꜣswt*)

'Executive at the Head of the Two Lands' (*iry-pꜥt ḥry tp tꜣwy*)

'Eyes of the King' (*irty nsw*)

'Fanbearer' (*ṯꜣw ḫw*)

'Favourite of the King' (*imi-ib nsw*)

'First Charioteer of His Majesty (Father)' (*ktn tpy n ḥm.f*)

'First Lieutenant of the Army' (*idnw tpy n pꜣ mšꜥ*)

'Flautist of the House of Mut (*wḏnit pꜣ ꜥ Mwt*)

'General' (*imy-r mšꜥ*)

'General of Herakleopolis' (*imy-r mšꜥ nn-nswt*)

'Governor of Upper Egypt' (*imy-r Šmꜥw*)

'Governors of Estates' (*ḥḳꜣw ḥwt*)

'Head of His Two Banks' (*ḫnt(i) idbwy.f*)

'Head of Upper Egypt' (*ḥꜣt nt tꜣ Šmꜥw*)

'Hereditary Lord' (*iry pꜥt*)

'High Priest of Amun' (*ḥm nṯr tpy n ʾImn*)

'High Priest of Arsaphes' (at Herakleopolis) (*ḥm nṯr tpy n Ḥry-š.f*)

'Keeper of Nekhen' (*mniw Nḫn*)

'Keeper of Pe' (*(i)r(i) P*)

'Lesonis' (*imy-r šn*)

'Marshaller of Troops' (*ṯsw pḏt*)

'Men of the Gate of the Harîm' (*rmṯ pꜣ sbꜣ n pr-ḫnr*)

'Messengers of the Vizier' (*wpwtyw nw ṯꜣty*)

'Noble of the King beloved of him' (*šps n nsw mrr(w).f*)

'Overlord of Nekheb' (*ḥr(i)-tp Nḫb*)

'Overseer of an Expeditionary Force' (*(i)m(i)-r mšꜥ*)

'Overseer of Attendants' (*(i)m(i)-r ḫnt(iw)-š*)

'Overseer of Cattle (of Amun)' (*imy-r mnmnt (n ʾImn)*)

'Overseer of Commissions in Nine Nomes' (*(i)m(i)-r wp(w)t m spꜣ(w)t 9*)

'Overseer of Everything which Heaven produces and Earth creates' (*(i)m(i)-r ḫt nb(t) ddt pt ḳmꜣt tꜣ*)

'Overseer of Fields' (*imy-r ꜣḥ(w)t*)

'Overseer of Horse (of the Lord of the Two Lands)' (*imy-r ssmwt (n nb tꜣwy)*)

'Overseer of the Eastern Foreign Lands' (*imy-r ḫꜣs(w)t iꜣbt(w)t*)

'Overseer of the God's Palace of Upper Egypt' (*(i)m(i)-r ꜥḥ-nṯr Šmꜥw*)

'Overseer of the Nomes of Lower Egypt' (*(i)m(i)-r spꜣ(w)t Tꜣ mḥw*)

'Overseer of the Royal Harîm' (*imy-r ipt-nsw*)

'Overseer of the Treasury' (*imy-r ḫtmwt*)

'Overseer of the Two Houses of Gold' (*(i)m(i)-r prwy nbw*)

'Overseer of the Two Workshops' (*(i)m(i)-r wꜥbt(i)*)

'Overseer of Upper Egypt in the Middle Nomes' (*(i)m(i)-r Šmꜥw m spꜣwt ḥr(yw)t-ib*)

'Overseer of Works' (*(i)m(i)-r kꜣt*)

'Royal Heralds' (*wḥmw nsw*)

'Scribe of the Royal Harîm in the Suite' (*sš ipt-nsw n pr-ḫnr ḥr šms*)

'Secretary of all Commands' (*ḥr(i) sštꜣ n wḏ(t)-mdw nbt*)

'Secretary of the King in all his Places' (*ḥr(i) sštꜣ n nsw m st.f nbt*)

'Settlement-governor' (*ḥḳꜣ ḥwt*)

'Sole Companion' (*smr wꜥt(i)*)

'Son of the God (i.e. the King)' (*sꜣ nṯr*)

'Standard-bearer of the Garrison' (*ṯꜣy-sryt n tꜣ iwꜥyt*)

'Town mayor' (*ḥꜣty-ꜥ niwt*)

'Troop Commander' (*ḥr(y) pḏty(w)*)

Glossary

Akhet The first season of the Egyptian Civil Calendar which was divided into three 4-month seasons, each month having 30 days.

Cataracts The course of the Nile is cut by six main cataracts, i.e. major areas of broken water created by barriers of hard rock running at right angles to the course of the river through which the Nile has had great difficulty in cutting its way. These areas of broken water have created sections of river that are difficult and sometimes impossible to navigate. They have, therefore, consistently served as obstacles to movement up and down the river, though they can be overcome either by cutting canals, by portage around them, or by skilful navigation, though in some cases this is only possible at times of high water.

Cohort The largest and most important subdivision of a Roman **legion**, though the term was also used to denote other categories of unit in the Roman military establishment. The size of a standard legionary cohort could vary considerably according to date and other conditions but would rarely exceed 500.

Coptic As a stage in the Egyptian language this term denotes the last phase of its development when it was written in an alphabet based on the Greek alphabet supplemented by signs taken over from Demotic to denote sounds that Greek did not have. The term is also used to refer to the Monophysite Christian church of Egypt. Its application to the artistic tradition associated with this church is best avoided since that tradition belongs within the broader context of the late antique art of the Eastern Roman Empire and the use of the adjective 'Coptic' to denote the Egyptian version obscures that important fact.

Deben A unit of weight of approximately 91 grams. From the early New Kingdom values were frequently expressed in terms of *deben* of gold, silver, or copper.

Delta The northern part of Egypt that begins at the point where the Nile forks in modern times to run to the sea as the Rosetta and Damietta branches. It is a classic Delta formation created by the deposition of alluvium in an ancient bay of the sea.

Dragoman A term that originally referred to the interpreters and guides widely employed in the Ottoman Empire. It is frequently, though not universally, used in Egyptological literature to translate the word *au* (ꜥw) which occurs in the common title 'overseer of *au*' (*imy-ro au*, *imy-r ꜥw*) borne by expedition leaders who operated outside the frontiers of Egypt.

Dynasty A term used for convenience in Egyptology for dating purposes. The Dynastic system is based on that of the Egyptian priest Manetho who used a framework of thirty dynasties as the basis of his history of Egypt written in Greek in the early Ptolemaic Period. (A thirty-first dynasty was subsequently added by another hand.) Despite its recognized deficiencies this framework is so firmly established that it continues to be used by all practitioners of the subject.

Epagomenal days The Egyptian Civil Calendar consisted of 12 months of 30 days each yielding a year (*renpet, rnpt*) of 360 days. This unit was brought *approximately* into line with the astronomical year by adding five days of holiday at the end of the year. These were known to the Egyptians as 5 *heryu renpet* (*5 ḥryw rnpt*), 'the 5 days on top of the year'. The term 'epagomenal' originates from the Greek translation of this Egyptian designation (*epagomenai hēmerai*).

Faience A glazed non-ceramic material used at all periods of Egyptian history in a wide variety of contexts. It is quite distinct from the glazed ceramic ware associated with Faenza in Italy.

Gymnasion The training grounds in Greek cities originally intended for athletic pursuits, but they quickly developed into centres for discussion and higher education. In the Greek cities of the Graeco-Roman world they often functioned as secondary schools. As such they were bastions of Greek culture, and membership was jealously guarded, being confined to the cities' Hellenized elites.

Heb-sed Lit. 'Festival of the Tail', a title referring to the fact that the king wore a bull's tail during the event. It was a festival designed to rejuvenate the king. Greek texts describe it as 'the Thirty Year Festival', and the 30th Regnal Year was certainly the date for a king's first *Heb-sed* in some cases, but the date of the first celebration varied according to period and circumstance. After celebrating his first *Heb-sed* a Pharaoh was at liberty to celebrate further events at much shorter intervals.

Hēmiolia A light, swift war galley much favoured by pirates but also used in Hellenistic fleets. It gained its name from the fact that it was propelled by one and a half rows of oars per side.

Horus (in relation to kings) Egyptian kings were regarded as incarnations of the god Horus. This was reflected by the fact that the first title in the king's formal title sequence was the Horus title. Therefore, kings could be designated 'the Horus x', 'the Horus y', etc.

Lapis lazuli A high-quality semi-precious stone, usually blue in colour, which was sourced ultimately from Afghanistan through trade links. It was widely used from the Prehistoric Period for and on high-status luxury objects of many different kinds.

Lector-priest Literally 'reader-priest'. The Egyptian term was *khery-heb* (*ḥry-ḥb*), 'scroll carrier'. These priests are distinguished in representations by a cloth band running diagonally across the upper body from the shoulder and usually carry a scroll. They were the most learned group of Egyptian priests, in particular the ritual experts required to ensure that cult activities were properly conducted.

Legion The basic tactical unit of the Roman army, roughly equivalent to a modern division. It consisted of elite heavy infantry, and during the period covered by this book would have been about 5,000 strong, when up to strength, though that ideal situation was rarely achieved.

Lower Egypt Egyptologists, like the Ancient Egyptians, orientate themselves southwards. Therefore, Lower Egypt is the *northern* part of the country, i.e. the Delta.

Manetho *See* **Dynasty**.

Maryannu Charioteer aristocracy who formed the warrior elite of the Hurrian kingdom of Mitanni as well as the elites of Syrian towns during the Late Bronze Age. Captured members of the group were incorporated into the Egyptian army.

Muu, **dance of** A funerary ritual sequence of great antiquity whose role has been much discussed and interpreted in a variety of different ways. Its function seems to have been to welcome the deceased to the Afterlife and to offer guidance on the journey thither.

Na'arin A mixed corps of Asiatic infantry and chariotry in the army of the Nineteenth Dynasty. The name is probably Semitic and originally meant 'youth', but it seems to have lost any association with age in Egyptian contexts.

Nomarch The governor of a **nome**.

Nome From the Greek *nomos*, a standard subdivision of Egypt throughout antiquity. Their number varies, but later canonical texts list 22 in Upper Egypt and 20 in Lower Egypt. During the Pharaonic Period they frequently appear as administrative units, but that is not invariably the case. During the Ptolemaic and Roman Period they are the basis for provincial administration. They always have important religious dimensions.

Nubia The Nile Valley south of the First Cataract.

Pavisade A defensive screen.

Pentērēs Lit. 'a five'. This was the standard line-of-battle ship in Hellenistic navies. Such vessels were ramming war-galleys propelled by two superimposed rows of oars (though sails could be used when not in action). The arrangement of oarsmen consisted of three to each of the lower oars and two to the upper. On this basis a rowing unit or 'room' consisted of five oarsmen, three below and two above, and it was this system that gave the ship its name.

Peret The second 4-month season of the Egyptian Civil Calendar (*see Akhet*).

Phalanx In the Macedonian and Hellenistic armies, a mass of heavy infantry equipped with a pike that could be as much as 7 metres long. It was their role to pin down the enemy infantry so that they could be attacked, as appropriate, by the heavy cavalry which was the main striking arm. This phalanx concept differs radically from that of the Classical city states and must not be confused with it.

Phratry This term is based on the Classical Greek *phratria* (lit. 'brotherhood') which was the subdivision of a tribe immediately below the tribe level. Its precise nature in Greek contexts is much debated, though its ultimate origin must surely lie in a perception of kinship, however much it may have diverged in the course of time. Be that as it may, the term has been taken over into modern anthropology to denote a kinship unit below the tribal level.

Polyreme A warship of the Hellenistic or Roman Period larger than the Classical trireme and propelled by oars manned by two or more oarsmen. The commonest and most useful type was the *pentērēs*.

Prehistory The standard distinction between Prehistory and History is the presence or absence of writing or a comparable information storage system such as the Inca *quipus* (a code based on strings of knotted cords). In the Egyptian context the Prehistoric Period ends with the establishment of the First Dynasty.

Punt Egyptian *Pwenet* (*Pwnt*). This term embraced a wide geographical area including Somaliland, Eritrea, and southern Sudan. It was visited by maritime expeditions throughout Egyptian history in search of exotic products such as frankincense, myrrh, ivory, ebony, animal skins, and live animals.

Regnal years The Egyptians did not use an absolute chronology, i.e. a system where there is one fixed date to which all others are related, like the birth of Christ or the Islamic *Hejira*, but a system of relative chronology whereby dates were expressed in terms of the regnal years of kings. Therefore, the accession year of each king was the beginning of a new count starting with Regnal Year 1, and that count continued until the year of the king's death. The accession of the next king brought with it a new Regnal Year 1.

Satrap From Old Persian *khshathrapāvan*. The governor of a satrapy or province of the Persian Empire.

Second Sophistic The most important cultural phenomenon of the first three centuries of the Roman Empire whose main centres lay in Athens and the Greek east. It took its inspiration from the rhetorical and educational agenda of the Sophistic movement of the Classical Period and its heavy emphasis on display oratory exercised a pervasive influence on literary and philosophical culture. Some of its practitioners were major political figures, and the movement, as a whole, became a significant vehicle for asserting Greek cultural identity.

Sem-priest A category of priest that features prominently in funerary rituals, particularly the all-important ceremony of the Opening of the Mouth. They are easily identified by their panther-skin overgarment.

Serekh A conventionalized representation of an Egyptian palace used as a frame within which the Horus name of a king could be written. The lower part depicted the palace façade, the upper provided the surface for the text. The Horus hawk would be placed on top.

Shaduf A device used for irrigation purposes that appears in the New Kingdom and is still occasionally seen in Egypt. It consists of a vertical support on which a horizontal beam is fitted which can be swivelled vertically or horizontally. One end of the beam is fitted with a counterweight to facilitate movement; the other is fitted with a container suspended on a rope. This container is dipped into a water source, raised, and then swivelled to deposit the water where it is required.

Shomu The third four-month season of the Egyptian Civil Calendar (*see Akhet*).

Slate palettes Very common artefacts in Egyptian Prehistory and the early Dynastic Period. In origin they were palettes used for crushing malachite for cosmetic purposes, but they were developed into elaborate votive offerings covered with detailed representations of historical events and other activities of high symbolic importance, though their practical origin is still reflected by the presence of a depression on one of the surfaces reflecting the palettes' cosmetic ancestry.

Sistrum A rattle designed to create a tinkling sound used in both religious and secular contexts. It consisted of an open metal frame fitted to a handle. The frame was fitted with horizontal wires carrying the metal elements that created the tinkling sound when the device was shaken.

Tax-farming A system of tax collection whereby a tax in coin was auctioned by the state and sold to highest bidder (the farmer/s). In Ptolemaic Egypt the successful tax-farmers would then arrange for the tax to be collected and deposited in state banks. Any surplus over the original bid would count as profit, but the farmers would be required to make good any deficit. For the state this system guaranteed the relevant tax return at minimal inconvenience, but the potential for abuse was enormous and frequently realized.

Testudo Lit. 'tortoise'. This was a tactic used in the Roman army whereby a body of troops protected itself from missile attack by arranging for all troops at the front, rear, and sides of a formation to present their shields vertically and for all troops within to raise their shields horizontally above their heads. This technique created a carapace that offered protection against missiles from all directions.

Theocracy Lit. 'rule by a god'. In Egyptological contexts the term normally refers to rule by the priesthood of Amon-re at Thebes during the later New Kingdom and Late Period who could claim access to the divine will through the god's oracle.

Theogamy Lit. 'divine marriage'. The term refers to the doctrine that the Pharaoh was the physical son of the god Re or Amon-re who visited the queen to engender the new ruler. The doctrine appears in literary texts such as the *Westcar Papyrus* and in iconographic form in the temple of Amenhotep III at Luxor and in Hatshepsut's great temple at Deir el-Bahri.

Titulary The official title sequence of Egyptian kings. In its developed form it consisted of five titles; the Horus title, the Two Ladies Title, the Golden Horus title, the King of Upper and Lower Egypt title (*praenomen*, the throne name), and the Son of Re title (*nomen*, the personal name). These could be copiously supplemented with epithets at some periods.

Tjeker One of the Sea Peoples who had settled during the late second millennium in the northern part of the Plain of Sharon in modern Israel.

Tympanum The semicircular section of a round-topped stele usually filled with iconographic material relevant to the main text.

Upper Egypt The southern part of Egypt stretching from the apex of the Delta to the First Cataract (*see* further **Lower Egypt**).

Uraeus The cobra incarnation of the goddess Wadjet who served as the protective deity of the kings of Lower Egypt. Her Upper Egyptian equivalent was the vulture goddess Nekhbet. Both feature repeatedly in the iconography of Egyptian kingship.

Web-**priest** Literally 'pure priest'. *Webs* were a common category of priest whose major role was to maintain the maximum level of ritual purity so that they could function in temple ritual without any danger of contaminating sacred objects or places. They were very numerous in large temples.

References

ADAMS, B. 1996. 'Elite Graves at Hierakonpolis', in J. Spencer (ed.), *Aspects of Early Egypt*. London: British Museum, 1–15.

ADAMS, B. and CIAŁOWICZ, K. 1997. *Protodynastic Egypt*, Shire Egyptology 25. Princes Risborough: Shire.

ADAMS, W. 1997. *Nubia: Corridor to Africa*. London: Allen Lane.

AL-AYEDI, A. R. 2006. *Index of Egyptian Administrative, Religious and Military Titles of the New Kingdom*. Ismailia: Obelisk.

ALDRED, C. 1980. *Egyptian Art in the Days of the Pharaohs: 3100–320 BC*, World of Art Library. London: Thames & Hudson.

ALLEN, J. P. 2002. *The Hekanakhte Papyri*, Publications of the Metropolitan Museum of Art Egyptian Expedition 27. New York: Metropolitan Museum of Art.

ALLEN, J. P. 2005. *The Ancient Egyptian Pyramid Texts*, Society of Biblical Literature 23. Atlanta: Society of Biblical Literature.

ALLEN, J. P. 2008. 'The Historical Inscription of Khnumhotep at Dahshur: Preliminary Report', *Bulletin of the American School of Oriental Research* 352 (November 2008), 29–39.

ALSTON, R. 1995. *Soldier and Society in Roman Egypt: A Social History*. London: Routledge

ALSTON, R. 2002. *The City in Roman and Byzantine Egypt*. London: Routledge.

ALTENMÜLLER, H. 1975. 'Feste', in W. Helck and E. Otto (eds), *Lexikon der Ägyptologie*. Wiesbaden: Harrassowitz, i. 171–91.

Ancient Egypt 2013. Editors, '(More) News from the Amarna Project Team', *Ancient Egypt* 14(1): 6.

ANDREWS, C. A. R. 1998. *Egyptian Mummies*. London: British Museum.

ARNOLD, D. 1999. *Temples of the Last Pharaohs*. New York: Oxford University Press.

ARNOLD, DOROTHEA 1996. *The Royal Women of Amarna*. New York: Metropolitan Museum of Art.

ASHTON, S.-A. 2001. *Ptolemaic Royal Sculpture from Egypt: The Interconnection between Greek and Egyptian Traditions*, BAR International Series 923. Oxford: Archaeopress.

ASHTON, S.-A. 2003. *The Last Queens of Egypt*. Harlow: Pearson Education.

ASTON, B. G., HARRELL, J. A., and SHAW, I. 2000. 'Stone', in Nicholson and Shaw (eds) 2000: 5–77.

AUSTIN, M. M. 2006. *The Hellenistic World from Alexander to the Roman Conquest: A Selection of Ancient Sources in Translation*. Cambridge: Cambridge University Press.

BABA, M. 2011. 'Pottery Production at Hierakonpolis in the Naqada II Period: Towards a Reconstruction of the Firing Technique', in Friedman and Fiske (eds) 2011: 647–70.

BÁCS, T., and PARKINSON, R. 2011. 'Wall-paintings from the Tomb of Kynebu at Luxor', *Egyptian Archaeology* 39: 41–3.

BAGNALL, R. S. 1993. *Egypt in Late Antiquity*. Princeton: Princeton University Press.

BAGNALL, R. S. 2006. *Hellenistic and Roman Egypt: Sources and Approaches*, Variorum Collected Studies. Aldershot: Ashgate.

BAGNALL, R. S. (ed.) 2007. *Egypt in the Byzantine World, 300–700*. Cambridge: Cambridge University Press.

BAGNALL, R. S. and RATHBONE, D. W. (eds) 2004. *Egypt from Alexander to the Early Christians: An Archaeological and Historical Guide*. Los Angeles: Getty and British Museum.

BAHUCHET, S. 1999. 'Aka Pygmies', in Lee and Daly (eds) 1999: 190–4.

BAINES, J. 1974. 'The Inundation Stela of Sebekhotpe VIII', *Acta Orientalia* 36: 39–54.

BAINES, J. 1982. 'Interpreting *Sinuhe*', *JEA* 68: 31–44.

BAINES, J. 1997. 'Temples as Symbols, Guarantors, and Participants in Egyptian Civilisation', in S. Quirke (ed.), *The Temple in Ancient Egypt. New Discoveries and Recent Research*. London: British Museum, 216–41.

BAINES, J. 1999. 'On *Wenamun* as a Literary Text', in J. Assmann and E. Blumenthal (eds), *Literatur und Politik im pharaonischen und ptolemäischen Ägypten: Vorträge der Tagung zum Gedenken an Georges Posener, 5.–10. September 1996 in Leipzig*. Cairo: l'Institut français d'archéologie orientale, 209–33.

BARD, K. A. and SHUBERT, S. B. (eds) 1999. *Encyclopedia of the Archaeology of Ancient Egypt*, London: Routledge.

BARGUET, P. 1962. *Le Temple d'Amon-Rê à Karnak: Essai d'exégèse*, Recherches d'archéologie, de philologie et d'histoire 21. Cairo: l'Institut français d'archéologie orientale du Caire.

BARNARD, A. J. (ed.) 2004. *Hunter-Gatherers in History, Archaeology and Anthropology*. Oxford: Berg.

BATES, O. 1917. *Ancient Egyptian Fishing*, Harvard African Studies 1. Cambridge, Mass.: Harvard University Press.

BAUD, M. 1999. *Famille royale et pouvoir sous l'Ancien Empire égyptien*, BdE 126. Cairo: l'Institut français d'archéologie orientale.

BAUD, M. 2010. 'The Old Kingdom', in Lloyd (ed.) 2010c: 63–80.

BECKERATH, VON J. 1999. *Handbuch der ägyptischen Königsnamen*. Münchener Ägyptologische Studien 49. Mainz: Philipp von Zabern.

BECKMAN, G. 1999. *Hittite Diplomatic Texts*, SBL Writings from the Ancient World 7. 2nd edn. Atlanta: Scholars Press.

BELL, L. 1985. 'Luxor Temple and the Cult of the Royal Ka', *JNES* 44: 251–94.

BELL, L. 1997. 'The New Kingdom "Divine" Temple', in B. E. Shafer (ed.), *Temples of Ancient Egypt*. London: I. B. Tauris, 127–84.

BENDER, B. 1975. *Farming in Prehistory: From Hunter-gatherer to Food-producer*. London: John Baker.

BIERBRIER, M. L. 1980. 'Terms of Relationship at Deir el-Medîna', *JEA* 66: 100–7.

BIERBRIER, M. L. 1982. *The Tomb-Builders of the Pharaohs*. London: British Museum.

BIETAK, M. 2005. 'Neue Paläste aus der 18. Dynastie', in P. Jánosi (ed.), *Structure and Significance: Thoughts on Ancient Egyptian Architecture*. Vienna: Österreichische Akademie der Wissenschaften, 131–68.

BINGEN, J. 2007. *Hellenistic Egypt: Monarchy, Society, Economy, Culture*, ed. R. S. Bagnall. Edinburgh: Edinburgh University Press.

BLACKMAN, A. M. 1915. *The Rock Tombs of Meir*, pt. II, Archaeological Survey of Egypt 23. London: Egypt Exploration Fund.

BLACKMAN, A. M. 1918*a*. 'Priest, Priesthood (Egyptian)', in Lloyd (ed.) 1998: 117–44.

BLACKMAN, A. M. 1918*b*. 'The House of the Morning', in Lloyd (ed.) 1998: 197–214.

BLACKMAN, A. M. 1919. 'The Sequence of the Episodes in the Egyptian Daily Temple Liturgy', in Lloyd (ed.) 1998: 215–37.

BLACKMAN, A. M. 1921. 'Worship (Egyptian)', in Lloyd (ed.) 1998: 168–82.

BLACKMAN, A. M. 1988. *The Story of King Kheops and the Magicians: Transcribed from Papyrus Westcar (Berlin Papyrus 3033)*. Edited for publication W. V. Davies. Reading: J. V. Books.

BLACKMAN, A. M. and FAIRMAN, H. W. 1946. 'The Consecretion of an Egyptian Temple According to the Use of Edfu', *JEA* 32: 75–91.

BLACKMAN, W. S. 1927. *The Fellāḥīn of Upper Egypt: their Religious, Social, and Industrial Life To-day with Special Reference to Survivals from Ancient Times*. London: Harrap.

BOHANNAN, P. 1969. *Social Anthropology*, London: Holt, Rinehart, & Winston.

BONNET, CH., and VALBELLE, D. 2005. *Des Pharaons venus d'Afrique*. Paris: Citadelles & Mazenod.

BONNET, H. 1952. *Reallexikon der ägyptischen Religionsgeschichte*. Berlin: De Gruyter.

BORGHOUTS, J. F. 1994. 'Magical Practices among the Villagers', in L. H. Lesko (ed.), *Pharaoh's Workers: The Villagers of Deir el Medina*. Ithaca, NY: Cornell University Press, 119–30.

BOURRIAU, J. 2000. 'The Second Intermediate Period (c.1650–1550 BC)', in Shaw (ed.) 2000: 184–217.

BOWMAN, A. K. 1990. *Egypt after the Pharaohs: 332 BC–AD 642: From Alexander to the Arab Conquest*. Oxford: Oxford University Press.

BOWMAN, A. K. 2000. 'Urbanisation in Roman Egypt', in E. Fentress (ed.), *Romanization and the City: Creation, Transformations, and Failures (Proceedings of a Conference held at the American Academy in Rome to celebrate the 50th Anniversary of the Excavations at Cosa, 14–16 May, 1998)*, Journal of Roman Archaeology Supplementary Series 3. Portsmouth, RI, 173–87.

BOWMAN, A. K. and RATHBONE, D. W. 1992. 'Cities and Administration in Roman Egypt', *Journal of Roman Studies* 82: 107–27.

BREASTED, J. H. 1906–7. *Ancient Records of Egypt: Historical Documents from the Earliest Times to the Persian Conquest*. Chicago: University of Chicago Press.

BREASTED, J. H. 1909. *A History of Egypt from the Earliest Times to the Persian Conquest*. 2nd edn. London: Hodder & Stoughton.

BRESCIANI, E. 1958. 'La satrapia d'Egitto', *Studi Classici e Orientali* 7: 132–88.

BREWER, D. J., and FRIEDMAN, R. F. 1989. *Fish and Fishing in Ancient Egypt*, Natural History of Egypt 2. Warminster: Aris & Phillips.

BROSIUS, M. 2007. 'New out of Old? Court and Court Ceremonies in Achaemenid Persia', in Spawforth (ed.) 2007: 17–57.

BROWMAN, D. L., FRITZ, G. J., and WATSON, P. J. 2005. 'Origins of Food-producing Economies in the Americas', in Scarre (ed.) 2005: 306–49.

BRYAN, B. M. 2000. 'The 18th Dynasty before the Amarna Period (c.1550–1352)', in Shaw (ed.) 2000: 218–71.

Busia, K. A. 1954. 'The Ashanti of the Gold Coast', in D Forde (ed.), *African Worlds: Studies in the Cosmological Ideas and Social Values of African Peoples*. London: Oxford University Press, 190–209.

Butzer, K. W. 1976. *Early Hydraulic Civilization in Egypt: A Study in Cultural Ecology*. Chicago: University of Chicago Press.

Caminos, R. A. 1954. *Late Egyptian Miscellanies*, Brown Egyptological Studies I. London: Oxford University Press.

Campagno, M. 2004. 'In the Beginning was the War: Conflict and the Emergence of the Egyptian State', in Hendrickx et al. (eds) 2004: 689–703.

Campagno, M. 2011. 'Kinship, Concentration of Population and the Emergence of the State in the Nile Valley', in Friedman and Fiske (eds) 2011: 1229–42.

Capponi, L. 2010. 'The Roman Period', in Lloyd (ed.) 2010c: 180–98.

Carney, E. D. 1987. 'The Reappearance of Royal Sibling Marriage in Ptolemaic Egypt', *Parola del Passato* 237: 420–39.

Carter, H. 1917. 'A Tomb Prepared for Queen Hatshepsuit and Other Recent Discoveries at Thebes', *JEA* 4: 107–18.

Castillos, J. J. 2011. 'The Development and Nature of Inequality in Early Egypt', in Friedman and Fiske (eds) 2011: 1243–53.

Chaniotis, A. 2005. *War in the Hellenistic World: A Social and Cultural History*, Ancient World at War. Malden, Mass.: Blackwell.

Childe, V. G. 1951. *Social Evolution*. London: Watts.

Childe, V. G. 1954. *What Happened in History*. Harmondsworth: Penguin.

Ciałowicz, K. M. 2011. 'The Early Dynastic Administrative-Cultic Centre at Tell el-Farkha', in Friedman and Fiske (eds) 2011: 763–800.

Clarke, S. 1916. 'Ancient Egyptian Frontier Fortresses', *JEA* 3: 155–79.

Clarke, S., and Engelbach, R. 1930. *Ancient Egyptian Masonry*. Oxford: Oxford University Press. Repub. 1990 as *Ancient Egyptian Construction and Architecture*. New York: Dover.

Clarysse, W., and Thompson, D. J. 2006. *Counting the People in Hellenistic Egypt*, Cambridge Classical Studies. 2 vols. Cambridge: Cambridge University Press.

Cline, E. H., and O'Connor, D. (eds) 2006. *Thutmose III: A New Biography*. Ann Arbor: University of Michigan Press.

Cline, E. H., and O'Connor, D. (eds) 2010. *Ramesses III: The Life and Times of Egypt's Last Hero*. Ann Arbor: University of Michigan Press.

Cohen, R., and Westbrook, R. (eds) 2000. *Amarna Diplomacy: The Beginnings of International Relations*. Baltimore: The Johns Hopkins University Press.

Confucius 1967. *Li Chi: Book of Rites: an Encyclopedia of Ancient Ceremonial Usages, Religious Creeds and Social Institutions*, trans. J. Legge, ed. Ch'u Chai and Winberg Chai from 1885 version. New Hyde Park, NY: University Books; London: H. A. Humphrey.

Connah, G. 2005. 'Holocene Africa', in Scarre (ed.) 2005: 350–91.

Coppens, F. 2009. 'Temple Festivals of the Ptolemaic and Roman Periods', in J. Dieleman and W. Wendrich (eds), *UCLA Encyclopedia of Egyptology*. Los Angeles: University of California (<http://escholarship.org/uc/item/4cd7q9mn>, accessed August 2013).

COUYAT, J., and MONTET, P. 1912. *Les Inscriptions hiéroglyphiques et hiératiques du Ouâdi Hammâmât*. Mémoires publiés par les membres de l'Institut français d'archéologie orientale du Caire 34. Cairo: l'Institut français d'archéologie orientale.

CRAWFORD, H. 1991. *Sumer and the Sumerians*. Cambridge: Cambridge University Press.

CRONE, P. 1986. 'The Tribe and the State', in J. A. Hall (ed.), *States in History*. Oxford: Blackwell, 48–77.

DARNELL, J. C. 2003. 'The Rock Inscriptions of Tjehemau at Abisko', *ZÄS* 130: 31–48.

DARNELL, J. C. 2004. 'The Route of Eleventh Dynasty Expansion into Nubia', *ZÄS* 131: 23–37.

DARNELL, J. C. and MANASSA, C. 2007. *Tutankhamun's Armies: Battle and Conquest during Ancient Egypt's Late Eighteenth Dynasty*. Hoboken, NJ: John Wiley & Sons.

DAVIES, N. DE GARIS 1903–8. *The Rock Tombs of El Amarna*, Archaeological Survey of Egypt, Memoirs 13–18. 6 vols. London: Egypt Exploration Fund.

DAVIES, W. V. 2003. 'Sobeknakht of Elkab and the Coming of Kush', *Egyptian Archaeology* 23: 3–6.

DAVIES, W. V. and FRIEDMAN, R. F. 1998. *Egypt*. London: British Museum.

DE BUCK, A. 1937. 'The Judicial Papyrus of Turin', *JEA* 23: 152–64.

DE BUCK, A. 1970. *Egyptian Readingbook: Exercises and Middle Egyptian Texts*. Leiden: Nederlands Instituut voor het Nabije Oosten.

DECKER, W. 1992. *Sports and Games of Ancient Egypt*. New Haven, Conn.: Yale University Press.

DER MANUELIAN, P. 1994. *Living in the Past: Studies in Archaism of the Egyptian Twenty-sixth Dynasty*, Studies in Egyptology. London: Kegan Paul.

DER MANUELIAN, P. 2006. 'The End of the Reign and the Accession of Amenhotep II', in Cline and O'Connor (eds) 2006: 413–29.

DESROCHES NOBLECOURT, CH. 2002. *La Reine mystérieuse: Hatshepsout*. Paris: Éditions Pygmalion/Gérard Watelet à Paris.

DIJKSTRA, J. H. F. 2008. *Philae and the End of Ancient Egyptian Religion: A Regional Study of Religious Transformation (298–642 CE)*, OLA 173. Leuven: Peeters.

DODSON, A. 2008. *The Tomb in Ancient Egypt*. London: Thames & Hudson.

DODSON, A. 2010a. *Poisoned Legacy: The Fall of the Nineteenth Egyptian Dynasty*. Cairo: American University.

DODSON, A. 2010b. 'Mortuary Architecture and Decorative Systems', in Lloyd (ed.) 2010c: 804–25.

DODSON, A. 2012. *Afterglow of Empire: Egypt from the end of the New Kingdom to the Saite Renaissance*. Cairo: American University.

DODSON, A., and HILTON, D. 2004. *The Complete Royal Families of Ancient Egypt*. London: Thames & Hudson.

DORMAN, P. F. 1988. *The Monuments of Senenmut: Problems in Historical Methodology*. London: Kegan Paul.

DORMAN, P. F. 1991. *The Tombs of Senenmut: The Architecture and Decoration of Tombs 71 and 353*. New York: Metropolitan Museum of Art.

DREYER, G. 1998. *Umm el-Qaab I: das Prädynastische Königsgrab U-j und seine frühen Schriftzeugnisse*. Mainz am Rhein: Philipp von Zabern.

DURKHEIM, E. 1912 (1995). *The Elementary Forms of Religious Life*, trans. K. E. Fields. New York: The Free Press.

EMERY, W. B. 1965. *Egypt in Nubia*. London: Hutchinson.

EMERY, W. B., SMITH, H. S., and MILLARD, A. 1979. *The Fortress of Buhen: The Archaeological Report*, Excavation Memoir 49 (= *Excavations at Buhen*, i). With contributions by D. M. Dixon, J. Glutton-Brock, R. Burleigh, and R. M. F. Preston. London: Egypt Exploration Society.

Epigraphic Survey. 1930. *Medinet Habu*, i. *Earlier Historical Records of Ramses III*. Oriental Institute Publications 8. Chicago: University of Chicago Press.

Epigraphic Survey. 1994. *Reliefs and Inscriptions at Luxor Temple*, i. *The Festival Procession of Opet in the Colonnade Hall: with Translations of Texts, Commentary, and Glossary*, Oriental Institute Publications 112. Chicago: Oriental Institute of the University of Chicago.

ERMAN, A., and GRAPOW, H. 1926–71. *Wörterbuch der aegyptischen Sprache*. Berlin: Akademie Verlag.

EYRE, C. J. 1994. 'The Water Regime for Orchards and Plantations in Pharaonic Egypt', *JEA* 80: 57–80.

EYRE, C. J. 1997. 'Peasants and "Modern" Leasing Strategies in Ancient Egypt', *JESHO* 40(4): 367–90.

EYRE, C. J. 1999. 'The Village Economy in Pharaonic Egypt', in A. K. Bowman and E. L. Rogan (eds), *Agriculture in Egypt from Pharaonic to Modern Times*, Proceedings of the British Academy 96. Oxford: Oxford University Press, 33–60.

EYRE, C. J. 2002. *The Cannibal Hymn: A Cultural and Literary Study*. Liverpool: Liverpool University Press.

EYRE, C. J. 2010. 'The Economy: Pharaonic', in Lloyd (ed.) 2010c: 291–308.

FABRE, D. 2004. *Seafaring in Ancient Egypt*. London: Periplus.

FAIRMAN, H. W. 1954. 'Worship and Festivals in an Egyptian Temple', *Bulletin of the John Rylands Library* 37(1): 165–203.

FAULKNER, R. O. 1937. 'The Bremner-Rhind Papyrus—III', *JEA* 23: 166–85.

FAULKNER, R. O. 1941. 'Egyptian Military Standards', *JEA* 27: 12–18.

FAULKNER, R. O. 1946. 'The Euphrates Campaign of Tuthmosis III', *JEA* 32: 39–42.

FAULKNER, R. O. 1953. 'Egyptian Military Organization', *JEA* 39: 32–47.

FAULKNER, R. O. 1985. *The Ancient Egyptian Book of the Dead*, ed. C. Andrews. London: British Museum.

FAULKNER, R. O. 1994. *The Egyptian Book of the Dead: The Book of Going Forth by Day*. San Francisco: Chronicle Books.

FELBER, H. 2002. 'Die demotische Chronik', in A. Blasius and B. Schipper (eds), *Apokalyptik und Ägypten: Eine kritische Analyse der Relevanten Texte aus dem griechisch-römischen Ägypten*, OLA 107. Leiden: Peeters, 65–111.

FIGUEIREDO, A. 2004. 'Locality HK6 at Hierakonpolis: Results of the 2000 Field Season', in Hendrickx et al. (eds) 2004: 1–23.

FINNESTAD, R. B. 1997. 'Temples of the Ptolemaic and Roman Periods: Ancient Traditions in New Contexts', in B. E. Shafer (ed.), *Temples of Ancient Egypt*, London: I. B. Tauris, 185–237.

FISCHER, H. G. 1997. *Egyptian Titles of the Middle Kingdom: A Supplement to Wm. Ward's Index*. 2nd edn, rev. and augmented. New York: Metropolitan Museum of Art.

FISCHER-BOVET, C. 2011. *Army and Society in Ptolemaic Egypt*. Rochester, Mich.: UMI Dissertation Publishing.

FISHER, M. M. 2001. *The Sons of Ramesses II*, Ägypten and Altes Testament 53. 2 vols. Wiesbaden: Harrassowitz.

FOWDEN, G. 1993. *The Egyptian Hermes: A Historical Approach to the Late Pagan Mind*. Princeton: Princeton University Press.

FOWLER, C. S., and TURNER, N. J. 1999. 'Ecological/Cosmological Knowledge and Land Management among Hunter-gatherers', in Lee and Daly (eds) 1999: 419–25.

FRACHETTI, M. D. 2008. *Pastoralist Landscapes and Social Interaction in Bronze Age Eurasia*. Berkeley and Los Angeles: University of California Press.

FRANKE, D. 1983. *Altägyptische Verwandschaftsbezeichnungen im Mittleren Reich*, Hamburger Ägyptologische Studien 3. Hamburg: Borg.

FRANKE, D. 1991. 'The Career of Khnumhotep III of Beni Hasan and the So-called "Decline of the Nomarchs"', in S. Quirke (ed.), *Middle Kingdom Studies*. New Malden: SIA, 51–67.

FRANKFORT, H. 1948. *Kingship and the Gods: A Study of Ancient Near Eastern Religion as the Integration of Society and Nature*. Chicago: University of Chicago Press. Repub. in Phoenix edn. 1978.

FRANKFURTER, D. 1998. *Religion in Roman Egypt: Assimilation and Resistance*. Princeton: Princeton University Press.

FRASER, P. M. 1972. *Ptolemaic Alexandria*. 3 vols. Oxford: Clarendon.

FRIEDMAN, F. 1994. 'Aspects of Domestic Life and Religion', in L. Lesko (ed.), *Pharaoh's Workers: The Villagers of Deir el Medina*, Ithaca: Cornell University Press, 95–117.

FRIEDMAN, R. F. 1996. 'The Ceremonial Centre at Hierakonpolis. Locality HK29A', in A. J. Spencer (ed.), *Aspects of Early Egypt*. London: British Museum, 16–35.

FRIEDMAN, R. F. 2000. 'Ceramic Nails', *Nekhen News* 12: 13.

FRIEDMAN, R. F. 2011. 'Hierakonpolis', in Teeter (ed.) 2011: 33–44.

FRIEDMAN, R. F., and FISKE, P. N. (eds) 2011. *Egypt at its Origins 3: Proceedings of the Third International Conference 'Origin of the State: Predynastic and Early Dynastic Egypt', London, 27th July–1st August 2008*, Orientalia Lovaniensia Analecta 205. Leuven: Peeters.

FRIEDMAN, R. F., and RAUE, D. 2007. 'New Observations on the Fort at Hierakonpolis', in Z. A. Hawass and J. E. Richards (eds), *The Archaeology and Art of Ancient Egypt: Essays in Honor of David B. O'Connor*. Cairo: Conseil Suprême des Antiquités de l'Egypte, i. 309–36.

FRIEDMAN, R. F., VAN NEER, W., and LINSEELE, V. 2011. 'The Elite Predynastic Cemetery at Hierakonpolis: 2009–2010 Update', in Friedman and Fiske (eds) 2011: 157–91.

FROOD, E. 2007. *Biographical Texts from Ramessid Egypt*, Writings from the Ancient World 26. Leiden: Brill.

FROOD, E. 2010. 'Social Structure and Daily Life: Pharaonic', in Lloyd (ed.) 2010c: 469–90.

GALÁN, J. M. 1994. 'Bullfight Scenes in Ancient Egyptian Tombs', *JEA* 80: 81–96.

GARDINER, A. H. 1905. *The Inscription of Mes: A Contribution to the Study of Egyptian Legal Procedure*, Untersuchungen zur Geschichte und Altertumskunde Aegyptens IV.3. Leipzig: J. C. Hinrichs.

GARDINER, A. H. 1916. 'An Ancient List of the Fortresses of Nubia', *JEA* 3: 184–92.

GARDINER, A. H. 1932. *Late-Egyptian Stories*, Bibliotheca Aegyptiaca 1. Brussels: Fondation Égyptologique Reine Élisabeth.

GARDINER, A. H. 1941–8. *The Wilbour Papyrus*. 3 vols. Oxford: Oxford University Press.

GARDINER, A. H. 1947. *Ancient Egyptian Onomastica*. 3 vols. Oxford: Oxford University Press.

GARDINER, A. H. 1953. 'The Coronation of King Haremheb', *JEA* 39: 13–31.

GARDINER, A. H. 1957. *Egyptian Grammar, being an Introduction to the Study of Hieroglyphs*. 3rd edn. rev. London: Oxford University Press.

GARDINER, A. H. 1960. *The Kadesh Inscriptions of Ramesses II*. Oxford: Griffith Institute.

GESTERMANN, L. 1987. *Kontinuität und Wandel in Politik und Verwaltung des frühen Mittleren Reiches in Ägypten*, Göttinger Orientforschungen 4, series Ägypten 18. Wiesbaden: Harrassowitz.

GINAT, J. 1997. *Blood Revenge: Family Honor, Mediation and Outcasting*. Brighton: Sussex Academic Press.

GLANTZ, D. M., and ORENSTEIN, H. S. 1995. *The Evolution of Soviet Operational Art 1927–1991*. 2 vols. London: Frank Cass.

GÖDECKEN, K. B. 1976. *Eine Betrachtung der Inschriften des Meten im Rahmen der sozialen und rechtlichen Stellung von Privatleuten im ägyptischen alten Reich*, Ägyptologische Abhandlungen 29. Wiesbaden: Harrassowitz.

GOEDICKE, H. 1963. 'Was Magic Used in the Harem Conspiracy against Ramesses III?', *JEA* 49: 71–92.

GOELET, O. 1994. 'A Commentary on the Corpus of Literature and Tradition which Constitutes *The Book of Going Forth by Day*', in R. O. Faulkner, *The Egyptian Book of the Dead: The Book of Going Forth by Day*. San Francisco: Chronicle, 137–71.

GOHARY, J. 1992. *Akhenaten's Sed-festival at Karnak*, Studies in Egyptology. London: Kegan Paul.

GOMBRICH, E. H. 1995. *The Story of Art*. London: Phaidon.

GOYON, G. 1957. *Nouvelles inscriptions rupestres du Wadi Hammamat*. Paris: Imprimerie Nationale, Librarie d'Amérique et d'Orient Adrien-Maisonneuve.

GRAINGER, J. D. 2011. *Hellenistic & Roman Naval Wars 336–31 BC*. Barnsley: Penn and Sword Maritime.

GRAJETSKI, W. 2003. *Burial Customs in Ancient Egypt: Life in Death for Rich and Poor*, Duckworth Egyptology. London: Duckworth.

GRAJETSKI, W. 2006. *The Middle Kingdom of Ancient Egypt: History, Archaeology and Society*, Duckworth Egyptology. London: Duckworth.

GRAJETSKI, W. 2009. *Court Officials of the Egyptian Middle Kingdom*, Duckworth Egyptology. London: Duckworth.

GRANDET, P. 1993. *Ramsès III: Histoire d'un règne*. Paris: Pygmalion/G. Watelet.

GRANDET, P. 1994. *Le Papyrus Harris I (BM 9999)*, BdE 109/1–2. 2 vols. Cairo: l'Institut français d'archéologie orientale.

GRIMAL, N.-C. 1981. *La Stèle triomphale de Pi('ankh)y au Musée du Caire: JE 48862 et 47086–47089*, Études sur la propagande royale égyptienne, 1 = Mémoires publiées par les membres de l'Institut français d'archéologie orientale du Caire 105. Cairo: l'Institut français d'archéologie orientale.

GROENEWEGEN-FRANKFORT, H. A. 1951. *Arrest and Movement: An Essay on Space and Time in the Representational Art of the Ancient Near East*. London: Faber & Faber.

GUÉRAUD, O. 1931–2. *ΕΝΤΕΥΞΕΙΣ: requêtes et plaintes adressées au roi d'Egypte au IIIe siècle avant J.C.*, Publications de la Société royale égyptienne de papyrologie: Textes et documents. Cairo: l'Institut français d'archéologie orientale.

HABACHI, L. 1957. 'Two Graffiti at Sehēl from the Reign of Queen Hatshepsut', *JNES* 16: 88–104.

HABACHI, L. 1984. *The Obelisks of Egypt: Skyscrapers of the Past*. Cairo: The American University in Cairo Press.

HAENY, G. 1997. 'New Kingdom "Mortuary Temples" and "Mansions of Millions of Years"', in B. E. Shafer (ed.), *Temples of Ancient Egypt*. London: Tauris.

HAGEN, F. 2007. 'Local Identities', in T. A. H. Wilkinson (ed.), *The Egyptian World*, Routledge Worlds. London: Routledge, 242–51.

HAMMOND, N. G. L. 1989. *The Macedonian State: The Origins, Institutions and History*. Oxford: Clarendon.

HARRINGTON, N. 2004. 'Human Representation in the Predynastic Period: The Locality HK6 Statue in Context', in Hendrickx et al. (eds) 2004: 25–43.

HARTMANN, F. 1923. Hartmann, *L'Agriculture dans l'ancienne Egypte*. Paris: Librairies-Imprimeries Réunies.

HARTUNG, U. 2004. 'Rescue Excavations in the Predynastic Settlement of Maadi', in Hendrickx et al. 2004: 337–56.

HAWASS, Z., and VERNER, M. 1996. 'Newly Discovered Blocks from the Causeway of Sahure (Archaeological Report)', *Mitteilungen des Deutschen Archäologischen Instituts, Abteilung Kairo* 52: 177–86.

HAWASS, Z., and VERNER, M. et al. 2010. 'Ancestry and Pathology in King Tutankhamun's Family', *Journal of the American Medical Association* 303(7): 638–47.

HELCK, W. 1958. *Zur Verwaltung des Mittleren und Neuen Reichs*, PdÄ 3. Leiden: E. J. Brill.

HELCK, W. 1974. *Die altägyptischen Gaue*, Beihefte zum Tübinger Atlas des Vorderen Orients, series B (Geisteswissenschaften) 5. Wiesbaden: Dr Ludwig Reichert.

HENDRICKX, S. 1994. *Elkab V: The Naqada III Cemetery*. Brussels: Musées royaux d'art et d'histoire, Comité des fouilles belges en Egypte.

HENDRICKX, S., and FÖRSTER, F. 2010. 'Early Dynastic Art and Iconography', in Lloyd (ed.) 2010*c*: 826–52.

HENDRICKX, S., FRIEDMAN, R., and EYCKERMAN, M. 2011. 'Early Falcons' in L. Morenz and R. Kuhn (eds), *Vorspann oder formative Phase?: Ägypten und der Vordere Orient 3500–2700 v. Chr.*, Philippika, Marburger altertumskundliche Abhandlungen 48. Wiesbaden: Harrassowitz, 129–62.

HENDRICKX, S., FRIEDMAN, R., and EYCKERMAN, M. et al. (eds) 2004. *Egypt at its Origins: Studies in Memory of Barbara Adams. Proceedings of the International Conference 'Origins of the State. Predynastic and Early Dynastic Egypt', Kraków, 28th August–1st September 2002*, OLA 138. Leuven: Peeters.

HERMAN, G. 1997. 'The Court Society of the Hellenistic Age', in P. Cartledge, P. Garnsey, and E. Gruen (eds), *Hellenistic Constructs: Essays in Culture, History, and Historiography*. Berkeley and Los Angeles: University of California Press, 199–224.

HIKADE, T. 2004. 'Urban Development at Hierakonpolis and the Stone Industry of Square 10N5W', in Hendrickx et al. (eds) 2004: 181–97.

HIKADE, T. 2008. T. 'Origins of Monumental Architecture: Recent Excavations at Hierakonpolis HK29B and HK25', in Friedman and Fiske (eds) 2011: 81–107.

HOFFMAN, M. A. 1991. *Egypt before the Pharaohs. The Prehistoric Foundations of Egyptian Civilization*, rev. and updated. Austin: University of Texas Press.

HÖLBL 2001. *A History of the Ptolemaic Empire*, trans. Tina Saavedra. London: Routledge.

HOLMES, D. L. 1989. *The Predynastic Lithic Industries of Upper Egypt: A Comparative Study of the Lithic Traditions of Badari, Naqada and Hierakonpolis*, Cambridge Monographs in African Archaeology 33, BAR International Series 469. 2 vols. Oxford: BAR.

HOLMES, R. 1985. *Firing Line*. London: J. Cape.

HORNUNG, E. 1999. *The Ancient Egyptian Books of the Afterlife*. Ithaca, NY: Cornell University Press.

HORNUNG, E., and STAEHELIN, E. 2006. *Neue Studien zum Sedfest*, Aegyptiaca Helvetica 20. Basle: Schwabe.

HUNT, A. S., and EDGAR, C. C. 1934. *Select Papyri*, ii. *Non-Literary Papyri; Public Documents*, LCL 282. Cambridge: Harvard University Press.

JACKSON, R. B. 2002. *Empire's Edge: Exploring Rome's Egyptian Frontier*. New Haven: Yale University Press.

JAMES, T. G. H. 1953. *The Mastaba of Khentika called Ikhekhi*, Archaeological Survey of Egypt 30. London: Egypt Exploration Society.

JEFFREYS, D. 2004. 'Hierakonpolis and Memphis in Predynastic Tradition', in Hendrickx et al. (eds) 2004: 837–45.

JIMÉNEZ SERRANO, A. 2002. *Royal Festivals in the Late Predynastic Period and the First Dynasty*, BAR International Series 1076. Oxford: Archaeopress.

JOHNSON, A.W., and EARLE, T. 2000. *The Evolution of Human Societies: From Foraging Group to Agrarian State*. 2nd edn. Stanford: Stanford University Press.

JOHNSON, J. 1983. 'The Demotic Chronicle as a Statement of a Theory of Kingship', *Journal of the Society for the Study of Egyptian Antiquities* 13: 61–72.

JOHNSON, W. R. 2001. 'Monuments and Monumental Art under Amenhotep III: Evolution and Meaning', in O'Connor and Cline (eds) 2001: 63–94.

JONES, D. 2000. *An Index of Ancient Egyptian Titles, Epithets and Phrases of the Old Kingdom*, BAR International Series 866. 2 vols. Oxford: Archaeopress.

KAARE, B., and WOODBURN, J. 1999. 'The Hadza of Tanzania', in Lee and Daly (eds) 1999: 200–4.

KAHL, J. 2001. 'Hieroglyphic Writing During the Fourth Millennium BC: An Analysis of Systems', *Archéo-Nil* 11: 101–34.

KAHL, J. 2006. 'Dynasties 0–2: Hetep-sekhemwy to Netjerykhet. The succession', in E. Hornung, R. Krauss, and D. Warburton (eds), *Ancient Egyptian Chronology*, Handbook of Oriental Studies: Section 1, The Near and Middle East (Book 83). Leiden: Brill.

KAHL, J. 2007. *Ancient Asyut: The First Synthesis after 300 Years of Research*, The Asyut Project 1. Wiesbaden: Harrassowitz.

KAISER, W. 1987. 'Die dekorierte Torfassade des spätzeitlichen Palastbezirkes von Memphis', *MDAIK* 43: 123–54.

KÁKOSY, L. 1963. 'Schöpfung und Weltuntergang in der ägyptischen Religion', *Acta Antiqua Academiae Scientiarum Hungaricae* 11: 17–30.

KANAWATI, N. 2003. *Conspiracies in the Egyptian Palace: Unis to Pepy I*. London: Routledge.

KANAWATI, N. 2010. *Decorated Burial Chambers of the Old Kingdom*. Cairo: Supreme Council of Antiquities.

KATARY, S. L. D. 1989. *Land Tenure in the Ramesside Period*, Studies in Egyptology. London: Kegan Paul.

KELANY, A., et al. 2009. 'Granite Quarry Survey in the Aswan Region, Egypt: Shedding New Light on Ancient Quarrying', in N. Abu-Jaber, E. G. Bloxam, P. Degryse, and T. Heldal (eds), *QuarryScapes: Ancient Stone Quarry Landscapes in the Eastern Mediterranean*, Geological Survey of Norway Special Publication 12. Norway: NGU: Geological Survey of Norway, 87–98.

KEMP, B. J. 1963. 'Excavations at Hierakonpolis Fort, 1905: A Preliminary Note', *JEA* 49: 24–8.

KEMP, B. J. 1968. 'Merimda and the Theory of House Burial in Prehistoric Egypt', *CdE* 43: 22–33.

KEMP, B. J. 2000. 'Soil (Including Mud-brick Architecture)', in Nicholson and Shaw (eds) 2000: 78–103.

KEMP, B. J. 2006. *Anatomy of a Civilization*. 2nd edn. London: Routledge.

KITCHEN, K. A. 1975–90. *Ramesside Inscriptions*. 8 vols. Oxford: Blackwell.

KITCHEN, K. A. 1982. *Pharaoh Triumphant: The Life and Times of Ramesses II, King of Egypt*. Warminster: Aris & Phillips.

KITCHEN, K. A. 1996a. *The Third Intermediate Period in Egypt (1100–650 BC)*. 2nd edn. rev. Warminster: Aris & Phillips.

KITCHEN, K. A. 1996b. *Ramesside Inscriptions Translated and Annotated: Translations*, ii. *Ramesses II, Royal Inscriptions*. Oxford: Blackwell.

KITCHEN, K. A. 1999. *Ramesside Inscriptions Translated & Annotated: Notes and Comments*, ii. *Ramesses II*. Oxford: Blackwell.

KITCHEN, K. A. 2000. *Ramesside Inscriptions Translated & Annotated: Translations*, iii. *Ramesses II, his Contemporaries*. Oxford: Blackwell.

KOBUSIEWICZ, M., et al. 2004. 'Discovery of the First Neolithic Cemetery in Egypt's Western Desert', *Antiquity* 78: 566–78.

KOEHLER, E. C. 2010. 'Prehistory', in Lloyd (ed.) 2010c: 25–47.

KOZLOFF, A. P. 2001. 'The Decorative and Funerary Arts During the Reign of Amenhotep III', in O'Connor and Cline (eds) 2001: 95–123.

KOZLOFF, A. P., and BRYAN, B. M. 1992. *Egypt's Dazzling Sun: Amenhotep III and his World*. Cleveland: Cleveland Museum of Art with Indiana University Press.

KRADER, L. 1968. *Formation of the State*. Foundations of Modern Anthropology. Englewood Cliffs, NJ: Prentice-Hall.

KRATZ, C. A. 1999. 'The Okiek of Kenya', in Lee and Daly (eds) 1999: 220–4.

KRUCHTEN, J.-M. 1981. *Le Décret d'Horemheb. Traduction, commentaire épigraphique, philologique et institutionnel*, Éditions de l'Université de Bruxelles, Faculté de Philosophie et Lettres 82. Brussels: Université Libre de Bruxelles.

KUHRT, A. 1995. *The Ancient Near East c.3000–330 BC*, Routledge History of the Ancient World. 2 vols. London: Routledge.

KURTH, D. 1997. 'The Present State of Research into Graeco-Roman Temples', in Quirke (ed.) 1997: 152–8.

LACOVARA, P. 1990. *Deir el-Ballas: Preliminary Report on the Deir el-Ballas Expedition, 1980–1986*, American Research Center in Egypt Reports 12. Winona Lake, Ind.: Eisenbrauns.

LACOVARA, P. 1997a. *The New Kingdom Royal City*, Studies in Egyptology. London: Kegan Paul.

LACOVARA, P. 1997b. 'The Riddle of the Reserve Heads', *KMT* 8(4): 28–36.

LACOVARA, P. 2006. 'Deir el-Ballas and the Development of the Early New Kingdom Royal Palace', in E. Czerny et al. (eds), *Timelines: Studies in Honour of Manfred Bietak*, OLA 149. I. Leuven: Peeters, 187–96.

LANDSTRÖM, B. 1970. *Ships of the Pharaohs: 4000 Years of Egyptian Shipbuilding*, Architectura Navalis. London: Allen & Unwin.

LAUER, J.-Ph. 1973. 'Remarques sur la planification de la construction de la grande pyramide. A propos de "The Investment Process Organization of the Cheops Pyramid" par Wieslaw Koziński', *BIFAO* 73: 127–42.

LEACH, B., and TAIT, J. 2000. 'Papyrus', in Nicholson and Shaw (eds) 2000: 227–53.

LEAHY, A.1985. 'The Libyan Period in Egypt: An Essay in Interpretation', *Libyan Studies* 16: 51–65.

LEE, R. B. 1984. *The Dobe !Kung*. New York: Holt, Rinehart & Winston.

LEE, R. B., and DALY, R. (eds) 1999. *The Cambridge Encyclopedia of Hunters and Gatherers*. Cambridge: Cambridge University Press.

LESKO, B. S. 1969. 'Royal Mortuary Suites of the Egyptian New Kingdom', *JARCE* 73: 453–8.

LESKO, L. (ed.) 2006. *Pharaoh's Workers: The Villagers of Deir el Medina*. Ithaca, NY: Cornell University Press

Lexikon der Ägyptologie 1972–92, ed. W. Helck, E. Otto, and W. Westendorf. 7 vols. Wiesbaden: Harrassowitz.

LICHTHEIM, M. 1975. *Ancient Egyptian Literature*, i. *The Old and Middle Kingdoms*. Berkeley and Los Angeles: University of California Press.

LICHTHEIM, M. 1980. *Ancient Egyptian Literature*, iii. *The Late Period*. Berkeley: University of California Press.

LICHTHEIM, M. 1988. *Ancient Egyptian Autobiographies Chiefly of the Middle Kingdom: A Study and an Anthology*, Orbis Biblicus et Orientalis 84. Freiburg: Universitätsverlag; Göttingen: Vandenhoeck & Ruprecht.

LICHTHEIM, M. 1992. *Maat in Egyptian Autobiographies and Related Studies*, Orbis Biblicus et Orientalis 120. Freiburg: Universitätsverlag; Göttingen: Vandenhoeck & Ruprecht.

LICHTHEIM, M. 1997. *Moral Values in Ancient Egypt*, Orbis Biblicus et Orientalis 155. Freiburg: Universitätsverlag; Göttingen: Vandenhoeck & Ruprecht.

LICHTHEIM, M. 2006. *Ancient Egyptian Literature*, ii. *The New Kingdom*. Berkeley and Los Angeles: University of California Press.

LLOYD, A. B. 1975. 'Once More Hammamat Inscription 191', *JEA* 61: 54–66.

LLOYD, A. B. 1976. *Herodotus Book II, Commentary 1–98*, Études préliminaires aux religions orientales dans l'Empire romain 43. Leiden: Brill.

LLOYD, A. B. 1978. 'Strabo and the Memphite Tauromachy', in M. B. de Boer and T. A. Edridge (eds), *Hommages à Maarten J. Vermaseren*. Leiden: Brill, ii. 609–26.

LLOYD, A. B. 1982. 'Nationalist Propaganda in Ptolemaic Egypt', *Historia* 31: 33–55.

LLOYD, A. B. 1988. *Herodotus Book II, Commentary 99–182*, Études préliminaires aux religions orientales dans l'Empire romain 43. Leiden: Brill.

LLOYD, A. B. 1989. 'Psychology and Society in the Ancient Egyptian Cult of the Dead', in W. K. Simpson (ed.), *Religion and Philosophy in Ancient Egypt*, Yale Egyptological Studies 3. New Haven: Yale Egyptological Seminar, 117–33.

LLOYD, A. B. 1992. 'The Great Inscription of Khnumhotpe II at Beni Hasan', in A. B. Lloyd (ed.), *Studies in Pharaonic Religion and Society in Honour of J. Gwyn Griffiths*. London: The Egypt Exploration Society, 21–36.

LLOYD, A. B. 1995. 'Philip II and Alexander the Great: The Moulding of Macedon's Army', in A. B. Lloyd (ed.), *Battle in Antiquity*. London: Duckworth and Classical Press of Wales, 169–98.

LLOYD, A. B. (ed.) 1998. *Gods, Priests and Men: Studies in the Religion of Pharaonic Egypt by Aylward M. Blackman*. London: Kegan Paul, sect. III.

LLOYD, A. B. 2000a. 'Saite Navy', in G. J. Oliver et al., *The Sea in Antiquity*. BAR International Series 899. Oxford: John and Erica Hodges and Archaeopress, 81–91.

LLOYD, A. B. 2000b. 'The Late Period', in Shaw (ed.) 2000: 369–94.

LLOYD, A. B. 2000c. 'The Ptolemaic Period (332–30 BC)', in Shaw (ed.) 2000: 395–421.

LLOYD, A. B. 2002. 'The Egyptian Elite in the Early Ptolemaic Period: Some Hieroglyphic Evidence', in D. Ogden (ed.), *The Hellenistic World: New Perspectives*. London: Classical Press of Wales and Duckworth, 117–36.

LLOYD, A. B. 2006. '*Heka*, Dreams, and Prophecy in Ancient Egyptian Stories', in K. Szpakowska (ed.), *Through a Glass Darkly: Magic, Dreams and Prophecy in Ancient Egypt*. Swansea: Classical Press of Wales, 71–94.

LLOYD, A. B. 2007. 'The Greeks and Egypt: Diplomatic Relations in the Seventh–Sixth Centuries BC', in P. Kousoulis and K. Magliveras (eds), *Moving across Borders: Foreign Relations, Religion and Cultural Interactions in the Ancient Mediterranean*, OLA 159. Leuven: Peeters and Departement Oosterse Studies, 35–50.

LLOYD, A. B. 2010a. 'The Reception of Pharaonic Egypt in Classical Antiquity', in Lloyd (ed.) 2010c: 1067–85.

LLOYD, A. B. 2010b. 'From Satrapy to Hellenistic Kingdom: The Case of Egypt', in A. Erskine and L. Llewellyn-Jones (eds), *Creating a Hellenistic World*. Swansea: Classical Press of Wales, 83–105.

LLOYD, A. B. (ed.) 2010c. *A Companion to Ancient Egypt*, Blackwell Companions to the Ancient World. 2 vols. Chichester: Wiley-Blackwell.

LLOYD, A. B. 2013. 'Expeditions to the Wadi Hammamat: Context and Concept', in J. A. Hill, P. Jones, and A. J. Morales (eds), *Experiencing Power, Generating Authority: Cosmos, Politics and the Ideology of Kingship in Ancient Egypt and Mesopotamia*. University Park, Pa.: Penn University Press.

LLOYD, A. B., SPENCER, A. J., and EL-KHOULI, A. 1990. *Saqqâra Tombs*, ii. *The Mastabas of Meru, Semdenti, Khui and Others*, EES Archaeological Survey of Egypt Memoir 40 (in collaboration with the British Museum). London: Egypt Exporation Society.

LLOYD, A. B., SPENCER, A. J., and EL-KHOULI, A. 2008. *Saqqâra Tombs*, iii. *The Mastaba of Neferseshemptah*, EES Archaeological Survey of Egypt Memoir 41 (in collaboration with the British Museum). London: Egypt Exploration Society.

LOPRIENO, A. (ed.) 1996. *Ancient Egyptian Literature: History and Forms*, PdÄ 10. Leiden: E. J. Brill.

LUCAS, A., and HARRIS, J. R. 1962. *Ancient Egyptian Materials and Industries*. 4th edn. rev. and enlarged by J. R. Harris. London: Edward Arnold.

MACCOULL, L. 1988. *Dioscorus of Aphrodito: His Work and his World*, Transformation of the Classical Heritage 16. Berkeley: University of California Press.

McDERMOTT, B. 2004. *Warfare in Ancient Egypt*. Stroud: Sutton.

McDowell, A. G. 1999. *Village Life in Ancient Egypt: Laundry Lists and Love Songs.* Oxford: Oxford University Press.

McNamara, L. 2008. 'The Revetted Mound at Hierakonpolis and Early Kingship: A Reinterpretation', in B. Midant-Reynes and Y. Tristant (eds), *Egypt at its Origins 2: Proceedings of the International Conference 'Origins of the State. Predynastic and Early Dynastic Egypt', Toulouse (France), 5th–8th September 2005,* OLA 172. Leuven: Peeters and Departement Oosterse Studies, 901–36.

Mair, L. 1972. *An Introduction to Social Anthropology.* 2nd edn. Oxford: Clarendon.

Manning, J. G. 2003. *Land and Power in Ptolemaic Egypt: the Structure of Land Tenure,* Cambridge: Cambridge University Press.

Manning, J. G. 2007a. *Land and Power in Ptolemaic Egypt: The Structure of Land Tenure.* Cambridge: Cambridge University Press.

Manning, J. G. 2007b. 'Hellenistic Egypt', in W. Scheidel, I. Morris, and R. Saller (eds), *The Cambridge Economic History of the Greco-Roman World.* Cambridge: Cambridge University Press, 434–59.

Manning, J. G. 2010. *The Last Pharaohs: Egypt under the Ptolemies, 305–30 BC.* Princeton, NJ: Princeton University Press.

Manning, J. G. 2011. 'Networks, Hierarchies, and Markets in the Ptolemaic Economy', in Z. H. Archibald, J. K. Davies, and V. Gabrielsen (eds), *The Economies of Hellenistic Societies, Third to First Centuries BC.* Oxford: Oxford University Press, 296–323.

Marchant, J. 2011. 'Ancient DNA: Curse of the Pharaoh's DNA', *Nature* 472: 404–6.

Marcus, E. S. 2007. 'Amenemhet II and the Sea: Maritime Aspects of the Mit Rahina (Memphis) Inscription', *Ägypten und Levante* 17: 137–90.

Martin, G. T. 1989. *The Royal Tomb at el-'Amarna,* ii. *The Reliefs, Inscriptions, and Architecture,* The Rock Tombs of el-'Amarna, 7, Archaeological Survey of Egypt Memoir 39. London: Egypt Exploration Society.

Martin-Pardey, E. 1976. *Untersuchungen zur ägyptischen Provinzialverwaltung bis zum Ende des Alten Reiches,* Hildesheimer Ägyptologische Beiträge 1. Hildesheim: Gebrüder Gerstenberg.

Martinet, E. 2011. *Le Nomarque sous l'Ancien Empire,* Les Institutions dans l'Egypte ancienne. Paris: Presses de l'université Paris-Sorbonne.

Masson, O., and Yoyotte, J. 1956. *Objets pharaoniques à inscription carienne,* Institut français d'archéologie orientale: Bibliothèque d'étude 15. Cairo: l'Institut français d'archéologie orientale.

Maystre, C. 1941. 'Le Livre de la Vache du Ciel dans les tombeaux de la Vallée des Rois', *BIFAO* 40: 53–115.

Mbiti, J. S. 1969. *African Religions & Philosophy.* London: Heinemann.

Meeks, D. 1971. 'Génies, anges, démons en Egypte', in D. Meeks et al., *Génies, Anges et Démons: Egypte, Babylone, Israël, Islam, Peuples altaïques, Inde, Birmanie, Asie du sud-est, Tibet, Chine,* Sources orientales 8. Paris: Éditions du Seuil, 17–84.

Midant-Reynes, B. 2000. *The Prehistory of Egypt: From the First Egyptians to the First Pharaohs,* trans. I. Shaw. Oxford: Blackwell.

Monson, A. 2012. *From the Ptolemies to the Romans: Political and Economic Change in Egypt.* Cambridge: Cambridge University Press.

Mooren, L. 1975. *The Aulic Titulature in Ptolemaic Egypt: Introduction and Prosopography*, Verhandelingen van de Koninklijke Academie voor Wetenschappen, Letteren en Schone Kunsten van België, Klasse der Schone Kunsten 78. Brussels: Paleis der Academiën.

Moreno García, J. C. 1999. *Ḥwt et le milieu rural égyptien du IIIᵉ millénaire: Economie, administration et organisation territorial*, Bibliothèque de l'École des hautes études. Sciences historiques et philologiques 337. Paris: Librairie Honoré Champion.

Moreno García, J. C. 2004. *Egipto en el Imperio Antiguo (2650–2150 antes de Cristo)*. Barcelona: Bellaterra.

Moreno García, J. C. 2007. 'The State and the Organisation of the Rural Landscape in 3rd Millennium BC Pharaonic Egypt', in M. Bollig et al. (eds), *Aridity, Change and Conflict in Africa: Proceedings of an International ACACIA Conference held at Königswinter, Germany October 1–3 2003*, Colloquium Africanum 2. Cologne: Heinrich-Barth-Institut, 313–30.

Moreno García, J. C. 2008.C. 'Review Article: la dépendance rurale en Egypte ancienne', *JESHO* 51: 99–150.

Morenz, L. D., and Popko, L. 2010. 'The Second Intermediate Period and the New Kingdom', in Lloyd (ed.) 2010c: 101–19.

Morkot, R. G. 1990. 'Nb-m3ʿt-rʿ—United-with-Ptah', *JNES* 49: 323–37.

Morkot, R. G. 1991. 'Nubia in the New Kingdom: The Limits of Egyptian Control', in W. V. Davies (ed.), *Egypt and Africa: Nubia from Prehistory to Islam*. London: British Museum with Egypt Exploration Society, 294–301.

Morkot, R. G. 2000. *The Black Pharaohs: Egypt's Nubian Rulers*. London: Rubicon.

Morris, E. F. 2005. *The Architecture of Imperialism: Military Bases and the Evolution of Foreign Policy in Egypt's New Kingdom*, PdÄ 22. Leiden: Brill.

Morris, E. F. 2010. 'The Pharaoh and the Pharaonic Office', in Lloyd (ed.) 2010c: 201–17.

Müller, H. 1938. *Die formale Entwicklung der Titulatur der ägyptischen Könige*, ÄF 7. Glückstadt: Augustin.

Mumford, G. 2010. 'Settlements—Distribution, Structure, Architecture: Pharaonic', in Lloyd (ed.) 2010c: 326–49.

Murnane, W. J. 1977. *Ancient Egyptian Coregencies*, Studies in Ancient Oriental Civilization 40. Chicago: The Oriental Institute.

Murnane, W. J. 1981. 'The Sed Festival: A Problem in Historical Method', *MDAIK* 37: 369–76.

Murnane, W. J. 1995. *Texts from the Amarna Period in Egypt*, Society of Biblical Literature. Writings from the Ancient World 5. Atlanta: Scholars Press.

Murnane, W. J. 2001. 'The Organization of Government under Amenhotep III', in O'Connor and Cline (eds) 2001: 173–221.

Murray, M. A. 2000. 'Cereal Production and Processing', in Nicholson and Shaw (eds) 2000: 505–36.

Musurillo, H. A. 1954. *The Acts of the Pagan Martyrs: Acta Alexandrinorum*. Oxford: Clarendon.

Naʾaman, N. 1981. 'Economic Aspects of the Egyptian Occupation of Canaan', *Israel Exploration Journal* 31: 172–85.

Naunton, C. 2010. 'Libyans and Nubians', in Lloyd (ed.) 2010c: 120–39.

NAVILLE, E. 1886. *Das aegyptische Todtenbuch der xviii. bis xx. Dynastie, aus verschiedenen Urkunden zusammengestellt und herausg. von E. Naville.* 2 vols. Berlin: A. Asher.

NELSON, H. H. 1942. 'The Identity of Amon-Re United-with-Eternity', *JNES* 1: 127–55.

NELSON, K., and Associates 2002. *Holocene Settlement of the Egyptian Sahara,* ii. *The Pottery of Nabta Playa.* New York: Kluwer Academic/Plenum.

NEWBERRY, P. 1893. *El-Bersheh,* pt. I, Archaeological Survey of Egypt 3rd Memoir. London: Egypt Exploration Fund.

NICHOLSON, P. T., and SHAW, I. (eds) 2000. *Ancient Egyptian Materials and Technology.* Cambridge: Cambridge University Press.

NUNN, J. F. 1996. *Ancient Egyptian Medicine.* London: British Museum.

O'CONNOR, D. 2001. 'The City and the World: Worldview and Built Forms in the Reign of Amenhotep III', in O'Connor and Cline (eds) 2001: 125–72.

O'CONNOR, D. 2009. *Abydos: Egypt's First Pharaohs and the Cult of Osiris.* London: Thames & Hudson.

O'CONNOR, D. 2011. 'The Narmer Palette: A New Interpretation', in E. Teeter (ed.), *Before the Pyramids: The Origins of Egyptian Civilization,* Oriental Institute Museum Publications 33. Chicago: Oriental Institute of the University of Chicago, 145–52.

O'CONNOR, D. and CLINE, E. H. (eds) 2001. *Amenhotep III: Perspectives on his Reign.* Ann Arbor: University of Michigan Press.

O'CONNOR, D. and SILVERMAN, D. P. (eds) 1995. *Ancient Egyptian Kingship,* PdÄ 9. Leiden: E. J. Brill.

OBSOMER, C. 1995. *Sésostris Ier. Étude chronologique et historique du règne,* Étude 5. Brussels: Connaissance de l'Égypte Ancienne.

OGDEN, D. 2000. *Polygamy, Prostitutes and Death: The Hellenistic Dynasties.* Swansea: Classical Press of Wales.

OGDEN, J. 2000. 'Metals', in Nicholson and Shaw (eds) 2000: 148–76.

OREN, E. D. (ed.) 1997. *The Hyksos, New Historical and Archaeological Perspectives,* University Museum Symposium Series 8 = University Museum Monograph 96. Philadelphia: University Museum, University of Pennsylvania.

PADGHAM, J. 2012. *A New Interpretation of the Cone on the Head in New Kingdom Egyptian Tomb Scenes,* BAR International Series 2431. Archeopress: Oxford.

PANTER-BRICK, C., LAYTON, R. H., and ROWLEY-CONWY, P. (eds) 2001. *Hunter-Gatherers: An Interdisciplinary Perspective,* Biosocial Society Symposium Series 13. Cambridge: Cambridge University Press.

PARCAK, S. 2010. 'The Physical Context of Ancient Egypt', in Lloyd (ed.) 2010c: 3–22.

PARKINSON, R. B. 1998. *The Tale of Sinuhe and Other Ancient Egyptian Poems 1944–1640 BC.* Oxford: Oxford University Press.

PARKINSON, R. B. 2002. *Poetry and Culture in Middle Kingdom Egypt: A Dark Side to Perfection,* Athlone Publications in Egyptology and Ancient Near Eastern Studies. London: Continuum.

PARKINSON, R. B. 2008. *The Painted Tomb-Chapel of Nebamun: Masterpieces of Ancient Egyptian Art in the British Museum.* London: British Museum.

PARSONS, P. 2007. *City of the Sharp-nosed Fish: Greek Lives in Roman Egypt.* London: Weidenfeld & Nicolson.

PARSONS, T. 1966. *Societies. Evolutionary and Comparative Perspectives*, Foundations of Modern Sociology. New Jersey: Prentice-Hall.

PARTRIDGE, R. B. 1996. *Transport in Ancient Egypt*. London: Rubicon.

PARTRIDGE, R. B. 2002. *Fighting Pharaohs: Weapons and Warfare in Ancient Egypt*. Manchester: Peartree.

PARTRIDGE, R. B. 2010. 'Transport in Ancient Egypt', in Lloyd (ed.) 2010*c*: 370–89.

PATCH, D. C. 2004. 'Settlement Patterns and Cultural Change in the Predynastic Period', in Hendrickx et al. (eds) 2004: 905–18.

PEACOCK, D. 2000. 'The Roman Period (30BC–AD311)', in Shaw (ed.) 2000: 422–45.

PEDEN, A. J. 1994*a*. *Egyptian Historical Inscriptions of the Twentieth Dynasty*, Documenta Mundi. Aegyptiaca 3. Jonsered: Paul Åströms.

PEDEN, A. J. 1994*b*. *The Reign of Ramesses IV*. Warminster: Aris & Phillips.

PEET, T. E. 1930. *The Great Tomb-Robberies of the Twentieth Egyptian Dynasty: Being a Critical Study, with Translations and Commentaries, of the Papyri in which these are Recorded*. 2 vols. Oxford: Clarendon.

PERDU, O. 2010. 'Saites and Persians (664–332)', in Lloyd (ed.) 2010*c*: 140–58.

PETRIE, W. M. F. 1909. *The Palace of Apries (Memphis II)*, British School of Archaeology in Egypt and Egyptian Research Account 15th Year. London: School of Archaeology in Egypt, University College.

PHILLIPPS, R., et al. 2012. 'Mid-Holocene Occupation of Egypt and Global Climatic Change', *Quaternary International* 251: 64–76.

PIANKOFF, A. 1955 (1977). *The Shrines of Tut-ankh-amun: Texts Translated with Introductions*, Bollingen Series 40/2. Princeton, NJ: Princeton University Press.

PINCH, G. 1994. *Magic in Ancient Egypt*. London: British Museum.

PIRELLI, R. 1998. 'The Monument of Imeneminet (Naples, Inv. 1069) as a Document of Social Changes in the Egyptian New Kingdom', in C. J. Eyre (ed.), *Proceedings of the Seventh International Congress of Egyptologists, Cambridge, 3–9 September 1995*. Leuven: Peeters, 871–84.

POLLARD, N. 2010. 'Military Institutions and Warfare: Graeco-Roman', in Lloyd (ed.) 2010*c*: 446–65.

POSENER, G. 1936. *La Première domination perse en Egypte: recueil d'inscriptions hiéroglyphiques*, BdE 11. Cairo: l'Institut français d'archéologie orientale.

POSENER, G. 1957. 'Le Conte de Neferkarê et du général Siséné (Recherches littéraires, VI)', *RdE* 11: 119–37.

QUACK, J. F. 2000. 'Das Buch vom Tempel und verwandte Texte: ein Vorbericht', *Archiv für Religionsgeschichte* 2: 1–20.

QUAEGEBEUR, J. 1975. *Le Dieu égyptien Shaï dans la religion et l'onomastique*, OLA 2. Leuven: University Press.

QUIRKE, S. G. J. 1990. *The Administration of Egypt in the Late Middle Kingdom: The Hieratic Documents*. New Malden: SIA.

QUIRKE, S. G. J. (ed.) 1997. *The Temple in Ancient Egypt: New Discoveries and Recent Research*, London: British Museum.

QUIRKE, S. G. J. 2004. *Titles and Bureaux of Egypt 1850–1700 BC*, Egyptology I. London: Golden House.

QUIRKE, S. G. J. and SPENCER, J. (eds) 1992. *The British Museum Book of Ancient Egypt*. London: British Museum.

RATHBONE, D. W. 2007. 'Roman Egypt', in W. Scheidel, I. Morris, and R. Saller (eds), *The Cambridge Economic History of the Greco-Roman World*. Cambridge: Cambridge University Press, 698–719.

REDFORD, D. B. 1984. *Akhenaten: The Heretic King*. Princeton, NJ: Princeton University Press.

REDFORD, D. B. 1997. 'Textual Sources for the Hyksos Period', in E. D. Oren (ed.), *The Hyksos: New Historical and Archaeological Perspectives*, University Museum Symposium Series 8 = University Museum Monograph 96. Philadelphia: University Museum, University of Pennsylvania, 1–44.

REDFORD, D. B. 2003. *The Wars in Syria and Palestine of Thutmose III*, Culture and History of the Ancient Near East 16. Leiden: Brill.

REDFORD, D. B. 2004. *From Slave to Pharaoh: The Black Experience of Ancient Egypt*: Johns Hopkins University Press.

REDFORD, S. 2001. *The Harem Conspiracy: The Murder of Rameses III*. DeKalb: Northern Illinois University Press; London: Eurospan.

REEDER, G. 1994. 'A Rite of Passage: The Enigmatic *tekenu* in Ancient Egyptian Funerary Ritual', *KMT* 5 (3): 53–9.

REEVES, C. N. 1990*a*. *Valley of the Kings: The Decline of a Royal Necropolis*. London: Kegan Paul.

REEVES, C. N. 1990*b*. *The Complete Tutankhamun: The King. The Tomb. The Royal Treasure*. London: Thames & Hudson.

REEVES, C. N. 2001. *Akhenaten: Egypt's False Prophet*. New York: Thames & Hudson.

REISER, E. 1972. *Der königliche Harim im alten Ägypten und seine Verwaltung*, Dissertationen der Universität Wien 77. Vienna: Notring.

REISNER, G. A. 1918. 'The Tomb of Hepzefa, Nomarch of Siûṭ', *JEA* 5: 79–98.

RICE, E. E. 1983. *The Grand Procession of Ptolemy Philadelphus*. Oxford: Oxford University Press.

RICHARDS, J. E. 2000. 'Weni the Elder and his Mortuary Neighbourhood at Abydos, Egypt', *Kelsey Museum Newsletter* (Spring), 6–9.

RICHARDS, J. E. 2002. 'Text and Context in Late Old Kingdom Egypt: The Archaeology and Historiography of Weni the Elder', *JARCE* 39: 75–102.

RIGGS, C. 2005. *The Beautiful Burial in Roman Egypt: Art, Identity, and Funerary Religion*, Oxford Studies in Ancient Culture and Representaion. Oxford: Oxford University Press.

RITNER, R. K. 1993. *The Mechanics of Ancient Egyptian Magical Practice*, Studies in Ancient Oriental Civilization 54. Chicago: Oriental Institute of the University of Chicago.

ROBINS, G. 1979. 'The Relationships Specified by Egyptian Kinship Terms of the Middle and New Kingdoms', *CdE* 54(108): 197–207.

ROBINS, G. 1983. 'A Critical Examination of the Theory that the Right to the Throne of Ancient Egypt Passed through the Female Line in the 18th Dynasty', *GM* 62: 67–77.

ROBINS, G. 1987. 'The Role of the Royal Family in the 18th Dynasty up to the Reign of Amenhotpe III: 2. Royal Children', *Wepwawet* 3: 15–17.

ROBINS, G. 1993. *Women in Ancient Egypt*. London: British Museum.

ROBINS, G. 2008. *The Art of Ancient Egypt*. London: British Museum.

ROEHRIG, C. H. 1999. 'Reserve Heads: An Enigma of Old Kingdom Sculpture', in Metropolitan Museum of Art, *Egyptian Art in the Age of the Pyramids*. New York: Metropolitan Museum of Art, 73–81.

ROSSEL, F., et al. 2008. 'Domestication of the Donkey: Timing, Processes, and Indicators', *Proceedings of the National Academy of Sciences* 105(10): 3715–20.

ROTH, A. M. 1992. 'The pss̆-kf and the "Opening of the Mouth" Ceremony: A Ritual of Birth and Rebirth', *JEA* 78: 113–47.

ROTH, A. M. 1993. 'Fingers, Stars, and the "Opening of the Mouth": The Nature and Function of the *nt̲rwj*-blades', *JEA* 79: 57–79.

ROWLANDSON, J. 1996. *Landowners and Tenants in Roman Egypt: The Social Relations of Agriculture in the Oxyrhynchite Nome*, Oxford Classical Monographs. Oxford: Clarendon.

ROWLANDSON, J. 2010. 'Administration and Law: Graeco-Roman', in Lloyd (ed.) 2010c: 237–54.

RYHOLT, K. 1997. *The Political Situation in Egypt during the Second Intermediate Period c. 1800–1550 B.C.*, Carsten Niebuhr Institute Publications 20. Copenhagen: Carsten Niebuhr Institute of Near Eastern Studies, University of Copenhagen/ Museum Tusculanum Press.

RYHOLT, K. 2000. 'The Late Old Kingdom in the Turin King-list and the Identity of Nitocris', *ZÄS* 127: 87–100.

RYHOLT, K. 2010. 'Late Period Literature', in Lloyd (ed.) 2010c: 709–31.

SADR, K. 1991. *The Development of Nomadism in Ancient Northeast Africa*. Philadelphia: University of Pennsylvania Press.

SAHLINS, M. D. 1968. *Tribesmen*, Foundations of Modern Anthropology. Englewood Cliffs, NJ: Prentice Hall.

SÄVE-SÖDERBERGH, T. 1946. *The Navy of the Eighteenth Egyptian Dynasty*, Uppsala Universitets Årsskrift 6. Uppsala: University of Uppsala.

SAWYER, R. D., with SAWYER, M. 1993. *The Seven Military Classics of Ancient China*. Boulder: Westview.

SCARRE, C. J. (ed.) 2005. *The Human Past. World Prehistory and the Development of Human Societies*. London: Thames & Hudson.

SCHÄFER, H. 1974. *Principles of Egyptian Art*, trans. J. Baines. Oxford: Clarendon.

SCHOTT, S. 1950. *Altägyptische Festdaten*, Abhandlungen der geistes- und sozialwissenschaftlichen Klasse. Jahrgang 1950.Wiesbaden: Akademie der Wissenschaften und der Literatur in Mainz in Kommission bei Franz Steiner.

SCHOTT, S. 1953. *Das schöne Fest vom Wüstentale. Festbräuche einer Totenstadt*. Akademie der Wissenschaften und der Literatur. Abhandlungen der geistes- und sozialwissenschaftlichen Klasse. Jahrgang 1952, 11. Wiesbaden: Akademie der Wissenschaften und der Literatur in Mainz, in Kommission bei Franz Steiner, 767–902.

SEIDLMAYER, S. J. 1996. 'Town and State in the Early Old Kingdom. A View from Elephantine', in J. Spencer (ed.), *Aspects of Early Egypt*. London: British Museum, 108–27.

SEIDLMAYER, S. J. 2000. 'The First Intermediate Period (*c.* 2160–2055 BC)', in Shaw (ed.), 2000: 118–47.

SEKUNDA, N. 2006. *Hellenistic Infantry Reform in the 160s BC*, Studies on the History of Ancient and Medieval Art of Warfare 5. Monograph Series AKANTHINA. Gdańsk: Foundation for the Development of Gdańsk University.

SERVICE, E. R. 1962. *Primitive Social Organization: An Evolutionary Perspective.* New York: Random House.

SERVICE, E. R. 1966. *The Hunters.* Foundations of Modern Anthropology. Englewood Cliffs, NJ: Prentice-Hall.

SETHE, K. 1904. *Hieroglyphische Urkunden der griechisch-römischen Zeit.* Leipzig: J. C. Hinrichs.

SETHE, K. 1928. *Ägyptische Lesestücke zum Gebrauch im Akademischen Unterricht.* Leipzig: J. C. Hinrichs.

SHAFER, B. E. (ed.) 1997. *Temples of Ancient Egypt.* Ithaca NY: Cornell University Press.

SHAW, I. (ed.) 2000. *The Oxford History of Ancient Egypt.* Oxford: Oxford University Press.

SHAW, I. 2006. '"Master of the Roads": Quarrying and Communications Networks in Egypt and Nubia', in B. Mathieu, D. Meeks, and M. Wissa (eds), *L'Apport de l'Egypte à l'Histoire des Techniques: Méthodes, Chronologie et Comparaisons.* Cairo: l'Institut français d'archéologie oriental, 253–66.

SHAW, I. 2007. 'Gurob: The Key to Unlocking an Egyptian Harem?', *Current World Archaeology* 23: 12–19.

SHAW, I. 2008. 'A Royal Harem Town of the New Kingdom: New Fieldwork at Medinet el-Gurob', in C. Ziegler (ed.), *Queens of Egypt: from Hetepheres to Cleopatra.* Monaco: Grimaldi Forum; Somogy Éditions d'Art, 104–15.

SHAW, I. 2009. 'Seeking the Ramesside Royal Harem: New Fieldwork at Medinet el-Gurob', in M. Collier and S. Snape (eds), *Ramesside Studies in Honour of Kenneth Kitchen.* Bolton: Rutherford, 207–17.

SHAW, I. 2010. *Hatnub: Quarrying Travertine in Ancient Egypt.* London: Egypt Exploration Society.

SHEDID, A. G., with SHEDID, A. 1994. *Das Grab des Sennedjem: Ein Künstlergrab der 19. Dynastie in Deir el Medineh.* Mainz am Rhein: Philipp von Zabern.

SIDEBOTHAM, S.E., HENSE, M., and NOUWENS, H. M. 2008. *The Red Land: The Illustrated Archaeology of Egypt's Eastern Desert.* Cairo: American University in Cairo Press.

SIMPSON, W. K. (ed.) 2003. *The Literature of Ancient Egypt: An Anthology of Stories, Instructions, Stelae, Autobiographies, and Poetry.* New Haven: Yale University Press.

SMITH, M. 2008. 'Osiris and the Deceased', in J. Dieleman and W. Wendrich (eds), *UCLA Encyclopedia of Egyptology* Los Angeles: <http://digital2.library.ucla.edu/viewItem.do?ark=21198/zz001nf6bg>, accessed August 2013.

SMITH, S. T. 1995. *Askut in Nubia: The Economics and Ideology of Egyptian Imperialism in the Second Millennium BC,* Studies in Egyptology. London: Kegan Paul.

SMITH, S. T. 2003. *Wretched Kush: Ethnic Identities and Boundaries in Egypt's Nubian Empire.* London: Routledge.

SMITH, W. S. 1981. *The Art and Architecture of Ancient Egypt.* 2nd edn. rev. with additions by W. K. Simpson. Harmondsworth: Penguin.

SOUROUZIAN, H. 2011. 'Investigating the Mortuary Temple of Amenhotep III', *Egyptian Archaeology* 39: 29–32.

SPALINGER, A. J. 2001. 'Calendars', in D. B. Redford, *The Oxford Encyclopedia of Ancient Egypt.* Oxford: Oxford University Press, i. 224–7.

SPALINGER, A. J. 2005. *War in Ancient Egypt: The New Kingdom*, Ancient World at War. Malden Mass.: Blackwell.

SPALINGER, A. J. 2010. 'Military Institutions and Warfare: Pharaonic', in Lloyd (ed.) 2010*c*: 425–45.

SPAWFORTH, A. J. S. (ed.) 2007. *The Court and Court Society in Ancient Monarchies.* Cambridge: Cambridge University Press

SPENCE, K. 2007. 'Court and Palace in Ancient Egypt: The Amarna Period and Later Eighteenth Dynasty', in Spawforth (ed.), 2007: 267–328.

SPENCER, A. J. 1982. *Death in Ancient Egypt.* Harmondsworth: Penguin.

SPENCER, A. J. 1993. *Early Egypt: The Rise of Civilisation in the Nile Valley.* London: British Museum.

STANLEY, M. D., et al. 2003. 'Nile Flow Failure at the End of the Old Kingdom: Strontium Isotopic and Petrologic Evidence', *Geoarcheology* 18: 395–402.

STRUDWICK, N. C. 1985. *The Administration of Egypt in the Old Kingdom: The Highest Titles and their Holders*, Studies in Egyptology. London: Kegan Paul.

STRUDWICK, N. C. 2005. *Texts from the Pyramid Age*, Writings from the Ancient World 16. Atlanta, Ga.: Society of Biblical Literature.

SZPAKOWSKA, K. 2003. *Behind Closed Eyes: Dreams and Nightmares in Ancient Egypt.* Swansea: Classical Press of Wales.

TAYLOR, J. 2000. 'The Third Intermediate Period (1069–664 BC)', in Shaw (ed.) 2000: 330–68.

TAYLOR, J. 2001. *Death and the Afterlife in Ancient Egypt.* London: British Museum.

TAYLOR, J. A. 2001. *An Index of Male Non-Royal Egyptian Titles, Epithets and Phrases of the 18th Dynasty.* London: Museum Bookshop Publications.

TEETER, E. (ed.) 2011. *Before the Pyramids: The Origins of Egyptian Civilization*, Oriental Institute Museum Publications 33. Chicago: Oriental Institute of the University of Chicago.

THOMPSON, D. J. 1997. 'Policing the Ptolemaic Countryside', in B. Kramer et al. (eds), *Akten des 21. Internationalen Papyrologenkongresses Berlin, 13.–19.8.1995*, Archiv für Papyrusforschung 3. Stuttgart: Teubner, ii. 961–6.

THOMPSON, D. J. 2012. *Memphis under the Ptolemies.* 2nd edn. Princeton, NJ: Princeton University Press.

TRIGGER, B. G. 2003. *Understanding Early Civilizations: A Comparative Study.* Cambridge: Cambridge University Press.

TROY, L. 1986. *Patterns of Queenship in Ancient Egyptian Myth and History*, Boreas: Uppsala Studies in Ancient Mediterranean and Near Eastern Civilizations, 14 = Acta Universitatis Uppsaliensis. Uppsala: Almquist & Wiksell.

TURNER, E. G. 1984. 'Ptolemaic Egypt', in *CAH* 7(1). 2nd edn. Cambridge: Cambridge University Press, 118–74.

TYLOR, J. J., and GRIFFITH, F. Ll. 1894. *The Tomb of Paheri at El Kab*, Egypt Exploration Fund 11. London: Egypt Exploration Fund.

Urkunden des aegyptischen Altertums 1903–. Ed. K. Sethe, H. Schäfer, and G. Steindorff. 8 vols. Leipzig: J. C. Hinrichs.

VAN DEN BOORN, G. P. F. 1988. *The Duties of the Vizier: Civil Administration in the Early New Kingdom*, Studies in Egyptology. London: Kegan Paul.

VAN DIJK, J. 1994. 'The Nocturnal Wanderings of King Neferkarē", in C. Berger, G. Clerc, and N. Grimal (eds), *Hommages à Jean Leclant*, iv. *Varia*, Bibliothèque d'étude 106/4. Cairo: l'Institut français d'archéologie orientale, 387–93.

VAN DIJK, J. 2000. 'The Amarna Period and the Late New Kingdom (c. 1352–1069 BC)', in Shaw (ed.) 2000: 272–313.

VANDORPE, K. 2010. 'The Ptolemaic Period', in Lloyd (ed.) 2010c: 159–79.

VAN ESS, H. 2007. 'The Imperial Court in Han China', in Spawforth (ed.) 2007: 233–66.

VAN NEER, W., LINSEELE, V., and FRIEDMAN, R. F. 2004. 'Animal Burials and Food Offerings at the Elite Cemetery HK6 of Hierakonpolis', in Hendrickx et al. 2004: 67–130.

VERCOUTTER, J., et al. 1970. *Mirgissa I*. Mission archéologique française au Soudan sous la direction de Jean Vercoutter 1. Paris: Direction générale des relations culturelles, scientifiques et techniques, Ministère des affaires étrangères avec le concours du Centre national de la recherche scientifique.

VERNUS, P. 2003. *Affairs and Scandals in Ancient Egypt*, trans. D. Lorton. Ithaca, NY: Cornell University Press.

VINSON, S. 1994. *Egyptian Boats and Ships*, Shire Egyptology 20. Princes Risborough: Shire.

VITTMANN, G. 1998. *Der demotische Papyrus Rylands 9*, i. *Text und Übersetzung*, ii. *Kommentare und Indizes*. Ägypten und Altes Testament 38. 2 vols. Wiesbaden: Harrassowitz.

VITTMANN, G. 2003. *Ägypten und die Fremden im ersten vorchristlichen Jahrtausend*. Mainz: Philipp von Zabern.

VOGELSANG-EASTWOOD, G. 2000. 'Textiles', in Nicholson and Shaw (eds) 2000: 268–98.

WARD, W. A. 1982. *Index of Egyptian Administrative and Religious Titles of the Middle Kingdom: With a Glossary of Words and Phrases Used*. Beirut: American University of Beirut.

WEATHERHEAD, F. J. 2007. *Amarna Palace Paintings*, Seventy-Eighth Excavation Memoir. London: Egypt Exploration Society.

WEEKS, K. R. 1998. *The Lost Tomb: The Greatest Discovery at the Valley of the Kings since Tutankhamun*. London: Weidenfeld & Nicolson.

WEEKS, K. R. 2006. *KV5: A Preliminary Report on the Excavation of the Tomb of the Sons of Ramesses II in the Valley of the Kings*, Publications of the Theban Mapping Project. Rev. edn. Cairo: American University in Cairo Press.

WEINSTEIN, J. M. 2001. 'Egypt and the Levant in the Reign of Amenhotep III', in O'Connor and Cline (eds) 2001: 223–36.

WENDORF, F., and SCHILD, R. 1998. 'Nabta Playa and Its Role in Northeastern African Prehistory', *Journal of Anthropological Archaeology* 17: 97–123.

WENDORF, F., and SCHILD, R. and Associates 2001. *Holocene Settlement of the Egyptian Sahara*, i. *The Archaeology of Nabta Playa*. New York: Kluwer Academic/Plenum.

WENGROW, D. 2001. 'Rethinking "Cattle Cults" in Early Egypt: Towards a Prehistoric Perspective on the Narmer Palette', *Cambridge Archaeological Journal* 11(1): 91–104.

WENGROW, D. 2003. 'On Desert Origins for the Ancient Egyptians', *Antiquity* 77: 597–9.

WENGROW, D. 2006. *The Archaeology of Early Egypt: Social Transformations in North-East Africa, 10,000 to 2650 BC*, Cambridge World Archaeology. Cambridge: Cambridge University Press.

WENKE, R. J. 2009. *The Ancient Egyptian State: The Origins of Egyptian Culture (c. 8000–2000 BC)*, Case Studies in Early Societies. Cambridge: Cambridge University Press.

WENTE, E. F. 1967. *Late Ramesside Letters*, Oriental Institute of Chicago Studies in Ancient Oriental Civilisation 33. Chicago: University of Chicago Press.

WEST, S. 1969. 'The Greek Version of the Legend of Tefnut', *JEA* 55: 161–83.

WHALE, S. 1989. *The Family in the Eighteenth Dynasty of Egypt: A Study of the Representation of the Family in Private Tombs*. Australian Centre for Egyptology, Studies 1. Sydney: Australian Centre for Egyptology.

WILKINSON, R. H. 1994. *Symbol and Magic in Egyptian Art*. London: Thames & Hudson.

WILKINSON, R. H. 2000. *The Complete Temples of Ancient Egypt*. New York: Thames & Hudson.

WILKINSON, R. H. (ed.) 2012. *Tausert: Forgotten Queen and Pharaoh of Egypt*. Oxford: Oxford University Press.

WILKINSON, T. A. H. 1996. *State Formation in Egypt: Chronology and Society*, Cambridge Monographs in African Archaeology 40, BAR International Series 651. Oxford: Tempus Reparatum.

WILKINSON, T. A. H. 1999. *Early Dynastic Egypt*. London: Routledge.

WILKINSON, T. A. H. 2003. *Genesis of the Pharaohs*. London: Thames & Hudson.

WILKINSON, T. A. H. 2010. 'The Early Dynastic Period', in Lloyd (ed.) 2010c: 48–62.

WILLCOCKS, Sir W., and CRAIG, J. L. 1913. *Egyptian Irrigation*. 3rd edn. London: Spon.

WILLEMS, H. O. 1983–4. 'The Nomarchs of the Hare Nome and Early Middle Kingdom History', *JEOL* 28: 80–102.

WILLEMS, H. O. et al. 2007. *Dayr al-Barsha, i. The Rock Tombs of Djehutinakht (No.17K74/1), Khnumnakht (No.17K74/2), and Iha (No.17K74/3): With an Essay on the History and Nature of Nomarchical Rule in the Early Middle Kingdom*, OLA 155. Leuven: Peeters.

WILLEMS, H. O. 2010. 'The First Intermediate Period and the Middle Kingdom', in Lloyd (ed.) 2010c: 81–100.

WILLIAMS, B. R. 1999. 'Nubian Forts', in Bard and Shubert (eds) 1999: 574–9.

WILSON, P. 2010. 'Temple Architecture and Decorative Systems', in Lloyd (ed.) 2010c: 781–803.

WINLOCK, H. E. 1941. 'Neb-Ḥepet-Rēʿ Mentu-ḥotpe of the Eleventh Dynasty', *JEA* 26: 116–19.

WOLF, W. 1931. *Das schöne Fest von Opet: die Festzugsdarstellung im grossen Säulengange des Tempels von Luksor*, Veröffentlichungen der Ernst von Sieglin Expedition in Ägypten 5. Leipzig: Hinrichs.

YOFFEE, N. 2005. *Myths of the Archaic State: Evolution of the Earliest Cities, States, and Civilizations*. Cambridge: Cambridge University Press.

YOYOTTE, J. 1952. 'Un corps de police de l'Egypte pharaonique', *RdE* 9: 139–51.

Index